Data Modeling for Everyone

Sharon Allen

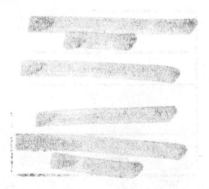

Curlingstone Publishing Ltd ®

Data Modeling for Everyone

curlingstone

Published by Curlingstone Publishing Ltd,
Arden House, 1102 Warwick Rd
Acocks Green, Birmingham B27 6BH. UK
Printed in the United States
ISBN 1904347002

Trademark Acknowledgements

Curlingstone has endeavored to provide trademark information about all the companies and products mentioned in this book by the appropriate use of capitals. However, Curlingstone cannot guarantee the accuracy of this information.

Credits

Author
Sharon Allen

Managing Editor
Fiona McParland

Commissioning Editor
Timothy Briggs

Technical Editors
Gareth Oakley
Craig Weldon

Indexer
Adrian Axinte

Cover Design
Corey Stewart, Astron

Proofreader
Agnes Wiggers

Technical Reviewers
Daryl Barnes
Sheldon Barry
Mike Benko
Robert Chang
Louis Davidson
Robin Dewson
Mark Horner
Arno Janssen
Rick Lowrey
Ella Moline
Helmut Watson

Production Coordinators
Rachel Taylor
Pip Wonson

Figures
Dawn Chellingworth
Rachel Taylor
Pip Wonson

About the Author

Sharon has enjoyed learning the intricacies of several careers since 1975 including Medical Assistant, Inventory Control Supervisor, Data Administrator, HTML & PL/SQL Programmer, and Data Warehouse Architect. This may sound a bit confused but it has given her a unique perspective and sensitivity to the goals and pressures of both business and information technologies. This has been a huge asset in the position of data modeler who works as an ambassador and interpreter between the two in order to successfully build data requirements and design data solutions.

Sharon could be role named as a Wife, Mother, Daughter, Sister, Friend, Author, Teammate, Data modeler, Programmer, Stained-Glass Crafter, Crocheter, Seamstress, Artist, Actress, Playwright, Vocalist, Housekeeper, Story Teller, Dragon Lady, Gardener, Teacher, and World Traveler. She knows that she doesn't fulfill any of these roles nearly well enough, but has a great time trying.

> **This book is dedicated to two special people in my life named Jack Kendell Allen – my father-in-law and my nephew. I miss you both.**

Acknowledgments

- ❏ To John Baker and Paul Yamor who let me try data modeling in the first place – Thanks for giving me a chance!

- ❏ To the gang who helped/s me learn this craft and how to wield it wisely – Wendell, Ted, Paul, Janet, Karen, Drew, Cindy, Ron, Dennis, Charles, Cory, Camelia, Sanjiv, Geraldo, Richard, Ella, Jan, Paul, David, Stuart, Wendell, Rich, Phil, Michael, John, Dave, Daryl, Danny, Brad, Yamile, Cindy, Rex, Arno, Steve, Rick, Jane, Susan – Thanks for taking the time to explain 'one more time' and share your wisdom and experience!

- ❏ To the pair who suggested their favorite publisher for me to submit a proposal to – Cindy Rutherford and Rich Hansen. Thanks a lot!

- ❏ To the IT writers who gave me an encouraging word – Sid Adelman, Larry English, David Marco, and Michael Brackett. Thanks for the vision of possibility!

- ❏ To the special people who kept me going when the going got rough – Doug, Tim, Dan, and Mike, (my gang), and Mom, Charlie, Arno, Ella, Gareth – I wouldn't have gotten here without you!

- ❏ To the team who made something out of my bumbling first attempts – my editors, reviewers, and development team – Three cheers!

- ❏ To everyone who has had to put up with me through this odyssey – Thanks for all the understanding and patience during my roller coaster highs and lows.

Data Modeler Blessing

May the Creator gather us into one entity defined as the members of the set Humanity.
May our primary key help us to recognize ourselves as irreplaceable and unique for all time.
May all our mandatory attributes be filled with good values and our optional attributes be
generously supplied.

May all our relationships be for good, gainful, and positive purposes building strong connections
in our travels as foreign keys both as recursions to ourselves, and intersections with other entities
in this universe.

And may any categorization be recognized as less a division, separating us from each other, and
more a highlighting of what makes us special.

Sharon Lee Allen 2002

Table of Contents

Table of Contents

Table of Contents

Table of Contents

Introduction

Data modeling is a skill set that is not immediately recognized in the IT world. While jobs for programmers and database administrators are regularly advertised, few companies employ people in a role titled data modeler. However, data storage design, and awareness of how data needs to be utilized within an organization, is of prime importance in ensuring that company data systems work efficiently. It's often only when systems start misbehaving, or can't cope with the data in a way that the users wish it to, that poor database design is exposed. How many times have you tried to cancel an utility account, only to find that the phone operators can't erase your records due to constraints in their data system? Instead of modifying or removing your details, you are forced into setting up another account. This is not only time consuming, but also a poor use of existing data. Efficient data modeling can ease such problems and ensure that each system is truly tailored to the needs of the users.

Relational databases provide a powerful means by which to store and manipulate vast volumes of data. The design of such systems is based on the mathematics of relational theory, advanced in the initial stages by E. F. Codd. This mathematical basis has meant that many of the standard database design titles are not easily accessible to many would-be modelers who want to know how to practically implement the theories they read about. This book focuses on giving the reader a background in the field of Enterprise data modeling. The physical implementation of these designs is beyond the scope of this book, and merits a title of its own, thanks to the complexities that can result in performance tuning the resulting application to run efficiently. The aim is to provide a practical guide to the 'what' and 'how' of data modeling, in a day-to-day task-oriented way, rather than from a theoretical best practices viewpoint. It is more than 30 years since the initial work of Codd and others, and yet we are still to see a commercial relational database that can be said to be truly relational. In the real world, theoretical perfection, as prescribed by Codd's own rules for a relational system, has to be compromised at the intersection with system performance. The art of data modeling is to recognize when to compromise, and when to adhere more strictly to these rules.

The book is split into three sections. The first five chapters deal with the basic tools that a data modeler has to have in their locker:

Chapter 1 begins our journey into data modeling by considering the very nature of data modeling, and its use within an Enterprise. It recognizes the various 'guises' in which data modeling makes its way into job descriptions within business, and gives an overview of the ultimate goals of modeling.

Chapter 2 looks at the terminology involved in relational modeling. This is where the mathematical basis of relational theory is left to others to expound, and the focus is on what the various concepts equate to in a real-world setting. We also introduce the syntax by which we graphically represent data models, focusing primarily on the notation that we'll use throughout the book.

Chapter 3 delves a little deeper into the theory underpinning the relational model, and considers the rules by which a database is assessed as relational. It then moves on to consider the process of normalization, by which data is broken down so as to adhere to the premises of relational theory. It also briefly touches on the practical nature of modeling, and where Codd's rules need to be bent so as to improve the performance of the given application.

Chapter 4 provides a guide to the various types of analytical models that we can be asked to produce as a data modeler, and the level of detail that we can choose to deliver. Tailoring your model to the needs of your audience is of key importance in this situation, since losing their ability to comprehend what you have modeled makes the exercise itself entirely futile. Knowing what level of detail is appropriate in different circumstances is important to determine quickly as a modeler, in order to make yourself an indispensable part of any development team. While project managers will want an overview of the model that you have devised, the programmers will need more detail in terms of the data types and size constraints they need to use in implementing your model. You need to be flexible in providing for a variety of needs.

Chapter 5 takes a look at how models fit into development projects. The design of a new application passes through several iterations, from the beginning of the project where the data elements that need capturing are outlined at a very general level of detail, to the final model provided for physical implementation as a database system, which is of a highly detailed and often complex nature. Ensuring that the model meets the needs of the project requires careful management of its extent, and effective communication between modeler and client.

The second half of the book looks to put the knowledge gained in the first half of the book to practical use by considering a sample system. To emphasize that the modeling techniques presented here are applicable to whatever system you happen to be working on, the chosen system is not a sample proprietary database such as Oracle 8*i* or SQL Server 2000, but rather the electronic version of the card game Solitaire.

Chapter 6 begins the process of modeling by capturing the scope of the modeling project. This is where the initial boundaries of the model are drawn, and the important concepts of the game captured in graphical format. By the end of this chapter, a very general model of the game is presented for further analysis. In the course of drawing up this model a general checklist of tasks is provided, to enable the reader to apply themselves to any general project.

Chapter 7 picks up this model and iterates through many of the same steps outlined in the previous chapter in developing the level of detail still further. It takes the concepts of the previous chapter and converts them into logical entities on the model. This process is something of a 'drill down' as the conceptual model of the previous chapter is fleshed out with more detail regarding the nature of the data in the system.

Chapter 8 illustrates the basic principles needed to take the logical model of the previous chapter and turn it into a model capable of being implemented as a physical database system. This is where the fine detail must be documented, and the room for errors is greatly diminished. A poor design here and the implementation problems for the development team may be myriad. It's important at this stage in the model development to be crystal clear as to the definitions of the various data elements, and how they are related together.

Chapter 9 considers the situation where budget and time constraints leave you in the position of trying to miss out the work highlighted in Chapters 6 and 7 and simply moving straight to a physical model. This is not an ideal situation for a modeler, but one where we can still apply basic practices to improve the integrity and longevity of the model. It outlines how you can take appropriate shortcuts and still provide verifiable detail in the model.

Chapter 10 considers the modeling needs of a data warehouse, a data store used to allow aggregation of historical data for reporting purposes. This presents a very different challenge to those of the previous chapters, since the data is structured very differently in a data warehouse, to improve the efficiency with which users can sum, aggregate, and manipulate data to provide reports and summary sheets. All the necessary terminology is presented here along with two sample applications illustrating how such data warehouse designs can be developed.

Chapter 11 looks at a different scenario altogether. While all the work up until this point has focused on building systems from scratch, this chapter considers the process of reverse engineering, where you attempt to model an existing system. This, in many ways, is the reverse process of the previous chapters, since you have to work your way back along the development chain, starting out with the physical elements in the database, in order to return to a logical model. This is often necessary in reappraisal of systems, such as when companies merge and need to verify what data is being collected in each system, or when looking to expand or enhance an existing system.

The final section of the book looks at the added value that the modeler can bring to a development team.

Chapter 12 considers what enhancements a modeler can provide to make the graphical models they produce for their clients more readable. Simple additions of text, abbreviations, icons, and color-coding can greatly enhance the readability of a model, and give it a life beyond the point when you are no longer associated with it. The more clarity a modeler can bring to their work, the easier it is for others to both follow and utilize their work.

Chapter 13 looks at additional 'value' issues in terms of the integrity and security issues surrounding the system data. Data integrity is of key importance to a system, since nonsensical values naturally reduce both the effectiveness of the application, and user confidence in its viability. There are a number of simple tests that a modeler can do to consider the nature of the data in the system, and flag any obvious problems for the rest of the development team. In cases where company-sensitive information is involved, there may need to be modifications to the model design to protect the data from being publicly exposed. While the DBA is often the first port of call in these cases, in restricting access to the databases being used, the modeler can aid the protection of data.

Chapter 14 looks at the nature of meta data, or 'data about data'. It discusses the need to document extraneous information, which often appears of little value within the development team, and which is generally lost over time since it exists only in the heads of the team and not in paper or electronic format. How to distribute data, and its use in repositories, for easy reuse is also discussed. As the number of database systems grows, so the number of model designs also increases. While each system will have its own specialist requirements, there are numerous occasions when previously modeled structures can be reused. This requires both easy access to previous models, and good documentation of such models, which is where meta data repositories can prove a valuable asset.

Chapter 15 is the final chapter in the book and gives a final heads up as to some of the best practices a modeler should aim for in their working environment. It highlights what traits a modeler should avoid, in order to ensure that the project succeeds, and reinforces this with some best practices. It then considers some further project details, such as ideas of how long each of the various modeling tasks will take, and some of the pitfalls to look for as you work your way through a project.

There is a glossary of terminology at the end of the book, which you can refer to when clarifying what you are reading about.

Who Is This Book For?

This book assumes no prior knowledge of relational modeling, or indeed programming constructs. It is aimed fairly and squarely at anyone who has a need for an easy-to-read, practical guide to relational data modeling. To that end it should have a broad appeal not only for developers and DBAs taking their first steps into database design, but also people such as data architects, information officers, and knowledge managers, who simply want a greater understanding of how their data can be managed efficiently. There are no specific software needs, since the book shies away from a specific database platform. Access to a PC with a version of Solitaire, or even a pack of playing cards, may aid understanding of the middle section of the book, but is not essential.

Conventions

To help you understand what's going on, and in order to maintain consistency, we've used a number of conventions throughout the book:

When we introduce new terms, we **highlight** them.

> **These boxes hold important information.**

Advice, hints, and background information are presented like this.

Words that appear on the screen in menus like the File or Window menu are in a similar font to what you see on screen. URLs are also displayed in this font.

In the book text, we use a fixed-width font when we talk about entities and tables. Take, for example, the `ProductPromotion` and `ProductPromotionNotification` entities. We also use this font style when highlighting statements used in database code, such as a SQL language `SELECT` statement, or when discussing `NULL` values.

There is almost no code presented in this book. However, on the few occasions when we show code examples then we show it as a gray box:

```
CREATE VIEW "Quarterly Orders" AS
SELECT DISTINCT
    Customers.CustomerID,
```

```
        Customers.CompanyName,
        Customers.City,
        Customers.Country
FROM Customers
RIGHT JOIN
Orders ON Customers.CustomerID = Orders.CustomerID
WHERE Orders.OrderDate BETWEEN '19970101' And '19971231'
```

Customer Support

We always value hearing from our readers, and we want to know what you think about this book: what you liked, what you didn't like, and what you think we can do better next time. You can send us your comments by e-mail to feedback@curlingstone.com. Please be sure to mention the book title in your message.

Errata

We've made every effort to make sure that there are no errors in the text or in the code in this book. However, no one is perfect and mistakes do occur. If you find an error in one of our books, like a spelling mistake or a faulty piece of code, we would be very grateful for feedback. By sending in errata you may save a future reader hours of frustration, and of course, you will be helping us provide even higher quality information. Simply e-mail the information to support@curlingstone.com, your information will be checked and if correct, posted to the errata page for that title and used in subsequent editions of the book.

To see if there are any errata for this book on the web site, go to http://www.curlingstone.com/, and locate the title through our Search facility or title list.

E-mail Support

If you wish to directly query a problem in the book with an expert who knows the book in detail then e-mail support@curlingstone.com. A typical e-mail should include the following things:

❑ The **title of the book, last four digits of the ISBN**, and **page number** of the problem in the Subject field.

❑ Your **name, contact information**, and the **problem** in the body of the message.

We *won't* send you junk mail. We need the details to save your time and ours. When you send an e-mail message, it will go through the following chain of support:

❑ Customer Support – Your message is delivered to our customer support staff, who are the first people to read it. They have files on most frequently asked questions and will answer anything general about the book or the web site immediately.

❑ Editorial – Deeper queries are forwarded to the technical editor responsible for that book. They have experience in all the topics discussed, and are able to answer detailed technical questions on the subject.

❑ The Author – Finally, in the unlikely event that the editor cannot answer your problem, he or she will forward the request to the author. We do try to protect the author from any distractions to their work; however, we are quite happy to forward specific requests to them. All Curlingstone authors help with the support on their books. They will e-mail the customer and the editor with their response, and again all readers should benefit.

The Curlingstone Support process can only offer support to issues that are directly pertinent to the content of our published title.

- What is Data?

- What is Data Modeling?

- Data Lifecycle

- How a Data Model Helps

- Who are the Data Modelers?

- Defining the Role

- Job Titles

- As-Is Support

- To-Be Support

- Summary

Data Modeling: an Overview

In this chapter we will take a look at what data modeling involves and who, within any given organization, actually does the modeling. We will look at:

- ❏ The nature of data versus information
- ❏ What data modeling is
- ❏ How data modeling helps in dealing with the lifecycle of Enterprise data
- ❏ Who actually performs data modeling tasks in the organization
- ❏ What activities the data modeler participates in

What Is Data?

Data is the description of facts, rather than information, which is the useful interpretation of data. As the ultimate goal of data is to provide useful information, it must be modeled in such a way to aid that aim. While once data was represented simply by text and numbers in a database, today its abstraction into digital format has expanded to include pictures, sounds, virtual 3D objects, and complex multi-media blends of all of those things. That evolutionary growth of the very nature of data is challenging us all as to how to use technology to its maximum capability.

Even the subjects and focus areas of data have changed. We used to think of data mostly in terms of Inventory and Accounts Payable systems. Now we add Ground Tracking Systems using dynamic uplinks to satellites that help us find our way around. We see Virtual Gaming allowing people from around the world to play and communicate with each other in real time. There is Online Shopping that remembers who we are and what we might be interested in, and cameras on public buildings using face recognition software to watch for trouble.

While people seem to want to collect ever-increasing amounts of data, they also want to have it manipulated in order to provide aggregates, trends, logic-driven prioritizations, derivations, and mappings of data to other things of importance about the data (meta data). In order to support those desires we need to provide data in structures that support different functionality like:

- ❑ Online Transactional-Processing (OLTP)
- ❑ Operational Data Stores (ODS)
- ❑ Data Warehousing (DW)

Our current view of data management tells us that we need to collect and store data in the most elemental, atomic, basic, and reusable parts possible. Only by doing that can we build relationships that support the creation of newly defined information. And since we frequently need to combine those basic data elements, we need to design appropriate storage and processing facilities that allow this to be accomplished.

The process we use to discover those basic data elements, determine how they relate to each other today, and define them so that they can be recognized and used in the future, is called data modeling.

What Is Data Modeling?

Data modeling is a technique that records the inventory, shape, size, contents, and rules of data elements used in the scope of a business process. The business process scope may be as large as a multi-disciplined global corporation, or as small as the receiving of boxes on a dock. The final product is something like a map accompanied by all the backup documentation needed to interpret it with complete clarity.

Some models are built to document very high-level ideas and are termed **conceptual** models. Some are built to document the theoretical purity of data element rules and structure, called **logical** models. And maybe the best known type of data model is the type that determines the actual design of a database, called a **physical** model. This model is the basis of the code written to create tables, views, and integrity constraints. These three basic types connect to each other loosely and can support each other as different views of a single business process.

A data model does not provide the full compliment of back end code that needs to be built to support an application. It does not contain security grants, or database link code. It doesn't show sizing and space needs (although some modeling software will let you add in those aspects). The data model is a blueprint for a database, *not* the database itself. It's a cornerstone of the development effort, but only one of the building blocks of designing an application.

The process of modeling can capture a representation of something that exists, the **As-Is** state of our physical data, so that we can view how the data is structured in an existing database, and what rules the database manages in an environment today. These views are generally restricted to a single application, or a set of tables in a restricted schema like a database. It could take hundreds of them to fully document the scope of an Enterprise, for example. It could also take hundreds of logical models to describe the more theoretical rules of the data, rather than how they were physically implemented. Similarly, there could also be many conceptual models covering all the business processes, although it is more likely at the higher level of the conceptual model, than it is at the other stages, to attempt to cover all the Enterprise activities in a single view.

> **A model helps us to view how we manage data now or did in the past.**

Data Modeling is also used to create designs for something new, the **To-Be**. Sometimes we create multiple To-Be designs, and the development team chooses which one to implement.

> **We model to try out options. There can be a number of solutions even for similar problems, and it isn't always easy to know the right one.**

However, whatever it is used for, data, in its elemental form, needs to be understood and should be cared for with a disciplined approach to its lifecycle. Before we continue looking at data modeling techniques, let's look at the lifecycle of a typical data element.

Data Lifecycle

What follows are the stages that new data goes through on its way from being used as a recent fact, to becoming a historic fact, and eventually becoming a forgotten fact. (A stage that we are having increasing difficulty believing in, due to repeated requests by clients to unearth their archived data or restore it from backups.)

This is not the lifecycle of an application development project, although many other processes can go through similar stages. These are the steps that any data element goes through:

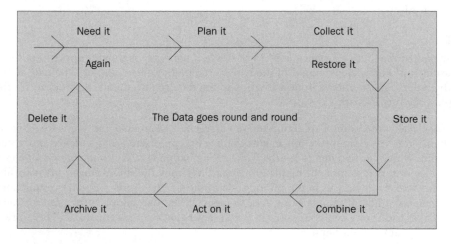

Need It

This is the point in time where someone asks for some data. What was the temperature in Des Moines yesterday? How many candy bars were bought before the PG movies last week? How many parking spaces are going to be available before second shift shows up? Let's consider the example of a Credit Card Transaction Chargeback Amount. Say you are a small retail firm, and you want to begin accepting credit cards to pay for purchases. You contact several different credit cards to find out how. One of the things you discover is that different credit card companies charge different fee amounts for using their service. The fees even differ under different circumstances. You realize that in order to understand what providing this service to your customers is going to cost you, you need to collect the service fee for each transaction separately to be able to analyze profitability better. This recognition of the need for a data element is step one.

Almost no data element is captured just because it exists. It needs to be of value to someone, or there need to be belief in a future value, to bring it to life. As you find out what the impact of the new data element is on the organization, you may discover other data elements also need to be available.

The 'Need It' phase is the recognition of a new fact, which needs to be available in order to accomplish a task. You now know you need a Credit Card Transaction Chargeback Amount in order to assess profitability in your business, determine Return on Investment (ROI) by looking at service usage and cost, and even plan next year's budget. So what happens after you know you need it?

Plan It

This is the stage where the exploration and analysis of the data element happens. Questions are asked about frequency, size, and business rules. Methods of capturing and storing it are explored. The security, reliability, and quality issues are looked into.

How much can a Credit Card Transaction Chargeback Amount be? Is it determined by the amount of the sale and so presented as a percent? Is it a flat fee per transaction? Do we know when we charge the customer what the service charge to the company will be, or are we charged at a later time? If so, how do we tie it back to the individual transaction? Is it credited back to us so the amount could be a + or a – value?

When we plan for it, we look at all sorts of different things about it and document as much as there is to know about this new data element, including where we think it fits with existing data elements. This may be in the form of a formal specification or a lively brainstorming session. What happens after you make a plan for it?

Collect It

This is the part of the lifecycle where you check to see if you were right and implement the plan. It's a time of testing and finally deployment of the chosen method of data creation. The data must be sufficiently understood to at least draft a solution to the data requirements, in order to be able to verify that the plan is going to work.

We start a collection of Credit Card Transaction Chargeback Amounts and see if we learned enough to manage them properly. Sometimes this means that we end up discovering we need more data elements or that we didn't plan for this one properly. This testing happens every time a new value (a real instance of the data element) comes into our hands to manage. We may find that things run smoothly for a period of time and then changes in the billing style of the Credit Card companies impact our understanding, use, and definition of this data element. When that happens the plan for the data element changes too. None of these stages in the life cycle have to be sequential. There are innumerable times when loopbacks might happen.

So now we feel comfortable that we have the process of collection of Credit Card Transaction Chargeback Amounts right. What next?

Store It

After collecting a certain amount of data, you must decide how to store it. Often the collection and storage requirements of the data differ, as we may want a narrow, fast database to collect real-time data, but a larger, less responsive one will be used for the storage. It may be collected in dozens of little individual credit card scanners, which need to be polled, have the data element applied correctly to the sales data from the cash registers, and finally aggregated together and sent on to a different environment. There may be security or accessibility issues that require parallel storage (in case of power or equipment failure).

This is also another point at which general monitoring of the process we created to collect this data element is critical. Time and quality performance are watched in order to increase both, and so satisfy the client's data needs. Credit Card Transaction Chargeback Amount may be important to us, but not important enough to cause a 20% increase in the complexity of completing a sale (causing incorrect billing and increased voids), or the negative impact on the speed of service time for completion of a sale. Many considerations happen when we look at how we are going to save and store our new data element.

But once we have collected and stored it to our satisfaction, what happens next?

Combine It

We start to use it to our advantage. This is a maturing of the data element itself. After it has been around a while, new ways to use it should start to spring up, especially if it is timely and reliable. Equally, any problems with the original analysis will have become apparent, and need revising. This is a time of integration with other data collections and highly complicated report writing. It means that the data element was well created and valuable to the data clients.

The Credit Card Transaction Chargeback Amount becomes a new variable, additive fact, or decision point in the Sales, Marketing, Finance, and Accounting departments. The data element becomes a popular new addition to the data element resource pool for the enterprise. It is referred to in the formula for Gross Sales and Net Sales. The data warehousing team is asked to provide it in the Monthly Sales Fact table. It becomes a part of the never-ending thirst for better understanding of the health of the enterprise.

So after it is aggregated, averaged, sliced, diced, racked, and stacked in reports and on screens all over the company, what can it do?

Act On It

It can become the foundation for action. It can even become the foundation for a new series of data elements that are used like a dashboard to effect decisions. This stage is only achieved if the data is understood and becomes a cornerstone of the data collection for the client. This is the crowning achievement for a piece of data. It has been proven to be a quality fact and can be relied on to support a decision. This data should have an auditable pedigree, in order to stand the scrutiny of doubt if the action doesn't get the expected results. In other words, you'd better know where it came from, and who thought it was a true fact.

This is, of course, the targeted goal of data, namely to be useful.

Credit Card Transaction Chargeback Amount can become the basis for a large decision, like a new program to provide a bank debit function for customers, which could be less expensive to the company than the charges from other credit cards. It can become the basis for daily small decisions, like offering discounts for cash sales of less than a certain value. It may even become the basis for a decision to cancel the credit card program and become the reason for its own removal from the data element inventory.

However, once the data element has established itself as a useful addition to the company data resource what do we do with it?

Archive It

We begin the process of archiving backup and historic copies for security and the ability to purge production data sets. Once data values have depreciated in relevance and value, they're moved to a nearby storage area. Only the data clients can determine where that boundary is. Setting it aside is fraught with its own challenges. How should the data be archived? How accessible should it be? How safe should the archive be? Should it be in the same format, structure, and rules as the 'live' data? The Credit Card Transaction Chargeback Amounts from the current week are critical to have available, the ones from last month are less so. The individual values from two years ago have almost lost their value. They may only have value now in aggregated form for trend reporting.

We probably begin to take slices of data out of the production systems and archive them in several ways. The data warehouse may keep a larger set of older data than any other application in the company, but even they may need to resort to removing transaction-level detail into near-line storage to keep performance at an appropriate level.

This is the golden retirement stage of data. It can still be useful but it is no longer of immediate relevance. What happens when the data values or data elements finally become obsolete?

Remove It

We delete them from all live environments. They fall off everyone's list of responsibilities. They may not be deleted the way we think of a transaction deleting a record, but they are gone for all intents and purposes from anyone's ability to use them. Over time their very existence fades away. Data values and data elements get tossed out when they are no longer of value; tapes are erased, backups deleted, whole collection tools like old applications, measuring devices, and storage devices are scrapped. Even if the data still exists (say on 8-inch floppy) the means to retrieve it may no longer be available.

This is the 'Rest in Peace' stage of data. The amount of data in our landfills is probably staggering although our perception of the value has changed over time. It is hard now to conceive of any data being worthless. But I do know that I still come across bone piles of tapes, disks, and clunky old machines that contain data that exists nowhere else, so it seems appropriate to note that this stage still does exist in the life of a data element.

When credit cards no longer exist, our Credit Card Transaction Chargeback Amount will be as useful as a collection of payroll information from 1912. Only historians will be interested, and they will only be interested in samples, not all of it. But that leads us into the next step that can happen to a data element.

Need It Again

This is where the data archeologists come in. Sometimes a need shows up for old data elements, or at least for the ability to pull a restricted selection of data elements out of data no one thought anyone would need, and that was deleted.

The data miners want to get a view of data over as much as ten or twenty years time to look for relationships between outlying factors and the behavior of company data. It seems that as soon as we decide no one needs it anymore and we toss it into a deep ocean trench, someone wants it back again. It was this need that really brought data warehousing to the importance it has today. Unfortunately even a data warehouse team has to pick and choose what it keeps based on the *known* understanding of need. We still lose data from lack of having an identified customer for it.

So you could say this is a rediscovery stage of data. It is usually extremely painful, and often expensive, to try to satisfy because nobody planned for it. It is very seldom that you can find a map of where data treasure is buried. But once you do, you need to restore it.

Restore It

This is the hard part if you haven't planned for an eventuality of this nature. This is the point where someone has to figure out how to get data out of files or media where the access tools don't exist anymore. Here we try to bring it back to life. We usually have to deal with the extra burden of lost understanding about the nature and rules of the data (in other words it may have to be analyzed to be understood again) as well as media corruptions and lack of usable tools.

How a Data Model Helps

We have talked about the lifecycle of data, because helping to manage and understand the company use of data elements is what data modeling is all about. Data models can be used to help in every stage of the lifecycle of data, bearing in mind that they need to be built differently according to the support requirement of the task in mind. Throughout iterations of these steps, the model can be used to help explain our understanding of the data to the client. This works both as a reality check (do I understand your business properly), and as a prompt to show what is missing in your understanding. This is particularly important during the first few stages of the lifecycle.

- ❑ In the 'Need it' stage, when the requirements are being gathered, a high-level concept model can be built to target whereabouts in the process that specific data element is created. It captures the definitions, descriptions of 'business world' vocabulary, and interview notes about the exceptions to the basic rules.

- ❑ In the 'Plan it' stage, all the little details can be discovered and documented in the data model. You can gather enough information to build actual data structures for the design and test stages of a project. The model in this stage is an evolving blueprint of the design and definition of many aspects of a data element.

- ❑ In the 'Collect it' stage, the model can be used to scope the test and verification scenarios for data gathering trials. You can actually build small subsets of the model that ease the ability to trace 'What if?' examples through the boxes and lines, discovering timing and security issues before trying it with an application.

- ❑ In the 'Store it' stage, many data models of the various local data structures can be used as a part of the requirements document to create a separate global repository. If data needs to be relocated, the model will confirm the basic rules required for the storage system.

- ❑ In the 'Combine it' stage, a model can act like a menu noting all the ingredient options and how they can be combined. Without a model as a map of what to choose, you are totally dependent on what the person assigned to help remembers. You can create a submodel with all the necessary elements to visually document the combination.

- ❑ In the 'Act on it' stage a model can be one half of the pedigree map. It can document what application, table, and column the data was pulled from. The original creation process can be documented in the form of an External (screen field) to Internal (table column) map. The data definitions and rules can document the quality and integrity goals of the structure. Stewardship and Security measures may also be a part of the model documentation. The model can therefore be added as part of the backup documentation for audit purposes.

❑ In the 'Archive it' stage, the data model can show the original and archived resting spots of the data element. It can show the structure with its rules and definitions of the data elements at the time of archival for later review in the case of restoration.

❑ In the 'Delete it' stage, the data model can be used to document the targeted full database, selected tables or columns, or possibly locations of data that is being proposed for surgical removal. It can be used as a map or catalog of the chosen deletions in order to be able to understand what they were when they were used.

❑ In the 'Need it again' stage, models, which were archived along with the data, can be used to refresh everyone's memory of what was actually archived. It can assist in targeting one specific area of data need rather than having to simply bring everything back from the grave.

❑ In the 'Restore it' stage, the data model can be used to build new data structures for the data to return to. They may not be named exactly the way they used to be due to uniqueness conflicts. You may need to plan a whole new structure for the return engagement.

We have covered what data is, and how models can be used to manage it. Now let's put a face on the Data Modeler role.

Who Are the Data Modelers?

This can be a tough question to answer. Finding the people in your organization with data modeling skills in their toolbox can be a challenge. Different companies use different titles for this position, and frequently append this skill to the job description of different job titles.

> Data modeling is often an additional skill set rather than a full-time job (not because there isn't enough work to keep a modeler busy, more due to the way department responsibilities have evolved).

Defining the Role

Data modeling as a profession doesn't seem to have established its own persona like database administration or programming. I have completely given up putting 'Data Modeler' down in occupation blanks on forms. Yet it is a profession unto itself, with its own internationally recognized professional organization DAMA (Data Management Association www.dama.org). Plus the skill of data modeling is brought up over and over in database development books as the discipline of choice towards building a quality database. Data modelers can be found doing the following, with or without a title that highlights the modeling skill set:

❑ Documenting, designing, and improving

❑ Guiding and advising

❑ Auditing / Enforcing

❑ Analyzing and researching

❑ Communicating

Let's now use a few metaphors to understand the data modeler's role.

Photographer

Think of the data modeler as a photographer for the National Geographic magazine. Depending on the assignment, they are either taking pictures of deep space Nebulas or inner space neutrons. They take pictures documenting reality at any level of detail and give the viewer the ability to find answers. Those beautiful, colorful, simple images provide easily recognized documentation. What would we do without pictures of our As-Is (current state) life?

A photographer does a similar job to someone *documenting* data structures already in existence (so called 'As-Is' data structures). The art of photography doesn't simply reflect true life but adds a little something, helping our understanding of the subject. Photographers use their skills to highlight and emphasize aspects that show the subject from a particular viewpoint, and focus our attention on something they have found to be important.

The data modeler working to document the current state of the Enterprise data is constantly updating a library of information relating to data elements, what they are, where they are used, how they are built, what they mean, and all of the details referring to their physical nature (data type, size, precision, default values, and so on.) The level of detail varies depending on the audience and purpose of the model.

Architect

Now think of the data modeler as an architect. Architects work to understand the owner's requirements, intended use, budget, resources, and future plans for a building. An architect would develop the blueprints for a museum and research facility, a design that would differ from a bakery or auto factory, since each design has to take into account multiple parameters. Then they oversee construction from a consultant and validation point of view. They stay a part of the build team and iteratively change the design if problems come up.

A Data Structure Architect describes someone *designing* a new data model, as we would in custom development projects. These are 'To-Be' (future state) designs. Quite frequently, several are offered to the clients and reviewed to find the appropriate final choice.

The data modeler working to build for the future is trying to design the best solution to a business problem. The solution may need to focus on flexibility, security, process improvement, data quality, or all of the above. They use their models of the 'As-Is' state of the data elements to discover the shortcomings and new data elements that are now needed. They may create a brand new solution or create a delta design that is an upgrade.

Upgrade Engineer

Upgrade Engineers (say in the Auto or Aerospace industry) frequently take existing machines, tools, or systems and try to make them better. They find ways to streamline steps and lower the energy requirements. They are constantly looking for ways to reduce moving parts to simplify construction and increase maintainability. They want to increase safety and reliability and satisfy new standards. And they want to reduce failure points to the lowest possible level while supporting critical parts with the highest amount of protection. Their prototypes are usually mini 'To-Be' proposals of solutions sent to a committee for review and approval.

This metaphor describes the Enterprise focus of an *improvement* style of data modeling. Data is an asset of the company. Ask any of the Finance department if they wouldn't prefer all assets to be maintained as inexpensively for as long a life as possible. A data modeler acting as an Upgrade Engineer will generally work only with physical data models. They will probably start with an 'As-Is' issue of some kind, followed up with one or more proposed 'To-Be' solutions.

Reference Librarian

Data modelers are people who it would be appropriate to approach if you were looking for a specific type of data. They can be the Reference Librarians of corporate data, especially if there is no Meta Data Management team. At the very least they know all of their designs inside and out.

Librarians ask you all sorts of questions about what you need. They head off to the various indexes and files and pull up all sorts of interesting references and descriptions of what you are looking for along with the locators of those references. They help point you in the right direction. The Data Reference Librarian can be analytical, and frequently creates several custom sub models incorporating data elements from multiple systems and sources, to be used for *guidance*.

Business Consultant

Given a complete and detailed enough set of requirements, a data business consultant can look at the specs of a project and provide feedback as to the company's ability to meet them, especially from the relationship rules built into a database design. The data business consultant can help solve a 'Make or Buy' decision. They provide *advice*, or perhaps a complete functional review of a software tool from a content and data restriction viewpoint. Frequently this has to be done with the help of a vendor if the database design or logical model of the tool is unavailable or private.

Buildings Inspector

Another metaphor of a data modeler can be that of an Inspector. Inspectors enforce rules issued by a higher authority in regard to a process, structure, or environment. Data modelers can do the same thing in an organization. They are frequently part of a review team enforcing naming, structure, use, integration, or data element definition standards for an enterprise.

Data Buildings Inspector is one of my least favorite roles to perform. It doesn't help you make friends, but it can be as vitally important as any of the other policing and monitoring functions that are needed to keep everyone honest. However, it is a part of the world of modeling and you might find them in an *audit* function in your corporation, attempting to enforce IT development rules.

A Data Modeler Charter

- ❑ To take responsibility for the Enterprise data element inventory and structure of the past, present, and future

- ❑ To document, design, research, guide, audit, or inspect everything there is to know about Enterprise data elements

- ❑ To enable and empower efficient, safe, maintainable, reliable, quality data structure development for the creation, maintenance, and accessibility of Enterprise data assets

Mostly a data modeler just wants to make life easier for people who need to use data as a second language, so they can leave at 5pm everyday to go play baseball with their kids. If they can depend on the documentation and designs that the data modeler can provide, it cuts their research and development time down considerably.

Job Titles

It is always fun to find out what the world calls people with your skill set these days, and find out what they have bundled it up with. I did a simple search for data modeling on www.Monster.com for the US, and here is what I found for one day of listings. It has gotten so that I don't know what to call myself anymore.

- ❑ Application Developer
- ❑ *Data Administrator*
- ❑ *Data Architect*
- ❑ Data Engineer
- ❑ *Data Modeler/Analyst*
- ❑ Database Administrator
- ❑ *Information Analyst*
- ❑ Programmer/Analyst
- ❑ Software Developer
- ❑ Systems Analyst

The ones in italics are the ones I would consider the better titles for data modelers. The key point to note is that most modelers are not just one thing. They are combinations of things, and data modelers are found all over an Enterprise.

> **Data modeling is often combined with other skills to create composite job titles and descriptions. This can make figuring out if you should apply for a data modeling job difficult to assess.**

As-Is Support

Data modeling tasks generally fall into one of two areas. They deal with what is now, or what could be in the future. We call these areas **As-Is** and **To-Be**.

> **As-Is tasks require discipline and orderliness. They are often repetitive, like auditing the current state of a database, and systematic, like profiling all the data values in a production system.**

As-Is tasks tend to be included in several areas such as the support of Configuration Management, providing impact analysis, promoting IT Standards, providing data integrity analysis, and researching existing techniques and tools.

Support Configuration Management

Configuration management is the process of controlling what an environment is. It may be the hardware/software compliment, or the data elements in the databases loading on a piece of hardware. There are some companies who have a whole department chartered to manage the configuration of at least the production data environment, although they may be managing the tools and content of several test environments as well. Data modelers participate in controlling data environment change, often through very detailed processes called **change control**. They maintain many different kinds of documentation tailored to fit the needs of the audience. These are the models, definitions, and mappings. They build and maintain:

❑ Enterprise-level conceptual data documentation

❑ Project logical data documentation

❑ Maps of data (logical/physical) objects into an Enterprise data library

❑ Physical data object documentation

❑ Data element relationship rule documentation

❑ Risk assessments

❑ Documentation of data element security needs

Sometimes this documentation is kept under the same controls as production code. It may be assessed, but not updated without going through the correct procedures of Check out, Change, Test, QA Review, Approve, and Check In.

Provide Impact Analysis

The data model library and meta data repository should be the first source for noting the ripple effects to an organization when there is a change to the Enterprise data. Y2K would have been much easier for most of us if there had been a central repository to start from. The modeler can look for impacts to and from:

❑ Alterations to data element definition and physical details

❑ Alterations to existing functions changing data deliverables

❑ Retiring applications, procedures, interfaces, concepts

❑ Incorporation off new applications, procedures, interfaces, concepts

Promote IT Standards

Data modelers are card-carrying members of the data quality team. They constantly promote data and data design standards, and are frequently called upon to participate in code, procedure, and document reviews. They frequently provide their expertise in the following:

- ❏ Assist in Test plan creation to test for Quality
- ❏ Planned integrity checks for denormalizations
- ❏ Promote proper relational integrity
- ❏ Promote standardized project documentation
- ❏ Promote Names based on RIS standards and platform requirements
- ❏ Build Definitions provided by the data element owner
- ❏ Promote standard sizes and data types
- ❏ Promote standard abbreviations
- ❏ Promote security for documented sensitive and critical data objects
- ❏ Promote standard nullability options
- ❏ Promote the creation and maintenance of documentation

Provide Data Integrity Assessments

They may assess the suitability of data design to highlight necessary concern over the existing data management environment, looking for areas of improvement in:

- ❏ Supportability – is this structure appropriate for future needs?
- ❏ Quality – does the existing structure promote quality data creation and updates?
- ❏ Integrity – are there business rule checks at the database level?
- ❏ Enterprise appropriateness – is this structure suitable for our company (are we trying to force a manufacturing application to manage contract documentation?)

Research Existing Techniques and Tools

Sometimes data modelers are tasked to be way out in front of the pack in early analysis and finding hidden or currently unknown data sources. This might mean that they have to be proactive and nosy instead of just working by request. This might also mean they need access to people, applications, machines, and documentation from all levels in order to accomplish the task. They may need to be able to interview both the CEO and a local machinist, or use the HR system in a test environment, or exercise a department's PC that they have set up to behave 'just so'. The data modeler needs an entrée to quite a bit to get their job done right.

- ❏ Documenting Business Process/Scope
- ❏ Document User requirements
- ❏ Mapping Business Processes to Data objects
- ❏ Discovering Data Structures not in Enterprise controlled environment, in other words, Desktop development

To-Be Support

To-Be support is different. This looks at Enterprise data with a view to the bright future of data management. To-Be support means designing, advising, and suggesting alternatives to the As-Is environment, which hopefully is already fully documented.

> **To-Be tasks involve creativity and innovative problem solving. They are less serial and more iterative, requiring a level of self motivation and management.**

Design New Data Structures

❑ Create the planned Enterprise conceptual/logical data view

❑ Design data element structure fixes for change requests

❑ Design new database architecture for custom development projects

Provide Expert Advice

We will be required to provide advice about proposed changes, and may be asked to be responsible for preventing redundancy in data, and duplication of effort when integrating new plans into the company's data environment. Any advice we offer will need to be backed up with explanations and examples of what could happen if the choice goes one way or the other. We:

❑ Research data element scope and provide options

❑ Provide recommendations about designs

❑ Suggest a Make or Buy decision

❑ Research and provide a recommendation on data manipulation or software design tools

❑ Suggest Risk mitigation options, especially for denormalization decisions

Provide Alternatives

We may have to build and maintain a summary of choices, recognized deficiencies, and unresolved needs.

❑ Plan Integration – Identify and suggest candidate data elements for integration

❑ Plan of Data organization – provide options in a 1/5/10 year Enterprise data management plan

Provide Expectation Assessments

We may assess the suitability of new data designs (Purchase software decision support tasks) and check database designs for:

- ❑ Risk Analysis
- ❑ Supportability
- ❑ Quality
- ❑ Integrity
- ❑ Enterprise appropriateness

Research New Techniques and Tools

The world of data management is broad and full of growth. Data modelers need to keep up with current developments to know if they are still making the right decisions and providing the best advice possible to their Enterprise. They need to attend conferences, read journals, and develop a good network of others who can share experiences. They need to pay attention to new and evolving:

- ❑ Tools – Hardware and Software
- ❑ Techniques – Modeling, Programming, Designing
- ❑ Directions of the Enterprise market
- ❑ Client Goals
- ❑ Enterprise Goals
- ❑ And whatever else might come in handy

Summary

Data modeling can be used for much more than just building a new database. It can be an integral step in the management of the lifecycle of data. The model can be there at the conception, birth, life, death, and restoration of data. It is certainly a great design technique, but it is also a great cataloging technique. It has become more prominent in recent years, thanks to the increasing volume and complexity of data stored by individuals and businesses.

We have discussed the nature of data modelers, and shown how they can be just about anyone on a development or data management team, since data modelers are very involved in all aspects of data design, build, maintenance, and rediscovery.

We also took a look at how modeling can be used in an 'As-Is' environment for:

- ❑ Configuration Management – every change is drafted, reviewed, approved, and acted on
- ❑ Impact Analysis – every change is analyzed for ripples and given a cost
- ❑ Development Standards – every structure is designed and reviewed for corporate consistency
- ❑ Quality Review – every existing data element can be assigned a steward for quality, security, criticality, sensitivity, and integrity issues
- ❑ Research of the current enterprise data environment

And how it can also be used in 'To-Be' conceptualization in order to:

- ❑ Design New Data Structures – providing new solutions to data challenges
- ❑ Provide Data design 'Make or Buy' advice – with a data model of the business rules, you can compare the data model of a proposed vendor solution to verify a good match
- ❑ Provide alternatives – helping to map directions for the future
- ❑ Assessments of what to expect – creating risk analysis, supportability, quality, and integrity due to proposals
- ❑ Research of new directions for data management

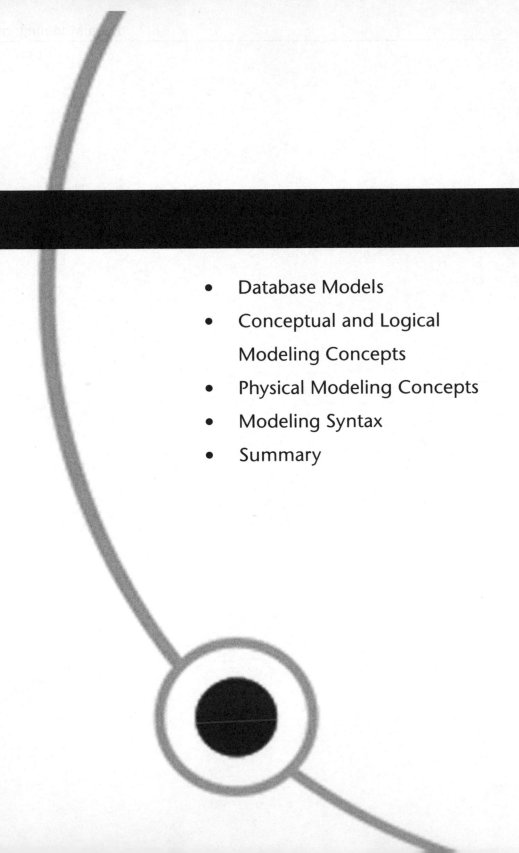

Relational Modeling

In order to be able to create relational data models, and develop truly relational databases, we need to understand what constitutes a relational database, be comfortable with the terminology involved in describing relational systems, and be aware of the different symbol sets we can use in representing relational systems in graphical format. To this end, in this chapter we'll consider:

- ❑ The nature of relational databases, and how they differ from hierarchical and network data management systems (DBMS).
- ❑ The terminology of relational databases:
  - ❑ Entities
  - ❑ Attributes
  - ❑ Keys (candidate, primary, foreign)
  - ❑ Relationships
  - ❑ Tables/ Views
  - ❑ Columns
  - ❑ Keys (primary, surrogate, alternate, foreign)
  - ❑ Constraints
- ❑ The IDEF1X modeling syntax and other notations available for a modeler's use in documenting data elements and business rules.

Database Models

Before we look at relational databases in more detail, we'll take a brief look at Hierarchical and Network Database Management Systems (DBMSs), since understanding their limitations will help you understand what the Relational approach is trying to solve.

Hierarchical

One of the hierarchical DBMSs still working today is an IBM product called **IMS** (**Information Management System**). It is basically a tree structure using a series of links to navigate from record type (table) to record type. Records (tables) include one or more fields (columns). Each tree must have a single 'root' record type. As an example of this type of system, consider the following class scheduling system at a college:

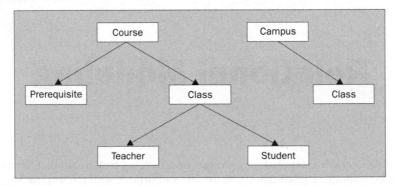

The problem with this system lies in children with more than one parent (such as Class in our example here). Many real-life data elements are like this, but unfortunately the Hierarchical DBMS can't handle this efficiently, since the two instances of Class are not easily related. Workarounds capable of dealing with this, usually require the creation of duplicate records or tables to satisfy the different needs, leading to data synchronization problems, since the same records appear in numerous places within the database.

Network

One of the big Network databases still tackling huge amounts of data management is IDMS (Integrated Database Management Systems). Network databases set out to solve the hierarchical problem of multiple parents. If we revisit our College database example, then in a Network database Campus is directly linked to Class through an owner / member link as shown below:

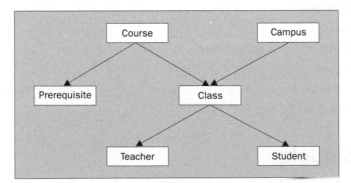

Unfortunately, in order to get from Teacher to Campus we must walk the tree back through Class. You can imagine that for a large database with many tables this may be a very long path. Futhermore, these paths are not easy to change nor new relationships easy to add once the database is created, making them rather inflexible.

Relational

Relational databases like Oracle, Microsoft SQL Server, and IBM's DB2 improve on both network and hierarchical database models, by enabling the matching of data fields at the database level. We will look in more detail at how this is achieved in a moment, but let's consider what a relational database model of our example would look like:

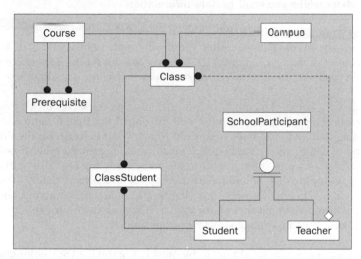

Don't worry about the lines and symbols we use here. We'll explain what they mean later in this Chapter.

This model allows `Class` to have three parent relationships, something which isn't possible in a Hierarchical database. It ensures that only one set named `Course` is necessary, which can be related to itself on occasions when the prerequisite of one course is that you have attended another course. It isn't possible for a Network database to contain a record like this, which is both a parent and a child of itself. In a similar fashion, teachers and students are recognized as `People`, allowing Isaac Asimov to be both a `Student` and a `Teacher` of a `Class`. Relational design emphasizes keeping only one record of like information. Getting to records can also be simpler in a Relational database. In this example you can connect the `ClassStudent` straight to the `Campus` without connecting to `Campus` directly.

Conceptual and Logical Modeling Concepts

Conceptual and logical modeling is used to capture the rules of data in a business activity. The emphasis is on how the data is used in a business environment. It is immaterial that the current tool only allows one e-mail address if the business keeps multiple e-mail addresses for their vendors. It doesn't matter if today's form has no space for a web site address if the business needs to know this information. Conceptual and logical modeling concentrates on documenting what is really happening with data, how it is being used, and what it needs to do in the future.

From this analysis we can then build tools that make using the data in this business correct fashion easy and fast. The database design will have rules built into the actual structure that promote quality, simple data value maintenance, and growth. Knowing what the rules are for the data in the business is the first step in designing an appropriate table structure in your database.

Entities

Entities are the foundation of relational data modeling. The industry definition of an entity is as follows:

> **An Entity is a person, place, thing, or concept that has characteristics of interest to the Enterprise, about which you want to store information.**

Note that entities are not tables. They are often physically implemented as tables, and are depicted in a similar manner to tables in data model graphics, but they are not tables. Tables are always physically implemented, while some entities are too conceptual to ever become actual tables.

Think about your house. Those of us out here in California find ourselves picking our housewares (books, CDs, wine bottles, pencils, and so on) up off the floor from time to time when the earth rattles too much. Everything that had once been organized is now lying in heaps on the floor. When you are faced with that kind of chaos, your natural instinct is to create organized piles of belongings; CDs go in one corner, the books stack up in another, and so on. Data modeling organizes distinctive data elements in a similar manner, grouping together elements that represent a person, place, thing, or concept. Fortunately they are not generally found in this chaotic a state in your company, though of course they don't generally have furniture to put them back into. We have to determine the needs of the system we are looking at and build suitable storage structures from scratch.

When clearing up your house you would begin by quickly organizing your belongings, generally by subject. All the multi-media goes in this corner, the kitchen stuff is over here, and broken bits are in a bin. In data modeling this would be the **conceptual analysis** phase. You have the elements that you are going to keep in large, very general, still unexplored piles (**conceptual entities**), and a pile of stuff that is out of scope (put there by purposely setting them aside for now). After this conceptual organization you go on to a more detailed organization. This time the multi-media is sorted into more distinctive groupings like Music, Movie, and Game. In data modeling terms we have identified our conceptual MultiMedia entity, representing this set of things, and we are now refining our understanding by developing logical entities in the form of Music, Movie, and Game. Each is a distinctive set with different important attributes. The composer or artist is important to how we store and retrieve music, but subject and title are the important factors in Movies.

Data modeling starts by organizing, in a conceptual abstraction, sets of relevant data. Through the use of a concept called normalization, which we'll look at in more detail in the next chapter, we purify and isolate the data logically into very distinctive, reuseable, elemental sets, which can be related and combined for different purposes. Finally we design physical storage structures (tables) to hold the data and manage it appropriately.

Entities are generally thought of as sets of entity classes, representing a person, place, thing, event, or concept. It is good to use this list to check against when you are looking at a group of instances to see if they could be an entity. So, if we think of an entity as a set, then both of the following are entities in an Order system:

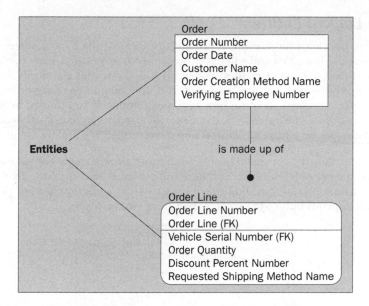

Equally, concepts such as Employee, Project, Department, Part, Vendor could all qualify as entities.

> **You need to be very careful with names in data modeling. Employee may be better titled Worker or even Support Person depending on the customers you are modeling for.**

What constitutes an entity is dependent upon the system being modeled. For example:

- ❏ to a Dog Breeder `Collie` may be an entity
- ❏ to a Veterinarian `Large Dog` may be an entity
- ❏ to a Pet Shop `Dog` may be an entity
- ❏ to a Property Rental firm `Pet` may be an entity
- ❏ to Vector Control `Animal` may be an entity

On a similar note:

- ❏ To a legal firm `Advice` may be a billable service or entity
- ❏ To a car dealer, `Advice` may only be an attribute of a `Salesperson` entity

The real trick to entities is deciding whether you have found an entity or an **instance** (one member of a set), or both, and the way to determine this is from the project scope and domain.

Conceptual or Logical Entities

It is good to remember that entities come in two major varieties, which have different purposes. The **conceptual entity** really is an idea and will never be deployed physically. They don't very often have further characteristics (known as **attributes**) associated with them, and are mostly used to communicate to teams about the subject areas and large concepts that are going to be analyzed further by a project. There are almost no rules about what can be a conceptual entity. If you think it helps tell the story, and you can give it a descriptive definition, you can generally use it as a conceptual entity. Conceptual entities will almost never be a table or physical object, since they are usually too generic.

Here is a little model showing conceptual entities capturing a few thoughts about our Order system. These entities are at a very high level. `Order` here will probably encompass individual orders as well as Supply Chain contracts. `Product` could be services, as well as audit functions or processes that help fulfill orders. It all depends upon what you discover from your analysis.

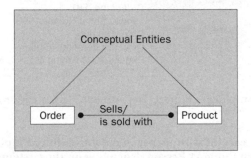

At the conceptual level the details are blurred. You may not actually have a full understanding of the scope of the concepts when you use these structures in your model. You will work with a person who is knowledgeable in the area of your analysis to build and validate your model.

Logical entities are a little tougher since, having been fully detailed and documented, they will quite often be the structure leading to a design of a table or physical object. When they are fully attributed they look like this:

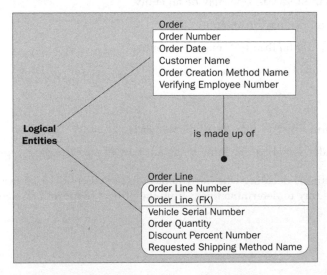

From this point on, when I talk about entities I'm referring to logical entities.

Instance or Entity?

An instance (or member of the set) defined by an entity correlates roughly to a row or record in a table, in the same way that an entity correlates to a table, but is not strictly defined as such. So for example, in a 'Jazz records' entity, we might find instances like 'Kind of Blue', 'Porgy & Bess', or 'Time Out'.

> **Instance means a single member of an entity, a member of the set. It may ultimately be a row or record in a table, but is not defined as such. In math it is called a tuple.**

Category Entities

Category structures, or **generalization hierarchies**, are used to partition an entity into subsets. Each subset is part of the whole so, for example, Trucks, Cars, Ships, and Airplanes are all subsets of Vehicles. Here is our Order system. Now we can see that we sell Vehicles, which can be broken down into Cars, Trucks, and Vans.

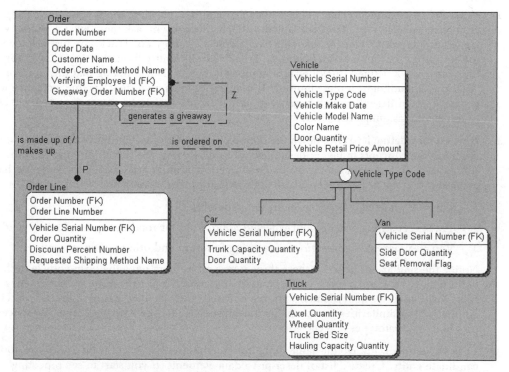

The entity whose set includes all of the members (in this case `Vehicle`) is referred to as the **supertype**. The divisions (in this case `Car`, `Van`, and `Truck`) are called **subtypes**. All subtypes share the data elements in the supertype but they may each have data elements that are unique and not shared between them. We use this modeling structure (Category) to document a cohesiveness that would otherwise be lost.

Child category entities sometimes feel like instances due to the fact that the subdivisions get more and more detailed. Once in a while you will even have a subtype entity that is only a set of one, so the difference between the instance and the entity gets very slim. Remember that an instance is a *member* of a set whereas an entity is an *idea* or the *set itself*.

> **A category structure manages a single set of instances by dividing them into types. This generally occurs due to differences in use, or the attributes belonging to each type.**

Obviously a `Collie` can be an instance of `Dog`, while `Truck`, `Car`, and `Van` can be instances of `Vehicle`. So how do you know if it is an instance, or member of a category? We have to observe or discover the 'natural use' of the set, in other words observe how and why things behave the way that they do in a given set, using guidelines that we'll look at now.

Defining Signs of a Category

These are the main clues to knowing whether or not you need to document a category structure:

❑   **What do the customers think**? This is your first and best check to see if you are working with an instance or an entity. Find out how the clients think. If you ask them what a Truck, Van, or Car is, do they think you are referring to a 'Vehicle'? If they do, Trucks are just instances of the set `Vehicle`. On the other hand, is 'Truck' with its ability to haul weight, have more than four tires, and a defined truck-bed size unique enough to their thinking that the concept 'Truck' is something complete in itself? Is it an entity in its own right, having existence which is considered different enough because of its use or structure to be categorized separately with useful attributes uniquely its own?

❑   **How do they define it**? Write down the definitions of the things you think could be an entity. Audition the concepts to be entities in textual form. Review the definitions and look for similarities. You may find concepts that seem very dissimilar are actually the same, or have a generalization entity that encapsulates the similarities. For example:

  ❑   Car = A wheeled *vehicle*, especially an automobile.

  ❑   Truck = A strong, usually four-wheeled *vehicle* used for road transport of heavy loads.

  ❑   Van = A large covered *vehicle* for carrying furniture and other goods by road.

  Notice the similarities between these three items; all of them have the term vehicle in their definition, have wheels, and seem to be used on a road. Notice the differences: Truck is specifically used for heavy loads, Vans are covered, and Cars are automobiles. If your clients emphasize the similarities you probably have instances. If they emphasize the differences you probably have subtypes of a category.

❑   **Look at Sample Data**. Do the same thing for data that the client will want to capture about the candidate entity. Create a list of descriptive data elements. If you start to see repeating patterns of attributes like Name, Weight, and Description over and over, you probably have a collection of instances rather than entities. They won't need a distinct enough structure to make it necessary to create them as different entities. On the other hand, if only Trucks require government inspections to be tracked, then Trucks have a different attribute to other Vehicles and may warrant their own category entity.

❑ **Count how many there are**. Another check is to find out if there is more than one instance of the candidate entity. Be aware this isn't a foolproof check however. Some entities have only one instance existing at the time of the analysis, but they have the *potential* for more later on. For example the 'Company' entity that refers to the enterprise itself may be a single instance now, but mergers happen all the time. Sometimes not allowing a single instance that is a very distinct concept to be an entity will reduce flexibility for the future.

Complete or Incomplete

Categories can be either **complete** or **incomplete**. Complete categories have all subtypes defined, whereas incomplete categories don't. A category may be incomplete because all of the categories are not known, they can increase over time, or you choose not to show them all. The decision to show them all is based on the importance of identifying the subtypes to the customers and/or the IT development team. If a subtype needs to be treated differently for security or processing, for example, then you may need to display it in the logical model to be able to map those types of requirements.

> **A complete category structure creates a subcategory that every instance in the set fits into. An incomplete category structure creates some, but not all subcategories that the instances would fit into.**

A child category entity can be a parent of another level of categorization, which can continue for unlimited levels. Just remember that every instance of every level must also be part of the set defined by the topmost parent category.

Inclusive or Exclusive

Categories can also be **inclusive** or **exclusive**. Inclusive means that any of the members of the supertype can be members of any (or all) of the subtypes. Exclusive means that each member can only be in one of the subtypes. So for instance in an inclusive category if we had a super-type entity called Dessert broken into four subtypes Frozen, Baked, Fresh, Flambé, the instance of Dessert named Cherries Jubilee would be a member of both Frozen and Flambé. However, in an exclusive category we would have to choose which one to assign the instance to, probably Flambé since the fire is the most distinctive feature.

Associative or Intersection Entity

An **associative** or **intersection** entity is a juncture between two entities. They are generally created as a resolution of a many-to-many relationship. We'll see more regarding such relationships later in this chapter. For now let's consider a simple example. Suppose there are people in our Sales department who have to follow up on Order issues. Each Order may need more than one Call back to resolve the problem. Each member of our Sales Staff can assist in the resolution of many Orders. You have a set (entity) of Orders and one of the Sales Staff, but a further Call Backs set, recording the call backs required to resolve the problems. This is illustrated overleaf:

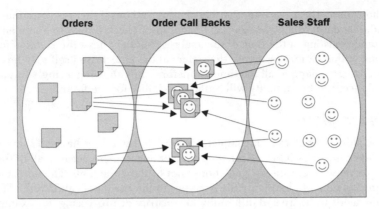

It would look like this in a model:

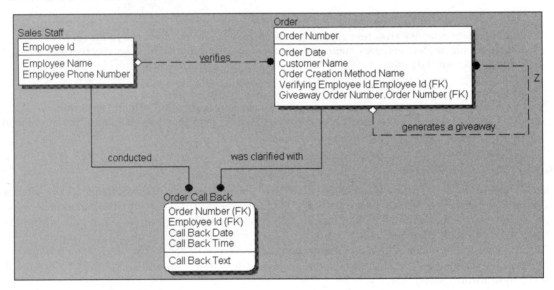

Example of Identifying an Entity

Determining entities all depends on the circumstances, scope, and purpose of the analysis. Let's consider my wallet and document the objects. I have on the desk one black plastic tri-fold wallet. Among the cards I have:

❑ Two Business Cards, One Driver's License, Two Club Memberships, One Bank Card, and Four Credit Cards (one Company, one Store, two Generic)

Among the paper I have:

❑ Five Store receipts, One canceled check, Two deposit slips, and Four ATM slips

Among the money I have:

❑ 17 pennies, 3 nickels, 1 Five dollar bill, and 4 One dollar bills

Some of these nouns are instances, some are entities, and some entities are here but haven't been named or discovered yet. The distinction between entities and instances will be different to an archeologist digging up my wallet 3,000 years from now and the Lost Property department at a college. Both of them will care about finding the wallet and will find capturing some information about its contents useful. However, each will require a different level of detail and, as such, the definition of an entity is in the eye of the beholder. Both will have an entity for the event, something that wasn't even on the list but is very important. It may be the Recovered Property event entity.

To the Lost Property department at the college Wallet is probably an instance. Does it matter to them that the property is a wallet rather than an umbrella? Only because they need to put the wallet in a safe and the umbrella in a box. They just see the objects as someone else's property and log them into the system accordingly. For them the entity is probably Property with Wallet as one type of property. The $9.32 recovered, and the name on the Driver's License may be enough for them, so Property and Recovered Property may be all they want to capture. In fact, they may be satisfied with Recovered Property, which is kept in a Log Book on the desk.

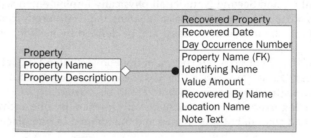

To the archeologist, on the other hand, Wallet may be important and distinctive enough to have its own entity. They may want to describe the size, material, and style, which will make it very different from finding VCRs and CDs. The contents of my wallet may even yield enough information to become part of someone's doctoral thesis about the inhabitants of Southern California in the early 2000s.

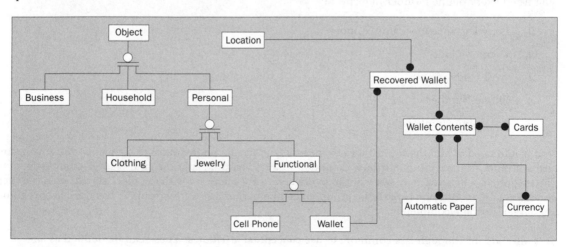

Attributes

Attributes are what most people think of as data. They exist as numbers, codes, words, phrases, text chunks, and even sounds and images, that are combined to be an instance in an entity. Attributes are *not* columns in a table, although they may grow up to be implemented that way some day. Attributes are simple separate, distinct, singular characteristics that describe or identify an entity. Attributes are the genes, the DNA of an entity. An attribute can be defined as:

> **An Attribute is a distinct characteristic for which data is maintained.**

Here again I am going to make a distinction between the logical world and the physical world. Attributes don't store data; they describe it. Some attributes never make it to being columns in their own right. It is very rare to see Century Number, Year Number, Month Number, Day Number, Hour Number, Minute Number, and Second Number all physically implemented separately. My point here is that they all qualify as attributes, since each has a meaning that is different from the combination. Each separate data element may be important to know and be defined by itself for some reason.

So what is an attribute? If we consider our `Order` entity above, then all the labels inside the entity (`Order Number`, `Order Date`, `Customer Name`, `Order Creation Method Name`, and `Verifying Employee Number`) are attributes. Every attribute has to be 'owned' by an entity. And in the world of logical relational modeling every distinct attribute is only 'owned' by one entity. It can be 'migrated' through relationships and shared, but it is created and maintained in one place.

Group Attributes

A **group attribute** can be defined as a combination of distinct logical attributes describing a single characteristic of an entity. `Address` is made up of many distinct data elements, as is `Phone Number`. If you listed every phone number in terms of:

❑ Long Distance Operator Number

❑ Country Code

❑ Area Code

❑ Phone Number

❑ Extension Number

you would need to add those attributes every time you need a phone number on the model. If you can use a `Phone Number` group attribute definition it saves you time later on. It also saves complexity at the beginning when you may not want to overwhelm your audience with details. I should point out here though that if an attribute is part of a group it can't be part of any other group. It has been absorbed into the larger attribute completely.

It is also possible, though less common, to use **conceptual attributes**. These can be defined as an abstraction of a characteristic of an entity. So, for example, you might add an attribute `Person Full Name` to your `Client` entity as a conceptual attribute placeholder. When it is finally fully logically attributed you may find it to be made up of five or more different logical attributes, such as:

- ❑ Title Code
- ❑ First Name
- ❑ Middle Name
- ❑ Last Name
- ❑ Generational Qualifier Code

As, for example, in Dr. Martin Luther King Jr. In fact you may need several middle names or titles in order to fully describe a name, depending on your clients' need.

> *An interesting note here is that you may generate a logical model that breaks out the definitive data elements only to have them compressed back together again in physicalization as a Full Name. However, keeping the logical attributes atomic in the physicalization will allow simple access to the data, such as sorting on Last Name, for example. Compressing the name back together makes it much harder to do that.*

If you aren't ready to fully detail an attribute into its most base parts, or you are going for simplicity in the early stages, use conceptual or group attributes. Not all modeling software can help you manage the ability to move between the details and the group attribute name. You may have to manage the association outside the model.

Now that we have talked about what attributes are and how much detail they can hold, let's talk about another aspect of attributes, namely the type of data they describe.

Attribute Classes (Types)

All logical attributes (conceptual and group attributes aren't precise enough to need this level of definition) must fit into one type of data or another. This is a very high-level classification of data meaning, which considers the use and definition of an attribute. It's very different from the domain of the attribute, which refers to the target data type in physicalization, such as VARCHAR, DECIMAL, and so on. However after saying that, scanning the look and data values of an attribute is a good test of your analysis and definition of attributes. So, for example, in our Order entity above we have attributes such as Order Number, Order Date, and Customer Name. We would expect the Order Number attribute to contain a number value, while Order Date should contain a date value. Similarly the Customer Name attribute should contain a text value.

What happens when, for example, you think you are looking at a list of Sale Amounts someone gathered from a pile of paper invoices and you discover dates mixed into dollar amounts? You ask around. Chances are a field on a form was used for several purposes, and contains two or more meanings. It could be that you have discovered a new business rule no one thought to tell you about, or you may have found one of the areas that can be enhanced with the clarification of data elements. The business process may be supporting a funny rule that states that if an invoice is a real invoice, the field contains the billing amount, but if it is a return for maintenance, then it contains the proposed return date. Stranger things have happened.

Every attribute must be able to be defined as one, and only one, class. If, for whatever reason, you have multiple classes of attributes with similar meaning in the same set, then choose the most specific type possible that is true for all occurrences. For instance if you are merging fields that seem to have many meanings, you may want to class the new attribute as just a text field. Or you may find that you can tighten the class from Number to Quantity or Amount because the data values are consistent enough to qualify for a more definitive class.

Here is my shortlist of attribute types, but you may want to add your own in time:

Type Word	Meaning	Data Domain
Amount	A monetary number	Number
Code	An alpha-numeric meaningful abbreviation	Text
Date	A calendar date – month, day, year	Date
Description	A textual account or portrayal	Text
Flag	A one letter or number Boolean set	Text
Identifier	A unique recognition tag in the form of a character and/or number, system generated ID or a GUID. This may be process driven, or nonsensical and insignificant to the data user	Text
Image	A non-language visual object	Blob
Name	A textual label	Text
Number	A place in a sequence	Number
Quantity	A number totaling a measurement by a unit	Number
Sound	An aural resonating object	Blob
Text	An unformatted language segment	Text
Time	A moment such as hour, minute, second, and so on	Time

Notice that this type of classification is not the domain. We reuse the domain of the data for many different classes or types. This classification becomes very important when we talk about naming standards of attributes.

Keys

Attributes play another role other than just describing characteristics of an entity. They are used to identify unique instances of the entity either as a member of a set (described as a candidate, primary, or alternate key) or as a reference to a member of a set (foreign key). These attributes, or groupings of attributes, are called keys.

> **A logical model key is one or more attributes used to uniquely identify an instance in an entity either as part of the entity or in reference to another entity.**

We'll consider each type of key in turn, beginning with candidate keys.

Candidate Key

> **A candidate key is one of one or more sets of single or multiple attributes used to uniquely identify an instance in an entity.**

Candidate Keys are **all** the optional choices for unique identification of an entity.

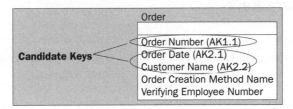

Candidate keys are expected to be unique forever as well as stable and never changing. In the above example, we have two candidate keys. Instances in the Order entity could be identified by:

❑ A unique number that we give them (Order Number)

❑ The combination of Order Date and Customer Name (assuming a customer can only order once a day, and each customer has a different name).

In Erwin 3.5.2 a Candidate key is also known as an Alternate key so we see the 'AK' notation. The first number tells us which alternate key the attribute belongs to. The second number tells us how many attributes go into making up the alternate key. Other software packages have different conventions.

Identifying the candidate keys provides us with some options. It may be that there are expected interfaces that would prefer one method of identification to another. This is another place where you will want to get sample data and test for uniqueness as well as stability.

Natural and Surrogate Key

Logical modeling focuses on data elements that are in the real world. They are numbers on invoices and checks, names of places and countries, longitude and latitude coordinates of reefs and landing strips, to name but a few. We generally don't make up attributes on a logical model. Natural keys are built out of attributes that exist in the real world.

> **A natural key is one of one or more sets of single or multiple attributes used to uniquely identify an instance in an entity that can be found existing in the Business world.**

Quite frequently however, natural keys are not stable or consistent enough to use in a physical design. Fortunately, database platforms have the ability to auto-generate numbers and apply them to records being created in a table. They have no meaning in themselves, but they provide a means of identifying a row. We call them **surrogate** keys.

> A surrogate key is a single attribute invented in a RDBMS to be used in uniquely identifying an instance in an entity. It has no natural occurrence that it mirrors from the business world.

A simple example of a surrogate key is an Order ID number. If you choose to implement them physically you need to take some special precautions to prevent duplicate data entry, since all they do is identify a row instance (rather than the member of the set) as being unique. For example, with an Order ID, and no forethought, you can insert the same order number over and over again.

Primary and Alternate Keys

> A primary key is the candidate key that is chosen to uniquely identify an instance in an entity.

Whatever identifier you choose has the potential of migrating through your system and into other systems. That identifier alone is the way back to the rest of the attributes owned by this entity. That means that whatever you choose to be your primary key should never be allowed to change. Otherwise anything referencing it could potentially lose the link.

In the modeling syntax we use throughout this book you will always find the primary key above a line in the entity giving it prominence in the list of attributes.

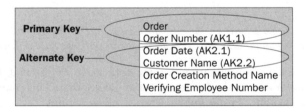

Whatever candidate keys are left over following designation of the primary key are now called **alternate** keys. Note that although the primary key is never referred to as an alternate key after this point it still retains that designation, having been a candidate key.

> An alternate key is one of one or more sets of single or multiple attributes not chosen to primarily identify an instance in an entity but which could uniquely identify an instance as well.

Foreign Key

> A foreign key is the complete compliment of attributes designated as the primary key of an entity that has migrated (or is shared) through a relationship to a new entity.

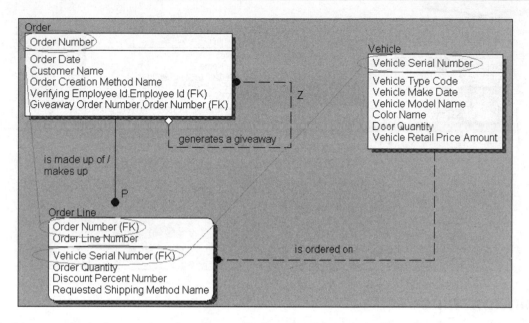

In this example, Order Number has migrated to be part of the primary key of Order Line. Vehicle Serial Number has migrated to Order Line as well. There are no limits to how many attributes you may need to migrate to an entity.

Foreign keys allow us to look backward to their source and find other attributes that are contained in that entity. Order Line can get Customer Name by tracing back and matching Order Number to Order. Order Line can also get Vehicle Model Name by tracing the foreign key backward and matching it. As long as one attribute has been identified in the parent entity as a primary key, then a foreign key (the entire set of identifying attributes chosen to be the primary key) will become part of the set of attributes in a related entity.

Role Names

Foreign keys do not have to keep the name of the attribute they came from. Note how Employee Id becomes a foreign key named Verifying Employee Id in Order and yet kept the name of Employee Id in Order Call Back. Role naming generally includes a definition change as well. The use of data in a new place may change its definition entirely. However, the rule of thumb is that they will keep their size and data domain. The only time there may be a difference is during a unification of columns (which we will talk about later).

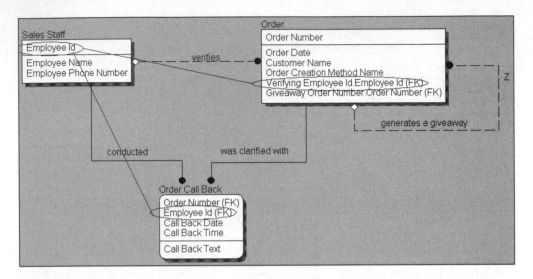

Relationships

> **Relationships are the logical links between entities.**

Relationships are represented on the model as lines drawn between entity boxes, with symbols detailing their meaning. So again these are potential physical constraints when you physicalize your logical model, but here they just note the references to connectivity between entities. Active verb phrases show their dynamic nature and the business process being supported by that link. Some of us call the Entity/Relationship sentences created by the noun and verb phrase **Business Rules**.

Relationships are two sided. With one exception, they show a link from one entity to another. It is by defining a relationship that foreign keys are migrated, creating the links by which instances connected together can be traced. We generally refer to those two sides as a **parent** (the source), and **child** (the target). Relationships are either:

❑ **Identifying** – in which case the parent primary key migrates into a primary key position of the child

or

❑ **Non-identifying** – where the parent primary key migrated into a non-key position

Each side of the relationship has a **cardinality** and **nullability** symbol. Cardinality tells us how many instances can be related to each instance in a parent entity. One parent entity can be related to child entities with a cardinality of:

❑ Zero or One

❑ One and only One

❑ Zero, One, or Many

❑ One or Many

❑ Specifically <Number>

❑ A range <Number> - <Number>

❑ Whatever it says about a multiple relationship

Nullability tells us whether or not child instances **must** be related to a parent instance. If the migrated key in the child instance *must* exist, then the nullability is termed **mandatory**, and NULL values are not allowed. If the migrated key in the child instance *may* exist, then the nullability is termed **non-mandatory**, and NULL values are allowed.

So the relationship combines information describing (Identifying/Non-Identifying) + (Nullability) + (Cardinality) + (Active verb phrase). When you read the relationship between two entities you get sentences that are easily determined to be true or false rules about how the data sets behave. Let's consider our Order example once again:

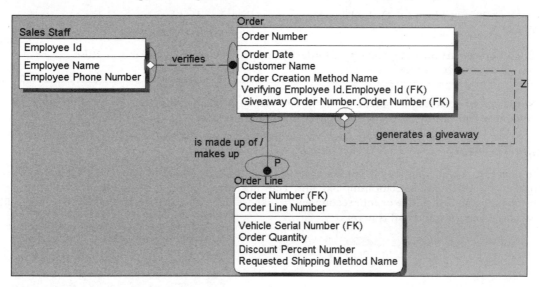

Each Order Line can only be identified if the Order who generated it is known. True or False? True. How about the verifying Employee Name? Do we need to know the employee who verified the Order to be able to identify the Order? No we don't, since orders are identified by a unique number (although we can select a smaller set of them by restricting the list to the person who verified them). If this were true you would not be able to use a nullable non-identifying relationship (noted by the diamond in this modeling syntax). There are no NULLs allowed in a primary key, which is where the primary key of the parent entity would be migrating to in an identifying relationship. We allow this relationship to be NULL because for a period of time an Order can exist without having gone through the process of verification. You need to watch things like that when you model.

Now let's look at the nullability and cardinality rules.

Relationship Rule	True or False
Each Order may own Zero or One Order Line	False
Each Order may own Zero, One, or Many Order Lines	True (if we can build orders before we make up our mind about the vehicle)
Each Order must own One and only One Order Line	False
Each Order must own One or Many Order Lines	False
Each Order must own 7 Order Lines (but no more and no less)	False
Each Order must own 1-7 Order Line (but no more than 7 and no less than 1)	False
Each Order must own the quantity of Order Line equal to today's calendar day (but no more and no less)	False

Note that only cardinalities that allow for a zero can be of NULL cardinality. So by combining the nullability and cardinality we specify the business rule exactly.

Many-To-Many

In conceptual modeling we can combine any of the cardinality choices on any side. There are no parents or children in a relationship like this. They are simply noted as being related and must be resolved by an associative or intersection entity (like we did with Order Line and Order Call Back earlier) when greater detail is necessary.

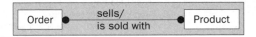

I would tend to classify this as the one conceptual relationship that we deal with (although it is allowable on Entity Relationship level logical models as well). It covers a broad concept and needs to be analyzed further to be of much use.

Recursion (Hierarchical) Relationships

This is a relationship of an entity to itself. The relationship line loops from itself to itself creating a funny looking structure sometimes called a 'Pig's Ear'. To continue our example here, let's say that every tenth Order over $50.00 gets a special giveaway. However, as Marketing is financing the giveaways they need a separate Order to maintain tax and finance autonomy from the Customer. The rule here is that a Giveaway Order must be the result of an Order counting process and only one Giveaway can be created by an Order. The result is a **recursion** from Order to Order.

A recursion creates a hierarchical tree, where a child can only have one parent. Using the Z for 'Zero or One' in this example, the recursion is a single link downward:

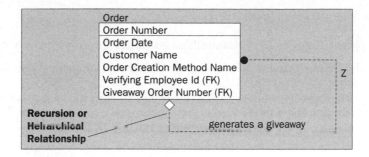

Network Relationships

A Network style relationship involves the same principle of bringing two or more of the same entity together, but is much more flexible than a recursive relationship since in this case a child can have many parents. We use them all the time to build Organizational charts and Parts trees. An example of an organizational chart is shown below:

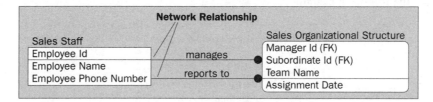

Let's say that we want to build a matrix of the people who manage teams, and those who participate in them. The recursive relationship wouldn't work, since it only allows a single relationship either up or down for the set members, and is too restrictive. In this case Employee can be both a Manager and a Subordinate. They can be on many teams, manage many teams, and participate in many teams.

This type of dual relationship has limitless possibilities for depth and breadth of the network. It has one risk that will need to be dealt with physically, namely that no record can be its own child or parent. It would cause an infinite loop where the query to get the details goes around and around, chasing its tail like a puppy.

Relational Model Business Rules

Business rules combine the entity and the relationship into sentences that can be reviewed by the clients for truth. Since everything becomes so atomic in the model they can seem pretty silly at times. For example, you might well think that we all know that 'One Week must have seven Days'. However, if a week is defined as a 'Sunday to Saturday period of time', then chances are that you will have two weeks every year that are not exactly seven days long; the first week in January and the last week in December. The first time I ran across 54 weeks in a year I was stunned, and we didn't catch it with the business rule review because we thought some of them didn't warrant review. This little oversight caused a week's worth of discussion due to the need for a 'Week over Week' analysis report. Obviously we broke the rule that you need to come to your analysis without preconceived notions and remain objective.

Business rules are built to read in both directions:

❑ 'Each' || parent 'Entity name' || relationship verb phrase || cardinality || child 'Entity name'

❑ 'Each' || child 'Entity name' || relationship verb phrase || cardinality || parent 'Entity name'

In the modeling syntax we are going to use, the standard way to write the verb phrases is in third person singular. A second business rule is then added to include the rules about nullability. They look as follows:

No Null Allowed

❑ Each || 'Child Entity name' || belongs to || cardinality || 'Parent Entity name'

Null Allowed

❑ Each || 'Child Entity name' || optionally belongs to || cardinality || 'Parent Entity name'

Let's consider the following example:

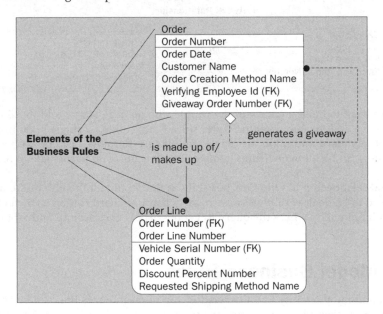

So we would build business rules like this:

1. Each Order is made up of Zero, One, or Many Order Lines.

2. Each Order Line makes up One and only One Order.

3. Each Order Line must belong to One and only One Order.

In this book we are going use a combination that departs slightly from IDEF1X standard, but allows us to review the business rules with the nullability factor included:

❑ 'Each' || parent 'Entity name' || nullability || relationship verb phrase || cardinality || child 'Entity name'

❑ 'Each' || child 'Entity name' || nullability || relationship verb phrase || cardinality || parent 'Entity name'

This gives us the following rule in our above example:

1. Each Order may be made up of Zero, One, or Many Order Lines.

2. Each Order Line must make up One and only One Order.

In reading these you can imply that an Order Line can't exist after the Order it's part of is deleted. Not only that, but an Order Line can't be part of more than one Order, and Order Lines can't be created until the Order exists.

> **Sometimes reading the implications derived from the rules is more important than the rules themselves, because you see how restrictive the rules actually are and realize that there are circumstances when they aren't true. The business rules must allow for every circumstance over the course of time.**

There is some disagreement in the world of modeling right now as to whether Entity/Relationship phrases are business rules or not. I guess I would say that they are just one type of business rule. A sentence like 'An Employee may be assigned to Zero, One, or Many Projects' sounds very much like a business rule to me. However, so does 'A customer can earn credit toward a free giveaway by purchasing $100 of product within three months of their first order'. Given the correct logical model, this business rule can be derived from several True / False decisions, however it is not a simple Entity/Relationship phrase. Business rules are more than just what can be modeled, but the model must support them.

Physical Modeling Concepts

It is in developing a physical model that all the care and concern you put into analyzing data elements and business processes really pays off. Entities are promoted to candidate tables, attributes to candidate columns, and relationships to candidate constraints. Many times there is almost a default 'take it like it is' process that happens in the first pass at developing the physical model. This is where the rubber hits the road so to speak. The fine-tuning you thought you did in your logical model needs to happen again, but with a much higher awareness of your model's permanent impact on the business. You can build logical models all day without affecting too many people. That is not the case now. Every name you choose, misspelling you make, size you make too small, data type you misjudge, and constraint you define incorrectly is going to have an impact on the entire development and maintenance teams for years to come. Fortunately the data modeler isn't alone in building the physical design since the DBA and programmers are generally involved in brainstorming and reviewing before anything is built. While there are still corrections and alterations made at this stage, it is crucial to have as well developed a design as possible, even in the case of development and test databases built to 'road-test' the design with a reasonable set of test data and queries.

Tables

Tables are called **files** or **records** in network and hierarchical DBMSs. They are the physical equivalent of an entity. When I speak to a business client who doesn't have any database background I equate tables to their spreadsheets or ledgers. A table is a singular container for data organized in rows and columns. And just like spreadsheets, tables can be linked together to provide a foreign key connection from a record in one spreadsheet to a record in another one.

Promoting an entity into a table isn't hard. In a data modeling tool it is simply a toggle of preferences from logical to physical. I actually have to remind myself that everything needs to be looked at from a new direction, namely that of the chosen RDBMS platform on which the physical model is expected to be deployed. DB2 has name length constraints, while SQL Server doesn't support comments on the tables and columns to save definitions at the database level. Every RDBMS that I have worked with has some personality quirk that impacts how I create the physical model. You need to learn your RDBMS to know its strengths and weaknesses.

I used the Oracle RDBMS option in the following examples and am using Underscore notation, replacing spaces in the column names with underscores.

In a simple logical-to-physical transformation logical entities become physical tables like this:

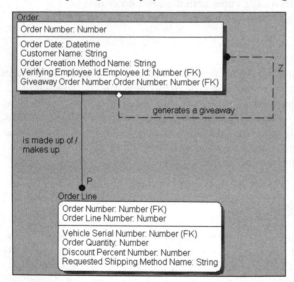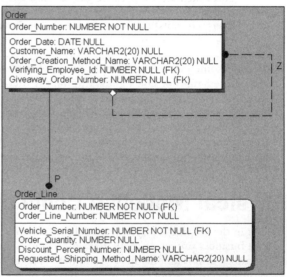

I have made the attribute data domains visible so that you can compare them with the default data types that are created in the physical tables. As you can see there have been few other changes during the transformation, other than the replacement of spaces with underscores. Sometimes getting physical is as simple as this. Remember that there are some rules we need to bear in mind regarding restricted words, depending on the programming language being used to code. You can't use simple names like 'Date' or 'Column' as a column name, for example. You may also want to shorten lengthy column names by creating a standard list of abbreviations. Different companies have different standards and approaches to the naming conventions of database objects.

We'll see more details regarding the transformation of a logical into a physical model in Chapter 8.

Operational Tables

The logical entities may not be the only tables that need to be created for an application database. Sometimes you need tables that have no entity source. I call these **operational** tables although you will also hear them referred to as **utility** tables. They exist simply to help manage the processes that need to happen in order to support the system requirements. You may, for example, need to model a table that deals with user security details, such as encrypted usernames and passwords required by the administrator. It may be that the programmer would like a table to store values that deal with the daily quantity of web page hits or captures errors for historic reference. Perhaps they want to be able to keep a batch load history for a couple of weeks before archiving it. There are thousands of these types of needs when you get to the physical model. These tables are not generally modeled on the logical model, but are added in the process of developing the physical model.

Views

A view is (generally) a temporary structure that is based on the results of a query but can be used in the same fashion (with a few restrictions) as a table. Views can be part of our design, in supporting the requirements and functionality of an application.

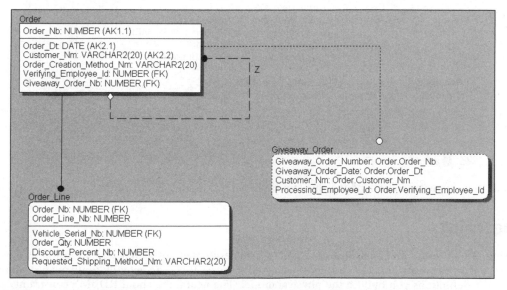

Notice that the column names in the view do not have to match the column names from their original tables. Many Views are created simply to give clients names that are easier for them to recognize. This View has been created to support a Giveaway Order screen for the Marketing department to be able to report on just the Giveaway Orders in their *ad hoc* query tool.

Column

All attributes, which you documented as representing business data elements, should be considered candidates to become columns. There are a few extra qualifications that need to be reviewed before they move into a physical design. They need to have a method of creation and maintenance, and should have a steward to verify the values. This is especially true in the case of independent entities such as 'Lists of Values', or sources of heavily relied-on data like zip codes and country names that become tables.

Try not to send an attribute on to a database design if no one is going to accept responsibility for the quality and maintenance of it. Having said that, the modeler does have some responsibility in verifying that the attribute has some chance of being a corporate asset rather than yet another bit of data dead weight to clog the RDBMS and lengthen the time for diagnosis, backup, or recovery. I would have told you this at the table level but it is deeper than that. Going over the attributes one last time with the business clients and determining whether they are important enough for someone to audit them for quality is a good test before you add them to the columns of a new table.

Operational Columns

Operational columns are very similar structures to operational tables. They are needed by the IT development team to be able to do their job easily and well. Almost all tables can use a set of columns that stamp them for analysis by creation or modification. Sometimes there is a flag column that a programmer uses to trace the stage of complex processes. As an example, consider the following physical design for our Order table:

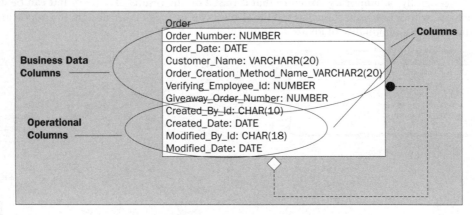

Again these types of columns don't show up in the logical model, but are added to the physical design.

Constraints

A simple way to think of a constraint is the physical deployment of a logical relationship, which represents a business rule. The more sophisticated software tools can actually build a constraint directly from the definitions you built in the physical model. The neat thing about RDBMS constraints is that they act like the law of Gravity; you can't break them unless you disable them.

> *There are some seriously complicated constraints that are also created in the RDBMS. Generally they cannot be shown as a simple line between boxes on your data model. These constraints, as database objects, are beyond the scope of our discussion here.*

Here is an example of a foreign key constraint:

```
ALTER TABLE Order_Line
     ADD  ( FOREIGN KEY (Order_Number)
                    REFERENCES Order ) ;
```

If your constraint says that a parent must have at least one child, then the RDBMS will actually prevent the insertion of a parent record without a corresponding child record. Deletions of records are prevented if they are connected through foreign keys to other tables. So the above constraint prevents the deletion of an `Order` record unless all the corresponding `Order_Line` records are deleted as well. This prevents the occurrence of **orphan** records, unrelated to any other values in the database, which impair referential integrity.

Modeling Syntax

Having covered the conceptual building blocks of entities, attributes, keys, and relationships, let's now look at the graphical symbols used to draw a relational model. There are a number of different modeling standards, and choosing which one of them to use in capturing your data analysis can be one of the most interesting (and confusing) issues that you'll have to deal with. While each style is similar, there are differences in the detail of how each building block is drawn. So far in my career, once the choice is made about the model drawing style at your company, it is almost set in stone. You will quite likely need to train the clients and the programmers in how to read the model so you may only want to do it for one drawing style. However, awareness of the strengths and limitations of a variety of different styles will help you in deciding what style is most useful in your work. Don't make up your mind too soon. While our focus here will be on the IDEF1X standard, we'll introduce three other modeling styles here.

The Symbols of Integration DEFinition (IDEF1X)

We will begin with IDEF1X because that is the notation we will use throughout the rest of the book. It is found in most CASE and modeling tools and is the language used in US Government projects, having been developed in the 1970s by the US Air Force, and revised by D. Appleton in 1993. I find it has gone through its testing period and is able to capture most of my discoveries about how data relates together. But unlike Latin it is not a dead language, it is growing to encompass some of the new UML and object modeling needs in the form of its latest incarnation IDEF1X$_{97}$.

Use of IDEF1X is a personal preference; you can generally draw the same analysis in many styles. Some have symbols covering concepts that others don't. For instance Barker can denote either/or whereas IDEF1X can't. Whatever you use you should learn it until you are very comfortable with it.

The symbols in IDEF1X are close enough to the other modeling styles to be recognizable and different enough to be confusing if you haven't used them.

- ❑ Entities are both square and round cornered boxes. Square cornered denotes a lack of dependence for identification on another entity. Round cornered denotes the opposite.
- ❑ Relationships are solid lines if the foreign key is identifying and dashed if it is non-identifying. Solid and dashed lines are completed with a set of terminating symbols that can be combined to cover a variety of cardinality and optionality rules.
- ❑ Entities that are categories have complete and incomplete symbols.
- ❑ Attributes are shown depending on the view.
- ❑ Primary keys are segregated from other attributes above a line.

No matter the choice of drawing style, what we are capturing is essentially the same. We might just draw it a little different depending upon the syntax we use. We'll now take a closer look at this notation.

Boxes

Boxes denote three different concepts. Logical models contain entities, while physical models contain tables and views. It is often hard at first glance to be able to decide whether you are looking at a logical or physical model for this reason.

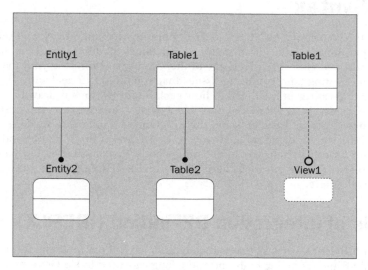

Here are some pretty basic rules about boxes on a model.

Dual Syntax

All of the boxes on a model represent either entities or tables/views. They do not mix. Entities and table/views are never used together. While they may look the same, logical and physical objects are never on the same model.

Singular Purpose

Boxes have one purpose. They are visual boundaries surrounding a data set. On a relational model this basically means two things:

❑   Boxes don't represent anything other than entities and tables or views.

❑   All entities or tables/views are represented as a box. They are not represented any other way. Even those copies representing discoveries from other logical analyses or actual objects in other databases, which will not be deployed, are still boxes on the model. They are usually noted with a distinctive color, text format, or naming convention to identify them appropriately.

Location Indifference

In IDEF1X boxes are not in any order. They are not arranged in any special way nor does placement mean anything. You get the same code no matter how you arrange them on the model. They are arranged to suit your desire to communicate data discoveries. You will find people get used to your placements and react negatively when you move things around. However, there is an argument from some that the physical creation order should order the model, so that everything that needs to be built first should be above later needs. There is also a feeling that all relationship lines should either be 'in the top and out the bottom' or on the sides noting the migrating key.

Concentrate on making the arrangement of the objects on your model a way to create a useful product for your customers. I have a tendency to try to use as little paper as possible so that I can print easier. This won't be useful if you are trying to work with someone who needs the creation precedence clearly noted by putting the independent entities above the dependent entities. Use your best judgment and be sensitive to your clients.

Corner Meaning – Dependent / Independent

The corners of the boxes denote the kind of dependence between each other. Square boxes denote independent entities or tables, while rounded boxes denote dependent entities or tables. If you need the primary key of Entity3 to migrate to identify Entity4, then Entity4 becomes a **dependent** entity. The same occurs with tables. Views are always dependent because they have no existence without the tables they are derived from.

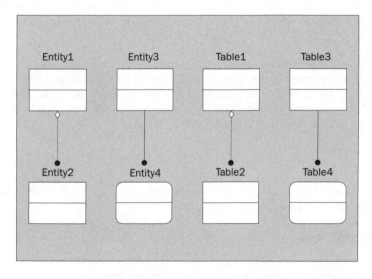

So, for example:

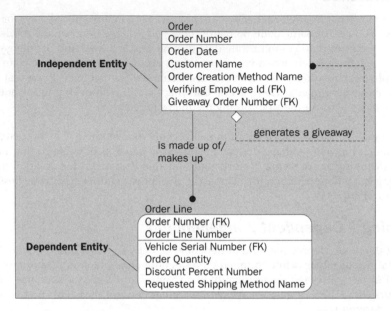

You can see from this example that an `Order Line` is dependent on `Order` for a portion of its identity. You need the `Order Number` identifier to be able to complete the identifier (or primary key) of the `Order Line`.

Remember that dependence is a state of having a portion of the complete identifier created in another entity or table, and is important to the sequencing of some data creation and deletion. I would like to say that it will be your visual clue to all sequential dependence but it isn't true. Certain of the mandatory relationships will also impact sequential tasks of creation and deletion of objects, constraints, and data, yet in IDEF1X they are not shown with a soft corner.

Lines

Lines are also for the most part the same on both the logical and physical model, and are used to segregate, connect, and note membership.

Lines within Boxes

Lines in boxes segregate the data elements into two types, those that act as a primary key or identifier and those that don't. Every text line above the line notes one separate data element that has been chosen to either completely, or uniquely, identify each member of the entity. You should only ever see one line in a box.

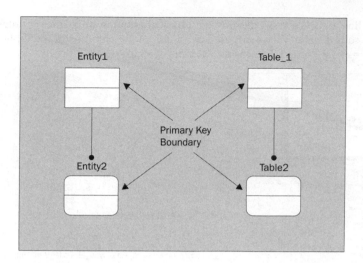

Relationships Between Boxes

Relationships, as we saw earlier, tie entities and tables together, and are also depicted using lines. These lines have a verb phrase explaining why the tie is there, but are also drawn so as to depict information about the relationship.

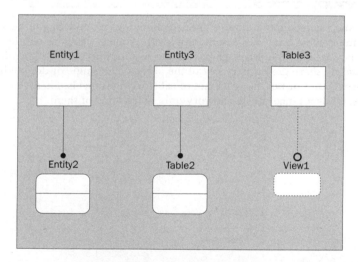

❑   Solid lines denote that the entire compliment of data elements above the line (the primary key of the parent entity or table) is migrating to the primary key position of the entity (or table) it is being related to. This is called an **identifying** relationship. We just looked at one between Order and Order Line. An Order Line can't exist without an Order.

❑   Long dashed lines denote that the entire complement of data elements above the line of the parent entity or table is migrating to a position below the line of the entity or table it is being related to. This is called a **non-identifying** relationship. The relationship between Order and Order to denote a Giveaway Order is non-identifying. A Giveaway Order could exist without an Order and one doesn't need the Order that triggered it to be created to identify it.

57

❑   The last line style is a short dash. It is a physical notation only since it notes that a view uses a table for source data. Views can use any, or all, of the columns in the table they reference. Our Giveaway_Order View is an example of that.

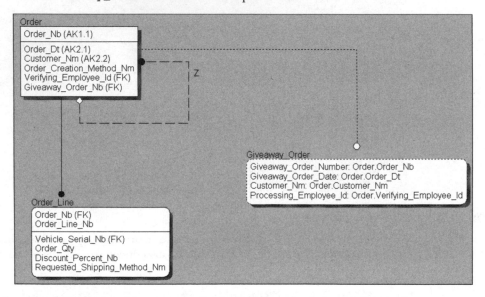

A further type of line we need to mention is used solely in logical modeling to denote a category grouping. As a reminder, we have one parent entity with as many category entities as required to document your analysis. The solid lines tell us that the relationship is identifying, in other words that the category entities all share the primary key of the parent. The single or double lines at the intersection tell us whether or not the entire set of category divisions is noted. A complete category notes all the types, while an incomplete category only notes some of them.

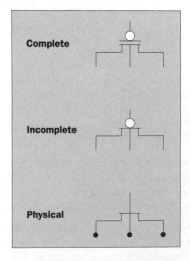

The physical notation is the default notation when you transform a logical model into a physical one. The same notation is used for both the complete and incomplete category.

Terminators

These symbols show up at the end of lines. They tell us how many of one instance in an entity or table is allowed, or required, to be related to an instance in another.

Cardinality Terminator

Cardinality covers the 'How Many?' part of the question. These symbols give us lots of flexibility in definition. They also help DBAs figure out ratio and sizing estimates in the physical world. The symbol is a combination of a dot and a notation.

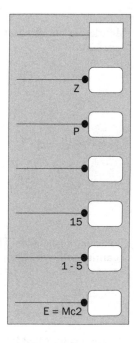

This is how they are read.

Relationship Line Terminator Symbol	Meaning	Infers	Example
Plain line	One and only one	Generally the parent or source	This is the parent terminator. It is used for child to parent business rules, such as 'Each Order Line makes up One and only One Order'.

Table continued on following page

Relationship Line Terminator Symbol	Meaning	Infers	Example
Z plus dot	Zero or One	Boolean decision	This is a child terminator. It is used for parent to child business rules, such as 'Each Order generates Zero or one Order'.
P plus dot	One or Many	Mandatory requirement of at least one	This is a child terminator. It is used for parent to child business rules, such as 'Each Order is made up of One or Many Order Lines'.
Dot	Zero, One or Many	Most flexible rule	This is a child terminator. It is used for parent to child business rules, such as 'Order is made up of Zero, One or Many Order Lines'.
< Number> plus dot	Specifically <N>	The most restrictive. That quantity only (always)	This is a child terminator. It is used for parent to child business rules, such as 'Each Calendar Year is made up of 12 Months'.
<N – N> plus dot	The range Number – Number	A range rule. Must be at least at the lower, but might be as high as the higher	This is a child terminator. It is used for parent to child business rules, such as 'Each Calendar Month is made up 28 to 31 Days'.
<note> plus dot	Whatever it says about a multiple relationship	A very complicated 'How many' that can't be stated any other way.	This is a child terminator. It is used for parent to child business rules, such as 'Each Customer under 12 and over 65 is offered a Ticket Discount'.

Note that this list includes two (at the bottom) that are not standard IDEF1X.

Nullability Terminator

This symbol says whether or not a relationship is required from all of the instances or not. This is read from the Child to the Parent, and in the case of a mandatory relationship will read as:

❑   Every Child `<Entity / Table>` instance *must* be related to a Parent `<Entity/Table>` instance

In the case of a null allowed relationship it will read as:

❑   Every Child `<Entity / Table>` instance *may not* be related to a Parent `<Entity/Table>` instance.

The symbol to denote this latter relationship type is an open diamond at the end of the line closest to the parent. So for example in our little Order model:

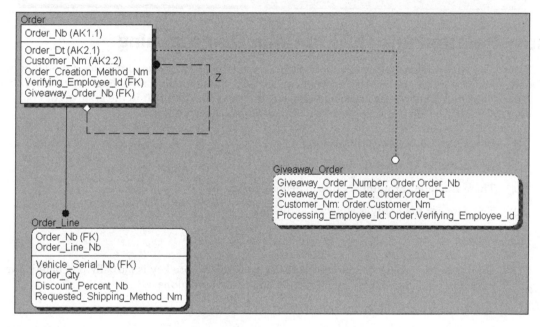

We only sell Vehicles so every `Order_Line` *must* have a `Vehicle_Serial_Number` it is related to. However, not every `Order` generates a `Giveaway Order` so although it *may* have one it isn't required.

View Terminator

The last terminator is the small dashed line and a hollow dot, which denotes a View. As a reminder here, Views are only found on physical models, and contain pre-packaged or filtered data from source tables. Everything in them is dependent for existence on the original sources. I tend to look at that empty dot as a ghost, since you model them for many different reasons but they have no substance on their own. It shows up as an empty terminator since the notation is only to show a dependency between the View and the source tables/s. You will find Views on models that have no relationships if they are referencing tables that are not on the model.

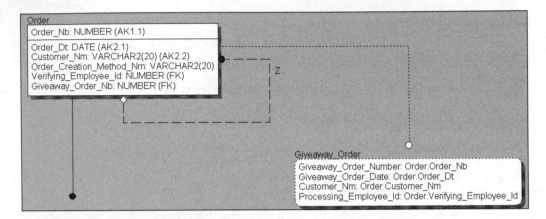

Entity-Relationship (ER) or Chen Diagramming

ER has been very popular, especially for conceptual modeling, and is one of the oldest modeling styles, having been first developed by Dr Peter P. Chen in 1976. Some modern modeling software has dropped ER from the choices they offer in recent years, so you may come across it in the archives of your company. Similar to most of the styles we'll discuss here:

❑ Entities are in square corner boxes.

❑ Relationships connect the boxes with a line.

❑ There is a letter or number code to denote cardinality.

❑ The name of the entity is attached to the box.

Unique to ER:

❑ Double border boxes denote a **weak entity type**, one whose key is partially populated as an identifying relationship to another entity and can't stand alone.

❑ Attributes are not shown.

❑ The relationships are nouns, rather than verb phrases.

❑ Rules should be read in a definite direction (left to right, top to bottom).

Here is an example of a Chen diagram and some pointers to the information it portrays:

❑ An Employee can do project work (proj-work) on many (M) Projects.

❑ An Employee can be the project manager (proj-mgr) of one (1) Project.

❑ A Dependent is only a dependent (emp-dep) for one (1) Employee. Since Dependent is a weak entity type, each instance of Dependent must have an Employee instance that identifies it.

❑ A Part can be a Component of many (M) parts.

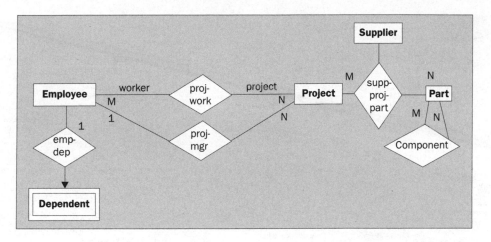

Chen (ER) is still used quite a bit and is very good at summary or conceptual analysis.

Information Engineering (I/E)

I/E, developed by Clive Finkelstein and James Martin in 1976, is very popular today among modelers and is generally an option in the popular modeling tools.

- ❏ It uses square and round cornered box conventions like we saw in IDEF1X for an entity. The square cornered boxes denote an independent entity, the round cornered boxes a dependent one.

- ❏ Attributes are shown. The entity box is divided to show the distinction of primary key and owned attributes. There is also the option of a simpler view without attributes.

- ❏ Relationships are lines between boxes with 'crow's foot' additions to denote cardinality.

The distinctive feature of I/E is the terminators of the relationship lines. I/E uses the famous 'Crow's foot' symbol to denote multiplicity, allowing for many different combinations of cardinality and optionality for parents and children. An interesting point to note here is that there are actually different versions of I/E that have subtle syntax differences. Some allow for an exclusive either/or notation and some don't. Get familiar with your own version.

Here is an example of an I/E diagram. You will notice that the notations map to IDEF1X fairly well. They are very similar to work with other than the category relationship. Where IDEF1X notes complete and incomplete categories, I/E notes them as exclusive (where one instance can only be grouped into one subtype) and inclusive (where an instance can be noted as more than one subtype).

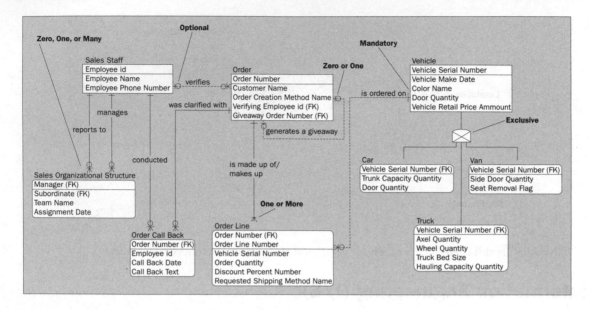

Barker Notation

Richard Barker's notation, developed in 1990, is used in Oracle's CASE design tools.

❑ The entity boxes all have round corners.

❑ The relationship line shows optionality as a dashed line, rather than a terminator symbol.

❑ Attributes are shown, but a line does not segregate the primary key. The primary key is coded with a # sign.

❑ Relationships are restricted to binary (true or false).

❑ The exclusion (either/or constraint) is an arc spanning relationships.

❑ Category or Subtype/Supertype relationships are shown as nested boxes.

Here is an example of what it looks like. And these are a few of the business rules that can be read.

❑ Each LINE ITEM is for either one PRODUCT or one SERVICE.

❑ Each PRODUCT is on many LINE ITEMs.

❑ The code is the primary identifier of PRODUCT.

❑ The name is an optional attribute of PRODUCT.

❑ Each ORDER is made up of many LINE ITEMs.

❑ Each LINE ITEM is at least partially identified by an ORDER.

❑ Each LINE ITEM is part of one ORDER.

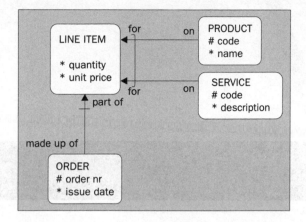

This image came from http://www.inconcept.com/JCM/December2000/halpin.html where you can read more about Barker notation.

Summary

In this chapter we looked at how RDBMS (Relational Database Management Systems) differ from network and hierarchical systems in relying on matching data fields (foreign keys) to create relationships between tables rather than the data pointers used in other systems. This concept, along with that of a single instance of each member of each set, is the basis for relational data modeling.

We were introduced to relational modeling terminology, and the concepts that we use every day to build conceptual, logical, and physical data models. We looked at:

- ❑ Entities (independent, dependent)
- ❑ Attributes (singular, group)
- ❑ Keys (candidate, primary, foreign)
- ❑ Relationships (identifying, non-identifying, category, view)
- ❑ Relationship Terminators (cardinality, nullability)
- ❑ Tables / Views (customer data sets, operational data sets)
- ❑ Columns (customer data elements, operational data elements)
- ❑ Keys (primary, surrogate, alternate, foreign)
- ❑ Constraints

And finally we looked over some alternatives in data modeling graphics, focusing on the IDEF1X notation that we'll use in all our models throughout this book.

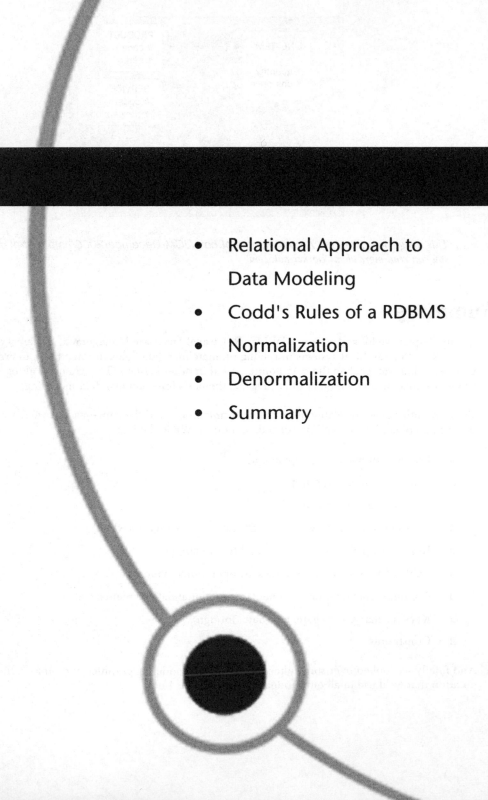

- Relational Approach to Data Modeling
- Codd's Rules of a RDBMS
- Normalization
- Denormalization
- Summary

Introduction To Relational Theory

In this chapter we are going to provide a basic review of relational theory. Although it is based on relational algebra and calculus we are not going to go into any actual math or logic proofs, nor will we go into a discourse on set theory. We'll concentrate instead on the implications it has for data organization using those concepts, in order to illustrate the solid foundation upon which relational modeling is based.

From there we will review the process of normalization, and see how it involves a series of rules by which we can test the relational nature of our data organization. We will finish up with a brief introduction to denormalization, the process by which we deliberately break some of the normalization rules in our design. In summary we will look at:

❑ A brief overview of the relational approach

❑ Codd's data management objectives and twelve rules of an RDBMS

❑ Normalization – Working with data so that it adheres to:

    ❑ Universal Relations

    ❑ First Normal Form

    ❑ Second Normal Form

    ❑ Third Normal Form

    ❑ Boyce – Codd Normal Form

❑ Denormalization – What is it, and why we might want to do it, including examples of:

    ❑ Derived Columns

    ❑ Deliberate Duplication of Data

    ❑ Disabling Constraints

Relational Approach To Data Modeling

Relational Theory, also referred to as Relational Database design, and/or the Relational Model, centers around the mathematical term **relation**. A relation in this context is a mathematical term referring to two-dimensional tables that have single valued entries. All entries in a column of the table are of the same data element, defined by a unique name, and have no positional or order significance. We often think that 'relational' is in reference to the use of relationships between entities and tables, but this is not the case.

In spite of being referred to as a relational theory, it isn't a 'theory' in the normal sense in that it does not have a succinct, well-defined list of 'premise-conclusion' statements. It wasn't originally written to explain data as it behaved in the storage structures at the time (since they weren't RDBMSs). It was developed to propose rules for organizing data in a new way, mostly to reduce redundancy and data maintenance anomalies. This means that it isn't just a database design standard, as we can use relational techniques to analyze data without any thought of physical deployment on a database platform. The concepts described by Dr Codd provide sound analysis and documentation goals for describing the details of data element behavior in a business activity.

The relational model provides a data organization technique that allows for consistency in storing and retrieving data, by utilizing recognized mathematical operations. A good point to remember though is that scientific models are used to reflect a sort of theoretical perfection that no one ever achieves in reality (hence our need sometimes to break the rules in real situations once you know how to manage it).

> *You can read more about the mathematics of relational theory in 'An Introduction to Dababase Systems' (Addison-Wesley, ISBN 0-201-14201-5).*

Origins of Relational Theory

In 1969 Dr Edgar F. Codd, an IBM mathematician wrote a groundbreaking report for his employees regarding storing large amounts of data. He expanded on these original thoughts in an article published the next year in *Communications of the ACM*, (Vol. 13, No. 6, June 1970, pp. 377-387), which is usually attributed with having begun the whole body of work in relational modeling.

> *You can find this article 'A Relational Model of Data for Large Shared Data Banks' at http://www1.acm.org/classics/nov95/toc.html.*

A database by Dr Codd's definition is 'a collection of time-varying relations … of assorted degrees'. Relation here is used in its mathematical sense of simply a set, comprised of records. So we might say today that a database consists of tables, which can contain records. These collections of records can change over time by insertion, deletion, and modification. These sets may have references to members of other sets through relationships. An instance or record of data is created and managed in only one set and is referenced everywhere else.

Notice there is no mention of computers or electronic formats. Databases by this definition are simply collections of data and can be organized relationally. You should also note that the writings by Dr Codd didn't give us the art of data modeling, a graphical syntax, or the relational approach whole and fully thought out. He described concepts and laid the foundations, which have been built on ever since.

Relational DBMS Objectives

We saw from our brief look at non-relational DBMSs in the last chapter some of the problems that both Hierarchical and Network database systems posed in terms of the means in which large amounts of data were stored. Dr Codd, while seeking to improve on these database models, outlined a series of objectives for a 'Relational' DBMS in an invited paper to the 1974 IFIP Congress.

You can find the article 'Recent Investigations in Relational Data Base Systems' in Information Processing 74, Proceedings of IFIP Congress 74, Stockholm, Sweden, August 5-10, 1974. (North Holland, ISBN 0-7204-2803-3).

These were the objectives he was striving for:

❑   To provide a high degree of data independence

❑   To provide a community view of the data of spartan simplicity, so that a wide variety of users in an Enterprise (ranging from the most computer-naïve to the most computer-sophisticated) can interact with a common model (while not prohibiting superimposed user views for specialized purposes)

❑   To simplify the potentially formidable job of the database administrator

❑   To introduce a theoretical foundation (albeit modest) into database management (a field sadly lacking in solid principles and guidelines)

❑   To merge the fact retrieval and file management fields in preparation for the addition at a later time of inferential services in the commercial world

❑   To lift data-based application programming to a new level, one in which sets (and more specifically relations) are treated as operands instead of being processed element by element

He goes on to list the four main components of his relational model. Codd felt that data collections are established not from an altruistic motive of keeping knowledge whether it's used or not, but to benefit the business by providing business clients with data that they need for their activities. And since that is true, why not underline the client needs as the drivers for database development in the future? So therefore we should organize data to:

1.   Simplify to the greatest practical extent the types of data structure employed in the principal schema (or community view)

2.   Introduce powerful operators to enable both programmers and non-programmers to store and retrieve target data *without having to "navigate" to the target*

3.   Introduce natural language (for example, English) with dialog support to permit effective interaction by casual (and possibly computer-naïve) users

4.   Express authorization and integrity constraints separately from the data structure (because they are liable to change)

While the first commercial RDBMS was the Multics Relational Data Store (MRDS) launched in 1978 by Honeywell, it wasn't until the early 1980s that RDBMSs became readily available to begin trying out his concepts.

Codd's Rules of a RDBMS

It was several years after his IFIP paper that Codd came up with his twelve rules, which we are still using today as the measure of the relational nature of databases. It is important to note that many of the DBMSs we consider relational today don't pass all the rules 100%. While they primarily act as a measure of the degree to which a database can be described as relational, it is also possible to use them in highlighting the importance of some of the aspects of physical modeling.

The goal of data modeling is not to follow all these rules religiously, but it is good to know the foundations that we are working with. These rules provide an indication of what a theoretically perfect relational database would be like, and provide a rationale for organizing data relationally. However, as we shall see in the course of this book, in physically implementing relational systems we break some of the rules in tailoring the performance of the database system for the needs of the client.

The proviso to these rules can be outlined as a 'rule zero', namely:

Rule 0

> Any system that is claimed to be a relational database management system, must be able to manage data entirely through its relational capabilities.

This means that the RDBMS must be self contained as far as data management is concerned. It can't require ties to outside factors to manage data. In other words while it is loaded on a given piece of hardware, and comes under the control of an operating system, it doesn't use any of the capabilities of these items in its data management. While a front-end tool, such as Enterprise Manager in SQL Server 2000, may help create database objects, such as tables, columns, and so on, the actual management of these objects is all performed within the database itself.

Rule 1: The Information Rule

> All information in a relational database is represented explicitly at the logical level in exactly one way – by values in a table.

This means that data elements aren't kept in a code block or a screen widget. All data elements must be stored and managed in a table.

Rule 2: Guaranteed Access Rule

> Each and every datum (atomic value) in a relational database is guaranteed to be logically accessible by resorting to a table name, primary key value, and column name.

This means that every value in every record in the database can be located by the table name, column name and unique identifier (as a key not as a physical storage locator number) of the record. It emphasizes two things:

❏ Firstly, the importance of naming in modeling. Every table must have a unique (meaningful) name (hopefully in the Enterprise but at least in the database).

❏ Secondly, the importance of choosing the data element(s) acting as its primary key.

Rule 3: Systematic Treatment of NULL Values

> NULL values (distinct from empty character string or a string of blank characters, and distinct from zero) are supported in the RDBMS for representing missing information in a systematic way, independent of data type.

This means that the database engine has to allow NULLs in any data type, and not zeros, spaces, or 'N/A'. This emphasizes the importance of the database supporting defined nullability and optionality as stated in the model.

Rule 4: Dynamic Online Catalog Based On the Relational Model

> The database description is represented at the logical level in the same way as ordinary data, so that authorized users can apply the same relational language to its interrogation as they apply to regular data.

This states that meta data about the actual data objects themselves should be available for use from tables, usually called system catalogs. These catalog or library tables contain the physical model in data element form. Some even carry the definitions of the tables and columns. So this emphasizes the public use of the results of your modeling efforts.

Rule 5: Comprehensive Data Sublanguage Rule

> A relational system may support several languages and various modes of terminal use (for example, the fill-in-blanks mode). However, there must be at least one language whose statements are expressible, by some well-defined syntax, as character strings, and whose ability to support all of the following is comprehensible: data definition, view definition, data manipulation (interactive and by program), integrity constraints, and transaction boundaries (begin, commit, and rollback).

This means that a relational database can work with one or several programming languages (SQL, T-SQL, and PL/SQL for example) that are extensible enough to cover all the functionality requirements of managing the environment. They must support data definition, view definition, data manipulation, integrity constraints, authorization, and transaction boundaries (BEGIN, COMMIT, and ROLLBACK).

For a modeler this means that you need to be aware of the rules of the programming language/s being used in your world before you physicalize. There will be a list of restricted words that you can't use for naming, for example.

Rule 6: View Updating Rule

> **All views that are theoretically updatable are also updatable by the system.**

Views are temporary sets of data based on the results of a query. Rule 6 proves that Codd was very forward thinking. This rule means that if a view can be changed bottom-up by changing the base values then it should also be possible for it to be changed top-down, which should ripple the change to the base values. This rule of Dr Codd's says that each view should support the same full range of data manipulation that direct access to a table has available. Up until recently views were very temporary arrays of data, accessible like a table but basically built as the answer to a query. That means that the data really lived elsewhere and was simply displayed through a view. Updating a view was impossible. You could only update the base data to impact the view. Materialized views (available in Oracle 8), indexed views (available in Microsoft SQL Server 2000), and some other new functionality (such as INSTEAD OF triggers in SQL Server 2000) changed all that. Given that a view knows where its data came from it can now push an update backwards to the origin.

Rule 7: High-level Insert, Update, and Delete

> **The capability of handling a base relation or a derived relation as a single operand applies not only to the retrieval of data but also to the insertion, update, and deletion of data.**

This rule underlines the mathematics of set theory that the relational database is built on. It says that records have to be treated as sets for all functions. First the set of records is identified and then they are all impacted the same way without having to perform single row processing. This states that data manipulation processes occur without dependence on the order of retrieval or storage in a table. All records are manipulated equally.

Rule 8: Physical Data Independence

> **Application programs and terminal activities remain logically unimpaired whenever any changes are made in either storage representation or access methods.**

This means that the data customer is isolated from the physical method of storing and retrieving data from the database. They do not need to worry about factors such as when data changes physical location from disk to disk, or that the size of their table changed for example. In other words the logical manner in which the user accesses the data must be independent from the underlying architecture (storage, indexing, partitioning, and so on). Such independence ensures that the data remains accessible to the user no matter what performance tuning of the physical architecture occurs.

Rule 9: Logical Data Independence

> Application programs and terminal activities remain logically unimpaired when changes of any kind that theoretically permit unimpairment are made to the base tables.

This rule strongly suggests that the logical understanding of data organization and the physical design choices of that data are completely autonomous. You should be able to change the database level design of data structures without a front end losing connectivity. This is difficult to implement. We can fool applications by designing a view or setting up a synonym to take the place of a table if the table needs to change drastically, but applications are very dependent on the names of physical structures.

Rule 10: Integrity Independence

> Integrity constraints specific to a particular relational database must be definable in the relational data sublanguage and storable in the catalog, not in the application programs.

A minimum of the following two integrity constraints must be supported:

- ❑ Entity integrity: No components of a primary key are allowed to have a NULL value (or value representing a NULL like N/A).

- ❑ Referential integrity: For each distinct non-NULL foreign key value in a relational database, there must exist a matching primary key value from the same domain. So in other words no parent record can be processed without all the impacts to the children records being processed at the same time. 'Orphan' records, those not related to others in the database tables, aren't allowed.

These integrity constraints must be enforceable by one or several programming languages (SQL, T-SQL, and so on).

Rule 11: Distribution Independence

> An RDBMS has distribution independence. Distribution independence implies that users should not have to be aware of whether a database is distributed.

This means that anyone using data should be totally unaware of whether or not the database is distributed (in other words whether parts of the database exist in multiple locations). Even from the physical model it shouldn't make any difference where the DBA chooses to set up the data storage, but it most certainly doesn't matter to the logical model. This was very forward thinking as SQL vendors are only just producing features allowing for the building of fully distributed databases.

Rule 12: Non-Subversion Rule

> If an RDBMS has a low-level (single-record-at-a-time) language, that low-level language cannot be used to subvert or bypass the integrity rules or constraints expressed in the higher-level (multiple-records-at-a-time) relational language.

All this rule is saying is that there should be no way around the integrity rules in the database. The rules should be so intrinsic to the object that you would need to rebuild the object to allow for breaking the data laws.

Normalization

Having considered the rules by which we determine the relational nature of a database, we now need to look at the process of **normalization** that we use in designing relational systems. Normalization can be defined as follows:

> Normalization – A data modeling technique, the goal of which is to organize data elements in such a way that they are stored in one place and one place only (with the exception of foreign keys, which are shared).

Entities as descriptive business concepts, and attributes as descriptive business data elements can be provided to the clients as a list. Every attribute must belong to one and only one entity (with the exception of foreign keys, which are shared), and every entity must own at least one attribute. The test to make sure you have the correct mapping of this is called normalization. If you have been diligent about creating atomic (singular) attributes then this process will be much simpler. Don't try to normalize a model before you have taken it to the greatest level of detail possible, with all attributes called out separately, and each data element well understood.

There are seven normal forms widely accepted in the modeling community, sequenced in order of increasing data organization discipline. By the time you are testing for Domain Key Normal Form you must have tested and organized the data elements to support the previous six Normal Forms. These rules are cumulative, and can be summarized as follows:

Name	Tests for the previous normal forms and:
First Normal Form (1NF)	The appropriateness of the primary key
Second Normal Form (2NF)	The dependence of all attributes on all aspects of the primary key
Third Normal Form (3 NF)	The dependence of any attribute on any attribute other than the primary key
Boyce – Codd Normal Form (BCNF)	Verifies that all data sets are identified and segregated

Name	Tests for the previous normal forms and:
Fourth Normal Form (4NF)	Verifies that all attributes are single valued for a member of the set
Fifth Normal Form (5NF)	Verifies that if the constituent parts of an entity were divided they could not be reconstructed
Domain Key Normal Form (DKNF)	Verifies that all constraints are the logical consequence of the definition of the keys and the domains (data value rules)

We will only consider the first three Normal forms in this chapter, as well as Boyce/Codd NF. This isn't because I don't think the others aren't interesting, but simply to try and reduce the complexity of normalization to make it more accessible here. On a more practical note, just getting to 3NF or BCNF is the goal of many project teams.

Up until now we have talked about data modeling with an emphasis on concept, relationships, and data understanding rather than data element organization. Normalization is all about organizing those data attributes into a format where relational data integrity is maintained as strictly as possible. Logical data models should adhere to the Normalization rules, in order that we can translate them into functioning physical data models. However, as we mentioned earlier, in implementing such physical models we will almost inevitably break some of the normalization rules in optimizing the performance of the system.

Universal Properties of Relations

This is the underlying set of preconditions that must be in place prior to the test for normal forms. They refer to that two-dimensional math form called a relation that relational design is based on:

❑ There must be no duplicate instances (members of the set).

❑ Instances are unordered (Top to Bottom).

❑ Attributes are unordered (Left to Right).

❑ All attribute values are atomic. No single column describing a single instance is allowed to hold multiple values at one time.

These concepts underpin the way we define entities and attributes. The primary key must ensure that there are no duplicates. Not only that, but a primary key must be defined, and the unique values must exist, for a member to be added to the set. There must be at least enough attributes to make a member of the set unique. In addition, it shouldn't matter in what order the instances (members of the set) of an entity are created.

The same goes for the order of the attributes. They end up in an order but it shouldn't matter what that order is (except for RDBMS needs). The attributes exist as sequence independent as the instances. The diagram overleaf illustrates that once the above universal properties are true (as supported by RDBMS and your analysis), you add layer on layer of tests for potential anomalies in the data organization. The satisfaction of each one depends on the core already being true.

Think of it as painting a house. First you prepare the surface, then you seal the wood, then you primer and finally you apply two top coats of paint. You cannot apply 3NF until 1NF and 2NF have already been tested and the design adjusted. It is a layering of data structure quality testing.

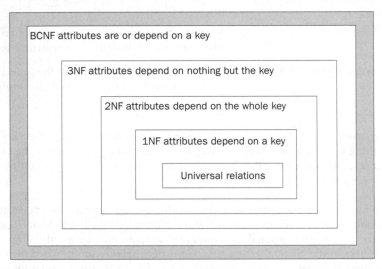

So first you put the generic universal relations right, by concentrating on the duplicate instances. For example, in the set of `Orders`, `Order 6497` is not allowed to appear more than once. In a similar fashion no attributes are allowed to have multiple values. So, for example, you can't store the data values 'Spokane, Miami, and LA' as a single `City` attribute; each value must be stored as an individual attribute. Test this by getting sample data and combing through it. These data issues will have to be resolved before a physical database can accept them if your logical design is used.

Why Check for Universal Relations?

Unwanted, or unmanaged, duplicates or multiples create serious issues in physical data management. They cause problems with:

- ❑ Consistent updates in all the places the data is stored
- ❑ Correct reporting with multiples in the mix
- ❑ Correct generalizations especially in math functions like sums and averages

So, for example, if your bank account current balance is stored as several duplicated values in the bank's database, then there is a chance that, if the relevant integrity constraints are compromised in some way, your balance will only be updated in one place on the database. All these values need to be updated in a synchronized fashion otherwise your latest salary payment may be missed off!

In all of these cases there is a chance of providing incorrect answers to simple data questions needed by the clients. The inability to provide correct answers lowers the value of the data. Having to be creative about getting correct answers due to these kinds of data storage issues increases the cost of managing the data. There's so much code out there that randomly picks the first instance of a duplicate row just because there is no other way of filtering out the duplicate records. There are also complicated blocks of code, involving complex query statements, coupled with 'IF ... THEN ... ELSE' statements, devised to parse through multiple values buried in one column in a table just to be able to report correctly.

First Normal Form (1NF)

Having obeyed the demands of the Universal relations, First Normal Form is then defined as follows:

> **First Normal Form (1NF) demands that every member of the set depend on the key.**
> **There are no repeating groups allowed.**

Here you are testing for any attribute, or group of attributes, that seem to duplicate. For example, any attribute that is numbered is probably a repeater. In our above car dealership example, we see Car Serial Number 1, Car Serial Number 2, Car Serial Number 3, and the corresponding Color attributes.

Another way to recognize that attributes repeat is by looking for a distinctive grouping that is within a different type. You could find something like *Home* Area Code and *Home* Phone Number, then *Cell* Area Code and *Cell* Phone Number, followed by *Work* Area Code and *Work* Phone Number for example.

Repeating groups of attributes denote at least a one-to-many relationship to cover the multiplicity of their nature. What do you do with them? You recognize them as a one-to-many relationship and break them out into a different entity. Then change the attribute names because now they occur only once. Finally you have to apply the universal rules for the new entity and determine what the primary key is. In this case each of the members of this set represents a sale of a car. You need both the Order Number and the Car Serial Number. In many Order systems this will be an Order-to-Order Line structure, because the sales are not for uniquely identifiable products.

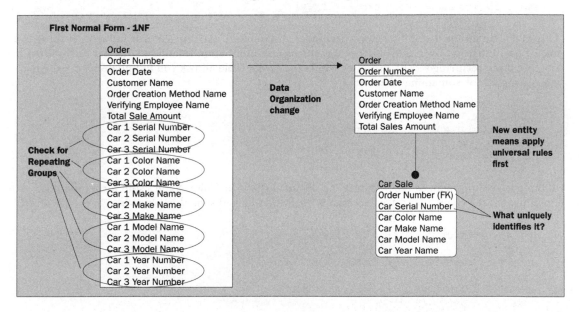

Why check for 1NF?

We check for first normal form in order to ensure:

❑   Consistent updates in all the places the data is stored

❑   Correct reporting with multiples in the mix

❑   Correct generalizations especially in math functions like sums and averages

Imagine trying to update all `Color Name` records in our `Orders` table from 'Dark Red' to 'Burgundy'. You have to find all the right places under all the right circumstances to get the update right, and issue code that looks something like this:

```
UPDATE Order
SET Car_1_Color_Name = 'Burgundy'
WHERE
Car_1_Color_Name = 'Dark Red';

UPDATE Order
SET Car_2_Color_Name = 'Burgundy'
WHERE
Car_2_Color_Name = 'Dark Red';

UPDATE Order
SET Car_3_Color_Name = 'Burgundy'
WHERE
Car_3_Color_Name = 'Dark Red';
```

This of course means that it'll be more likely that an instance of `Color Name` is missed, resulting in a loss of data integrity. By making a set that contains just information relating to one car sale, rather than keeping three recurring sets of attributes within the Order table allows you to update with a single call, which would look something like this:

```
UPDATE Car_Sale
SET Car_Color_Name = 'Burgundy'
WHERE
Car_Color_Name = 'Dark Red';
```

In the pre-1NF-normalized table finding the distinct list of Car Color Names sold for a month is complicated, since you would have to issue a query that looked something like this:

```
SELECT DISTINCT Car_1_Color_Name FROM Order
UNION
SELECT DISTINCT Car_2_Color_Name FROM Order
UNION
SELECT DISTINCT Car_3_Color_Name FROM Order
```

However, having modified the data to conform to 1NF leaves us with a single statement of the form:

```
SELECT DISTINCT Car_Color_Name FROM Car_Sale
```

Now imagine what happens to the reports, screens, and procedures when the clients need to increase the number of Car Sales allowed on an Order. Suppose they want to be able to sell 100 at a time on a bulk order. If we remove the repeating group from Order to satisfy 1NF then there is no impact at all and a huge order of 500 separate Car Sales is no issue whatsoever.

Second Normal Form (2NF)

Having obeyed the demands of the Universal relations and 1NF:

> **Second Normal Form (2NF) demands that every aspect of every member of the set depends on the whole key.**

Look at the Car Sale entity below, which violates 2NF. If we assume that Car Serial Numbers are unique around the world and never repeat (I think this is true at least for new cars) then car buffs would tell you that the Make, Model, and Year can be found out just by knowing the Serial Number. None of the values for those attributes should change during a sale. Even the Color of the car probably doesn't change due to a sale; most of us choose the color of the car based on how it is offered on the lot.

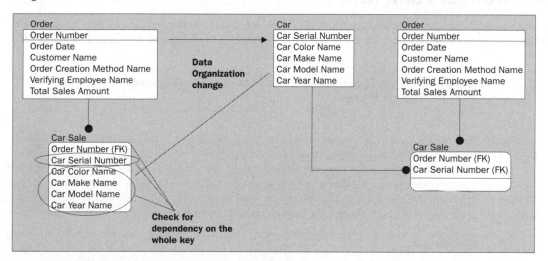

The normal forms between 2NF and BCNF work with this issue of attribute ownership. Every attribute needs to be 'owned' by the correct entity. They need to be completely identifiable by one and only one primary key, namely the key of the owning entity. Then they are shared by relationships to other entities that link the information.

In this case testing for 2NF has caused us to move the information about Cars to a separate Car entity with an identifying relationship back to the sale of the car.

Why check for 2NF?

This time you don't need to worry about repeating less than atomic attribute values (like Car Make Model Year Text), repeating instances in an entity (like the Order table without a primary key), or repeating occurrences of an attribute in an entity (like Car 1 Color Name, Car 2 Color Name, Car 3 Color Name). This time it is repeating information across *instances* of an entity that concerns you.

In a `Car Sale` instance table (examples of what data could look like in a design), the data would look like this before applying the test for 2NF.

Order Number	Car Serial Number	Car Color Name	Car Make Name	Car Model Name	Car Year Number
001	928374	Silver	Toyota	Camry	2002
002	928374	Silver	Toyota	Camry	2002
003	928374	Silver	Toyota	Camry	2002
004	928374	Silver	Toyota	Camry	2002

Suppose we have had a whole rash of bad luck selling Serial Number 928374. For some reason people keep bringing it back. We have sold it four times now. Look at all the information about that car being duplicated over and over. Breaking out `Car` as a separate entity prevents this type of inter-instance duplication. This data doesn't change with each `Order`, since it is now owned by the `Car` itself.

Third Normal Form (3NF)

Now we check for what are called **transitive dependencies**. These are attribute values dependent on attributes other than the key. In this case, having satisfied the demands of the Universal relations, 1NF and 2NF:

> **Third Normal Form (3NF)** demands that every attribute of every member of the set depends on nothing but the key.

Look at the `Car` entity. Can a `Car Model Name` of `Camry` have a `Car Make Name` of `GM`? No only `Toyota` makes `Camry`. Can a `Camry` have a `Car Year Number` of `1975`? No, the Toyota Camry wasn't offered until 1983. There are dependencies between the values of Make, Model, and Year of a Car. These dependencies create a set of true facts about cars that can be used over and over by many different members of the set of Cars. That means they need to be kept in a new entity we will call `Car Manufacturer Type`. We will change the organization to include this new entity and relate it to `Car`.

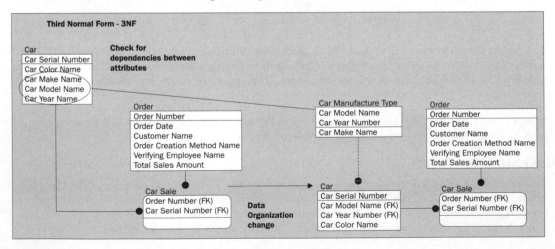

Resolving the transitive dependency gave us another clue that we needed another entity. This process creates simpler, more atomic sets of things for us to manage.

Why Do We Check for 3NF?

We are reducing duplication again and adding quality checks. This time let's look at an instance table of Car.

Car Serial Number	Car Color Name	Car Make Name	Car Model Name	Car Year Number
928374	Silver	Toyota	Camry	2002
876978	Black	Toyota	Camry	2002
987678	Red	Toyota	Echo	2002
986765	Blue	Toyota	Camry	2002
234590	Purple	Chrysler	P T Cruiser	2002
093485	Black	Volkswagen	Beetle	2001

Just knowing the Model Name of the car should tell us the Make Name. Volkswagen can't be the Car Make Name of a Camry. Nor can a P-T Cruiser be a Toyota. The relationship of Make to Model is a concept unto itself. We also know that Camry wouldn't be valid for any car older than 1983 so the Car Year Number is also part of the concept about Make and Model.

Boyce/Codd Normal Form

Having obeyed the demands of the Universal relations, 1NF, and 2NF, and 3NF:

> **Boyce – Codd Normal Form (BCNF) demands that every attribute must be a fact about a key and that all keys are identified.**

Look at the Order entity again. Order Date is a fact about the Order Number key, but Customer Name isn't, since the name of the customer is a fact about customers. Orders just reference customers, so any information about the customer would be inappropriate in the Order entity. How about Order Creation Method Name? Actually it is one of a small set of Order Creation Methods. Finally we need to recognize that Verifying Employee Name isn't a fact about the Order Number key, and that Employees are another data set that should be referenced by the Order.

If the values are part of a restricted list, they need to be brought out and analyzed for what identifies them. This process builds reusable data sets that add a great deal of quality to the data sets.

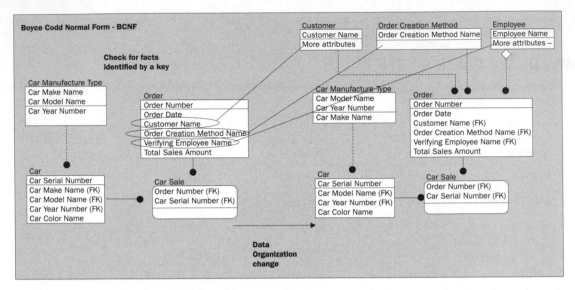

BCNF says that every attribute must be a fact about the entity identified by its primary key, or needs to be a foreign key originating elsewhere. It is very much a test for there being a 'place for everything and having everything in its place'. Think of the BCNF test as the final sweep for the restrictive 'List of Values' that the application will want to provide for the clients. It segregates all attributes into sets, and tests to see whether or not they stand alone.

So we pull out the concepts of `Customer`, `Order Creation Method`, and `Employee` and build three new entities. You may wonder how `Employee Name` changes into `Verifying Employee Name`. That is through a process called **role naming** where the migrating primary key changes names to clarify the role it plays in the new entity. We will look in more detail at role naming in Chapter 4.

If you can take your entities and attributes through to BCNF you have done a pretty thorough job of capturing the essence of relational modeling. From here it is simply a question of translating the logical design into a physical design and adding enough physical characteristics to the model to make it into a complete blueprint to create database objects.

This seems to be a really tedious exercise, especially if you are analyzing more than the nine data elements we started with. After a while you will get so good at this that it will come to you automatically. In practice we don't test each entity over and over again like we did to explain each of these forms. The structure will just not feel right and we will fix it without giving any real thought to whether we just fixed a 2NF or BCNF violation.

Denormalization

Denormalization is a process that happens in the final physical model designing and testing phases of a development project. It purposely undoes some of the relational concepts we just went over that drive logical analysis and design, in order to aid application performance. It may, for example, be more convenient to have some degree of redundancy in your physical design, such as having `Customer Name` in both the `Order` and `Customer` tables in our above example. Or indeed, we may wish to use a trigger for the `Order Creation Method` rather than build a table of three records.

Denormalization is carried out after weighing up the benefit that it will bring to the performance of your application, as set against a loss of relational integrity in the data. As such it can be very powerful, and very harmful. Without an understanding of what it is trying to achieve, all the hard work you have put into adhering to the various levels of Normal form will be undone, and the system will suffer as a result. Equally, if you are unaware of how it can be used to optimize the performance of the physical implementations of your designs, then you won't always produce the most client-friendly applications possible. Bear in mind that 'denormalized' doesn't mean 'un-normalized'. Un-normalized database designs (those which never went through the rigors of logical analysis) can't be said to be denormalized, since they were never normalized in the first place.

Denormalization should be done with the delicacy of brain surgery, and involve experience from across the entire development team. The DBA will be heavily involved, and programmers will also have suggestions. There may even be some Enterprise oversight committee who will review and approve the choices of denormalization for the final physical design. I have introduced it here so that, as a data modeler, you won't be too taken aback when the logical designs you created, built only to support the documented and proven worth of normalization, are apparently mangled in their physical implementation, without a thought as to what data anomalies these decisions could cause. Denormalization, when carried out efficiently, includes built-in safety nets to ensure that data integrity is maintained.

Derived Columns

While you don't logically model derived values, we deal with them all the time in reports and screens. You want to see values such as Order Total Amount and the Expected Arrival Date, which can be derived from the base elements. It is often tempting to store these values in a column, rather than waste I/O recreating them at every request, as part of the denormalization process. This, however, necessitates the creation of coding (stored procedures), to ensure that any change in the base values is reflected in those values derived from them. This safeguard must be maintained at all times otherwise the data passed to the client is inaccurate and worthless.

Derived columns can be good choices, especially in the cases of non-volatile, complicated, time-consuming, high-use formula results. Last year's budget at the department rather than the G/L level would be a good candidate. There is a pretty low chance that someone is going to change the proposal now and everyone wants to know what the target is. Keeping the department level proposal rolled up from lower-level details may be an appropriate storage of derived data. The Order Total is another matter. The RDBMS is wasting I/O time to get you a total. Leave it to the Data Warehouse team to save the denormalized value and keep the total derived through an automated synchronization process.

Remember that you may not need to consider derived columns, if you can generate the derived values by some other means, such as materialized views. If you are able to use views, then you can maintain the highly normalized form of the database, and simply update the view when the base values change.

Deliberate Duplication

Another thing you don't model logically is duplicate attributes. Remember that, from the point of view of normalization, we want one thing in one place owned by one entity. On the other hand I have six pairs of scissors in my house. I denormalized them because nobody ever seems to put them back where I can get to them and I waste time searching for them.

Some database table structures are huge and complicated. It might take five or more table joins to get the Product Code of a Product or the Hire Date of an Employee. Duplicating columns has as much risk as saving derived columns, since you are deliberately introducing redundancy into the database. You need to look at the cost of getting the value dynamically versus the cost of refreshing the duplicates every time the base attribute is updated for a specific record.

The risk here is similar to that which we saw in the case of derived columns, since we must have code in the form of a stored procedure or trigger, in order to ensure that the values are updated on each occasion that the base value changes. Duplicated columns should also be protected from being updated by any other process, and only retrieve data from a single approved source.

Deliberate Removal or Disabling of Constraints

I am not referring here to the temporary disabling of constraints for loading or emergency data management. This is full-time deliberate removal of relationships that have been discovered in the logical analysis, probably to enhance insert, update, or delete transaction speed.

Every time an insert, update, or delete fires on a table that is shackled with constraints, the constraints fire, taking time and doing their job of stopping bad things from happening. Sometimes this isn't an optimal physical design. Some tables take a beating in continual processing. Others need to be able to take in less than quality records that can be cleaned up at a later date.

This seems a little like removing the seat belt from your car because it wrinkles your tie. The whole purpose of the analysis is to document the rules of the business. This particular denormalization should be a last resort for data that has no chance of integrity. The best you can do is batch a QA check on a regular basis and mail the results to someone who might care enough to fix things.

Deliberate Undoing of Normalization Forms

This is another form of denormalization. Just go backward through the normal forms and undo all the changes you made to make your analysis relational. You will get closer and closer to one huge flat file. I am not going to say that a huge flat file is never the right database design, but I haven't come across one yet that is in a transactional system. Data warehouse dimensional designs are a whole other ball game.

You deliberately go back to repeating groups, transitive dependencies, partial key dependencies, and even keyless tables. Each of these decisions has to be made with the knowledge of what could happen to the data residing in structures built this way.

Summary

A relational database adheres to a greater or lesser extent to the twelve rules of a RDBMS drawn up by Codd. In developing a relational system we use the process of normalization, verifying the relational nature of our data organization against the various degrees of normal form. We considered 1NF, 2NF, 3NF, and BCNF, and showed how they help us verify that:

❑   Single membership of an instance in a set is recognized by a stable unique identifier.

❑   All the attributes in an entity depend on all the identifying attributes.

❑   None of the attributes depend on any other attributes other than the identifying attributes.

❑   Any attributes which can be recognized as a set unto themselves have their own entity and identifying key.

We then looked at the power and risks of denormalization, the process by which we break the rules of normalization, in order to improve application performance. It is something that requires experience, in order to tailor its use appropriately for any given application, but can prove invaluable in enhancing the user experience of the application in question.

- **Model Development**
- **Conceptual Analysis**
- **Logical Analysis**
- **Physical Analysis**
- **Reverse Engineered Analysis**
- **Analysis is in the Detail**
- **Summary**

Levels of Analysis

Having looked at the theory behind relational data modeling, the terminology that we use in discussing relational models, and what the notation we use in our models looks like, we now need to discuss the types of data models that we can construct, and the level of data element detail that we include within them. Data models as deliverables can be tailored to the needs of the client, with appropriate levels of detail.

We will look at the following types of model in this chapter:

- ❑ **Conceptual** – This model type relates thoughts or big subject areas together. It is used in project scope reviews or as a data area table of contents, and involves creating logical groups for greater definition.

- ❑ **Logical** – Contains detailed subjects related together. The objects in this model are named and built with as much detail as necessary for the logical data requirements to be understood. The goal is to isolate and present each distinct data element, documenting as much about it as possible. Business rules documented in the relationships (rules relating entities) can be used as a True/False test prior to writing code.

- ❑ **Physical** – Table structures designed to manage the detailed subjects. Database object naming standards are applied here, and these models provide a blueprint for database design.

- ❑ **Reverse Engineering** – Analysis of data management structures that already exist (either as a custom development or a vendor product). The thing that separates reverse engineering analysis from conventional physical analysis, is that you may need to include things on the model that don't necessarily exist physically at the RDBMS level. This can include things such as relationships that never made it to constraints, and instead are managed in screens or procedures.

In creating conceptual, logical, and physical models there is a progression in the level of detail you need to provide. The closer you get to a physical model, the more aspects you need to define of the elements and the more detailed choices you have to make. This is what makes modeling such an iterative process since in double-checking the detail in the definitions within your physical model, you will frequently have to refer back to your logical and conceptual models to verify the existence of data elements, and the relationships between them. We will look at the level of detail provided in each of these modeling phases in terms of:

❑ **Entity-Level** – Logical high level used for scope and planning or a simplified review at the beginning of a project. This view contains only (core) entities, their definitions, and (preliminary) relationship lines.

❑ **Key Based** – This view contains only entities, primary keys, (preliminary) relationship lines, and foreign keys and the definitions.

❑ **Fully Attributed** – Most detailed level of analysis containing entities, primary keys, (preliminary) relationship lines, foreign keys, attributes, and definitions.

Model Development

Most professions have several levels of analysis that they go through before they are finished creating something. Professional photographers do a Polaroid first to do some general checks before they move on to the real film. Design engineers start with a sketch, to draft, to final release of a drawing. Doctors do an office check-up, to a physical, to a complete physical, and nowadays to a series of MRI and sophisticated scanning before attempting a complicated surgical procedure.

Data modelers do pretty much the same thing. They gather information in an iterative process that moves the knowledge from concepts to logical to physical designs. It is the safest and most commonly taught method of modeling. Yes, you will find shortcuts being taken everyday, but that doesn't mean that this isn't the best way to analyze and develop data structures.

You should also know that the process can move backwards. This is generally called **reverse engineering**. If you have the finished form to work from, it is possible to work backwards and create a logical from a physical and a conceptual from a logical. It isn't unheard of and can be quite useful, for example when trying to extract data from an old system for use in a new one.

In creating a data model there are several stages of development depending upon the project goal you have been set. Sometimes you are developing models to capture currently undefined data dynamics to support the building of a new application. In cases like that you are moving through a fairly well-defined lifecycle of analysis, in developing a future 'To Be' model, as listed below. Other times you may be working with a project whose goal it is to integrate several systems and retire portions as being redundant and costly to the enterprise. In cases like that you may be skipping around these steps going from 'As-Is' to 'To-Be' models in a more iterative and reactive mode.

These are only in a general order, and not all projects work through these steps. Bear in mind that as greater understanding of the system is acquired, so it is often necessary to return to one of these steps in order to verify particular details.

❑ **Proposal & Planning** – The development proposal review board usually needs a conceptual design to explain the intended scope of a project. This helps to justify funding especially if you can show, in your preliminary research, what concepts will be new additions to the Enterprise.

❑ **Detailed Requirement Gathering** – Building on your initial requirement gathering this stage verifies and enhances the conceptual design to increase the confidence that the scope was well defined. You may even decompose very high-level concepts downward to produce several conceptual designs, if the project is large enough to need to be separated out into subteams.

- **Logical Design** – The conceptual design is used to help steer the logical analysis modeling in the gathering and detailing of specific data elements (attributes) and organizing them into normal form tested and verified entities. We need our non-technical clients to review what we have discovered along the way. They need a logical model with full names and very descriptive relationship verb phrases.

- **Physical Design** – The logical model is then made into a concrete, database-specific physical model. It often goes through a process of renaming (to support the target RDBMS standards) and creating 'physical only' objects used to manage the tables operationally. This physical analysis results in the model that can be used to create RDBMS objects. Programmers working to create, or maintain, a set of tables need a completed and up-to-date physical model to learn with and eventually write code from.

- **Design Review** – This evaluation phase refers back constantly to the logical and physical design. It becomes the communication method for noting the changes to the team in understanding and as the prototype system is developed.

- **Implementation** – Finally, it goes into production. The whole set of conceptual, logical, and physical models, definitions and mappings become part of the department-controlled reference documentation. This is the set of documents that are the most difficult to keep synchronized with reality since things change without your involvement.

- **Vendor or Legacy Solutions** – Reverse-engineered analysis models are generally a physical design or mostly physical designs. Sometimes it becomes necessary to add relationship lines for clarity even when the constraints don't exist. Otherwise you have a model full of freestanding boxes that is not terribly useful even if you organize them in alphabetical order. They need to be more than an inventory of physical objects. As Company mergers become more frequent, reverse-engineered design of similar existing systems becomes necessary to be able to compare data rules. Vendor packages need to be compared with existing company business rules and policies to verify a good fit before purchase. Legacy systems need to become a fully understood and known quantity before they are targeted for replacement.

Not a Flow Diagram

A data model at any level of analysis isn't a process or business flow diagram, though hopefully your project team is developing these models too, as they are another level of analysis that will contribute heavily to the success of the project. While relational data models perform the same role as a flow diagram in acting as a representational window into the real depths of analysis that have been captured, they don't tell a comprehensive coherent story from start to finish. In fact relational data models don't have a 'Start' and 'Finish' box. In Chapter 2 we looked at the graphic symbols that are used to 'tell a story' to the reader of a model, but there are also layers of information in a model that do not show on the diagram. These include items such as long informative definitions for each of the textual labels on the model, and lists of allowed values, notes, critical data rules, and quality checks documented and available for the enterprise.

> **Data models provide a data structure in terms of the mathematics of logic, rather than the business organization's rules.**

Data models capture rules at a much lower level of detail than most business processes. This point is one of the things that seem to be the most confusing about data models to the beginner, since they tend to think that a model should explain all of the business rules. A data model can only document primary business rules explicitly in the graphical view. These are the business rules so basic that no one actually thinks about them as business rules. There may be client-specific business rules that can be inferred from the model, but these can't be captured in graphical format. To determine such rules you need to examine the documentation accompanying the graphical data model.

Take for example the business rule that:

❑ Each Customer must have a CreditRating of 'Satisfactory' or better to be notified by Marketing of a ProductPromotion.

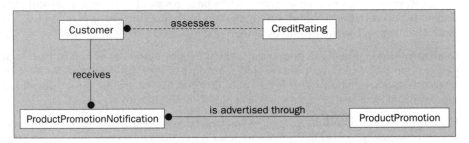

The model can't cover the value 'Satisfactory' or the 'or better' part of the rule in a relationship rule. Those are members of a data set that is configured to support this rule. It isn't visible in the graphic. This can cause some distress among your clients if they expect to find their 'rules'. Those rules will probably be managed in code, based on requirements and business rules documented elsewhere.

> **You need to manage the expectations of the team as to what the model can provide them with.**

Data Relationship Rules

The data model does an excellent job in noting all the primary business rules verifiable from the one we outlined above:

❑ Each Customer must have a CreditRating

❑ Each Product may be advertised by a special Promotion

❑ Each Customer may receive a ProductPromotion

❑ Each ProductPromotion is developed by Marketing

❑ Each MarketingDepartment representative may deploy a ProductPromotionNotification

❑ Each Credit Rating must be attained for a Product Promotion

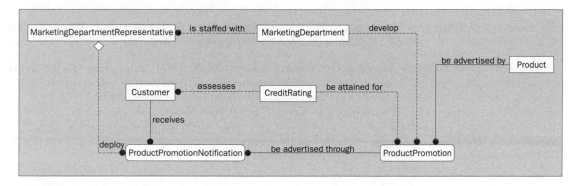

Note that this model shows many rules at a very simple level by pairing concepts or (eventually) sets. These are referred to as **binary** relationships. There are exceptions, on occasions when a concept is complex enough to need three or more relationships in order to describe it. However, at this level, even these can be read as pairs. Take, for example, the `ProductPromotion` and `ProductPromotionNotification` entities. While there are many relationships to these entities, we are able to read each of the relationship lines as simple relationships between two entities. You might not even recognize that `ProductPromotion` was connected to so many sets without the graphic to highlight the fact.

> Data models do not document the underlying data or concept connectivity the way they are exercised in business situations.

Conceptual Analysis

Conceptual models are reference only documents. They capture and document the first look at the arena of data processing. Ideally they are built without a single thought as to what, how, and where a physical deployment might be. Conceptual modeling is often overlooked as having little intrinsic value, but think about it. Someone has to become acquainted with the project scope. They have to interview the makers and processors of the data elements. They have to trace documentation through paths of creation, auditing, publication, saving, and distribution. They have to follow both common happenings as well as gather up stories of anomalies. Then they need to jot down process improvement opportunities. They have to take all that knowledge back to their desk, mull it around in their head, and create a simple, easy-to-read graphic that covers the whole thing.

The definition of a concept is:

❑ A thought or opinion, general notion or idea, especially one formed by generalization from particular examples.

And that is exactly what you are targeting to capture in a conceptual level of analysis. You are documenting unique identifiable data set types, which are intrinsically necessary to the successful management of whatever the charter of your project says needs to be managed. It could be one or more business processes. It could be almost anything that requires the gathering and management of quality data to create a successful outcome.

93

Conceptual modeling is not a trivial task. This type of model centers on discovering and analyzing organizational and user data requirements. We are focussing on what data is important. When the data model encompasses the entire Enterprise, it is called the **Enterprise** or **Corporate** data model.

This type of model can either document the current environment (As-Is) or future plans (To-Be). It may be used to support strategic or tactical analysis of the corporate data inventory. When data modeling involves senior-level managers, it can help them focus on current data management and look for opportunities to improve it. For example, a conceptual model that encompasses more than one project, or one department, or one business process can show in a very simple fashion the most used data concepts (like Calendar, or Employee) simply by the quantity of relationship lines linking them to other conceptual entities.

Entities in a Conceptual Model

Remember from Chapter 2 that entities are not tables. They are basically nouns that capture an idea of the necessary ingredients in their process. Things like:

❑ People or Mechanisms that do things

❑ Material or Requests that need to be changed

❑ Product or Deliverables that need to be created

❑ Thresholds or Control concepts that need to be applied

❑ Time, Geography, Budget, Organizing structures that need to be referred to

❑ Logic points that need to be used to govern 'if this – then that' decisions

They shouldn't be too specific or too general, since we are capturing information at a high level. They have single noun names and a good definition that encapsulates what you discovered on your trips through the environment being analyzed. Conceptual entities are guides to the more detailed logical entities that come next.

Relationships in a Conceptual Model

These are the verbs that tie the entities together. They are not physical, but notes describing the dependencies that appear to exist between entities. In addition to any information you need to document regarding specific business rules, these relationships should capture the following details about the relationship:

❑ **Category** – We introduced categories in Chapter 2. Conceptual categories can be useful to note big separations in concepts that need to be treated one way as an aggregate and another way as a specific member. Geography is a great example of a conceptual category. An enterprise may use sets such as Continent, Nation, State, Province, and City, as part of the set Geography. Yet each one may need to be broken out as a subtype to be able to document different business rules relating to their particular group. For example, a Film Company makes contracts with Nations to release rights to a film. However, the Films are shown in Cities.

We will look at many categories throughout the book. It is a very useful data model construct to display the similarity and differences of entity families.

❑ **Verb Phrase** – Generally you want verb phrases to be simple connective phrases that note that this 'happens' to that, creating simple sentences. In the conceptual model it may not be as easy as a simple verb. Parts may be used as spares, or to build, or rework, a product. People can manage, support, be assigned to, assist, train, and hire other People. Draw a line for each to show the separate business rules binding the entities together.

❑ **Cardinality** – This is the choice you need to make for the line terminators. It notates 'How Many' children there have to be for every parent. This is the cardinality definition. There are two terminators for every line. Conceptual models tend to use the most generic ones, the 'One' or 'Many' notations, but you can use any of them you think you need. If you need a refresher as to the notation we use to denote cardinality then look back to Chapter 2.

Conceptual Model Example

Here is what the conceptual model would look like for an advertising and marketing department. You can see that this is a pretty high-level view. Notice though that all we are looking at are the entities and relationships. There are really only four basic concepts in the model, namely who does the task, what is the task, who are the targets, and how do I communicate with them.

We kept the names specific enough to help the client see the process and yet generic enough to cover large areas of data. The relationship names are simple and instructive to someone who isn't as familiar with the business area.

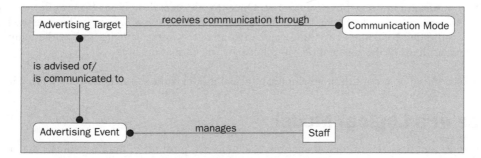

Logical Analysis

Logical analysis uses conceptual analysis as a launch point and drives downward to fully document the 'sets' or entities that must be created and related together in order to support the scope of the project. We discover and document each separate data element. They are all recognizable in their entities, and every aspect of that entity that the clients are interested in becomes an attribute. We then keep them as simple sets and relate them together so that they can be used to create all of the different combinations that are required to satisfy the needs of the project.

Beginning with a conceptual model at least gives us a certain feel for differentiation, which we separate more and more, until we have the base data parts, sorted out. This is very iterative, since in the course of analysis you may well change your mind as to how to group elements together. That is the nature of the process, refining your definitions until all the data elements are defined appropriately.

We call this process 'logical' analysis because of the mathematics that it sprang from. Whether you are talking about the logical model of a network, hierarchical, object-oriented, or relational analysis, you are sinking your toes into the math that started the whole thing.

> **A well-documented logical analysis provides a framework for organizing sets to provide consistent answers to questions.**

The logical analysis delves deep into the very nature of the data elements that the conceptual analysis scoped together as being necessary to support a process. Due to that need for depth and details we add a new level of detail to the model, in terms of the actual attributes or data elements that each entity consists of. We will find the identifiers in the form of candidate keys and promote one of them to be the primary key of that entity. We will begin the process of defining domains and tightening up the relationship aspects like cardinality and nullability. And then we need to test it against the Normal forms for quality.

The logical analysis is probably the most taxing portion of modeling for a project. This is where you lay out the foundations for the project. Mistakes here are very serious. The ripple they create when you discover you were wrong can cripple a project's ability to deliver on time or on budget. What makes logical analysis troublesome is that it is very difficult to move down from the conceptual analysis to the true data elements and true data sets. And once you do, validating it is still a surprising and enlightening experience. Not only that but you must allow yourself enough time in this phase of your analysis to prevent going from logical to physical too fast. Once the physical design has been built the ripple effects of a new understanding or key concept can be very costly. Take some time to make sure the logical model has solidified by doing everything you can think of to verify, validate, test, and attempt to break your understandings of the sets (entities) and business rules (relationships).

You will see the steps required in developing a logical model from a conceptual model in Chapter 7.

Entities in a Logical Model

Entities represent data sets in logical analysis. Each one is a pure set of building blocks that are related together to create information. For example, to answer the question 'what number is valid to call a person at work?' we need to relate Person + Company + Phone (type Company Phone) correctly.

Whereas the conceptual entities were broad ideas these are narrow. In fact I would say (barring ridiculous levels) the narrower the better. You have to drive the logical analysis down until you can actually see the business data element in their most atomic form.

Attributes

These are all the things that the clients feel they need to store to be able to do their jobs. The attributes are the things you want to remember about the entities. They are the descriptors. You may find them originally in reports or spreadsheets that the clients use now to manage a process. You have to find every one of them and add them to the model in the correct entity. When we do the tests for Normal forms we are really verifying the placement of the attributes into the proper entity home.

Candidate Keys

The attributes are reviewed to see if they can act as a non-changing unique identifier of a member of the set of rows in the entity. Candidate keys are often the natural identifiers of things in the world at this stage of analysis but you may be adding in a surrogate key at this point also. Candidate keys can be single attributes like serial numbers that stay with the railcar for its entire life. However, some keys are composites made up of combinations of attributes like date, time, route, location, airline, and seat class for your airline reservation for your vacation. Remember from Chapter 2 that an entity can have more than one candidate key, but only one of these is then selected to be the primary key; the rest are noted as alternate keys.

In logical modeling it doesn't matter what order multi-attribute keys are in. It will however matter when you physicalize the model in terms of the eventual performance of the application.

Logical Domains

Our attributes will have to be of a particular data type, or **domain**, such as integer, string, boolean, and so on. Specifying domain here, before we get to the physical model, makes creating the physical model much easier, and also highlights anomalies in the data by providing an expectation of what the data will consist of. With that expectation defined you have the means of testing reality to see if it is what you thought it would be. For example, if you have an attribute designated as a time domain, and you find the word 'Noon' (as opposed to the time value 12:00PM) or 'After 6' in the real data, you will have to rethink the attribute with the clients. Either it is a Time attribute or it is a Text attribute. Programmers count on numbers, dates, time being what they say they are. Otherwise they have to put in all sorts of complicated translation and check code into their programs. Sometimes they have to anyway, but they would rather know up front than find out by trying to load data without planning for those anomalies. Of course if you can't find anomalies like this in the current dataset it doesn't mean that a user in the future won't want to enter data in this way. You have to try to foresee these kinds of issues and resolve them with the client as early as possible.

Logical domains represent the lowest common denominator among RDBMS data types and may be one of the following:

- ❏ BLOB – A binary large object, generally a picture or graphic formatted object. This also includes LOB (large objects) like music or video

- ❏ DateTime – Values that must fit within the Gregorian Calendar and a 24 hour clock

- ❏ Number – The entire set of symbols noting a sequencing at any precision. This data type does include symbols for positive and negative values

- ❏ String – Any character including numbers and complex characters like accent marks and tildes

- ❏ Unknown – no domain specified

Remember that these are simple in comparison to physical RDBMS data types. So, for example, the logical data type NUMBER(5,2) would in one RDBMS translate to NUMERIC(5,2) and in another to DECIMAL(5,2). Logical analysis is done without any thought about the tool or platform, which it will eventually be built in or deployed on.

Role Names

You will either be forced into creating role names (because the same attribute name cannot exist in any entity more than once) or you will want to for clarity. Either way it is an important element of logical analysis. Employee ID makes perfect sense in the `Employee` entity, but what is it doing in an entity concerned with advertising campaign attributes? Is it the Employee who launched the campaign, the author, the person who approved it, the manager, or the web master in charge of the web site with it on? Role names clarify just what a migrated key is doing there.

In a similar manner, Employee ID may have a recursive relationship to itself, such as Employee to Manager (each Employee must be managed by one, and only one, Employee). You can't have Employee ID noted twice (once for the Employee record identifier, once for the Manager). If you want those recursions to exist you *have* to role name the foreign keys so that they can exist. Besides you have the same problem. Why are they there? You can't tell if they all read as Employee ID. Is this their manager, administrative assistant, the person who hired them, gave them their review, or recommended them for promotion? Who are they?

You may find that the clue to the name you wish to use for the role name is in the verb phrase of the relationship. Take, for example, 'Each Employee must be managed by one, and only one, Employee'. In this case, the verb 'managed' changes the EmployeeID into ManagerID as the name of the foreign key using a role name.

Relationships in a Logical Model

Logical analysis evolves from the generalities of conceptual analysis. So while the many-to-many relationship is legal, the point of logical analysis is to get the data elements organized as closely as possible to whatever level of Normal form that you are targeting. Many-to-many relationships must be resolved at some point along the way. Entity detail models allow many-to-many notation, but all other detail levels require a resolution. We saw how to do this, through the use of intersection (associative) entities, in Chapter 2.

Other than that relationships are pretty much the same. They are the pathways that primary keys travel to connect the data sets together.

Categories

Categories in logical analysis are used to provide the subtypes of an entity to provide more detailed sets to assign attribute ownership or detailed relationships to. For example, when we are talking about types of phone number only 'Company' phone numbers are allowed to have an Extension Number whereas 'Mobile' phone number are not. Showing this in a category provides an insight in the physicalization as to why an attribute should be `NULL` allowed. In this case the Extension Number attribute should be `NULL` allowed since some phones won't have one.

This is also an extremely useful technique to expose anomalies. Noting the seven different types of vehicles to the owner of a 'Classic Car' business that you are doing a Sales system for, may jog her memory into remembering that sometimes she sells motorcycles too. You unearth a portion of the current business data that has been shoehorned into tables and columns they don't fit very well in.

Categories may also highlight different business rules. The category for `Books` at a library may note that they have `PublicAccess` and `PrivateCollection` books, with only `PublicAccess` books allowed to be checked out. To reflect this, would require that only `PublicAccess` books should be provided to the `Checkout` entities through a relationship.

Identifying or Non-identifying

The conceptual analysis has only a limited understanding of whether relationships between the concepts are identifying or non-identifying. There is no concept of key migration here. We simply do our best to capture our understanding of existence dependencies. It isn't until we start to get the migrations of the foreign keys and the definitions of the primary keys analyzed that this differentiation becomes important.

As a reminder here, if you need the identifying attribute/s from one entity to identify a different entity, then this is defined as an identifying relationship. For example you need to know the State Identifier from the entity State to uniquely identify a record in County entity. Otherwise you couldn't distinguish between the record for Orange County, California and Orange County, Florida. Other times you are just making reference to another entity in a non-identifying fashion. For instance in the example coming up you will see that Employee has a non-identifying relationship to Communiqué. The Person getting the message, how it was routed to them, what message it was, and the date/time it got to them identifies a single row of Communiqué. Who it was that sent the message is informational only.

Verb Phrase

Every different verb needs a different relationship in order to capture the multiple roles that the migrating member of the data set can play. Notice how many relationships we have in just this tiny model:

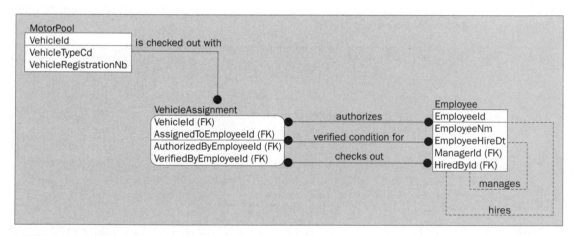

Often you will find a key entity loaded down with relationships. Keep them as simple as possible and try to avoid 'has' and 'is' unless you are stumped. Most relationships aren't all that hard to describe.

Cardinality

Now the detail levels of cardinality come into play. Detail the terminators of the relationships as much as possible, and make the rules as restrictive as the data rules are. The objective here is to determine a representation of how the data is shaped that will help in the physicalization, and give the clients a very black and white view of the world you are creating to store their data in. As a result it needs to be as restrictive or non-restrictive as they are in reality. Remember that rules noted now in the structure can bring huge gains in quality and integrity as you progress to a physical analysis.

May or Must

The logical analysis is the place to put the finishing touches to the relationships. It puts restrictions on the allowed nullability. As a reminder here we use NULL to denote the absence of any value, in other words an empty data element. Values such as 'N/A', 'Unknown', or '---' are not NULLs but data values representative of meaning to someone. If a relationship is a possible but not mandatory, such as 'a Sale may or may not have a Service Contract included' then we say that the relationship is NULL allowed, and denote it as follows:

Logical Analysis Example

What happened to the simple four conceptual entities that we started with? They evolved into the unique sets of values that need to be managed and related together to allow maximum integrity and flexibility. We will see more about the development of such models in Chapter 7. It is sufficient here to point out the inclusion of category structures, resolution of the many-to-many relationships, and the inclusion of attributes with key designations.

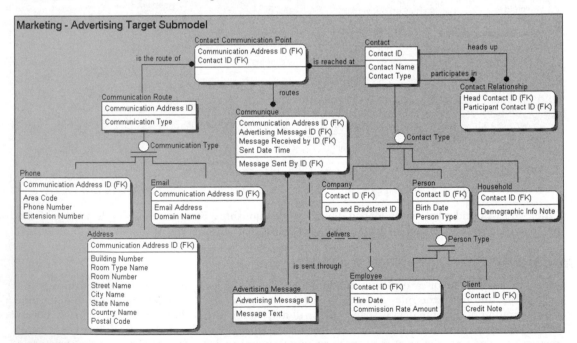

Let me include a conceptual to logical mapping just for curiosity sake while noting that most of the Staff and Advertising Event entities are not in this submodel. It expands to be even bigger than this!

Conceptual	Logical
Staff	Contact
Staff	Person
Staff	Employee
Advertising Event	Advertising Message (subset of the Event entities)
Advertising Event	Communiqué
Advertising Target	Contact
Advertising Target	Company
Advertising Target	Person
Advertising Target	Household
Advertising Target	Client
Advertising Target	Client Relationship
Advertising Target	Client Communication Point
Communication Mode	Communication Route
Communication Mode	Phone
Communication Mode	Address
Communication Mode	E-mail

Physical Analysis

Now that we have covered the logical analysis, let's consider the next step, physical analysis. If we have done the 'due diligence' of serious logical analysis, this analysis is more a continuation of the process aimed at building database objects. However, as we have emphasized, if our understanding of the data increases during this phase of the analysis, then we may have to revisit the logical model in order to verify entity or relationship definitions.

In this phase of analysis we need to make a decision on what tools to use to write the front end and the RDBMS choice to deploy the tables (SQL Server, Oracle, Access, DB2 for example). We can't go very far until we do that. Different RDBMSs and programming tools have different quirks that you need to be aware of. There are the size constraints of the table and column names, the system's 'reserved words' (such as SELECT, INSERT, DELETE and so on), and quirky database-specific things like being unable to migrate more than one column in a foreign key.

> **Being familiar with the database and programming language domain you are designing will assist you in proceeding with the physical design.**

101

We call it physical because unlike a logical model, a real RDBMS database can be built from a physical model. It is going to be a tool to provide someone hopefully with a means of saving time, effort, pain, money, and headaches. We are now going to take all the logical analysis that we so faithfully documented and figure out how to make it a real working data storage environment. This analysis takes the plan drawing and moves it into the final blueprint.

The first default action in moving a model from logical to physical is to change entities to tables, and attributes to columns. That is a first draft of the structure but there is a whole lot more needing figured out before it can be deployed. We need to determine exact parameters for the naming standards, sizing, and data types. We may also want to expand the model to include operational tables or columns. None of these things have been included in the analysis yet. And then we need to test it again for quality against the Normal forms. Normalization should have been completed in the logical analysis, but additions to the model discovered in this phase need to be retested.

Tables

Tables are the file structures that data will be organized into. Each row is one member of a set. Each column is one fact about that member. You will see the words entity and table used interchangeably in some books but, as we have previously stated, they aren't the same. Tables are physical implementations of the logical definitions contained in entities. The first task here is usually renaming the logical entity name with a proposed table name.

Entities don't care where they might end up someday. In fact one logical analysis could be the basis for several different physical analysis designs depending on different deployment platforms with different structures and different naming conventions. Entities are above all that since they are theoretical; tables are practical.

Columns

Columns have a similar relationship to attributes as entities have to tables. They show up by default if you are using modeling software to assist you in the move from logical to physical, since attributes are moved to columns without much impact other than the fact that columns can't contain blanks. In other words, you need to state that a data value is NULL if there is no value associated with it; you can't simply leave it as a blank entry. Your first task with them will probably be renaming to shorter, abbreviated forms, in order to comply with whatever name length restrictions may exist in the RDBMS you are targeting.

Quite frequently a development group has standards that include adding columns (termed operational columns) that weren't in the original inventory of attributes. You might be asked to add a set of something like this to every table:

Column Name	Definition
CreateId	The person or process who created the record
CreateDtTm	The date and time the record was created.
CreateLocationId	The environment identifier where the record insertion request originated from

Column Name	Definition
ModifiedId	The person or process who last modified the record
ModifiedDtTm	The date and time the record was last modified.
ModifiedLocationId	The environment identifier where the record update request originated from

Such columns provide the programmers and DBAs with the means to troubleshoot data and processing issues by allowing them to see who created a record, when it was created, and where it came from. These are generally not logical attributes from a client perspective.

After renaming and adding new columns you have another set of analysis to perform. This time you need to add new information at the column level.

Primary Keys

This is the last change point for primary keys.

> **After the tables have been built the impact of changing a primary key is really painful.**

Check one last time for the appropriateness of the current choice. The team may wish to go with surrogate keys rather than natural keys. Every table needs to be thoroughly reviewed and have the primary key approved from the perspective of current use and future needs.

Physical Domains

This is a very detailed task. You can do a data profile of existing data if it is available to give yourself a leg up, but ultimately the client should be responsible for some of these answers, since it's is going to be their new tool. Some of these questions will have been asked during the logical analysis. Now is the time to verify and really emphasize the need to finalize the decisions.

- ❑ Is this a fixed or variable length field?
- ❑ If it is a data field will you ever want to see time also?
- ❑ How big do you want the column be?
- ❑ What kind of number do you need to store (-/+)?
- ❑ How many decimal points do you need?
- ❑ Should we restrict the values?
- ❑ Is there a way to prevent incorrect data?
- ❑ Do you want to set up a default on insert?

Relationships / Constraints in a Physical Model

Relationships in the physical model are candidates for implementation as constraints in the RDBMS. Unfortunately some platforms aren't able to deploy them. The rules in a constraint can be deployed as triggers, scripts, and stored procedures. If constraints aren't going to be used, you may want to map them to whatever has been chosen to take its place in preventing integrity and quality issues.

An example of the constraints from the model we just looked at is as follows:

```
ALTER TABLE Employee
      ADD  ( PRIMARY KEY (EmployeeId) ) ;

ALTER TABLE Employee
      ADD  ( FOREIGN KEY (HiredById)
                          REFERENCES Employee ) ;
```

Security

And finally, once we have all the tables, columns, and extra information available, we need to map the client community, noting what privileges they can have. We need a way to group the clients. They generally have groupings something like this:

❑   Owner – can do anything

❑   Administrator – can do almost anything

❑   Special groups – have restricted power to carry out certain operations

❑   Viewers – can only see

The DBAs may implement security by only giving clients access to tables through the granting of appropriate INSERT, UPDATE, and DELETE privileges. It is up to them to devise the specifics of the security policy that needs implementing, but you need to give them an overview of what is needed. Once you establish the general groups the clients want to maintain, you set up a CRUD diagram for all the tables and columns. CRUD stands for Create, Read, Update, and Delete. These are the general privileges that the DBA can set up for them. From this diagram all the Security roles can be created in whatever security method is being developed. You may want to do a separate or combined view of this type of grid:

Special Marketing Group Security Analysis				
Table/Column	**Create**	**Read**	**Update**	**Delete**
Emp.Emp_id		X		
Emp.Hire_Date		X		
Emp.Cons_Rate_Amt				
Emp.Emp_Name		X		
Emp.Emp_Birth_Date		X		

You will see here that the Marketing group isn't allowed to view the Commission rates of Employees. The other thing this will bring out is whether or not the clients need to partition the data in some way other than table and column. Quite frequently we find clients needing to restrict even Read access to the data based on Geography or Department. Cases like that may cause you to return to the model and perhaps develop other views to be able to support this requirement. Hopefully it isn't newly discovered at this stage of development and you knew it was coming all along.

Unfortunately the model itself isn't very good at documenting this portion of the analysis; it is another mapping document separate from the model itself.

Physical Analysis Example

We will leave a fuller discussion of the issues involved in developing a physical model from a logical one until Chapter 8. At this point we will simply present a physical model, based on our earlier logical one, which we drew up for our marketing department. To give some insight here, the following table shows how I mapped the logical entities to physical ones:

Conceptual	Logical	Physical
Staff	Contact	Contact
Staff	Person	Contact
Staff	Employee	Employee
Advertising Event	Advertising Message (subset of the Event entities)	AdvertisingMessage
Advertising Event	Communiqué	Communiqué
Advertising Target	Contact	Contact
Advertising Target	Company	Contact
Advertising Target	Person	Contact
Advertising Target	Household	Contact
Advertising Target	Client	Contact
Advertising Target	Client Relationship	ContactRelationship
Advertising Target	Client Communication Point	CommunicationPoint
Communication Mode	Communication Route	CommunicationRoute
Communication Mode	Phone	CommunicationRoute
Communication Mode	Address	CommunicationRoute
Communication Mode	E-mail	CommunicationRoute

The physical analysis in this case bring us to a model that looks like this:

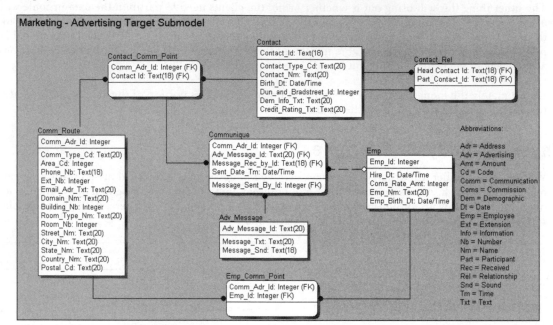

The key decisions made in this case are as follows:

❑ All the Contact attributes were rolled up to Contact (a choice in category structure physicalization) except in the case of Employee. This means that almost all the attributes are NULL allowed. The logic for what columns can be filled in is being managed through code based on the Contact_Type_Cd.

❑ The choice was made to give Employee its own table for security reasons rather than roll it up with the rest of the Contacts. That meant that the relationship to Comm_Route which holds their addresses, phone number, and e-mail addresses, needed a new intersection table called Emp_Comm_Point.

❑ All the Communication Routes were rolled up to one table (a choice in category structure physicalization). It means that except for Comm_Type_Cd all the attributes are NULL allowed. The logic for what columns can be filled in is being managed through code based on the type code.

Reverse Engineered Analysis

We have devoted the whole of Chapter 11 to reverse engineering modeling since it is an extremely necessary modeling activity. The goal of reverse-engineered analysis is to develop a graphic identifying the existing database objects to aid tasks such as redevelopment, redesign, or performance tuning. What makes it tough is that you are working backwards from the existing system implementation, and don't have any of the development notes or models to work with. Instead of coming 'Top-Down', from the logical model, you are moving 'Bottom-Up', beginning with the physical model, and working backwards to develop and document a logical (and possibly even a conceptual) model.

You almost need two physical models. One that is the exact physical truth representing the database and another, which documents what the data rules actually are even if they are being managed in the front end or through stored procedures. The exact truth can be most depressing. I have built models using this technique that show hundreds of tables, named in abbreviations which no one has the key to, without a single database constraint in sight to show where the data migrates from or to. Models like this have a place but they don't answer the real questions.

Most of your data model customers want to be able to recognize data elements. They want to look at the model to see how difficult the task of bulk loading newly acquired data is going to be. They want to check the size constraints of the Last Name of people in the system.

Definitions can be really difficult. Who knew what was supposed to be in those tables or columns compared to the reality of today? You may have to resort to data profiling and publishing what you found rather than a textual description of what that element is. Be sensitive to ways the clients have broken the database rules provided in the original implementation. For example, the column may be mandatory but the only values in there are spaces or N/A (rather than NULL). Things like this should be checked for and prevented in a check constraint but you will find that they often have forgotten to add that in. In the world of Reverse engineering it is more important to document what is real rather than what was intended.

Analysis Is in the Detail

In the first half of this chapter we have looked at the different types of model we develop as we move from our initial design phase towards our physical model, iterating through our definitions in order to verify their accuracy and validity (a 'top-down' approach). We also touched on reverse-engineered models, where we look at an existing physical model and work backwards to determine a logical model (a 'bottom-up' approach). Each type of model has a particular role to play in representing the state of the data we are modeling, and there are different levels of detail which we can give in such models as we will see now.

At one time I believed that entity level models were always the beginning place for a new design. I have learned over time that it is really up to the modeler as to how they want to approach a data problem. 'Top-Down' analysis has a tendency to begin with concepts that fit better into an entity (simple) level of detail model, whereas, Bottom-Up, analysis tends to begin with an FA (complex) detail level. Most models have the ability to be translated into all three no matter where they started. In practice you may well end up performing both top-down and bottom-up analysis at the same time with the hope of verifying your process by the meeting of these two analyses at some mid point.

Entity Level

Entity level models tend to have simplicity in both the entity quantity and the relationship complexity. It is not necessary to resolve the many-to-many relationships by building intersection/associative entities at this level. But don't think that is a hard and fast rule since you can have entity models which have no many-to-many relationships. The decision should follow an importance or prioritization goal of your own. Entity models are generally not physical data models because of this high degree of flexibility. Physical data models must adhere to the rules of creating RDBMS objects, while entity modeling allows much syntax that is simply not physically deployable. Let's consider our marketing department example once again. An entity level diagram in this case would look something like this:

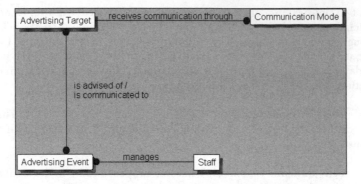

An alternative view of this model includes definitions along with the conceptual entity names, providing an additional level of detail with which to work. This is particularly useful in team review meetings, for example:

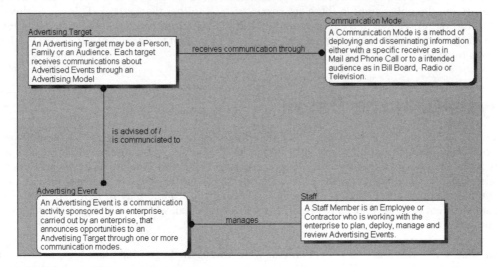

When To Use Entity Level Detailing

This level of detail is very suitable for:

❑   Scope documentation – projects

❑   Beginning business client reviews

❑   Overview documentation – Enterprise models

❑   Top Down analysis

Sometimes details can overwhelm an audience, whether it is your project manager, your business client, or a review committee. As I said earlier, an entity model can be backed into from a detailed design, or indeed a starting place for original analysis. However, keeping everything synchronized can be a real challenge. Either way the entity model should be the best choice for reviewing general content and rules of use. An entity model is most useful as a tool to communicate with the members of the team who are more interested in the fact that their business requirements have been captured.

Key Based (KB)

Data models detailed to the key based level concentrate on keys and their migrations along the paths of relationships. Why concentrate on keys? Keys are very powerful indicators that you have separated out similar concepts, and ensured that there is no duplication of entities in your model. They are required to be understood for integration and extraction efforts, and should be chosen with care and thought for the Enterprise data future. What makes a set member distinct should matter very much to you, and you may need to work with a set of sample data for each entity to verify this level of analysis.

However, I do admit that this level of analysis seems to be seen the least often in data modeling circles. Entity level is used constantly to create the simple view, while a fully attributed (FA) model is the ultimate goal for anything that is going to be deployed (as we shall see shortly). KB should be the one that is used to review the entities and their identifying attributes to watch for redundancy, incompatibility, and inconsistency. That step is often combined into the creation of the fully attributed model.

Here is an example of a logical KB model, again based around our marketing department example:

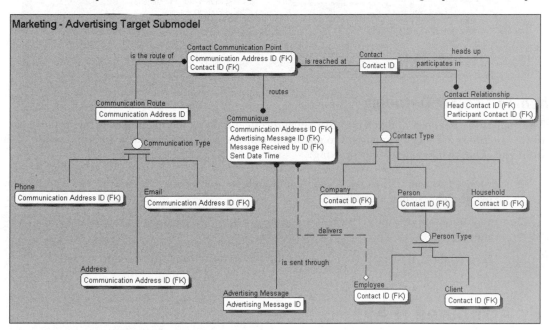

You can see at a glance that some entities are using the same identifier. For example, the Phone, Email and Address entities all use Communication Address ID as their identifier. Such identifiers are often opportunities to aggregate entities into one table in the logical to physical transformation. In this case we could combine Phone, Email, and Address in a singe Communication Route entity. The choice to roll up a category structure is very visible this way. There are obviously other considerations and other options to designing such a table, but a key based detailed model provides a useful means by which to carry out such a review.

Here is a KB physical model. Now you can even review the data types and sizes of the primary key. This model would be useful for index order or naming convention reviews, for example:

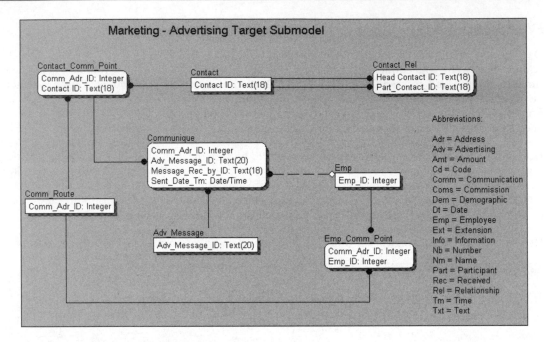

When To Use KB Detailing

The goal of the KB level of detail is to display and concentrate on the identifiers of the instances or rows. Identifiers are hugely important to anyone needing to work with the data without the use of the front end. This style is suitable for showing:

❑ Proposed or actual keys of a system – to highlight the currently chosen primary and foreign keys and check their suitability

❑ Integration opportunities and issues – to see what other systems are using as the PK of the same entities

❑ Merging data (retiring systems, acquiring new data) – to map source to target transformation issues

Fully Attributed (FA)

A data model with the full compliment of attributes is termed fully attributed. Logical and physical models can be taken to this level of detail, and it is the detail level that most often is associated with a data model. The one that has all the attributes or columns clearly defined.

I don't really believe in FA conceptual models so I won't try to show you what one would look like. They can become immense, with too much information to be able to find what you are looking for easily. In general all of the entities would be conceptual and so would the attributes. It might be a useful concept collector but I have never found the need for one. However, it could be a useful strategic tool if used correctly.

The FA logical is the final level of analysis to capture the business rules and data elements of a business process. You can use this model to walk through all the requirements that deal with creating, modifying, deleting, or displaying data. There is an enormous wealth of other information (especially the definitions) that is not visible on the graphic, which is also a part of the FA model.

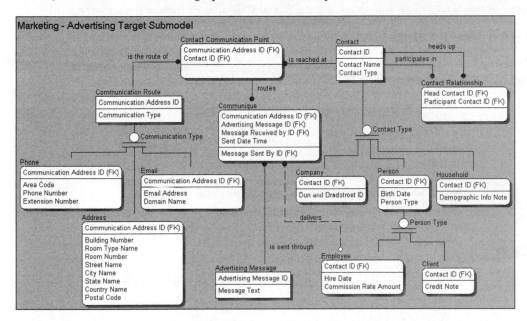

Here is an example of a FA physical model:

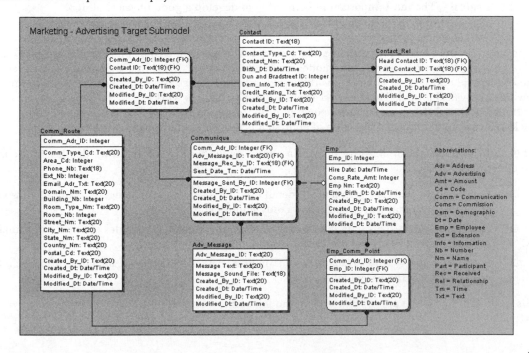

The FA physical model is the database schematic. It should show all the tables and columns needed to support both the business process and the operational management of the application. The FA physical is the source of information for the DDL to create database objects and must be developed with the rigor needed to successfully accomplish that task. A reverse-engineered FA data model ought to have captured the details to be able to rebuild the physical database structure if necessary.

When To Use FA Detailing

The goal of the fully attributed data model is to capture and present all of the data elements necessary to satisfy the charter of the project. The charter may be a development project for a new custom application, or it may be to create a model of a legacy system. These are generally the most important models to the IT community. This style is suitable for many tasks including:

❑   Fully analyzed data element requirements (logical)

❑   Blueprints for databases (physical)

❑   Delta points for change control (logical & physical)

❑   Visual data load/unload ordering documents (physical constraints)

❑   Impact analysis (data type, data element, data size)

Summary

This chapter has considered the various analysis styles you can use to document data elements. These can be summarized as:

❑   **Conceptual** – The highest level beginning place.

❑   **Logical** – The most important to being able to develop a good physical design.

❑   **Physical** – The most detailed one that creates the DDL to generate a database object.

A 'top down' approach to the modeling of a system will begin with a conceptual model and work down through a logical model to a physical model for implementation. This process develops details regarding the conceptual entities that you begin with, breaking out attributes and relationships as you progress towards a physical model. There are occasions when you have to work with a 'bottom up' approach, working backwards from an existing system, in order to develop a logical model (and sometimes further back to a conceptual model). This type of approach is termed reverse engineering analysis.

At each of these stages of analysis, there is a choice as to the level of detail we display in the model we develop:

❑   Entity Level – This is a high level of detail used for scope and planning, or a simplified review at the beginning of a project. It shows only entities and attributes.

❑   Key Based (KB) – This is an intermediate level of detail, which includes entities, and primary key attributes (usually natural keys if possible).

❑   Fully Attributed – Most detailed level of analysis. All attributes listed, including all foreign keys migrating from the parent table.

It is important to use the appropriate type of model, and level of detail, tailored to the needs of your particular situation. We will consider the scope of projects in the next chapter.

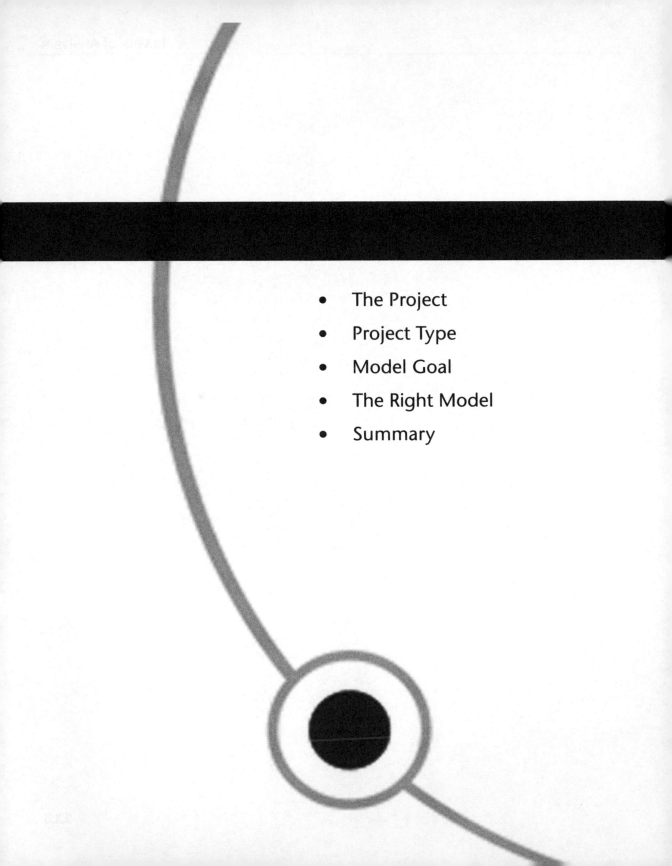

How Data Models Fit Into Projects

In this chapter we're going to see how everything we've been looking at comes together with the project to drive the creation of a data model. We'll look at what you need before you begin modeling, and what model or models you might want to build to make the project a success.

This isn't a book about project management, so although we will look at some of the tasks and stages of a project, we won't go through a software development methodology in detail. What we will do is look at all the stages in light of the data modeling tasks that accompany them. To that end we will look at:

❑ Project parameters
❑ Selecting the right model for the job

The Project

Up until now we have been focusing almost exclusively on data modeling, its history, techniques, and definitions. Now we need to look at how to launch a data model into the furious currents of Enterprise activity. Most often a modeling task will be nested inside a data management project, although from time to time you will model outlying structures that may help the team determine interface and integration options.

Such projects arise because someone, somewhere in the Enterprise has determined that the data requirements have changed and need to be managed differently. Understanding this data need is extremely important for us to be able to help provide a data storage solution. The person suggesting the project may have done a preliminary business process study, and determined that productivity could be increased with a new automated way to capture and report on data that is currently being managed manually. They may have read about a new business process that they think will make the company more profitable. They may be required to change certain internal data rules to respond to external data rule changes. Their study may or may not have focused on data storage structures. Many times the data element inventory and design changes are just one (critical) part of the overall enterprise changes that need to happen to support a business process change.

As a data modeler for an Enterprise you must always keep in mind that you serve two masters, in determining how to best respond to data storage requests. You need to help make the short-term goals of the project successful, and you need to pursue the long-range goals of Enterprise data management. Balancing these two things often takes some creative compromising. You will generally find that project team success is judged in terms of adherence to time and budget constraints, whereas Enterprise success is more focused on whether the solution provided the ability to meet the requirements and quality of design. As a result you have to balance quality and functionality with time and cost.

Project Management

Before starting to think about building a data model, we need to learn about the project. We can't begin without knowing the basics. A survey of intended Enterprise goals (financial, quality, growth, simplification, expansion), and the high-level expectation of how to achieve them, needs to be completed in order to guide the project. What's also important at this stage is to determine the methodology the project will follow. In meeting the project goal you may well follow a formal project methodology, involving systematic, planned undertakings with very clear goals, teams, budgets, and stages. On other occasions you will head towards the goal in a more spontaneous manner, taking action to supplement and enhance productivity, or to fight one of the short-term data 'fires' that crop up everyday in an Enterprise. However, bear in mind that quick fixes have a habit of staying around for a lot longer than generally anticipated, and we should still endeavor to approach seemingly informal projects with the same care and process as larger ones.

In a formal project there will probably have been a feasibility step that determined a set of generic goals, assessing whether or not the goals were reasonable, accomplishable, and appropriate to the strategy of the Enterprise. You may be given this information in a Chartering/Kickoff/or formal Project Start meeting that brings all the key team members together for the first time to begin detailed project planning. In a less formal project your team may have to gather and write down their own understanding of the goals in the form of a short list of assumptions. Either way, at this point you need to draw up an initial scope for the project, outlining the expected results as the boundary markers for exploration. The initial scope will include:

❑ Definitions of goals to be included. For example, creating a central, managed list of customers with a purchase history

❑ Goals to be excluded. For example, the Marketing department's potential customers, or the Sales department's canceled customers

❑ Assumptions made. For example, this list of customers will be a list available for Enterprise use, managed by Accounts Receivable

All the project documentation needs to be kept up to date and relevant, to ensure that the entire team is working from the most recent revision. It is a good idea to determine at the beginning of a project how we intend to ensure that everyone has the correct copies. There may be a numbering, dating, and/or location standard that will help prevent 20 versions of the scope statement floating around to confuse the team.

Scope

I would say that the most critical factor to the success of any project is the definition of the scope. This is an iterative process, since the scope may need to be modified over the life of the project as the analysis makes more and more detail understandable. It drives the direction of the exploration, which in turn drives a tighter control of the direction. Don't expect the first draft of the scope to survive without alterations.

I'm sure we could all come up with several instances of incorrect or misunderstood scope (and by association requirements) causing incorrect decisions to be made that waste time and money. I have seen requirements documents, software prototypes, and even (as painful as this was to witness) complete Alpha test systems shared proudly with the clients only to be told they were insufficient to meet the intended scope. This seems to happen most often when the business clients and the project team don't stay in close communication with each other at least through the design phase. The scope needs to be interpreted, clarified, tested, and detailed by both the customers and the development members of the team. Scope, assumptions, definitions, and outcomes are elements best confirmed with the customer in writing or by e-mail, as a means to confirm that there is 'project clarity' amongst the respective parties. Critical amendments and iterations also need formal acknowledgement since ambiguity, misperception or vagueness can often lead to expensive over-runs.

The scope statement is usually a short document describing the goal. Descriptions of what isn't being dealt with are as important of what will be, especially if there could be any confusion among those who are not as close to the analysis. End product customers are the most important to keep up to date. The language used to describe scope can be critical. Saying that the project will automate 'inventory processes' is probably too broad. Does that include receiving, shipping, rework, manufacturing, scrap, return, credit, restock, samples, and supply chain management? It is imperative to clarify this. It may be all of that, or it may be just the conjunction of those processes where they impact 'On-Hand' quantities. The scope should contribute heavily at the beginning of the project to a 'Glossary of Terms', to ensure that the whole project team understands the terminology used as the same thing. I would include all acronyms as well, since I have, for example, used acronym lists in aerospace projects where the same letters can mean as many as fifteen different things depending on the context.

Project Standards

Standards are the ground rules that govern the process of any project. They may cover the available development methodologies, Enterprise preferred hardware/software choices, deliverable formats for project plans, requirements, functional specifications, even data element naming on the models. They may be developed internally or adopted from external sources.

Many shops don't worry about creating such formal rules to manage their process with. On the other hand even small companies may need to use some formal development guidelines to be eligible to participate in bidding for certain contracts (such as government or military ones for example). The development and management processes of the Enterprise's data may also be part of the judgment criteria used in external quality rating systems of Enterprises.

We are going to briefly look at a few formal process controls that could be used as standards in a project:

- ❑ Methodology
- ❑ ISO9001 - International Standard Organization – standard 9001
- ❑ CMM - Capability Maturity Model

Methodology

Formal methodologies, when used correctly and, maybe more importantly, consistently, can become an awesome tool to get the best results possible out of a project. They will impact not only the final deliverable of the project, but also the plan for delivering, maintaining, enhancing, monitoring, and judging the effectiveness of it. Equally, when used incorrectly they may steal the focus of the team from solving a problem for a client and redirect the effort into a document generation process.

Formal methodologies are like checklists. They remind us of all the myriad aspects of analysis and planning that we should do even if we don't have the time or resources to do them. The nice thing about formal methodologies for a modeler is that the various stages of model development are often actually called out as deliverables at established steps in the process.

I have used many different methodologies. My first was a 'Top-Down' approach starting with a very formal set of analysis steps. The RAP (Requirements Analysis Planning) stage discovered current business processes, identified deficiencies, and scoped one or more projects to mitigate them. The emphasis here was on documenting everyone's viewpoint (current and future), from the business client, through the technical team, and into the Enterprise. This provided the tactical, technical, and strategic dynamics at play in the project. This stage developed documentation from Scope to Detail Requirements (including Activity and high-level data models).

Each project that the RAP identified was then planned and deployed utilizing another set of formal steps. The PDM (Prototype Development Methodology) built on the analysis of the RAP to develop software and business process enhancement for the Enterprise. The emphasis here was to provide a framework for iterating through design, development, and maintenance of an automated system utilizing prototyping as a means to refine the definition of requirements, and allow the business clients to experience the functionality of the system in a timely fashion to fine tune it to meet their needs. This stage developed from further enhanced Project Plans to fully tested, deployed, documented Software (including conceptual, logical, and physical data models).

Some big companies like large aerospace firms may have developed their own Software Project Management methodology. There are CASE (Computer Aided System Engineering) tools that have inherent processes. And there are consulting firms that have created their own methodologies, which they will teach and share. You will find most methodologies need Enterprise sponsorship, training, and support to make them an integral part of the software development process.

ISO 9001

Bidding for some contracts (government or industry) requires that a company must comply with standards established by an outside regulatory department. One of the most common that we in IT are being judged by is ISO 9001. ISO 9001 is a quality standard in the industry, which has been established by the International Organization for Standardization (ISO), and is equally applicable to anyone producing furniture, rocket ships, or video games. The emphasis is in management of processes. It has a two-step approach, which requires that a company keep records that:

- ❑ Define and document what they are going to do
- ❑ Audit what was done against the plan

They have a website at www.iso.org, where the ISO series is described as *"A network of national standards institutes from 140 countries working in partnership with international organizations, governments, industry, business and consumer representatives. A bridge between public and private sectors."*

This certification doesn't put an auditor or ISO committee in the company. It verifies that good practices were being used consistently at the time the company was certified (and hopefully are still being used). It gives customers a certain level of confidence in the level of documentation and support they can expect.

You can see the benefits immediately. Using this type of standard the project team takes the time to plot out the detailed tasks necessary to accomplish the goal and then uses that as a checklist to verify that all the tasks have been accomplished. And since all projects have an iterative understanding of the plan, a simple feedback mechanism sets up self-correcting documentation.

Getting an ISO compliance rating (there are 15,000 different ones) is a big deal, and you will see companies putting banners on their buildings noting that they are certified. In order for a company to claim it is ISO 9001 compliant it must go through a series of audits leading to certification. The company may need to go through a lengthy process of training, analyzing, and altering current practices, and setting up a self-correcting audit function to maintain ISO requirements. Your models may become part of the documentation proving the level of data management and software tool development.

Capability Maturity Model

The Capability Maturity Model (CMM) for Software is a software process maturity framework to help organizations to assess and improve their software development process. The Software Engineering Institute (SEI) at Carnegie Mellon University developed it in response to a request by the US government for a method of assessing software contractors. This gives everyone the ability to compare projects and products against an objective, common measurement, and takes some of the 'gut feel' factor out of the judgement for success.

Again, there are no process steps. These are levels of compliance and achievement, like a ladder or staircase leading upward to higher quality levels. It is a great way to assess how your team is managing data and gives you a 'next level' of control to shoot for. Here are the five levels they defined:

1. **Initial** – The software process is characterized as *ad hoc*, and occasionally even chaotic. Few processes are defined, and success depends on individual effort and heroics.

2. **Repeatable** – Basic project management processes are established to track cost, schedule, and functionality. The necessary process discipline is in place to repeat earlier successes on projects with similar applications.

3. **Defined** – The software process for both management and engineering activities is documented, standardized, and integrated into a standard software process for the organization. All projects use an approved, tailored version of the organization's standard software process for developing and maintaining software.

4. **Managed** – Detailed measures of the software process and product quality are collected. Both the software process and products are quantitatively understood and controlled.

5. **Optimizing** – Continuous process improvement is enabled by quantitative feedback from the process and from piloting innovative ideas and technologies.

You can find out more about this standard and how to implement it at www.sei.cmu.edu/cmm.

If your organization is using CMM to understand and improve their process areas, the current level may already be understood. Key process areas are identified to achieve the next level. So, for example, the key process areas at Level 2 focus on the software project's concerns related to establishing basic project management controls. They are Requirements Management, Software Project Planning, Software Project Tracking and Oversight, Software Subcontract Management, Software Quality Assurance, and Software Configuration Management. Modeling standards and model management may be a part of that process.

Project Team

Models are communication tools, so they need to be able to depict information in a form that can be understood. As we discussed in the previous chapter, we can develop conceptual, logical, and physical models with different levels of detail (entity, key based, or fully attributed). This allows us to create submodels where some levels of detail are invisible (like data types and relationship verb phrases in an entity level detail model) to your given audience. You may, for example, want to create submodels of just subject areas, for discussion with your business clients, if the full model is too large. You may want to concentrate on names and leave the domains invisible at this stage in your discussion. You have to choose how to present your analysis in the most constructive way possible.

With this in mind, let's look at who the model customers are.

Project Initiators/Sponsor

The project initiators are generally the group of people who are sponsoring the project. They are frequently management business-type customers who have a limited understanding of what the data model is trying to capture for them. They will probably need a simpler style model to be able to follow what you are saying, generally a conceptual or logical model which is pretty tightly focused on their area of knowledge. You may even need to have a model using their business terms in the naming or only provide a definition view so they can follow along.

These people don't need to know the internal workings of your model, but they do need to know the general outline, as well as any pointers towards the bottom line of cost and resource allocation that you can give. They will probably have different priorities than your organization will. Be careful how you explain your analysis to prevent misunderstandings. Their priorities are very important so make sure they know you are aware of that. Be aware though not to misrepresent complexity as being simple, nor indeed simplicity as being complex. One can cause a completely unreal expectation about time and budget and the other can cause a devastating loss of faith in your integrity.

Business Team

The business team generally represents the group of people who will be impacted the most by the deployment of the results of the project. They are the business liaison with the development team. Although the development team may be involved in the initial series of interviews and fact finding with the actual users of the final product, the business team will spend much of their time fielding data and process issues. They resolve them by taking them back to their management (the project sponsors) or further exploring details in the user community. The people they represent will either have their process impacted with a new tool or their data sources impacted by your project. This means that the business team generally has a huge vested interest in the success of the project.

Business team members need to learn how to read even the detailed models at least at the logical level. They need to understand down to the level of data element size and nullability whether you have captured their requirements adequately. However, the fact that they need to learn means that you have to be doubly sensitive to their frustrations, and will need to help them recognize the mappings of model elements to screen and report designs. Only the business team can tell you if your analysis and design are wrong for their needs. These are the people that you will be doing most of your upfront model reviews with.

Development Team

The development team may also have a sort of liaison to the data modeler (often the DBA and/or a senior programmer or lead). At some level the team will have to work with the results of the model (in table design) and will want to know all the rules (the same way the business team needs to). Hopefully the team will want to understand the data model even if they have never worked with one before. They should recognize how the model maps to the structures in the database. Still, especially in large projects, you will want to create submodels to reduce the clutter and allow them to focus on their assigned portions of the tasks the same way you restricted views by subject areas for the business team. The development team is often not as interested in the logical model as they are the physical model. Once you have completed your analysis with the business team of the logical rules they are itching to see a physical design. You may need to do several physical designs in order to point out options for category structures and physical implementation denormalization options. Make sure they are very clear about the Pros and Cons of each option when you need to work with them.

Extended Development Team

Don't forget the members of the team that aren't full time on the project but are critical to the overall success. The Infrastructure team is going to need estimates of bandwidth to move the data around. The Training group may need to see how complex this is going to be to teach. The Helpdesk may need to add extra operational data elements to be able to troubleshoot issues. Project managers want to look at how the design is shaping up. The Test team will want to begin making test scenarios based on the business rules. Even the Software Quality team may want a model to look over.

Budget and Schedule

I hesitate to put this in, but we are as bound to the available resources of our company as any other department. Managing data costs money. Someday someone will finally come up with a generic formula to create a dollar value on creating, managing, and storing data for those of us who have to weigh the choice of intrinsically limited, but quick and cheap, designs vs. more flexible, but slightly longer development, and therefore more costly designs. In the meantime data modelers are often on the front lines when it comes to recognizing a serious increase in complexity than the original understanding scheduled for. We can create visual representation of scope creep on the model using color or version comparisons. This means it is our responsibility to help manage expectations and share risks with the project manager.

Project Lifecycle

All projects whether formal or informal tend to go through certain stages. You will find many different pictures of what project lifecycles look like, one of the more common being the 'Waterfall' lifecycle, which is a classic 'Top-Down' analysis style. It provides us with a good set of steps but the original 'Waterfall' design only showed the steps related in one direction (downwards). Once a team (completely) finished one step they went on to another (never to return to a previous step).

Over time we have come to the conclusion that this is a naive way of describing what actually happens in a project. Most lifecycle diagrams now attempt to show parallel processing and feedback loops that note the team can return to any step appropriate to iron out issues, or respond to new understanding. This could be categorized as a **Semi-Structured** lifecycle. In general, there are starting or planning tasks that deal with strategy, analysis, and design, and there are execution tasks dealing with building, testing, and deploying. They have a general flow from one to the next. However, within a single project each of these processes could be active concurrently, or they could be approached from steps traditionally considered a long way down the development path.

I tried to capture the idea of a general path and the whirlpool of swinging back around to any place along the lifecycle if necessary in the following diagram. Notice that most of the steps don't simply move from one process to another. There are overlaps that will make it difficult to decide if you are in the Strategize or Analyze step, or the Design or Build step. Most of the time you are probably combining steps to move the project forward.

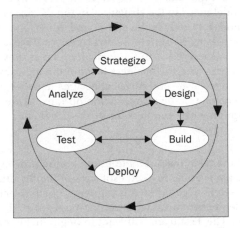

You can find more about project lifecycles at www.yourdon.com, where Edward Yourdon calls this iterative, parallel, messy lifecycle activity a **radical** implementation of a structured project lifecycle. At its most extreme he states that the radical implementation would involve 'all activities in the structured project lifecycle ... taking place simultaneously', while the opposite extreme would be a conservative sequential approach 'finishing all of one activity before commencing the next'. He rightly points out that you will probably never work in either extreme but rather take a 'middle of the road' approach, blurring the boundaries of the steps between each other, as appropriate for the project in hand.

The benefit of going over these steps is not to compartmentalize and order them. It is to provide a list of steps that need to be accomplished, provide some concept of dependency, and acknowledge that you do what you have to do to get the job done. Needing to backup to earlier steps in the lifecycle may be a sign of a part of the project which is misunderstood, mismanaged, or out of control. However, in doing so the team should be able to weed out all 'controllable' mistakes in order to improve the final product delivered at the end of the project. Such a lifecycle can also help in performance appraisal in post-project analysis.

Let's now take a look at the different steps in the process with an emphasis on the modeling tasks.

Strategize

The strategy step in a project works through survey, feasibility, options, risk, and usually prioritization to see when the need should be satisfied. It was probably initiated by an outside organization requesting data management ingenuity to fix a problem. Having identified a need, this stage is a high-level identification of business clients, description of current deficiencies, and debate concerning the 'should' and 'ought' aspects of solving the problem as well as gathering options about 'how' and guessing about time, budget, skills, resources, and enterprise return on investments.

Good strategy needs a lot of information. This is an intelligence-gathering step where quite a few educated guesses are made about impacts, costs, risks, and benefits. The modeler may be asked to provide anything from 'As-Is' systems models to conceptual data flows or vendor application data scopes. This step should create something that could be called a **Vision document** whose main purpose is to organize the thoughts of the key decision makers and get the project moving. It should be able to capture both the objectives and the scope, although alternatives and risks may still be on the table.

At the end of this step there is at least a list of the make or buy, build from scratch or enhance legacy, in-house or consultant, domestic or international, expected availability, security, and administration decisions that need to be made. Alongside that list a proposed budget, schedule, and team are generally organized.

A note of caution here. If the Manufacturing department has used the same multi-part forms for the last 20 years to manage their data, they will be temporarily impacted by any change to their process. They may not recover in time to prevent a negative month or two in performance. Enterprise-critical tasks need to have special concern given to them before you can replace even an old, awkward legacy process with a cool new solution.

A list of deliverables from this stage is:

- ❑   Project Proposal
- ❑   Business Objectives and Risk Analysis
- ❑   Project Charter
- ❑   Options, Feasibility, and Scope
- ❑   Enterprise development schedule

Analyze

This is the step where the detailed requirement gathering happens, and is pivotal to any project. It is expected that at the end of it you should know everything you require in order to develop a solution for your customers that will solve the problem described in the project charter or vision statement. At this stage the business team has one or more subject matter experts (SMEs) to represent them on the team. The SME explains, describes, and clarifies point after point until everyone is satisfied that they have at least a general understanding (which will improve over time) of the data and functional needs. This is the foundation of the requirements documentation. (Unavailability of the SMEs at this point can seriously impact the schedule of a project. Their leadership and commitment is a critical success factor.)

During the gathering of information to create the requirements documentation the team will gather up documentation and samples representing the processes, screens, and reports they might need to support or replace. This exhausting process can take the form of Joint Application Development (JAD) sessions, interviews, prototyping, and observation, and may involve the team delivering any of the following:

- ❑   A set of **use cases**, tracking data elements by processing them on paper and describing the nature of the management process.
- ❑   A **Business Process Flow** diagram, using a modeling tool like BPWin or Visio. This maps out the activity steps at a high level, sequentially noting dependencies and controls between them.
- ❑   A **Work Breakdown Structure** (WBS) that divides the effort of the project into smaller and smaller details. This provides a hierarchical outline to help create a detailed project plan.

There will be an infrastructure and hardware assessment. The team may even work up test cases to make sure they have gotten all the exceptions and failure points identified.

Sometimes all this documentation is overwhelming for the team, but even the smallest document could become important as understanding matures. The team needs to develop their own methods of controlling the information, which may require the assignment of a librarian for this phase in the case of large projects.

The modeler needs to keep a clear head and pick out the distinct data element usage and relationship rules. Develop a dictionary of data elements, use, and concepts from the very start. Capture the definitions and shape of the data as you go. The traditional requirements document may not call out this level of detail but it will make every step after this one easier.

This stage generates a blueprint, a control document with a comprehensive set of requirements. However, you have to take responsibility at this stage to make sure you gather everything you need to know to build a fully attributed data model. Requirements or functional specification documents don't usually go down to the level of detail that any member of the technical team needs to do their job. From the modeler's perspective, the requirements document needs to have immense depth of detail at the logical data element level. So stay involved. Encourage mockups and hand-drawn concepts of screens and reports so that you can double-check your data elements.

By the time this stage is completed you should have an almost complete paper system that can act as the instructions for the next stage. Not only that, but you should have determined any need to alter scope, budget, schedule, or resources due to critical issues that have been discovered during your analysis. The further along the path you go before noting a problem, the more troublesome it will be to fix. Trust me, no effort is wasted here, and you, as a modeler, may be called upon to create models at levels of analysis from conceptual through to logical fully attributed before the Analysis stage is complete.

A list of deliverables from this stage is:

- ❑ Updates to previous documents
- ❑ Evaluation of 'As-Is' environment through:
    - ❑ Development of conceptual, logical, and physical models
    - ❑ Assessment of Hardware / Infrastructure
    - ❑ Assessment of Business Rules, Business Process/Flow Diagrams, and/or Use Case Scenarios
- ❑ Development of 'To-Be' requirements through:
    - ❑ Development of conceptual, and logical models
    - ❑ Draft Business Rules, Business Process/Flow Diagrams, and Use Case Scenarios
    - ❑ Production of a detailed Project Plan outlining functional requirements, gap and impact analysis, proposed options and solutions, evaluation of vendor solutions, and mock up reports.

Design

The design step (which may cover redesigning or optimizing existing tools) covers both the information technology architecture (technology, network, programming platform, and so on) and the application architecture (client front end, middle tier, database, security). Choices made on one side may impact the other side. All the final detail decisions have to happen now.

This stage covers absolutely everything that needs to be built to support the new tool. That includes training documentation, maintenance tools, audit functions, backup and recovery solutions, Internet use, client licensing issues, hardware enhancements, testing and release needs, and even customer feedback management. When you look at the list of tasks, designing the application is actually only one of a mountain of concerns.

The data modeler at this point is focusing on Data Flow diagrams, State diagrams (especially when you have flows of data that you need to understand in order to determine what states the data will be in in different situations), and the physical fully attributed model. However, the modeler is not usually alone, and can call on the help of DBAs and programmers in determining performance options and any operational objects required. You may need to create many small submodels to back up documentation for screens, procedures, and reports. Remember to keep them all in sync with each other.

A list of deliverables from this stage is:

❑   Updates to previous documents

❑   Development of 'To-Be' environment through production of:

   ❑   Data Flow and State diagrams

   ❑   Physical model

   ❑   Business Rules, Business Process/Flow Diagrams, and Use Case Scenarios

❑   Technical Requirements in the form of:

   ❑   System Specifications (hardware and infrastructure)

   ❑   Application Distribution Model

   ❑   User Interface, Screen & Report, and Physical Navigation design

   ❑   Installation and Program Specifications

   ❑   Data Conversion Specification

   ❑   Security Specification

   ❑   Archive / Recovery Specification

   ❑   Test Strategy

Build & Test

As I told you at the beginning many of these steps can be active in parallel to each other, and the build stage is really coupled with test and actual design. It is not until we have done some testing that we may confirm whether an aspect of our design works or is fully optimized. Many modelers spent a lot of time in the 'design - build (proof of concept) - test' cycle. It almost appears to be a whirlpool for a while.

One thing the data modeler is often asked to help with is the generation of the DDL. The final fully attributed physical model should be the template for the generation of the tables and constraints. The modeler is also needed to test the screens and reports to verify the design in terms of data definition and integrity between the data elements. You can use the model to double-check the precedence of record creation or deletion. As the modeler you often know better than anyone what you expect to see in the fields and on the reports. You may also have test case documentation as a guide of expected results to check against.

A list of deliverables from this stage is:

- ❑ Updates to previous documents
- ❑ Finalization of Documentation
    - ❑ Physical model
    - ❑ Final Technical Specification
    - ❑ Deployment Strategy
    - ❑ Test Case Scenarios
    - ❑ Test Statistics – Change Management
    - ❑ Software
    - ❑ Training and Help Tools

Deploy

This is the goal. Finally the team moves the code out of test and into production. You have a party and move into maintenance mode. I always judge an application's success on the enhancements that are suggested right away. When the business clients want to tie it to other systems or combine new data sources or build new dashboard screens you have truly done a good job.

At this stage all of the various models and analysis levels need to be revisited and examined against the final physical model to make sure they are all in sync and the final data dictionary needs to be as production ready as the code.

A list of deliverables from this stage is:

- ❑ Updates of previous documents
- ❑ Post project evaluation meeting notes
- ❑ List of expected next steps

Project Type

There are many different types of Information Technology projects that require data model support. We are going to look at three in particular, in terms of the types of models they will need. Remember that data models aren't *just* a pictorial of entities or tables. Every bit of analysis documented on that picture could be presented in text, and the diagram is only one product provided by the modeler to support a project. We'll focus here on Enterprise, Transactional, and Data Warehouse/Enterprise Reporting-type projects. From the modeler's perspective:

- ❑ Enterprise project models are concerned with capturing the dynamics of the storm in large brush strokes.
- ❑ Transactional project models are concerned with capturing the raindrops, one at a time.
- ❑ Data Warehouse/Enterprise Reporting project dimensional models are concerned with gathering the raindrops and providing different ways of selecting and aggregating them simply and accurately.

Enterprise

An Enterprise-level project is generally sponsored to document a very high-level view of business processes. It is often a strategy-type project that is looking at the current data environment with an eye to enhancing or streamlining it in the future. It may be an ongoing project to create an abstract view of the entire Enterprise or it may have a more restricted focus. Such projects allow an assessment of pedigree of the data being used, and how it relates to other areas of the organization, or indeed to external suppliers or customers. Rarely will such projects aim to create a software product. Instead the focus will generally be on giving an overview of the data used in business processes, through the development of a conceptual model. These models aggregate common ideas into one entity. For instance if both the Inventory and Marketing applications keep a full-blown physical copy of the Item records, then the Enterprise model will show one conceptual reference to 'Item'. These conceptual entities can then be mapped through logical and physical data models to actual implementations.

With Enterprise project models the modeler needs to pay special attention to the names they choose, since these high-level concepts can be easily misinterpreted. For instance 'Account' in the Sales group may have a very different definition from 'Account' in the Finance group. Definitions always help maintain clarity, but Enterprise project models need to be especially careful because many different audiences review them.

Enterprise projects tend to use conceptual models to document:

❑   General Areas – which are entities

❑   Conceptual Relationships – showing business process connections

❑   Notes – which document special circumstances

❑   Legends – explaining notations on the model

Transactional – OLTP

Transactional projects deal with building or enhancing software applications that create new Enterprise data records (a single instance in a table which is a member of the data set). The main purpose is to provide a tool to collect new or modify existing records in some structured way. These are Sales, Inventory, HR, and Accounting systems to name just a few. Transactional projects can contribute to Enterprise projects with any conceptual model created to abstract the business. These conceptual models are generally a more detailed view because of the focused scope.

A Transactional project doesn't always result in custom development of a new database although a new piece of software is generally the goal. Transactional projects have a 'Make or Buy' step somewhere after detailed analysis. They need to be able to compare the data elements and business rules that are used in a company with an 'Off the Shelf' solution. The model used here is generally a fully attributed logical model. What good is buying an HR package if you need to be able to matrix people into different departments at a percentage of support but the HR system will only allow them to work for one? Either you will need to change the way you do business or you need to find a more flexible HR solution.

Transactional projects tend to use all types of models to document the analysis needed to reach the goal.

- ❑ Conceptual models – Capture general/abstract concepts as entities, business process connections as conceptual relationships, notes documenting special circumstances, and legends explaining the notation used in the pictorial model.

- ❑ Logical models – Capture specific data sets as entities, data dependencies and usage as data relationships, notes documenting special circumstances, and legends explaining the notation used in the pictorial model.

- ❑ Physical models – Capture tables and views as data access/manipulation structures, and constraints as relationships.

Data Warehouse – Enterprise Reporting

Data Warehouse or Enterprise Reporting projects are launched to deal with providing quick, efficient, correct data reporting for the Enterprise. Data Warehouse projects focus on historical data to support trend analysis, data mining, and 'What Happened? And Why?' reporting. Enterprise Reports projects are concerned with Operational Data Stores (ODS), collections of nearly current data for operational reporting.

You may need to support this type of project with every type of data model we have gone over (conceptual, logical, physical). You may also need to utilize a specialized physical modeling design called a dimensional design style. We already talked about normalization in the relational theory chapter. Dimensional modeling techniques denormalize by design. It organizes data to get it out of the database quickly, simply, and expediently. We'll consider this type of design in more detail in Chapter 10.

Quite often this style of model is used in the client-accessible portion of a data warehouse or an operational data store (ODS). There may be other normalized layers involved to support the system. There are fewer tables and therefore less joins which can increase query return performance by orders of magnitude. Pre-calculated and pre-aggregated data is the rule not the exception. These data structures are built to be used by the general public with a drag-and-drop query tool so it is built to prevent confusion and stress. Data organized dimensionally is data with training wheels on it. It has built-in safety nets, like full-named tables and columns for clarity, pre-aggregation to prevent math errors, pre-formatting to speed the output and create consistency in reporting, and derivations based on enterprise-controlled formula rather than *ad hoc* answers. This data has been collected, reviewed, and blessed before publishing.

Data Warehouse and Data Warehouse/Enterprise Reporting projects use every means available to ensure quality, speed, and ease of viewing. They tend to use all types of models to document the reported data, as we outlined for Transactional projects.

Project Style Comparison

Here is just a short list of things that you could use to recognize what the models from each project will provide. Data Warehouse projects will be focused on historic data, whereas Enterprise Reporting will be focused on current data.

Factors	Enterprise	Transactional	Data Warehouse – Enterprise Reporting
Build database objects	No	Yes	Yes
Maintain database objects	No	Yes	Yes
Document database objects	No	Yes	Yes
Manage relationship rules	Yes	Yes	Yes
Database inventory	No	Yes	Yes
Project deliverable	Yes	Yes	Yes
Data element definitions	Yes	Yes	Yes
Column definitions	No	Yes	Yes
Business Interface analysis	Yes	No	No
Cross-application Data element analysis	No	Yes	Yes

In Transactional and Data Warehouse/Enterprise Reporting:

❑ The focus is almost always at the data object level. You can follow all the data elements and see how they relate in one application.

❑ Models are needed to create physical structures. They iterate through abstraction, analysis, and physical design.

❑ There are easy to recognize boundaries. The scope of most transactional data models is one distinct application. The scope of a dimensional data model is either one environment like the data warehouse or the Operational Data Store (ODS).

❑ The scope is always based on the project, whether it is focusing on the invoice module of the Sales application or looking to create an entirely new Sales application.

❑ Products are more frequently kept up to date. All the models keep their value by staying in sync with the database. They should be versioned and archived with every release and structure fix. Since these models are blueprints of a database, the programmers and DBAs may well constantly refer to them.

While in the case of an Enterprise model:

❑ The focus is more generic, providing an overview of all the data elements.

❑ Concentrate on abstraction.

❑ There are more loosely defined boundaries, due to the interconnectivity of business processes and external, as well as internal, data needs.

❑ There's often a simple goal of exploring a subject area/business process to determine what it involves.

❑ Products may not be revisited until a new project is launched to explore an adjacent business process.

Model Goal

Models are deliverables. Therefore they must be created to satisfy a need. They have a goal they need to accomplish. You will have many goals through the life of a project, and recognizing what these goals are will help you pick the analysis level of your model. We are going to look at three basic goals for building a model for a project, namely Abstraction, Data Element Analysis, and Physical Design.

Abstraction Models

If your goal is to make complex ideas as simple to understand as possible you are usually going to use a conceptual model. For example, here is the first conceptual model of the Shipping department for a start-up company. It captures ideas referring to an entire warehouse full of products being sold and shipped in very simple syntax. This could be the beginning of a custom development project.

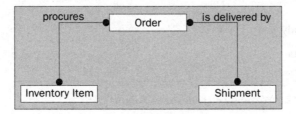

For the most part if your goal is to look at the abstract, then you will capture thoughts and ideas about how things are now, or how they could be in the future, in the conceptual model. They are often garbled scribbles on whiteboards or enthusiastic ramblings of someone who had a brilliant thought in the middle of the night. Conceptual models tidy up the chicken scratchings into something that can be presented and talked about with customers who may or may not be database aware. At this level you are representing big data areas. Models like this become part of the decision making process which begins a project.

Maybe the brilliant thought is about legacy systems and how to increase functionality to reduce costs and service the customer better. You could have two conceptual models that might look like this:

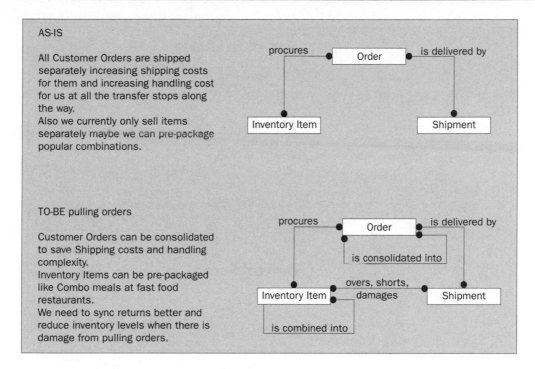

Both the models above look simple enough. However, if we consider the second one, then it tells us that there is a possibility that the Inventory Item, Order, and Shipment data are currently all being managed in separate applications. Perhaps the data flows are currently flat files that are ported from one application to the next and batched at the end of the day, causing a timing issue. If the Shipping manager and Inventory manager both want to be able to track the impact of shipping companies on inventory levels, and who is currently handling product, this may currently be almost impossible because it is all manual. As a result, this little model may be filled with a year's worth of scope. It may even need to be parsed down into smaller projects to improve handling of budgeting and resourcing. The model is just a tool to get data management discussions going.

Abstracting is an important way to clear away the details and focus, providing a simple model with which to begin discussion of pros and cons, cost, and feasibility studies. Don't be afraid of getting things wrong at this stage as long as you are prepared to change them, or even to remodel again from scratch.

Data Element Analysis Models

Analysis models are generally the ones built after a project is launched. They have all sorts of customers with all levels of expertise. You will likely be using every analysis level, and level of definition, at your disposal to be able to capture and communicate back what you have discovered or are theorizing. We use the conceptual entity levels to set up and verify data scope, anticipated integration, and high-level business rules. Analysis models are working models. They may have lots of notes on them while everyone figures out how to move to the next step.

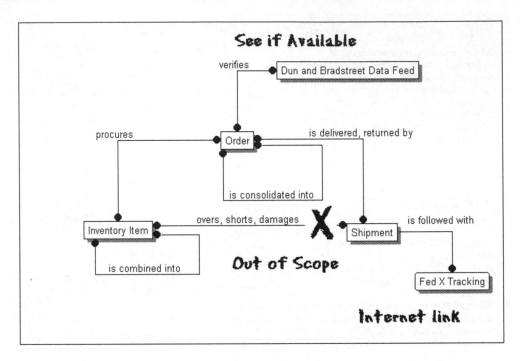

We expand the conceptual entity-level model into a logical entity-level model and finally to a logical fully attributed model. The analysis being captured on the model documents every stage of understanding as the team figures out what needs to be done. In this case, if you need to impact multiple systems, you may need to do a reverse engineering effort to understand the 'As-Is' of the systems themselves to compare to your logical fully attributed and find the delta changes that need to occur.

Physical Design Models

Design models are the ones at the database schema level. These are generally the physical models although new discoveries should be updated on the logical level as well. So you may be impacting both from time to time. The Physical design/s may be a series of options that are debated and argued over by the whole development team until all of the processing, performance, naming, structure, and sizing issues have been worked out. As an example, consider the following model, which uses a class word abbreviation naming standard, Camel notation, and data types to support an Oracle platform:

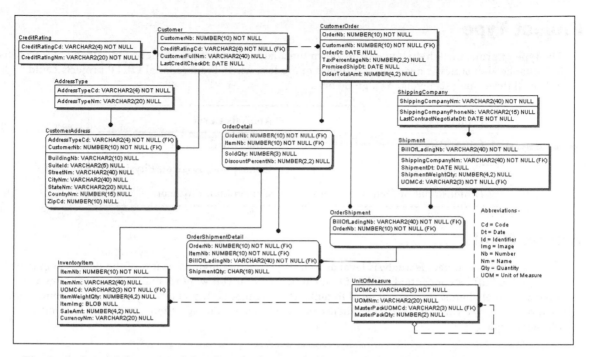

The final physical design model is the one that gets built, sometimes many times as it progresses from development, through testing, and finally to production deployment. Once the database has been built from the model, you may be called upon to create submodels to support other efforts. The screen and report developers need to know the names of the tables and columns; as do the back-end procedure and initial load teams. Your models will be very popular at this point and, since everyone wants the latest version, you'll be kept on your toes trying to keep them updated.

All iterations should be versioned. At this point in the game you don't know if you are going to have to loop back to an earlier version or not. Large teams can be difficult to keep up-to-date. You may need to keep a control log of the changes so that you can keep track of them. This is also the last time prior to production release that the clients can point out something that was missed. Any changes required at this point must be reviewed by the team as a whole, since what seems like a simple change can impact screens, menu structures, reports, and even security. This is often a place where a team holds a late discovery for a 'Phase 2' effort. One of the documents that is part of finishing up the project is this set of enhancements. You may have 'To-Be' or delta models showing the changes that need to occur to support those enhancements. Physical models (and submodels) support building the tables, testing initial load processes, screen tests, report verification, and various other pre-release validation steps.

The Right Model

During the course of this chapter we have seen how projects develop, what controls there are within them, and what model types we can use to aid the goals of the project. To round off here, we'll look at how all of these things come together to help us decide what model to choose. Data models go through similar maturing and iteration processes as a full project. At the height of a project you will be moving rapidly between different models, from conceptual to logical to physical and back to logical, as you find out that there are exceptions to the business rules that the clients didn't mention earlier.

Project Type

The type of project will help you narrow down the analysis level of the models. Enterprise-level projects for instance almost never need physical levels of models, while Transactional OLTP projects could utilize all three analysis levels. As a guide here:

Project Type	Analysis Level
Enterprise	Conceptual
Transactional	Conceptual, Logical, Physical
Dimensional or Data Warehouse	Conceptual, Physical

Model Goal

Your task helps you decide analysis level as well. If you want a high overview of the data system then you need to build a conceptual model. On the other hand, if you want to analyze business rules and analyze data elements, then you'll need to build a logical model. If you already know everything there is to know about the rules of the data elements and need to design tables, then you'll want to build a physical model.

Model Goal	Analysis Level
Abstract	Conceptual
Analysis	Conceptual, Logical
Physical Design	Physical

Customer Need

Now you need to determine the customer of your model, in order to decide what level of definition you want to work with. If your customer is someone who wants a general rundown of the data involved in the project then you want an entity-level model. If you are working with someone who is concentrating on integration opportunities or key design choices then you need a key based view of the model. If the customer is someone who needs to see all the gory details then you want a fully attributed model.

Customer Need	Analysis Level
Overview	Entity
Focused Identifier/Uniqueness	Key Based
All the details	Fully Attributed

Choose one option from these three ways to narrow the definition of your product, and you will see what model you need to build. Here is a mapping showing the combinations of ideas that focus the product definition of a model.

Project Type	Model Goal	Customer View Need	Analysis Level	Level of Definition
Enterprise	Abstract	Overview	Conceptual	Entity Level
Transactional	Abstract	Overview	Conceptual	Entity Level
Transactional	Analysis	Overview	Logical	Entity-Level
Transactional	Data Element Analysis	Focused Identifier/Uniqueness	Logical	Key Based
Transactional	Data Element Analysis	All the details	Logical	Fully Attributed
Transactional	Physical Design	Focused Identifier/Uniqueness	Physical	Key Based
Transactional	Physical Design	All the details	Physical	Fully Attributed
Data Warehouse / Enterprise Reporting	Abstract	Overview	Conceptual	Entity Level
Data Warehouse / Enterprise Reporting	Data Element Analysis	All the details	Logical	Fully Attributed
Data Warehouse / Enterprise Reporting	Physical Design – normalized or dimensional	Focused Identifier/Uniqueness	Physical	Key Based
Data Warehouse / Enterprise Reporting	Physical Design – normalized or dimensional	All the details	Physical	Fully Attributed

> **Remember that if the model doesn't communicate what you are trying to get across to your audience then it is useless.**

These are still just high-level definitions of what is on a model and the details that show up. You have an almost unlimited set of choices, especially if you are using one of the modeling software packages. Making these choices just helps you narrow down what kind of model you are building and therefore what your checklist of information is. You still need to be aware of the level of understanding (rather than what they want to know) of your model customer, the needs of the project, and any methodology or external standard you need to be aware of.

Model Tips

Here is a shortlist of things you should keep in mind when modeling:

- ❏ Picking the level of analysis and detail of a model depends on many factors.
- ❏ Staying within scope is a challenge.
- ❏ Being wrong on a model can be a good thing. It stimulates discussion.
- ❏ There is no 'One Right' model. There are several serving different purposes. Not all of them are schematics for databases.
- ❏ Sometimes the 'correct' solution isn't the 'best' solution for the Enterprise.
- ❏ Models are products and have customers. Be customer-oriented.
- ❏ Stay objective. Feedback for designs or analysis is meant to enhance not criticize.
- ❏ Finding a way to keep the team in sync with each other at every model iteration requires a creative publish and deploy mechanism.
- ❏ Every model you build helps you to build the next one.
- ❏ You will need a second pair of eyes to look for your mistakes. You can be too close to see them.

Summary

We looked at how data models can be used to document and communicate data rules, from the business data creators to the technical data tool machinists. We saw that all projects have scope, standards, budget, and schedule constraints to consider, and detailed the steps called out by most development lifecycle descriptions, in terms of strategizing, analyzing, designing, building and testing, and deploying. The data modeler is often involved from the first strategizing stage through to the building and testing stages. We also reviewed project types that help focus the data model needs:

- ❏ Enterprise
- ❏ Transactional
- ❏ Dimensional

We saw how the data model can be a very flexible product to support many different goals. It is a critical factor to the success of a project, since without these models developers can't successfully move on to the design phase. Insufficient detail in the analysis stage of the project simply forces the team to revisit ground that the SMEs probably feel they have already described in detail. We also looked at how data models grow and mature throughout the life of the project. They evolve and iterate in a radical non-linear fashion very much like the projects and tasks they support. They can be used by the entire team to build, and verify, solutions to the challenges defined in the project scope.

Models in general should be constructed with an expectation that all the due diligence of definitions and accumulating project-specific 'value added' knowledge into the model, is going to be part of the task. Data models certainly have to start someplace, but they should continue to mature until you could hand one to a new team member and they could follow your analysis and design like a storybook.

- **Model the Business**
- **The Objectives**
- **The Scope**
- **The Approach**
- **Document the Process: Top Down**
- **Document the Process Rules:**
  Bottom Up
- **Building the Conceptual Model**
- **Checking the Business Rules**
- **Summary**

Building a Conceptual Model

This chapter is the beginning of the tutorial. It will give you the opportunity to see how some of the principles we looked at in the first section of this book can be applied to discover and document the data area of a business process. We will concentrate on the 20% of conceptual design tasks that returns 80% of the value of doing one. Instead of analyzing a process unknown to you, we will model the game Solitaire. I hope most of you are familiar with it. This will help you concentrate on the process of modeling, rather than the process of discovery. Many of you will have it on your PC; those without can simply get out the playing cards and work through the examples at your desk.

In the course of this chapter we will:

❑　Go over the Top down and Bottom up approach to analysis

❑　Gather the information for our conceptual model using both methods for comparison

❑　Organize, refine, and scope it

❑　Use the information to define subject areas and objects of importance, as well as the relationships between them

❑　Build a Transactional Conceptual E/R data model

Model the Business

Solitaire may not seem like a typical example of a business process. In fact it may seem more like a system or an application that has already been programmed, so why use it in this exercise?

The application Solitaire on your PC was built on rules gathered from a manual process. That manual process is called a game to us, but it could just as easily be something else, like managing a checkbook or planning a party. It could even be a serious business process like scheduling freight delivery or planning the next fiscal budget. Many business processes now have automated tools to support them. Have you ever visited a trucking hub? It is a routing station for freight. The point of the game there is to use your equipment as close to weight and volume capacity as possible at all times, stop as few times as possible, and deliver with speed, safety, and care.

Data modeling works by first gathering the data elements that are required to support a process or activity. You need to be able to dive into a totally manual, partially automated/manual, or fully automated process and find the underlying activity in order to get an unobstructed and objective view of the data elements and their rules. If you don't you will only have a view of what data elements there are today and how the rules have been built around them.

I want you to think beyond 'Solitaire – the application' for a moment and see the business process underneath. All processes have:

❑ Rules

❑ Equipment

❑ People

❑ Goals

❑ Durations

❑ The ability to win or lose

❑ The ability to get better over time

Solitaire is on your machine. You can test out the rules as we go along. But I want you to concentrate on the process underneath rather than Solitaire the application. If it doesn't happen with a deck of cards then it is out of the scope of this tutorial. We are focusing on the process and the data elements involved in the process. The game on your system is just for convenience, since I don't think Curlingstone is going to market this book with a pack of cards.

When I first learned data modeling it was with a company called DACOM. Using their methodology you would never even begin to data model without first creating an activity model (IDEF0). A good activity model goes down to a level where you actually see each data element and how they support the people or machines doing a job (along with a lot of other good information about Controls/Rules, process dependencies, teams, equipment, feedback loops, and timing constraints).

Unfortunately we don't always have the opportunity to do process analysis beforehand. And even if we do have an Activity or Process model, we often have to provide an overview that aggregates the hundreds of individual data elements for the team. You may need a way to aggregate the information together into an easily understood and recognizable overview of the data area of a business process.

What you need is a conceptual model.

The Objectives

What are you trying to accomplish? You are going to draw a picture that portrays the data scope of a business process. You are also going to refine and clarify all the individual descriptions of a process until it is distilled into a single truth (or as close as you can get it). In order to do that you need to:

❑ Become informed enough to explain and defend the discoveries

❑ Learn the vocabulary of the environment

- ❑ Identify the concepts or data elements, and determine the rules between them
- ❑ Validate the scope
- ❑ Build an Enterprise Conceptual E/R model

The building of the conceptual model may be part of a project whose only objective is to explore a business process for discovery of areas of potential custom or purchased software support. On the other hand it may be part of a project that has already decided that a software tool would greatly enhance a business unit's ability to do a quality job in the most profitable way possible. Either way, the creation of the conceptual model is generally the first task for the data modeler, right after the Kickoff and Charter sessions.

> **Data Modeling is not done in solitary confinement. We are always part of the team. So although we are going to work quietly together from the platform of this book, we need to keep in mind that what we are analyzing would generally be a part of someone's daily activities. You need to meet with them and start to learn about their process. Try to keep an open mind even if you are experienced with this business area. Making assumptions without validating them will cause you problems later on. You may be responsible for the model, but you share the responsibility with the Business Process Owners for getting the full scope of their concepts documented.**

In learning about the client try and pick up as many souvenirs as possible, such as:

- ❑ Department charters or goal statements
- ❑ Samples of forms and/or reports
- ❑ Organization charts
- ❑ Desk top procedures
- ❑ Training manuals

Looking at the current system's paperwork will not only give you an idea of the nature of the current data, but also of the likely lifetime and evolution of the data to be handled in the new system. Take a digital camera with you and document how the physical world uses data elements. Simply getting a map of the company's site, with the names of buildings and departments, will help you remain clear in your discussions with the client. Get, or make, a dictionary of terms. Find out if there is a professional dictionary to translate the technical terms into layman's terms. In short, do everything you can do to get familiar with the world you are about to document.

The Scope

Scope means the area covered or the limits to which you are going to analyze. Analysts in general and modelers specifically are constantly fighting to get a better, more solid wall around the scope. It's usually a variable through an entire project. Documents and signatures are helpful but managing the scope is one of *the* most difficult tasks for most project managers.

How are we going to find the scope of our tutorial? We are going to put the process 'Solitaire' into an organization framework and discover how it is going to be used. Just imagine that you are the data modeler in an Information Services department on a college campus. Your boss tells you that the Psychology department has decided to do some research into the Solitaire phenomenon, investigating the addiction level of employees to the game. Questions have come up about positive feedback and the ratio of wins vs. losses. They want to gather some data and check it out. So they want you to document the activity.

Whether verbal or written, scope is answers to questions. It is the first thing you have to discover. You ask:

Q. Who is the customer?
A. Here is the name and phone number of a contact in the Psychology department.

Q. Is this only about Solitaire?
A. Yes.

Q. Computer Solitaire or cards?
A. It's the game aspect they are concentrating on, not how they play it.

Q. Why do they want to look at Solitaire data?
A. To see if they can figure out why everyone wastes time playing it.

Q. Do they want to capture all the details of all the games?
A. They seem to, but you had better validate it with them.

Q. What is the goal of building them a conceptual model?
A. They want to see if it is feasible and within budget to build a little application to build a data mart for statistical analysis.

Q. What is the timeline?
A. As soon as possible.

Q. Do you want to review my work?
A. Yes. Let's go over it before you deliver it to them.

Many times defining a scope is more like this than actually having a scope document to work from. This informal conversation set up the initial boundaries of the model for you. It gave you the following information to work with:

❑ Your client is the Psychology department, with a specific contact to speak to.

❑ The client is looking at Solitaire to determine why it proves so popular with people.

❑ It is the game not the application that is important. You need to include an analysis of both even if you only have access to one or the other.

❑ The exact scope of your model is not clear at this stage. You should therefore work with a larger scope than may actually end up being necessary.

❑ There is a potential for a continuation of the data analysis to a physical database design in the future. You need to keep that in mind when you gather information.

❑ The schedule is tight and you need to be prepared to work with a programmer (really soon).

Of course now that you have a basic idea of what the scope is, you should document it and start a project notebook to give you a place to return to and refresh your memory of what exactly was agreed to in the beginning.

The Approach

Over the years I have found that, unlike an airplane, an analyst can mix approaches to get the best of both concurrently. In fact you would find it more of a chore to restrict your analysis to just one. These are the ways we will approach gathering data concepts about Solitaire.

Top Down

Using this approach we discover and draft a description of the business process. That description supplies you with concepts that will be used as a starting place. This approach allows the process to tell the story about the data. This is a functional or process-driven analysis. You concentrate on how things *work*. You need to, as the name implies, start at the top and drill downward increasing the level of detail in an iterative fashion. Without it you may miss:

❑ Assumptions that everyone expects you to know

❑ Future developments that could change your direction

❑ Opportunities to increase the quality, usability, accessibility, and enterprise data

With it you gain:

❑ An understanding of the way things fit together, from high to low levels of detail

❑ A sense of the political environment that may surround data

❑ An enhancement of your understanding of data importance

❑ The guide to the level of detail you need for different audiences

Know the Strategic Goals

Find out what the strategic objectives are for the process, group, department, and company. Strategic goals include all of the plans to do the right thing at the right time to accomplish a long-term goal. Don't just concentrate on data management or the business area you are analyzing. Find out about the directions they are moving in. Are there mergers on the horizon? Is a new web-based business being discussed? Is there a push for lowering the cost of operations? Almost any Enterprise strategic goal will have some intrinsic impact on the world of data management.

Strategy is part of every process. You as the data modeler need to be able to clearly state two things:

❑ What is the data going to need to be able to support?

❑ How will we know if it is right?

Interview People

In Top Down analysis, people are the best source of your information. You need to find out from:

- Managers of the Process – How it should work
- Process Experts – How it really works
- Customers of the data – What they need to get
- Suppliers of the data – How to get what is needed
- Handlers of the data – How they build it

Bottom Up

The Bottom up approach focuses instead on the inventory of *things* in a process. It implies an in-depth understanding of as much of the process as can be known at this point. This is much easier to do at your desk, since we are quite used to dissecting screens, forms, and reports to get to data and data rules. Using this approach you discover and draft a list of potential elements without regard to how they are used. The list is usually made up of a mixed set of very low-level, detailed notions and high-level concepts. The trick is to aggregate them to the same level of detail. This is a data-driven analysis. You concentrate on what things *are*. You concentrate on the parts rather than the process. You need to, as the name implies, start at the bottom and aggregate up increasing your level of aggregation, again in an iterative fashion. Without it you may miss:

- Data areas that everyone expects you to know
- Relationships
- Fuzzy, currently undefined areas that need extra work to bring them to the same level of understanding

With it you gain:

- An understanding of the things involved
- A sense of the quality levels that may be inherent to the data
- An enhancement of your understanding of data definitions

Know the Tactical Goals

Tactical goals include all of the activity to do the right thing at the right time to accomplish a short-term goal. Tactics is also part of every process. You need to be able to clearly state two things:

- What is the data?
- How will we know if we have it all?

Interrogate Tools, Products, Processes

In Bottom Up analysis, the current environment is the best source of your information. It may not fit the strategic goals, but you need this information to be able to effect change. You need to find out from:

❑   Tools – What data do they use and how

❑   Process – How the data is created, used, moved, stored, accessed

❑   Data Products – What they provide

❑   Data Interfaces – Who, What, Where, When, and Why they are currently in place

Document the Process: Top Down

For our first pass we are going to concentrate on the steps that the process must pass through to be successful. You may find these in Process flows, Training manuals, or other 'How to' documentation. You may also find that the only source of how things work is in the memories of the people doing the tasks. Top down analysis often requires extensive interviewing, double-checking inconsistencies with descriptions, sequencing, and criticality of the tasks. For our small process you can play the game a while and note down what you do.

We are going to do the following to build our conceptual model using the Top Down approach of Solitaire:

❑   Decide on your discovery source/s.

❑   Create a list of activities and activity descriptions

❑   Discover the most important elements in the activities

❑   List and define the elements

❑   Validate the activities with the business process community

❑   Group the elements into concepts and validate the concepts against the scope statement

❑   Define the concepts and relate them together

❑   Validate the conceptual model

Solitaire Activities

First we try to build a list of process steps. Play the game if you are unsure about how it flows and the rules you must obey. So what is going on with Solitaire? If it was a business process you might refer to department documentation, training class materials, textbooks, or written procedures. You could refer to an application spec or Users Manual if you are looking at a process already supported by an automated tool. However, remember that these are the rules of the application, and won't necessarily fit the business process anymore. In the case of Solitaire you could refer to a book of Card Game Rules, or discover the essence of the process by playing it yourself. However you do your discovery you want to create a high-level description of what happens.

Solitaire Process Steps

By following the process outlined above, here are the process steps I discovered myself:

❑   The Player shuffles a Deck of 52 playing Cards.

❑   Lay 7 Cards face down to create Piles in a line from left to right.

❑ Skip the Card farthest on the left and lay another Card face down on top of each of the remaining 6. Continue by skipping one more Pile with each pass until you have 7 Piles of Cards in quantities of 1,2,3,4,5,6,7.

❑ Turn over the top Card of each Pile. (This is the Status that the Game begins in.)

❑ There is a Pile of Cards that is face down in the upper left corner. (If you are playing by hand you are probably holding it.) This is the Draw Pile. It has 24 cards.

❑ Including the Draw Pile, there are 8 Piles of Cards on the Playing Area and empty Spaces indicate that 4 more Piles are possible. That makes 12 Piles of Cards.

❑ In the Playing Area are 7 Piles. The first has 1 Card. It is Face up. All the other six have 1 Card Face up and an increasing number of Hidden Cards stacked underneath them. These are Processing Piles 1-7. The amount of Cards needing to be processed is the number of the Pile from left to right minus 1. The total Cards in the Processing Piles originally equal 28 in the quantity configuration 1,2,3,4,5,6,7.

❑ Above the playing piles are 4 discard piles. Remove 3 Cards from the Draw Pile in order. Turn them over so the third Card down is visible and made available for processing at the beginning of each Play.

❑ The end of each Play occurs when no other Moves are available and a new Card must be drawn from the Draw Pile.

❑ Move the available Card from the Draw Pile to an appropriate Processing Pile or to the Discard Pile. Move all other available Cards from one Pile to another.

❑ You can play until there are no more available moves.

❑ Every Game ends in a Win or Loss.

Winning looks something like this played manually:

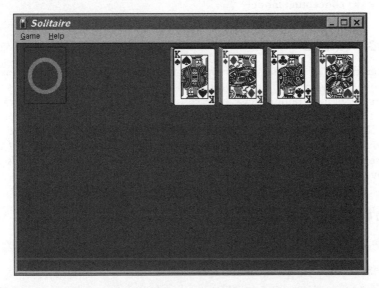

or like this played electronically:

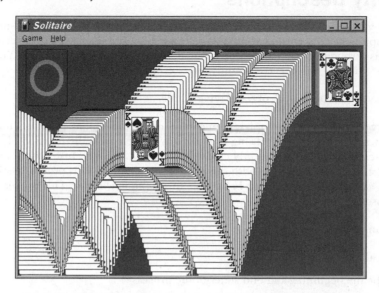

Losing looks something like this. There are a lot of cards left on the playing area that can't be moved.

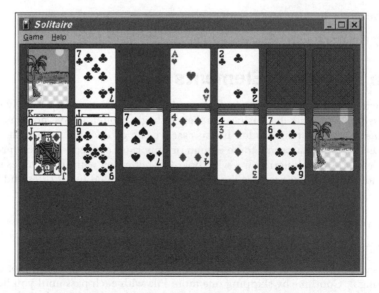

Even if you get a good written description of the process, it's important to try it out for yourself. Most procedures leave out a wealth of assumed knowledge and experience. In this case we assume that the reader knows what an Ace and a King look like, can distinguish between different colored suits, and understands that the model when played with cards by hand, is slightly different to that played on the PC.

Build Activity Descriptions

We now have a very small list of activities involved in the process of Solitaire. You need to have a complete description of the activities so that there is no confusion over what is covered in the activity. You may get this through documentation or you may need to write them yourself. You need this to validate your list with the business community. For example:

❑   The Player shuffles a Deck of 52 playing Cards.

The player in a Solitaire game is completely in control of the movement of cards within the rules controlling allowable movement. Shuffling is an activity that changes the position of one card to another. The deck is restricted to suit only cards. It excludes the Joker, Instruction, and or Advertising cards. A Solitaire game always begins with the cards being shuffled. This process begins with a player rearranging the cards randomly without being able to see the new order. This process completes when the player chooses to.

Activity descriptions should:

❑   Define all of the elements

❑   Describe the beginning and end states of the process

❑   Describe the trigger mechanism for the beginning activity

❑   Describe any dependencies or feedback loops

❑   Identify any controlling rules, mechanisms, or other activities

Identify the Important Elements

We now know what the activity of Solitaire looks and feels like. We would probably consider ourselves at least acquainted enough with the business process to begin modeling. We now need to determine the relevant concepts required for our model. In this case we can go over the rules with a highlighter and find just one of everything that seems to be a noun or important concept. In a real project you may not have a list of rules yet, so brainstorm on a whiteboard or better yet with sticky notes that you can easily move around and group. In our case, we'll go back over the bulleted list of rules and highlight in bold the key words:

❑   The **Player** shuffles a **Deck** of 52 playing **Cards**.

❑   Lay 7 Cards face down to create **Piles** in a line from left to right.

❑   Skip the Card farthest on the left and lay another Card face down on top of each of the remaining 6. Continue by skipping one more Pile with each pass until you have 7 Piles of Cards in quantities of 1,2,3,4,5,6,7.

❑   Turn over the top Card of each Pile. (This is the **Status** that the **Game** begins in).

❑   There is a Pile of Cards that is face down in the upper left corner. (If you are playing by hand you are probably holding it.) This is the **Draw Pile**. It has 24 cards.

❑   Including the Draw Pile, there are 8 Piles of Cards on the **Playing Area** and **Empty Spaces** that indicate that 4 more Piles are possible. That makes 12 Piles of Cards.

❑ In the Playing Area are 7 Piles. The first has 1 Card. It is Face up. All the other six have 1 Card Face up and an increasing number of **Hidden Cards** stacked underneath them. These are **Processing Piles** 1-7. The amount of Cards needing to be processed is the number of the Pile from left to right minus 1. The total Cards in the Processing Piles originally equal 28 in the quantity configuration 1,2,3,4,5,6,7.

❑ Above the playing piles are 4 **Discard Piles**. Remove 3 Cards from the Draw Pile in order. Turn them over so the third Card down is visible and made available for processing at the beginning of each **Play**.

❑ The end of each Play occurs when no other **Moves** are available and a new Card must be drawn from the Draw Pile.

❑ Move the **Available Card** from the Draw Pile to an appropriate Processing Pile or to the Discard Pile. Move all other available Cards from one Pile to another.

❑ You can play until there are no more available Moves.

❑ Every Game ends in a **Win** or **Loss**.

Basic naming standard: Entity names are always singular.

Next write them up on sticky notes, or something that will allow you the freedom to rearrange them. We'll tabulate here for simplicity:

Player	Deck	Card
Card Pile	Status	Game
Playing Area	Empty Space	Draw Pile
Hidden Card	Processing Pile	Discard Pile
Play	Move	Available Card
Win	Loss	

Define Your Elements

We need to be able to clearly define our discovered elements. Many times we are fooled by different names meaning the same thing and similar names for different things. You have to be able to recognize them for what they are by whatever words, labels, slang, and technical terms are being used to identify them. You will want to gather as much information you can at this stage. It will help you with further analysis. You may want to add in:

❑ Definition – A statement of precise meaning with a clarity of detail that creates common understanding

❑ Example – An instance which illustrates the general concept

❑ Includes – A shortlist of common and recognizable examples which belong

❑ Excludes – A shortlist of common and recognizable examples which don't belong

You will also find when you are defining things that some names just aren't complete enough and need to be changed for clarity sake. For instance Pile would be better described here as a Card Pile. You may even want to further qualify it to Solitaire Card Pile if you need to work with an Enterprise meta data customer for the model at a later date. If this were a game company we were supporting it could be important to be able to differentiate the concepts.

> **Don't write sloppy definitions such as Card Pile = A pile of cards, or circular definitions such as Game = A contest. Contest = A game!**

Remember that the more effort you put into your definitions, the greater chance you will have of successfully communicating your discoveries to the project team and model reviewers.

Name	Definition
Available Card	A card which is assessed to be able to be used in a Play by satisfying many rules.
Card	One of 52 unique game pieces used in playing games bearing pictures of figures or numbers organized by suit. Example: Queen of Clubs, 2 of Diamonds.
Deck	The complete set of 4 suits of 13 cards making a collection of 52 individual cards. Does not include Jokers, Instructions, and extra vendor cards.
Discard Pile	The location of the activity in Solitaire where a Card is removed completely from play. Only an Ace can begin a Discard Pile.
Draw Pile	The location in Solitaire where a Card is stored until such time as it is moved to the Waste Pile for processing.
Empty Space	A pile that has no cards.
Game	A contest played for sport or amusement according to rules made up of many small decisions, which affect the outcome. In this instance Solitaire.
Hidden Card	A card with the back visible.
Lose	The inability move all the Cards to a Discard Pile.
Move	The change in position of a card from one pile to another.
Card Pile	A collection of cards, which behave differently in the game of Solitaire. Example: Draw Pile, Discard Pile, Processing Pile.
Play	A Play is completed when the entire set of Available Cards are assessed resulting in a Move or Pass.
Player	A participant in the game of Solitaire.
Playing Area	The table or screen where the game is being carried out.

Name	Definition
Processing Pile	The location of the activity in Solitaire where cards are matched from the Draw pile according to playing rules. All processing piles are originally set up through the layout of a game. If during the processing of the cards, a pile is emptied – a King may be moved to the pile position and used to process more cards.
Status	The state of concluding a Game of Solitaire. Example: Win, Lose, Quit.
Win	The completed movement of all the Cards to a Discard Pile.

Validate Your Work

Now you should review your list with the business community to see if what you have documented is correct in their eyes. You may want to list them on a flip chart or on sticky notes and do a 'True & False' session. Include absolutes like 'Always' or 'Never' to force recognition of business process anomalies. Jot down new discoveries. Make sure your take your definitions with you. That way even if you choose a name for the entity that isn't instantly recognized by the client, once they read your definition they will see what you meant. In fact at this point element names are really handy shortcuts to the definitions. The definitions are the real knowledge.

You may need to iterate this process if there is dissent with the business process owners about what is correct. I have found sometimes that conflicting descriptions are actually true. You need to add to your activity descriptions how that can be and allow for it in the conceptual model. You may find that your business processes have variations as well. Many people will describe what they think is the only way to do something without knowledge that subtle variations may exist even within your Enterprise. The International community or even different departments supposedly using the same Business process may have different rules. You need to make it part of your responsibility to know.

Aggregate into Concepts

Now you need to group like things together. You are looking for build aggregations that would best cover the concepts in the process. Eventually, as we make these groupings, we can look for a generic label to describe them. Here is how I would group them and why. The following concepts deal exclusively with one complete game:

❑ Game, Win, Lose

This is the only person I see:

❑ Player

Now we list all the concepts relating to cards. Hidden and Available cards have to do with the status of a card, not the card itself. However, at this level there is no problem noting that they are about the same general topic. We should note that it is a judgment call on our behalf, as to whether to group them here or with Status.

❑ Card, Hidden Card, Available Card

The following concepts have to do with groupings of cards:

❏ Pile, Empty Space, Draw Pile, Discard Pile, Processing Pile, Deck

This one has to do with location:

❏ Playing Area

These have to do with the details of allowed and specific moves of cards:

❏ Play, Move

The one left over reminds us that in order to play a game we must be able to recognize the existing state. State of being in business processes may include the ability to recognize approval or availability states, versions, time durations, and maturing states like Part > Assembly > Product.

❏ Status

Now what? Look at the descriptions of why I pulled things together and give them a title. You get a much shorter list from my groupings than we started with. We are reducing and refining, and yet also increasing and simplifying. We are coming up with a way to express the activity of Solitaire in the simplest concepts possible, in order to make Solitaire approachable to almost any audience. At this stage our conceptual model can be broken down as:

Who	Description
Player	The person playing the game

What	Description
Game	Solitaire the activity
Card	The playing pieces for the game
Card Pile	A collection of playing pieces in the game

Where	Description
Playing Area	Where the game is held
Card Pile	Where the cards move

When	Description
Move	The rules of playing and the actual plays
Status	The state of a Play, Move, or Game

And all of that added together describes Solitaire from a very high but recognizable level. Did we leave anything out? Let's try doing this 'Bottom up' and see if the details match the aggregated names we have come up with to label our concepts. Remember we are usually doing this concurrently.

Document the Process Rules: Bottom Up

This time we are going to concentrate on the data elements that the process needs to be able to function. We are going to find the data elements and the rules they work by in Solitaire. Although much Bottom Up analysis is done with some kind of documentation or visible sets of data examples, in this case we don't have Solitaire data reports. Since what we are concentrating on is actually the manual game we will write out the rules ourselves to find the details. I hope you will see the overlap with the Top Down processing tasks we consider earlier.

Document the Rules of the Activity

The activity list we created didn't deal at all with many vital concepts that are buried in the rules of Solitaire. There is nothing in the activity steps describing the identification and description of a Card suit, what role color plays, the importance of the Ace and King, or even the way the Game can be won or lost. These are the data elements and the rules that control Solitaire. Just write them out and sort them a bit so they are not so freeform.

Card Rules:

- ❏ 52 Cards are played with. These exclude Jokers, Instructions, and Advertisings cards found in the Box
- ❏ Suits are Club, Heart, Spade, Diamond
- ❏ Suits are Red or Black
- ❏ Cards are Face Cards – Jack, Queen, King, or Number Cards 2-10, or Ace

Move Rules:

- ❏ A Play is completed when the entire set of Available Cards are assessed resulting in a Move or Pass.
- ❏ Cards that are Red move over Black Cards and vice versa
- ❏ Cards move from either the Draw Pile or another Processing Pile
- ❏ Cards move over another Card in decreasing order – King to two
- ❏ The Discard piles are populated in ascending order according to Suit – two to King
- ❏ Cards move to the Discard Pile from the Draw Pile or Processing Piles.
- ❏ Once a Card has been placed on the Discard Pile, it can't be moved back to the Pile it came from
- ❏ Once a Card has left the Draw Pile, it can't be moved back to the Draw Pile
- ❏ Only Aces can move to empty Discard Piles
- ❏ Only Kings can move to empty Processing Piles

Pile Rules:

- ❏ The first Card in the Discard pile is an Ace
- ❏ It doesn't matter which of the 4 piles a specific Ace ultimately moves to

Game Rules:

- ❑ There is only one Player for a Game
- ❑ You Lose if you cannot move all the Cards to a Discard Pile
- ❑ You Win when all the Discard Piles show Kings, or the Draw Pile and all of the Processing Piles are empty

Working with details like this allows us to identify relevant details to be flagged for review. We will look at them carefully and determine if they have a bearing on our conceptualization. It isn't a good thing to leave all the detailed analysis to the logical and physical model. At times it's the details that determine an aspect of a conceptual design. So we need to be aware of details that may affect our conceptual model.

Build Rule Descriptions

You need to define the rules as well in order to validate your understanding.

- ❑ Kings can move to empty Processing Piles. Kings are special cards in the Playing deck. They are allowed to move from the available position of any pile (other than the Discard pile) to any empty Processing Pile. This includes moving from one Processing Pile to another. This allows access to another card that was blocked by the King.

Rule descriptions should include not only all of the applications of the rule, but also all of the exceptions to the rule, as well as any results from the application or exception to the rule.

Identify the Important Elements

This should feel the same as when we discovered the nouns in the activities, though our list this time should include a different, wider range of nouns.

Card Rules:

- ❑ 52 Cards are played with. These exclude **Jokers**, **Instructions**, and **Advertisings** cards found in the **Box**
- ❑ **Suits** are **Club**, **Heart**, **Spade**, **Diamond**
- ❑ Suits are **Red** or **Black**
- ❑ Cards are **Face** Cards – **Jack**, **Queen**, **King** or **Number** Cards 2-10, or **Ace**

Availability Rules:

- ❑ A Card is **Available** if it is **Face Up** and the **Top Card** of a Pile that isn't the Discard Pile
- ❑ A Card is **Blocked** if it is Face Up and **Under** other Cards of a Pile that isn't the Discard Pile
- ❑ A Card is **Unavailable** if it is **Face Down** or in the Discard Pile

Move Rules:

- ❑ A **Play** is completed when all **Available Cards** are assessed resulting in a **Move** or **Pass**
- ❑ Cards that are Red move over Black Cards and vice versa
- ❑ Cards move from either the **Draw Pile** or another **Processing Pile**
- ❑ Cards move over another Card in **Decreasing Order** of face value – King to two
- ❑ The **Discard piles** are populated in **Ascending Order** according to Suit – two to King
- ❑ Cards move to the Discard Pile from the Draw Pile or Processing Piles
- ❑ Once a Card has been placed on the Discard Pile, it cannot be removed from the Discard Pile
- ❑ Once a Card has left the Draw Pile, it cannot be moved back to the Draw pile
- ❑ Only Aces can move to empty Discard Piles
- ❑ Only Kings can move to empty Processing Piles

Pile Rules:

- ❑ The first Card in the Discard pile must be an Ace
- ❑ It doesn't matter which of the 4 piles a specific Ace ultimately moves to

Game Rules:

- ❑ There is only one **Player** for a **Game**
- ❑ You **Lose** if you cannot move all the Cards to a Discard Pile
- ❑ You **Win** when all the Discard Piles show Kings, or the Draw Pile and all of the Processing Piles are **Empty**

Again write them up on sticky notes, or something that will allow you freedom to rearrange them. When using a Bottom Up analysis method, you may have hundreds, and there is much more danger of being fooled by two words that really mean the same thing. We'll tabulate them here for simplicity:

Card	Joker	Instruction Card
Advertising Card	Box	Suit
Heart	Club	Spade
Diamond	Red	Black
Jack	Queen	King
Ace	Face Card	Number Card
Availability	Face Up	Top Card

Table continued on following page

Blocked	Under	Unavailable
Available	Face Down	Play
Available Card	Move	Pass
Draw Pile	Process Pile	Discard Pile
Ascending order	Descending order	Player
Game	Win	Lose
Empty Space		

Define Your Elements

We just did this with the Top Down elements, so you may be able to reuse some of that work here. You still need to be able to clearly define your discovered elements. Even definitions become iterative through understanding. Make sure that you go back and update anything you enhance with more information.

Name	Definition
Ace	One of 4 playing Cards bearing a single pip which is the first Card in a Discard Pile in Solitaire
Advertising Card	A Card found in a deck that is not used for playing purposes
Ascending order	The ordering of Cards first with the Ace, then the Number Cards 2-10, then the Jack, Queen and King
Availability	The checking process to determine whether or not a Card is available to be used in a Play
Available	The status of a Card allowing it to be used in a Play
Available Card	A Card which is assessed to be able to be used in a Play by satisfying many rules
Black	The color traditionally associated with the suit of Clubs and Spades
Blocked	A status denoting that a Card cannot be played. It is Face Up and Under other Cards of a Pile that isn't the Discard Pile
Box	The usual container of a deck of Cards. Not all decks have boxes
Card	One of 52 unique game pieces used in playing games bearing pictures of figures or numbers organized by suit. Example: Queen of Clubs, 2 of Diamonds
Club	One of 4 Suits used in Playing Cards. The others are Diamonds, Hearts, and Spades. Clubs are Black
Descending order	The order of Cards by King, Queen, Jack, then the Number Cards 10 – 2, finishing with the Ace

Name	Definition
Diamond	One of 4 Suits used in Playing Cards. The others are Clubs, Hearts, and Spades. Diamonds are Red
Discard Pile	The location of the activity in Solitaire where a Card is removed completely from play. Only an Ace can begin a Discard Pile
Draw Pile	The location in Solitaire where a Card is stored until such time as it is moved to the Waste Pile for processing
Empty Space	A pile that has no Cards
Face Card	A Card in a Deck which has a figure pictured on the face
Face Down	The position of the Card where the Back is facing the Player, Cards are Unavailable in this position
Face Up	The position of the Card where the suit and designator can be read. Not all Face Up cards are available
Game	A contest played for sport or amusement according to rules made up of many small decisions, which affect the outcome. In this instance – Solitaire
Hearts	One of 4 Suits used in Playing Cards. The others are Diamonds, Clubs, and Spades. Hearts are Red
Instruction Card	A Card included in a deck that has the steps describing at least one game. This is not a playing Card
Jack	The Face Card ordered between the 10 and the Queen
Joker	A Card included in a deck that has neither Suit nor a position in a Suit. There are generally 2 provided and are used in some games but not Solitaire
King	One of 4 playing Cards bearing a figure representing the leader of a royal family which is allowed to change positions to an empty Processing Pile in Solitaire
Lose	The inability move all the Cards to a Discard Pile
Move	The change in position of a Card from one pile to another
Number Card	A Card in a Deck which does not have a figure pictured on the face. These are numbered between 2–10
Pass	The completion of a Play that does not include a Move of a Card
Play	A Play is completed when the entire set of Available Cards are assessed resulting in a Move or Pass
Player	A participant in the game of Solitaire

Table continued on following page

Name	Definition
Processing Pile	The location of the activity in Solitaire where Cards are matched from the Draw pile according to playing rules. All processing piles are originally set up through the layout of a game. If during the processing of the Card, a pile is emptied, a King may be moved to the pile position and used to process more Cards
Queen	A Card positioned between the Jack and the King
Red	A color traditionally associated with the suit of Hearts and Diamonds
Spade	One of 4 Suits used in Playing Cards. The others are Diamonds, Hearts, and Clubs. Spades are Black
Suit	One of 4 divisions of Cards. Clubs, Spades, Hearts, Diamonds
Top Card	A Card positioned on a Pile closest to the Player
Unavailable	The status of a Card as not being able to be moved in a Play
Under	The position of a Card beneath another Card
Win	The completed movement of all the Cards to a Discard Pile

Once again you should review your list with the business community to see if what you have documented is correct in their eyes. Use a similar technique for review whenever possible so that the relationship between you and the business process owners strengthens over time. Familiarity in this case encourages a relaxed and comfortable working environment.

Compare Methods

Since we are using the bottom up method to verify that we captured the concepts correctly in our top down approach, we are going to try to match all of the lower level elements to a higher level element.

Top Down Concepts	Bottom Up Elements
Player	Player
Game	Game
Card	Ace, Advertising Card, Available Card, Black, Box, Card, Club, Diamond, Face Card, Heart, Instruction Card, Jack, Joker, King, Number Card, Queen, Red, Spade, Suit
Card Pile	Discard Pile, Draw Pile, Empty Space, Processing Pile, Ascending Order, Descending Order
Playing Area	
Move	Move, Pass, Play
Status	Availability, Available, Blocked, Face Down, Face Up, Lose, Top Card, Unavailable, Under, Win

We seem to have been able to fit all of the details into a more generic concept. So I think we have a good starting place for a conceptual data model. I do want to have you do one more double check before we accept that we have all the concepts. Go back and read the definition of the top down concepts and compare them with the bottom up elements. The definition of the bottom up elements should always be of narrower scope than the top down concepts. For instance:

- ❑   Move = The change in position of a Card from one pile to another.
- ❑   Play = A Play is completed when the entire set of Available Cards are assessed resulting in a Move or Pass.

Should we be using Move as our concept or Play? Play seems to incorporate the elements of Move and Pass. I think we should change our list to use Play.

This type of comparison is also a good gauge of analysis to come. Card looks to have a great deal of diverse aspects, but that doesn't mean it is more important. It just means that when we move on to the Logical design it may explode into many more entities than Playing Area, which seems pretty isolated and self-contained.

Building the Conceptual Model

We now have a set of potential conceptual entities. We need to work with them a bit to finally create a conceptual data model. We are going to:

- ❑   Expand the definitions
- ❑   Review the potential entities, and choose an appropriate set of entities
- ❑   Relate the entities
- ❑   Validate the business rules and publish the model

We have defined seven potential entities for our conceptual data model of Solitaire. Let's go over them one by one. We will further enhance the definitions and see which ones we want to use. This is what we have so far:

Name	Definition
Card	One of 52 unique game pieces used in playing games bearing pictures of figures or numbers organized by suit. Example: Queen of Clubs, 2 of Diamonds
Card Pile	A collection of cards, which behave differently in the game of Solitaire. Example: Draw Pile, Discard Pile, Processing Pile
Game	A contest played for sport or amusement according to rules made up of many small decisions, which affect the outcome. In this instance – Solitaire
Play	A Play is completed when the entire set of Available Cards are assessed resulting in a Move or Pass

Table continued on following page

Name	Definition
Player	A participant in the game of Solitaire
Playing Area	The table or screen where the game is being carried out
Status	The state of a Play, Move, or Game

Enhancing Conceptual Definitions

At least half of conceptual entities are difficult to define just because they are so commonplace that we tend to define them in a circular fashion. However, at this point we need to have a list of crystal clear definitions. This ensures that any errors or inconsistencies are highlighted before the model is adopted in the physical design phase. As an example we currently have:

❏ **Card** = One of 52 unique game pieces used in playing games bearing pictures of figures or numbers organized by suit. Example: Queen of Clubs, 2 of Diamonds

Fight to be as specific as possible. If we are not specific enough in our definitions, we could end up spending hours creating a model based on a false assumption. So in our case, the phrase 'game pieces' would be too easy to confuse with tokens or dice. We need to be more specific.

❏ **Card** = One of 52 specific combinations of suit and numbers (or face), usually displayed in rectangular form that are used to play games. Example: Queen of Clubs, 2 of Diamonds

We also need to add restrictions to our definition to remove any misunderstanding that we have analyzed every use of Card. We are concentrating on Cards as they are used in Solitaire. We need to remove as many ways of misunderstanding the concept we are analyzing as possible.

❏ **Card** = One of 52 specific combinations of suit and numbers (or face), usually displayed in rectangular form that are used to play games, in this instance Solitaire. Example: Queen of Clubs, 2 of Diamonds

It would also be a good idea to explain that there are other cards and what they mean to our analysis. That gives up a definition like this:

❏ **Card** = One of 52 specific combinations of suit and numbers (or face), usually displayed in rectangular form that are used to play games. In this instance Solitaire. Example: Queen of Clubs, 2 of Diamonds. Excludes – additional rectangular paper stock that is included in a sold pack, such as Jokers or Instruction cards.

With a definition like that it would be pretty hard to misunderstand what we mean by Card in this conceptual model.

You should feel free to specifically call out what isn't included in a definition of an entity. In some worlds, such as manufacturing, Card would have a larger meaning than we are using. When you are targeting integration those notes will be extra helpful. You should also document what is not known, to allow for further discussion. In this case, for example, it might be that no one knows what the function of the Joker cards is.

Name	Definition
Card	One of 52 specific combinations of suit and numbers (or face), usually displayed in rectangular form, that are used to play games. In this instance Solitaire. Example: Queen of Clubs, 2 of Diamonds Excludes – additional rectangular paper stock that is included in a sold pack, such as Jokers or Instruction cards
Card Pile	A temporary and changeable area used to process a collection of cards, which behave differently in the game of Solitaire. A Card Pile does not have to have a Card in it to exist. Example: Draw Pile, Discard Pile, Processing Pile
Game	A contest played for sport or amusement (according to rules) made up of many small decisions, which affect the outcome.
Play	A Play is completed when the entire set of Available Cards are assessed resulting in a Move or Pass during a game of Solitaire
Player	A person who actively chooses a course of action to manipulate a game to its conclusion
Playing Area	The location where a game of Solitaire is being carried out. Example – Home, Work, Park, Table, or Screen
Status	The state of a Play, Move, or Game in the course of a game of Solitaire. Example Complete, Win, Lose, Pass

Go through the list one more time. Does every concept seem to be at the same level of detail? I keep looking back at Status. It doesn't quite seem to fit with the rest. My assessment is that it is a very critical but more detailed concept. I vote we remove it from the conceptual model.

> *Just because you move something off the conceptual model doesn't mean you need to lose the analysis you have done. Keep it in the notes to flow down to the logical data model analysis.*

If you are using a modeling software package you might have a picture of conceptual entities at the definition level that look something like this:

Player
A person who actively chooses a course of action to manipulate a game to its conclusion

Playing Area
The location where a game of Solitaire is being carried out. Example - Home, Work, Park, Table, or Screen

Card
One of 52 specific combinations of suit and numbers (or face), usually displayed in rectangular form that are used to play games. In this instance Solitaire. Example: Queen of Clubs, 2 of Diamonds Excludes - additional rectangular paper stock that is included in a solid pack, such as Jokers or Instruction cards.

Card pile
A temporary and changeable area used to process a collection of cards, which behave differently in the game of Solitaire. A Card Pile does not have to have a Card in it to exist. Example: Draw Pile, Discard Pile, Processing Pile.

Game
A contest played for sport or amusement according to rules made up of many small decisions, which affect the outcome

Play
A Play is completed when the entire set of Available Cards are assessed resulting in a Move or Pass during a game of Solitaire

Adding Relationships

Now we need to figure out the relationships between the entities. This task is challenging since you need to be as specific but as flexible as possible with your naming. A relationship between two entities captures a business rule. The ones in a conceptual model are very high level. They are not capturing relationships between data sets, but rather data between concept sets. There is no concept of Normalization in most conceptual models. The attributes are not filled in, there are no primary keys, and nothing is migrating. You are trying to identify connections or links between the concept entities. You want to note if it is conditional or restricted in some way.

They make complete sentences. Entities are the nouns in the sentences and relationships are the verbs. The restrictive nature of how they are built is a challenge to sentences that don't fit easily into this organizational structure:

Each\<Entity A singular>\<may or must>\<have something to do with>\<some quantity of>\<Entity B plural>

We are going to match every entity against every other entity to see if there are relationships. Then we are going to review them to see if they make sense together. Try to start with an entity that is key to tying everything together. I would pick Player or Game.

Player Relationships

Let's start with relationships to and from Player.

Player to Game

❑ **Each Player \<may or must>\<do what?to>\<how many> Games.**

Fortunately we are working on the conceptual model of a very small activity, so the verb phrases should be fairly simple to find. The key is to create as active a verb as possible between Player and Games. My data model training always considered 'is' or 'has' to be cheating, while 'Takes part in' is likely to be too passive. This is probably one of those horrible times when our language has defaulted a noun name based on the verb. Try 'plays', although 'manipulates' may speak more to our Psychology department. It is always a good idea to reread the definitions of your entities when you are relating them together. Review the definitions:

❑ Player – A person who actively chooses a course of action to manipulate a game to its conclusion.

❑ Game – A contest played for sport or amusement according to rules made up of many small decisions, which affect the outcome.

❑ **Each Player \<must> play \<1 or more> Games.**

Is that true? It is if you assume that a person can't be a Player unless they play a game.

❑ **Each Game\<must>\< be played by>\<one and only one> Player/s.**

Is that true? Yes! That means that you could expand the sentences to include their definitions and it would still be true.

❑ **A person who actively chooses a course of action to manipulate a game to its conclusion must play one or more contests ... for sport or amusement (according to rules) made up of many small decisions, which affect the outcome.**

This is a good method of verifying your definitions, relationship verb phrases, and the proposed relationship. The relationship can be represented as follows:

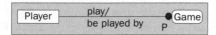

Player To Card

A Player does what to Cards? It seems to me that a Player shuffles, deals, chooses, moves, and discards Cards. They all seem perfectly valid to me. See what I mean about these conceptual model verb phrases? We need to find a generic, more aggregated verb to use in the conceptual model. All of those clear, specific, real verbs suggest a fairly complicated structure is going to be needed at the logical level to capture it all. Don't lose the fact that you have discovered many specific relationships. Note it down for the logical analysis phase.

- ❑   Player – A person who actively chooses a course of action to manipulate a game to its conclusion.

- ❑   Card – One of 52 specific combinations of suit and numbers (or face), usually displayed in rectangular form, that are used to play games. In this instance Solitaire. Example: Queen of Clubs, 2 of Diamonds. Excludes – additional rectangular paper stock that is included in a sold pack, such as Jokers or Instruction cards.

How about manipulates?

- ❑   Each Player must manipulate 1 or more Cards
- ❑   Each Card must be manipulated by 1 or more Players

That looks like this:

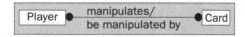

Player To Playing Area

- ❑   Player – A person who actively chooses a course of action to manipulate a game to its conclusion.

- ❑   Playing Area – The location where a game of Solitaire is being carried out. Example – Home, Work, Park, Table, or Screen.

This one is pretty easy.

- ❑   Each Player must play in one or more Playing Areas
- ❑   Each Playing Area may be played in by zero, one, or many Players

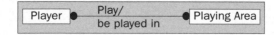

163

Player To Play

❑ Player – A person who actively chooses a course of action to manipulate a game to its conclusion.

❑ Play – A Play is completed when the entire set of Available Cards are assessed resulting in a Move or Pass during a game of Solitaire.

So does a Player make a Play? Maybe they direct a Play? I vote for direct. It has a flavor of control and execution.

❑ Each Player must direct zero, one, or many Plays

❑ Each Play must be directed by one and only one Player

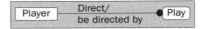

Player To Card Pile

❑ Player – A person who actively chooses a course of action to manipulate a game to its conclusion.

❑ Card Pile – A temporary and changeable area used to process a collection of cards, which behave differently in the game of Solitaire. A Card Pile does not have to have a Card in it to exist. Example: Draw Pile, Discard Pile, Processing Pile

Is there a direct connection between Player and Card Pile? Players are the ones who set up the game after the shuffle in the manual game. A Card Pile is then built by a Player.

❑ Each Player must build zero, one, or many Card Piles

❑ Each Card Pile must be built by one and only one Player

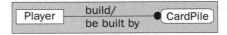

Player To Player

Don't forget to check for recursive relationships. If the Psychology department wanted to track how Solitaire spread from person to person through a Teacher/Student relationship we would need a recursive relationship here. Remember them? They connect an entity to itself. I don't remember anything in the scope about tracking this so we will assume for the moment that it is not included.

Review Player Relationships

Player is indeed a key to relating everything together. In fact the model looks a bit like a spider at this point.

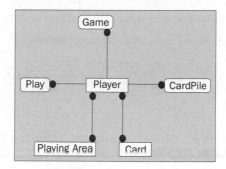

Not all of these relationships are going to make it through the iterative review process. You start with an assumption and then check and double-check; changing your mind from one iteration to the next. Right now all of the relationships we created made sense. Let's go on connecting the relationships and see how we feel.

Game Relationships

Now let's go on to Game relationships. Remember we have already done Game to Player since every relationship is two-way.

Game to Card

Again review the definitions to keep the concept fresh in your mind.

- ❑ Game – A contest played for sport or amusement (according to rules) made up of many small decisions, which affect the outcome.

- ❑ Card – One of 52 specific combinations of suit and numbers (or face), usually displayed in rectangular form, that are used to play games. In this instance, Solitaire. Example: Queen of Clubs, 2 of Diamonds. Excludes – additional rectangular paper stock that is included in a sold pack, such as Jokers or Instruction cards.

Does a Game directly relate to a Card? A game of Solitaire couldn't happen without them.

- ❑ Each Game must be played with exactly 52 Cards.

- ❑ Each Card may be used in zero, one, or many Games.

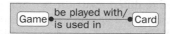

Game to Playing Area

- ❑ Game – A contest played for sport or amusement (according to rules) made up of many small decisions, which affect the outcome.

- ❑ Playing Area – The location where a game of Solitaire is being carried out. Example: Home, Work, Park, Table, or Screen.

This relationship shows that although we are going through all of the Game relationships at one time, Playing Area is actually the parent entity. One Game is located in one Playing Area. I don't think I have ever found anyone moving a game of Solitaire. They quit and start a new one if they want to.

- ❑ Each Game must be located in one and only one Playing Area

- ❑ Each Playing Area may house zero, one, or many Games

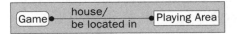

Game To Play

- ❑ Game – A contest played for sport or amusement (according to rules) made up of many small decisions, which affect the outcome.

- ❑ Play – A Play is completed when the entire set of Available Cards are assessed resulting in a Move or Pass during a game of Solitaire.

This one seems easy. Games are made up of Plays.

- ❑ Each Game must be forwarded with one or more Plays

- ❑ Each Play must forward one and only one Game

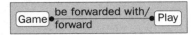

Game To Card Pile

- ❑ Game – A contest played for sport or amusement (according to rules) made up of many small decisions, which affect the outcome.

- ❑ Card Pile – A temporary and changeable area used to process a collection of cards, which behave differently in the game of Solitaire. A Card Pile does not have to have a Card in it to exist. Example: Draw Pile, Discard Pile, Processing Pile.

Is there a direct relationship between Game and Card Pile? Is it the same relationship that Game has with Cards? Every Game uses 52 Cards. Every Game uses the same set of Card Piles.

Here is another place where you are going to have to make an educated assumption. There are many relationships that are so stable we almost don't understand why we would document them. For instance Company to Department. Aren't all departments part of the company by default? Yes, but if we merge with another company we may need to differentiate the two Shipping Departments. You are the modeler. You choose what relationships to note and which one to leave as implied. I choose to leave Card Pile to Game as implied for the moment. I may choose to do the same thing with Cards when we do the final review.

Game To Game

Is there a relationship of Game to Game? One certainly could follow the other. Since the Psychology department is looking at feedback statistics let's assume that they will want to gather information about how many games in a row a person wins or loses.

- ❑ Each Game may precede zero or one Game

- ❑ Each Game may be preceded by one and only one Game

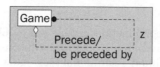

Review Game Relationships

You can see the relationships are starting to pull the entities together. When we look at the business rules that are generated, you will see the conceptualized story of the Solitaire process.

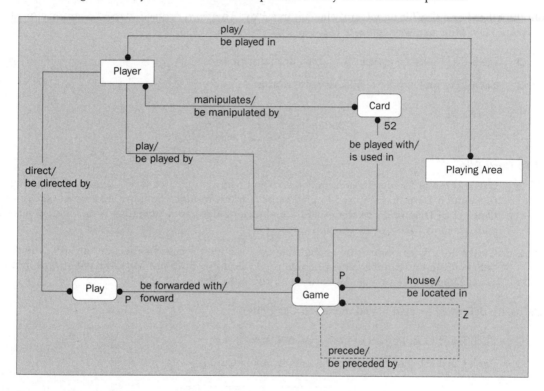

Card Relationships

Now let's look at Cards.

Card to Playing Area

- ❏ Card – One of 52 specific combinations of suit and numbers (or face), usually displayed in rectangular form, that are used to play games. In this instance Solitaire. Example: Queen of Clubs, 2 of Diamonds. Excludes – additional rectangular paper stock that is included in a sold pack, such as Jokers or Instruction cards.

- ❏ Playing Area – The location where a game of Solitaire is being carried out. Example – Home, Work, Park, Table, or Screen.

I don't see a relationship of Card to Playing Area. A Game is played with Cards and a Game is played in a Playing Area. That means that Cards are in the Playing Area because they are a part of a Game.

Card To Play

❑ Card – One of 52 specific combinations of suit and numbers (or face), usually displayed in rectangular form, that are used to play games. In this instance Solitaire. Example: Queen of Clubs, 2 of Diamonds. Excludes – additional rectangular paper stock that is included in a sold pack, such as Jokers or Instruction cards.

❑ Play – A Play is completed when the entire set of Available Cards are assessed resulting in a Move or Pass during a game of Solitaire.

On the other hand Card is an integral element in a Play. They are assessed, passed over, or moved during a Play. How can we aggregate that into one verb?

❑ Each Card may be used in zero, one, or many Plays

❑ Each Play may use zero, one, or many Cards

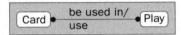

Card To Card Pile

❑ Card – One of 52 specific combinations of suit and numbers (or face), usually displayed in rectangular form that are used to play games. In this instance Solitaire. Example: Queen of Clubs, 2 of Diamonds. Excludes additional rectangular paper stock that is included in a sold pack, such as Jokers or Instruction cards.

❑ Card Pile – A temporary and changeable area used to process a collection of cards, which behave differently in the game of Solitaire. A Card Pile does not have to have a Card in it to exist. Example: Draw Pile, Discard Pile, Processing Pile.

Cards are definitely located in and moved to Card Piles.

❑ Each Card must be part of one or more Card Piles

❑ Each Card Pile may contain zero, one, or many Cards

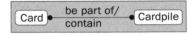

Card To Card

Is there a relationship of Card to Card? Absolutely. Remember all the status types referring to Cards under other Cards?

❑ Each Card may cover zero or one Card

❑ Each Card may be covered by zero or one Card

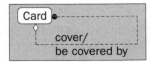

168

Review Card Relationships

We are starting to see relationships that may in fact be redundant. Player to Card Pile to Card, Player to Play to Card, and Player to Card is starting to look suspicious.

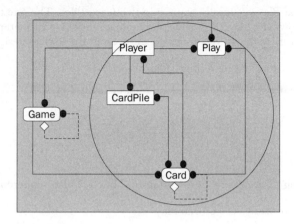

Playing Area Relationships

Let's now consider Playing Area.

Playing Area To Play

- ❏ Playing Area – The location where a game of Solitaire is being carried out. Example – Home, Work, Park, Table, or Screen.

- ❏ Play – A Play is completed when the entire set of Available Cards are assessed resulting in a Move or Pass during a game of Solitaire.

I don't think that a direct relationship exists between Playing Area and Play. Do you?

Playing Area To Card Pile

- ❏ Playing Area – The location where a game of Solitaire is being carried out. Example – Home, Work, Park, Table, or Screen.

- ❏ Card Pile – A temporary and changeable area used to process a collection of cards, which behave differently in the game of Solitaire. A Card Pile does not have to have a Card in it to exist. Example: Draw Pile, Discard Pile, Processing Pile.

I don't think one exists here either. Nor does there seem to be a recursive relationship to Playing Area.

Play Relationships

Now we'll consider Play.

Play To Card Pile

- ❏ Play – A Play is completed when the entire set of Available Cards are assessed resulting in a Move or Pass during a game of Solitaire.

169

❑ Card Pile – A temporary and changeable area used to process a collection of cards, which behave differently in the game of Solitaire. A Card Pile does not have to have a Card in it to exist. Example: Draw Pile, Discard Pile, Processing Pile.

The problem here is that Plays generally happen in two Card Piles. The one the Card moved from and the one it moved to. However, since this is the conceptual model we can wrap the relationships together for the moment, and let the detailed relationships show up in the logical design.

❑ Each Play must occur in one or more Card Piles

❑ Each Card Pile may be changed by zero, one, or many Plays

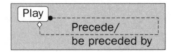

Play To Play

Do Plays have relationships to other Plays? Certainly. They are also sequential.

❑ Each Play may precede zero or one Play

❑ Each Play may be preceded by zero or one Play

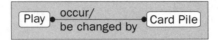

Review Play Relationships

We continue to add relationships. By now you can see that there is probably something wrong. The relationships seem to be creating a maze or web. We are just about ready to clear some of it up.

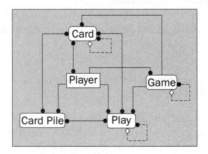

Card Pile Relationships

What about Card Pile?

Card Pile To Card Pile

There are rules that govern the movement of Cards from one type of Card Pile to another. The Draw Pile can only provide Cards to the Game. The Discard Pile can only receive Cards from the Game. Processing Piles can do both. Here is a structure you don't see very often. It is a many-to-many recursion.

❑ Each Card Pile may send to zero, one, or many Card Piles

❑ Each Card Pile may receive from zero, one, or many Card Piles

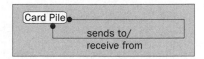

Checking the Business Rules

Next you need to take the list of business rules to the process experts and ask them if you captured what they were trying to tell you. Read them through once yourself to get a feel of the level of detail you are documenting. What is really amazing is that this is the high-level conceptual model. Wait until we get to the fully attributed logical model.

These are in forward (F) and then reverse (R) relationship sentence structure. Many modelers will remove the reverse sentences for simplicity (and to prevent the reviewers from being overwhelmed). This is your call. I prefer to show them both.

- ❑ F – Each Player must play one or more Games
- ❑ R – Each Game must be played by one and only one Player
- ❑ F – Each Player must manipulate one or more Cards
- ❑ R – Each Card must be manipulated by one or more Players
- ❑ F – Each Player must play in one or more Playing Areas
- ❑ R – Each Playing Area may be played in by zero, one, or many Players
- ❑ F – Each Player must direct zero, one, or many Plays
- ❑ R – Each Play must be directed by one and only one Player
- ❑ F – Each Player must build zero, one, or many Card Piles
- ❑ R – Each Card Pile must be built by one and only one Player
- ❑ F – Each Game must be played with exactly 52 Cards
- ❑ R – Each Card may be used in zero, one, or many Games
- ❑ F – Each Game must be located in one and only one Playing Area
- ❑ R – Each Playing Area may house zero, one, or many Games
- ❑ F – Each Game must be forwarded with one or more Plays
- ❑ R – Each Play must forward one and only one Game
- ❑ F – Each Game may precede zero or one Game
- ❑ R – Each Game may be preceded by one and only one Game
- ❑ F – Each Card may be used in zero, one, or many Plays
- ❑ R – Each Play may use zero, one, or many Cards
- ❑ F – Each Card must be part of one or more Card Piles
- ❑ R – Each Card Pile may contain zero, one, or many Cards
- ❑ F – Each Card may cover zero or one Card

- ❑ R – Each Card may be covered by zero or one Card
- ❑ F – Each Play must occur in one or more Card Piles
- ❑ R – Each Card Pile may be changed by zero, one, or many Plays
- ❑ F – Each Play may precede zero or one Play
- ❑ R – Each Play may be preceded by zero or one Play
- ❑ F – Each Card Pile may send to zero, one, or many Card Piles
- ❑ R – Each Card Pile may receive from zero, one, or many Card Piles

> **Every sentence must be true with no if, ands, or buts. Sometimes leading the clients through the maturing of the business rules helps them see problems early. You may even find business rules that your client overlooked, or thought were unimportant. This serves to highlight the fact that you have grasped the underlying process you have been asked to model.**

Checking the Relationships

After you get feedback from the clients on the business rules you will want to go over the relationships one more time. We need to both look for redundant relationships, and review the identifying and non-identifying nature of the relationships.

Adding relationships by comparing each entity to the others often leaves us with extra relationships in the conceptual model. Relationships are a little more difficult to manage in the conceptual model, since we aren't setting up primary keys nor are we migrating them as foreign keys. This is documentation of concepts relating to each other. We don't have the rules of normalization to help us out here. It is time to make sure all the relationships are valid. Some of them may have fallen off in the Business rule verification, but generally you find you still have some when you start to look at the model as a whole.

I have removed the second verb phrase for simplicity and changed the verbs to have a bit more of an active voice. Active verbs are always to be preferred in modeling. Take a moment to trace the lines and see if you can read the model we created.

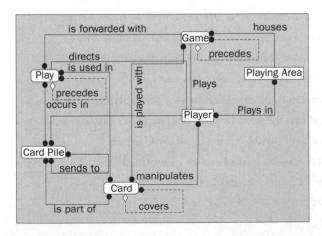

Now let's focus on some of the relationships that may not be truly necessary to document this process. Let's start with Player again. I am removing the cardinality so that we can concentrate on just the relationship for the moment.

❑   A Player plays in Playing Areas

However we also know these two facts:

❑   A Player plays Games

❑   A Playing Area houses Games

If we know the Player participating in a Game and we know a Game is played in a Playing Area then we already know what Playing Areas the Player plays in. Our scope emphasizes the desire to capture information about Players and Games. We are not expecting to need to know where Solitaire Players might hang out if they aren't playing. We will know where they play based on the Games they play. Remove the relationship between Playing Area and Player. The relationship is true, but in this case unnecessary.

Now while we are here let's review whether Playing Area to Game is identifying or not. Do you think that a Playing Area is descriptive or identifying for a Game? I think it is probably descriptive so change the relationship line to a non-identifying relationship. How about Player to Game? Do you think that a Player is descriptive or identifying of a Game? Hmmm. Games don't really have a natural identifier that I can think of. They would probably be noted as the first, second, or third game of a Player. I am going to guess that this relationship is identifying. The clients told us they want to follow the game life of a Player.

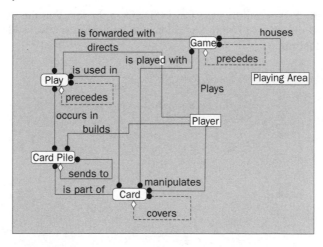

Let's try it again. We know that:

❑   A Player directs Plays

We also know that:

❑   A Player plays Games

❑   A Game is forwarded with Plays

Do we need the relationship of Player to Plays? Don't all of the Plays belong to one Game? Don't we already know the Player who played the Game? Sure we do. The relationship of Player to Play is redundant. Take it out. Now double-check for identification. Is the Game descriptive or identifying for a Play? I think it must be identifying because the same Play could happen in more than one Game.

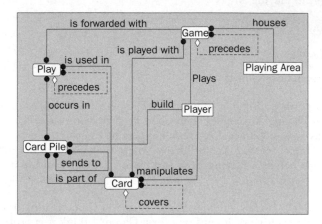

Follow down the relationship line to the next step.

❑   A Player builds Card Piles.

❑   A Play occurs in Card Piles.

So we already know the Player building the Card Piles from the fact that the Play is part of a Game. This relationship is redundant too. The many-to-many relationship is always identifying so you don't need to worry about that one.

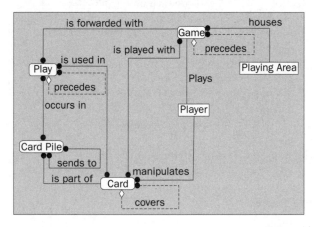

Now look at the Player of the Game and the Card.

❑   A Player manipulates Cards.

❑   A Game is played with Cards.

However, every Game is played with the same 52 and the Player is moving the same 52. What is important about the Cards is what Play they are used in don't you think? If a Player is playing a Game, and the Game itself is made up of Players, and the Players use Cards, then we need neither the relationship of Game to Card or Player to Card.

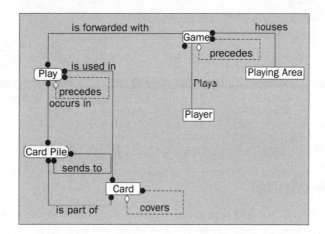

Finally let's look at the relationships around Play, Card Pile, and Card. If every Play occurs in Card Piles, and every Play uses Cards, is the relationship between Card and Card Pile necessary? Can you move a Card to be a part of a Card Pile if it isn't a Play? I suppose that depends on whether the original layout of the Game is considered a Play. When in doubt, go back to the definitions.

❑ Play – A Play is completed when the entire set of Available Cards are assessed resulting in a Move or Pass during a game of Solitaire

That looks to me like the original layout is not considered a Play. At this point I would call the clients and ask some questions about the original layout of the game. Since I know them very well, I will tell you that a Game to them starts with the first Play. The layout is out of scope. But wait. What about the rules that connect Card Pile to Card? What about the Kings and Aces who play special roles in special Card Piles? Perhaps there is a reason to keep the relationship in after all. But if that is the reason we are keeping the relationship, we need to rethink the verb to reflect this thought. We are not using the relationship the way we had originally expected. We don't need to remember what Card Pile they are a part of; we can derive that through Play. We are using the relationship to note that Kings can begin empty Processing Piles and Aces can begin empty Discard Piles. Change the verb to 'begins'.

You may want to add some titles and identification to the model itself. Rearrange the boxes and lines to suit your needs. Many people prefer to arrange the model so that the parents are above the children. I prefer to organize the model based on how I want to review the story. In this case Game is the main focus, so it takes the top position. But you have to decide what works for you.

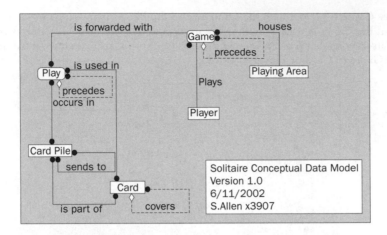

is forwarded with

houses

Game

precedes

is used in

Play

Playing Area

precedes

Plays

occurs in

Player

Card Pile

sends to

Solitaire Conceptual Data Model
Version 1.0
6/11/2002
S.Allen x3907

Card

is part of

covers

Publishing the Model

Now it is time to polish your model for printing. Check your spelling in the names, definitions, and relationships. Even the good modeling software won't help you with that. Add notes, and make sure you create your True/False questions test from the model. Also add in any points that need clarification. Publish your definitions. Remember, definitions at this point can't be too detailed. Make notations of things that are not as well analyzed as you would like. And put your name, e-mail, and phone number on everything so you can gather feedback.

The next step is validation with your peers, your manager, and the clients. That way you should have covered all the bases. This step is very important and sometimes quite a challenge to your people skills. You need to help people understand what they are looking at. You need to practice patience and try to teach them basics about modeling at the same time you are helping them to understand this particular model. Make sure that you take notes in your meetings. You will need to stay open to suggestions at this stage, to iterate new thoughts into the model.

> *Sometimes it is helpful to ask your peers if you can do a model walk-through with them before anyone else. Modeler to modeler. They may have some insight to offer before you report your findings to the outside world. They may help with names and relationships from past experience.*

Summary

In this chapter we have begun to apply the principles that we learned about in the first half of the book. We looked at the game of Solitaire and broke down the processes of the game methodically to discover the concepts, which are the foundations of our model. We used two methods, namely 'Top Down', focusing on the actual process of the game itself, and 'Bottom Up', focusing on the data elements buried in the Game rules.

We validated the analysis by comparing the results of those two methods and continued focusing until we determined the concepts we were going to document as entities. We defined them and began to build business rules between them by comparing each one with every other one, one at a time.

Then we took the relationships and built a list of business rules for the clients to validate in a True/False kind of review. We then began the process of verifying from an overview perspective that all of the potential business rules were actually necessary. We found several redundant relationships that could be deleted because the information could actually be deduced from other relationships. Finally we cleaned up the model, created nice documentation, and went on the road with it doing model reviews with the team to verify our analysis and understanding of their business.

We have created a conceptual data model of Solitaire. In the next chapter we will push the analysis down to the detail level of a fully attributed logical data model.

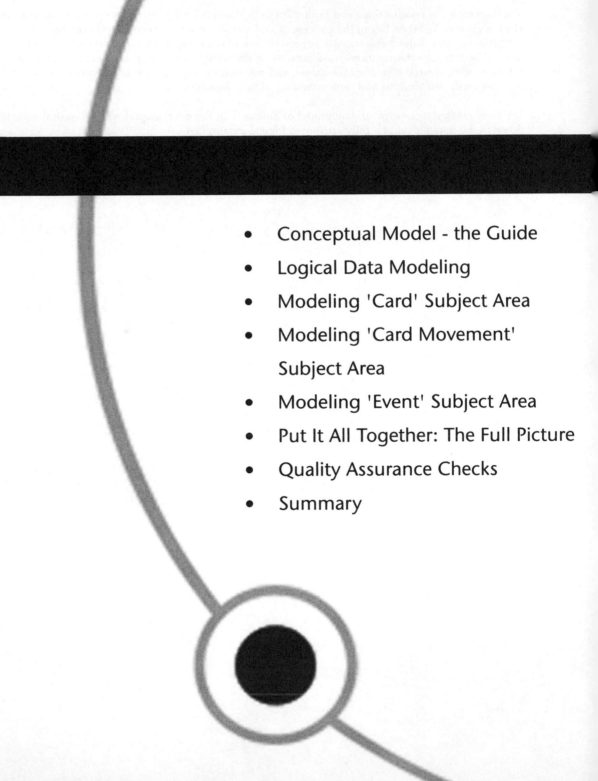

Building a Logical Model

This chapter covers building a fully attributed logical data model based on the conceptual model we created in the previous chapter. Throughout this chapter we will discover and document the data elements and their relationships needed to support and describe the process of Solitaire. We will cover each step along the way, sometimes having to loop back to change the model with new discoveries.

To this end we will:

- ❏ Review the conceptual model and build logical subject areas
- ❏ Propose entities for each subject area
- ❏ Determine the attributes and decide on a primary key
- ❏ Outline relationships between entities which will provide the foreign keys
- ❏ Apply several different quality assurance checks, especially the rules of normalization

I want to give you a real sense of the decisions that happen along the way; when to add in elements or attributes, when to take them out, and how to work through to a finished product. Data modeling is a very iterative process and involves a maturing of understanding.

We just finished building the conceptual model for an activity called Solitaire. The model included concepts for participants, location, materials, and rules; areas of interest involved in most business activities. However, there are no recognizable data elements yet. We have only built a concept model, a very handy gadget, but nowhere near a data map for Solitaire. What we want to do here is develop the logical data elements using the conceptual model as a scope definition. Each of the logical entities will be tested by mapping back to the conceptual model entities. The result of this mapping will be the building of a fully attributed logical data model.

Conceptual Model – the Guide

One of the points of this tutorial is the iterative, maturing, layered approach you can use to go from conceptual to logical to a physical data model (the draft database design). The conceptual model in this case is to a data modeler what a rough draft is to an artist. It captures basics about elements, placement, understanding, and can be mapped back to the scene for further clarification. We will work to discover what lies within the concepts we found. The conceptual model is part of the scope of our next analysis.

While you don't always have the time to create a conceptual model to help target the next steps, you do need to have a direction and boundaries. We all know the dangers of scope creep. Data element scope creep happens in one of two ways. First we find ourselves adding new activities and concepts forcing a top down increase. For instance, we could easily fall into analyzing data involved with setting up a study for the Psychology department, finding funding, assigning roles, and getting permission to gather information from subjects. We could suddenly find ourselves modeling historical aspects of the games or cards, or even expanding the playing area into a series of geographic entities and relationships. None of these things are in the original description of the task, nor on the current conceptual model. Losing focus this way widens the scope of the model.

Secondly, we drive the analysis of the concepts into details that aren't necessary, creating a bottom up increase. Each of the conceptual entities we documented will act as a pointer to the next places to explore. Think of conceptual entities as volumes in an encyclopedia set. Each of them is a holder for detailed aspects about one single concept. Some of those aspects are also out of scope. For example, there are owned attributes about cards that we don't care about in the least, such as tensile strength, combustion temperature, length, width, height, or weight. We don't care about them, but someone in the Enterprise could. We need to be very concerned that we get not only the right entities but the right attributes as well. Losing focus this way deepens the scope of the model.

In summary, we have to stay focused on what is needed for our project. The conceptual entities and their definitions are one way of maintaining that focus.

> **Every data analysis that we do can overlap the scope of another analysis. The better the job we do in capturing the real-world logic of how the data naturally interacts with each other, then the more chance we have that those elements will integrate and be useful to another project.**

Remember, that this part of the process is still very much exploratory, since we are going to create a first draft. We will do our best to capture it all, but the view will be skewed simply because it was us doing it. A different modeler will bring a slightly different vocabulary or different understanding due to their real-world experience. Eventually though, with enough validation, everyone comes to roughly the same finished product because we are looking at how the business data actually behaves.

Expect that even the best analysis can only yield a partially correct or complete view. Don't be disappointed when you have to revisit your model a few times. You probably cannot get any better than 80% right on the first try.

I can't emphasize enough how important it is to keep the client community involved in your analysis. You need to stay in contact with subject matter experts, project sponsors, process owners, business partners, and those who will ultimately exercise your designs. Maintaining close contact through iterative reviews is one of the ways to mitigate the risk of project failure.

Let's remind ourselves here how our conceptual model for Solitaire looked when we finished:

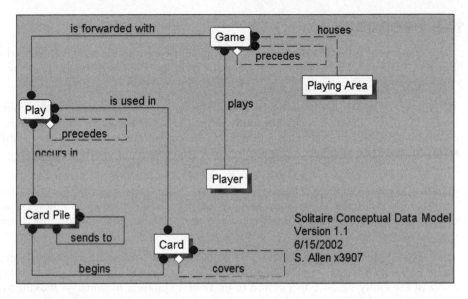

We are going to use the conceptual model as a guide for building our logical model. But it can only take us so far at which point we will lay it aside and use other sources to increase our understanding of the details needed for a fully attributed logical model. We will use it to:

❑   Validate the scope of our understanding of the concepts involved in the client's process

❑   Group the concepts together to form subject areas to focus on

❑   Find the logical entities (via the concept definitions)

❑   Forge the first logical relationships (using the concept relationships)

❑   Map the logical elements back to conceptual elements

Validating the Model

In order for the conceptual model to be able to act as a springboard into the next model, it needs to be validated by the process owners. We mentioned this at the end of the last chapter but it bears repeating. The business clients need an opportunity to look over your understanding and agree or disagree with the story it tells. You are not always the modeler who develops the conceptual model you are working with. Make time for a meeting to go over it and expand your understanding. Even if you were the author, business processes can change very quickly. Time lags are dangerous in analysis that builds on itself.

> **Keeping the business owners involved will help keep you from wasting time due to misunderstandings, uncommunicated changes, or model problems.**

So take time to go over the entity names and definitions, the business rules, and the scope, to ensure that you have captured all the important information in an accurate manner.

Using the Feedback

Here we are back in your office at the university. You have the conceptual model, validated by your clients, hanging on the wall like a satellite picture of the campus. The following points came out of the validation discussion with the client:

❏ The `Playing Area` isn't important to them. The study restricts to work environments. This means that you can either delete the entity or gray it out as a shadow entity. Shadow entities generally depict concepts that are out of scope (for one of many reasons), but are still a valid reference. I will leave it here just to show you what a shadow looks like.

❏ They missed the concept of a `Move`. You explained that it is one of the steps in a `Play`. You read the definition to them. They decide that that `Move` is a lower level element than the other concepts (be aware that it could just as easily have gone the other way). You make a note of the importance of this noun to the clients. You will probably find it an appropriate entity in the completed logical model.

❏ They also disagreed with the definition of `Player`. They want to be able to have people in the `Player` list who have not necessarily played a game yet. They want you to change the name of the entity `Player` to `Person` to make that apparent to someone looking at the model. They also admit they haven't really decided yet what they want to capture about the people who participate in the study. They are still working on it.

This means that we are now working with the following entities:

Name	Definition
Card	One of 52 specific combinations of suit and numbers (or face), usually displayed in rectangular form, that are used to play games. In this instance Solitaire. Example: Queen of Clubs, 2 of Diamonds. Excludes: additional rectangular paper stock that is included in a sold pack, such as Jokers or Instruction cards
Card Pile	A temporary and changeable area used to process a collection of cards, which behave differently in the game of Solitaire. A Card Pile does not have to have a Card in it to exist. Example: Draw Pile, Discard Pile, Processing Pile
Game	A contest played for sport or amusement (according to rules) made up of many small decisions, which affect the outcome
Play	A Play is completed when the entire set of Available Cards are assessed resulting in a Move or Pass during a game of Solitaire
Person	A potential participant in a study being conducted by the Psychology department

Scope the Subject Areas

We are working with a really small conceptual model so it is going to be a little difficult to not simply use each conceptual entity as the scope for a **subject area**. A subject area is generally a set of data organized to reflect a specific area of business such as Finance or Sales. I use the term subject area to mean a set of data organized to increase the ability of a project team or team member to focus on an area of interest.

Some people would say that this definition overlaps with the concept of submodel. It does. Subject areas are usually sub-models of larger models. They are also stand-alone models that map into a complete Enterprise conceptual model. In our case we will loosely group the conceptual entities into the areas we want to attack together, as follows:

Subject Area Name	Conceptual Entities	Description
Card	Card	The materials needed to play the game of Solitaire
Card Movement	Card Pile	The movements of Cards between Card locations and the rules regarding allowed plays
	Play	
Event	Game	The completed event of a single game of Solitaire including the person involved
	Person	

You might ask, why like this? Start with something that seems simple. The Card seems very defined and easy to analyze to me. Often you will find that static objects like forms, materials, and machines are already well defined and can be analyzed quickly and easily. Leave anything that the clients are still working on until last, to give them the best opportunity to complete their own tasks. Remember when we validated the model we learned that the clients aren't too sure what they want to capture about Person. Combine concepts into groupings that make sense to you.

Notice that there are some relationships that pass between the subject areas. We will be building each subject area and then combining them into the analysis already completed. The relationships we see on the conceptual model that link those entities together will help us find the logical relationships.

Logical Data Modeling

We are now truly going to exercise Dr. Codd's views on how to organize data into sets. Conceptual is too high a view for that, and physical often has to respond to the actual platform and programming language that the data is going to be manipulated in. The logical data model is the relational model. The others are tools that contribute to it or are derived from it. So we will define each of the subject areas we are focusing on with:

- ❑ Entities
- ❑ Attributes
- ❑ Candidate, and eventually, primary keys
- ❑ Logical data types and domains
- ❑ Relationships , cardinality, nullability

Modeling 'Card' Subject Area

You can be forgiven for thinking that we did this before in the previous chapter. When we did our bottom up analysis to build the conceptual model, we listed details and rolled them up to concepts. These became our conceptual entities. In logical modeling we are pushing down to details. There is often a feel of déjà vu when it comes to the logical model, especially using such a low level example of conceptual modeling. You should also note that we don't always do our modeling tasks in the serial fashion followed in this tutorial. Quite often you move from understanding to understanding at many analysis levels, sometimes even through many models at the same time.

As you will recall from the previous chapter, we defined Card in our conceptual model as follows:

❑　Card = One of 52 specific combinations of suit and numbers (or face), usually displayed in rectangular form, that are used to play games. In this instance Solitaire. Example: Queen of Clubs, 2 of Diamonds. Excludes: additional rectangular paper stock that is included in a sold pack, such as Jokers or Instruction cards.

Card Entity Analysis

I want to encourage you to pull out your cards again. Picturing them in your head is a good way to start but it is like analyzing without a source. You are going to forget things. Make a list of the things you find. Group them together if it is obvious to you that they make a grouping.

❑　Red/Black

❑　Clubs, Hearts, Spades, Diamonds

❑　Ace, King, Queen, Jack

❑　Number –10, 9, 8, 7, 6, 5, 4, 3, 2, Ace

❑　52 – Deck

❑　Single Card

❑　Back Design

❑　Front

Notice that we aren't sure at this point if an Ace is a Face or Number Card. We will need to clear this up at some point with the clients. Remember that we are looking for simple grouping of things to put into sets (entities). For example, Red and Black are values, rather than sets, since they are atomic in nature and would quite likely have similar information (attributes) available about them. Combined together they are members of the Color entity (set). Granted in this example the set is very small, with only two members, but it is still a valid set. Sets (entities) can be singular or complex concepts. For example, a member of the set of Ingredients used in a Bakery could be Water, Salt, or Baking Powder. It is just a simple list of every basic ingredients combined together (using a Recipe) to create a Baked Good. On the other hand Baked Goods may be compound concepts like Recipe, Lot, and Package. You might need to know all those concepts to truly identify members of the Baked Good set because in your enterprise Donuts have a different pricing structure based on value of the ingredients, freshness, and quantity in the box.

Try to use entity names that are simple and easily understood. I see sets in this instance in terms of Color, Suit, Face Card, Number Card, Card, Deck, and Card Side. Are you wondering why Color and Suit are both entities when everyone knows that Diamonds are always 'Red' and Clubs are always 'Black'? I have separated them out to illustrate a point. Each of these things is a singular, definitive concept. They have a restricted set of members. They have the potential of owning attributes distinctly necessary to knowledge pertaining to their set. They have the potential of requiring business rules based on their membership. Note these potential entities down on a whiteboard, or start a new model in your software tool, putting Card, which is our subject area, in the center and the rest of the words in a circle around it. These are your first draft entities of Card, and it is time to pause and make sure that you know what you mean by all of them. Again, as in our conceptual definitions, the names are just the shorthand for the concepts that we are capturing, and we need to write down definitions to ensure we know what we are talking about.

Entity (Logical Element) Name	Definition
Card	One of 52 unique game pieces used in playing games bearing pictures of figures or numbers organized by suit. Example: Queen of Clubs, 2 of Diamonds.
Card Side	One of two faces of a Card. The Back and the Front.
Color	One of 2 hues used in the definition of the suit of a Card. Red, Black.
Deck	The complete set of 4 suits of 13 cards making a collection of 52 individual cards. Does not include Jokers, Instructions, and extra vendor cards.
Face Card	A Card in a Deck which has a figure pictured on the face.
Number Card	A Card in a Deck which does not have a figure pictured on the face.
Suit	One of 4 divisions of Cards. Clubs, Spades, Hearts, Diamonds.

Card Category Analysis

Category relationships, as we discussed in Chapter 2, simplify the list of entities by noting that some sets are simply subsets. A category always has a **master** (also described as **supertype**) entity that contains the full conceptual set, with branches off it to further define individual members (known as **subtypes**) in the set. These subtypes can have their own unique attributes. To distinguish between category entities we use a **discriminator** (a hollow circle in IDEF1X notation) at the intersection point; all the branches come off it.

Finding the categories is sometimes a good place to start enhancing your entity list, because they almost always need to be seen as a team and are generally pretty easy to recognize. Some modelers prefer to leave them until later in the process. My own personal preference is to get them gathered up so I can recognize their need to share attributes and relationships. Recognizing them as a family unit can be helpful in simplifying the model. If you find they confuse your team then you can build a submodel with them left out.

What clues do we have that there is a category structure buried in the list of entities?

Face Card	*A Card in a Deck* which has a figure pictured on the face.
Number Card	*A Card in a Deck* which does not have a figure pictured on the face.

We recognize that we have entities that sound very similar, both being described as a card in a deck. Categories are recognizable because:

❑ They behave very similarly. For example, Insurance for Property, Life, Travel

❑ They behave slightly differently. For example, need assessed value of property, need medical condition of person covered, need duration and destination

❑ They share some attributes. For example, Beneficiary, Cost, Terms and Conditions

❑ They have some different attributes. For example, Title search, Health status, State of Political environment

❑ The clients expect to see them grouped together. They think of these as types of policies no matter how different they are from each other

> **Don't underestimate the need to pay attention to what the client expects to see. As we mentioned in the previous chapter, we should, wherever possible, use existing terminology and relationships familiar to the client, rather than inventing our own, or using more generic terms.**

We know that there are Number and Face cards in the deck. Do we need to note that Cards are divided into these subsets? Let's test it.

❑ Behave similarly? Yes they are part of a deck

❑ Behave differently? Yes you can derive the order of the Number cards but the Face cards have to have their order noted

❑ Share attributes? Yes, they share the attributes Name and Suit

❑ Special attributes? Yes, number vs. picture. Plus Face cards have a preceding Face card

A further point we need to note here is whether the categorization of Card Type into Face Card, and Number Card is a complete or incomplete category? Since we decided that the Jokers, Instruction, and Advertising Cards were out of scope, there are no other Card Types we haven't discovered, making it a complete category, which we denote as following:

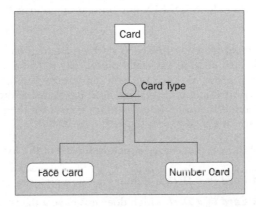

Categories are usually decision points for procedural processing, and so are important to the logic management of the data in the physical design. A programmer will assume that all the records can be treated the same unless you document a distinct type differentiation with a category. For example, the entity Account at a bank is often categorized into many different types. This allows the programmer to note that a customer will have many different rules applied based on the type of Account they have. The customer will not need to order checks if they only have a Savings account.

Card Relationships

Our next task is to tie all the entities together with relationships. Remember that a relationship has an optionality (optional or mandatory) and a degree of cardinality (how many), as we saw in the previous chapter. We will draft the relationships using the identifying solid line. We revisit that as we put in attributes and can test with foreign keys. Let's start with the relationships to and from Card.

Card To Suit

We start by reviewing the definitions:

❑ Card: One of 52 unique game pieces used in playing games bearing pictures of figures or numbers organized by suit. Example: Queen of Clubs, 2 of Diamonds

❑ Suit: One of 4 divisions of Cards. Clubs, Spades, Hearts, Diamonds

When we write our Business rule we get:

❑ Each Suit must differentiate many Cards.

❑ Each Card must belong to one (and only one) Suit.

That means we change the relationship verbs into 'differentiates / belongs to' for the model to keep 'active voice'. So there is a one-to-many relationship from Suit to Card. Draw a line between them and put a dot at the many end, near the Card. Write in the verb phrase.

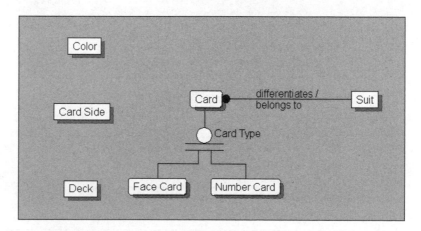

Card To Color

How about Card to Color?

❑ Card: One of 52 unique game pieces used in playing games bearing pictures of figures or numbers organized by suit. Example: Queen of Clubs, 2 of Diamonds

❑ Color: One of 2 hues used in the definition of the suit of a Card. Red, Black

Cards have Colors, that seems pretty obvious. But wait, all Diamonds and Hearts are Red, while all Clubs and Spades are Black. If you know the Suit then you already know the Color on the Card right? Therefore the relationship isn't to Card, it is to Suit.

Color To Suit

❑ Color: One of 2 hues used in the definition of the suit of a Card. Red, Black

❑ Suit: One of 4 divisions of Cards. Clubs, Spades, Hearts, Diamonds

    ❑ Each Color must illuminate 2 Suits

    ❑ Each Suit must be illuminated by one (and only one) Color

The change to active voice gives us 'illuminates / is illuminated by'. These Card relationships are very stable. They are probably stable enough that you might want to document using the restriction of 2. There aren't very many times you will ever use the ability to call out how many relationships there are. The only reason you might hesitate here is if you think that other types of cards might be added into this set in the future. Draw a line from Color to Suit with a dot by Suit. Add the number 2 by the dot and write in the verb phrase.

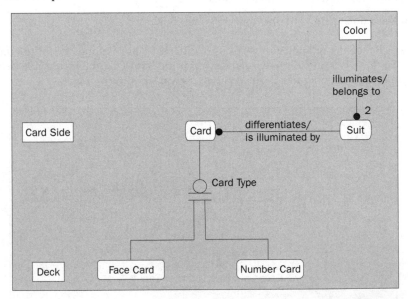

Use strong, detailed verbs. Bring as much life to the model as you can.

Card To Deck

Where does Deck fit in?

- ❏ Card: One of 52 unique game pieces used in playing games bearing pictures of figures or numbers organized by suit. Example: Queen of Clubs, 2 of Diamonds

- ❏ Deck: The complete set of 4 suits of 13 cards making a collection of 52 individual cards. Does not include Jokers, Instructions, and extra vendor cards. Each Deck must include 52 Cards.

- ❏ Each Card belongs to one (and only one) Deck.

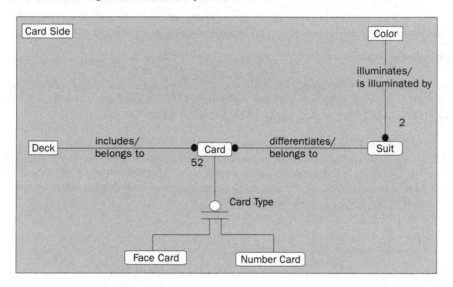

Again, this is a very stable relationship. You may feel like noting the 52. Remember that we may well want to use this model in future projects, which may involve two decks of cards, no use of face cards, include the use of jokers, and so on.

Card To Card Side

- ❏ Card: One of 52 unique game pieces used in playing games bearing pictures of figures or numbers organized by suit. Example: Queen of Clubs, 2 of Diamonds

- ❏ Card Side: One of two faces of a Card. The Back and the Front.

Now let's look at Card Side, the members of the set are 'Back, Front'... If you weren't thinking too hard you would attach Card Side to Card. Every Card has both a Back and a Front. Every Card has two Card Sides. That's pretty simple. In fact, it is almost too simple. So ask yourself if there is anything interesting about the business rules. The easiest way is to go back to the details of the set. How about Back? Isn't the business rule that the whole Deck must share a Back design? I believe some game software even has the back card design as an option. So although every Card has a Back it is the design, shared by the Deck, which may be interesting and important.

Let's add Back Design as an entity to our model, and write down a relationship between Back Design and Deck. If we were modeling the virtual world of the computer game it would be:

❑ Back Design: The pattern or color used to decorate one side of every card in a Deck.

❑ Each Deck may be decorated with one or many Back Designs

Since you only have one Deck, which can be redecorated at will, then when we write it the other way, it will read as follows:

❑ Each Back Design may decorate zero or one Deck

But as we are looking at Solitaire, in terms of the game being played with a physical pack of cards we actually have the following relationships:

❑ Each Deck must be decorated with one and only one Back Design

❑ Each Back Design may decorate zero, one, or many Decks

As you can see we have a very different relationship. This leads us back to the scope of our model. Our task was to look at the manual process of playing Solitaire. We should not move into the field of the virtual game, so should focus on the original definitions we came up with.

> **When analyzing a process that can happen in two completely different environments (Teller deposits and ATM deposits for example) be careful to look at the details of the activity from both worlds. Don't assume that the business rules for the data are the same because the final product is the same.**

So let's go with:

❑ Each Deck must be decorated with one and only one Back Design.

❑ Each Back Design may decorate zero, one, or many Decks.

In active voice that would be 'decorates / is decorated by'.

Well, it seems to me that the discovery of Back Design kind of changes our understanding of Card Side. Back isn't a side of a card anymore, but rather a picture, or a Back Design. So following that logic do we need a Front Design? Front Design is interesting since:

❑ Each Card must have exactly One Front Design

❑ Each Front Design defines exactly One Card

This is a one-to-one relationship. In the world of logical modeling this is extremely suspect, though they do occur from time to time. However, in this case the Front Design of a Card pretty much is the Card. So let's remove Card Side and Card Front from the model. Make a note to yourself that we have considered these to be unnecessary. We may need to come back to these when we come to review the model with the client. Here's what our model currently looks like:

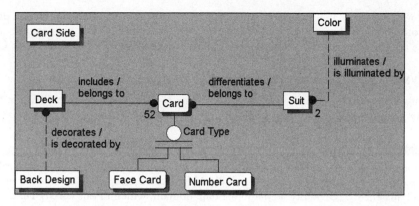

So here is Card with all the relationships that we found. Now we need to refresh our entity definition documentation and to start adding in some attributes.

> **Every time you perform a task to add value to the model you may impact the results of a previous analysis step. Don't neglect to update your model at each stage.**

Card Entity Details

At this stage we have a list of the potential entities used in the Card Subject Area. Now we need to flesh out these entities, by determining the appropriate attributes. In order to begin adding the attributes let's consider the complete list of the entities we have drawn up for Card:

Object Name	Definition
Back Design	The pattern used to decorate one side of every card in the Deck
Card	One of 52 unique game pieces used in playing games bearing pictures of figures or numbers organized by suit. Example: Queen of Clubs, 2 of Diamonds
Color	One of 2 hues used in the creation of the suit of a Card. They are Red and Black
Deck	The complete set of 4 suits of 13 cards making a collection of 52 individual cards. Does not include Jokers, Instructions, and extra vendor cards
Face Card	A Card in a Deck which has a figure pictured on the face
Number Card	A Card in a Deck which does not have a figure pictured on the face
Suit	One of 4 divisions of Cards. Clubs, Spades, Hearts, Diamonds

Try to start with an entity that has no parents, in other words one that does not have a dot next to it. They live completely on their own and only share their attributes with the entities that are related to them. These are the simplest, most atomic lists of things in your model. Let's start with Color.

Color Analysis

At this point we need to refer back to the list of attribute types that we gave in Chapter 3, to give us the flavor of any given attribute, and help us determine what the attributes are in this case.

Color Attributes

We have the members of the set already; they are Red and Black, which means that the relevant attribute type is Name. So the attribute where 'Red' and 'Black' is documented is `Color Name`. Put `Color Name` in the box signifying the `Color` entity, and add the data domain, which in this case is Text.

There are two very important things we need to keep in mind when we begin to develop attributes for an entity. Attributes should be both single valued, and non-derivable. The best way to explain this is to show an instance table of something breaking the rules.

Test for Single Values

The best way to test your ideas about attributes is to gather up a set of data from the field and look it over to see if your understanding of the way the individual values combine together is correct. Here is an example of having too many values in an attribute. Modeling the first draft of the attributes of Book seems simple enough. You would be very tempted to just start adding in the basic attributes without really thinking about the reality of those elements.

```
Book
## ISBN Number : Number
A₧ Title Name : String
A₧ Author Name : String
? —many more attributes : <unknown>
```

ISBN	Title	Author
1-861000-87-1	Instant UML	Pierre-Alain Muller
1-861004-7-61	Professional SQL Server 2000 Database Design	Louis Davidson
1-861004-10-9	Professional Java Data	Danny Ayers, John Bell, Carl Calvert Bettis, Thomas Bishop, Bjarki Holm, Glenn E, Mitchell II, Kelly Lin Poon, Sean Rhody, Mike Bogovich, Matthew Ferris, Rick Grehan, Tony Loton, Nitin Nanda, Mark Wilcox

I would tend to say that most books in our libraries have a single author. We tend to think of books that way, but the reality is that books are often written by a team of authors. Author therefore cannot be an owned attribute of Book. Author Name is quite likely owned by a separate entity that deals with the allowed multiplicity of Author to Book.

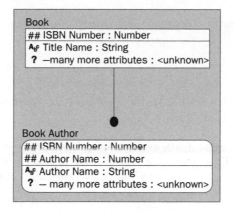

Test for Derivability

The second thing to watch out for in attributes is the derivable values. For instance we might be tempted to model student like this:

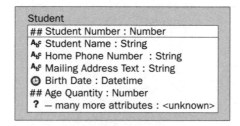

One of the things we need to do in our Kindergarten school is test the age of those being enrolled. They are not allowed to attend school earlier than 4.5 years of age. We might think we need an attribute to store the age of the student. However we already know their birthdate and from that we can derive their age. Deriveable attributes have no real function in a logical model. However, your team may choose to implement a physical column and maintain it with procedures and triggers. Attributes are the most basic facts known about an entity.

Color Key

The entity `Color` is pretty simple. We only have one attribute to work with, namely `Color Name`. Since you can always determine the difference between Red and Black with the name it becomes a candidate key. What would another candidate key be? We could create a Color ID if it seems appropriate. `Color Name` is a natural key, since it exists as a real-world data element, while `Color ID` would be a surrogate key where we would assign a number to a color to identify it. In the logical model we try to avoid surrogate keys if we can; they are more often a change made for the physical model. Try to approach each entity list of candidate keys with an open mind. Neither style of key is always the answer.

Let's promote `Color Name` from candidate key to primary key for the logical model, moving `Color Name` above the line in the entity box of your software model.

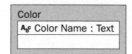

For a reminder of what constitutes candidate and primary keys look back to Chapter 2.

Color Definition

Now add in your definition.

❏ Color Name = The textual label identifying one of two hues used in the creation of the suit of a Card. They are Red and Black.

Let's break this down and see what it tells us. 'The textual label' tells us that we need Name as our attribute type. 'Identifying' tells us that Color Name is the primary key, while the rest of the sentence provides the definition of the entity Color as 'one of two hues used in the creation of the suit of a Card. They are Red and Black.'

Color Foreign Key

Having identified Color Name as the primary key of Color, the relationship between Color and Suit now looks like this on our model:

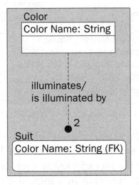

As you can see we now have our first migrating attribute, since Color Name appears in the Suit entity too. The FK following Color Name indicates that it is a foreign key, and will be automatically flagged as such by modeling software.

Color Relationship Check

We need to determine whether the relationship between Color and Suit is an identifying or non-identifying relationship. That means whether or not you need the source data element to identify a member of the target set. In this case it's whether or not you need to know what color a suit is to identify it. Since Clubs, Hearts, Diamonds, and Spades are completely recognizable even in black and white as an image or by name text the answer is no, and the relationship between Color and Suit is non-identifying. We denote this relationship with a dashed line, and move Color Name below the line in the Suit entity:

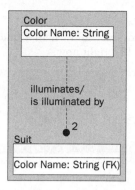

That concludes what we need to do for this entity. Each one goes through the same steps:

- ❑ Determine the attributes
- ❑ Determine the candidate keys
- ❑ Determine the primary key
- ❑ Write a definition for each attribute
- ❑ Follow all the foreign keys to their destinations and check for identifying or non-identifying status

Suit Analysis

Now let's consider Suit, and begin by looking at what attributes we have.

Suit Attributes

There are four suits in the set, namely Hearts, Clubs, Spades, and Diamonds. These are the Suit Names, and each Suit has a color (Color Name), which is the foreign key from Color. Is there anything else? How about the fact that each suit has a special symbol? Let's add in Suit Symbol Image as an attribute.

You may be saying that the attribute type Image is a bit redundant here, since Suit Symbol seems pretty self-explanatory. However, remember that Suit Symbol could be a description not an image, or an ID in a symbol set. It could even be a text block where the history of the symbol is noted.

Suit Key

Now we have some choices. Suit Name identifies Suit, although Suit Symbol Image is unique and completely recognizable as well. We could also consider a Suit ID as a candidate but I don't think it necessary in this instance, since Suit Name or Suit Symbol Image satisfies the test for natural keys in terms of existence and stability. Let's use Suit Name as the primary key (PK) and Suit Symbol Image as an alternate key (AK).

Suit Definition

Make sure you have the data type domain from the attribute type list correct and write up the two new attribute definitions:

- ❑ Suit Name – The textual label identifying one of 4 divisions of Cards. They are Clubs, Spades, Hearts, and Diamonds.
- ❑ Suit Symbol Image – The non-language visual object representing a Suit in a deck of cards.

Suit Relationship Check

Now we need to look at the relation to `Suit` and whether that relationship seems to be identifying or non-identifying. Here is what it looks like right now:

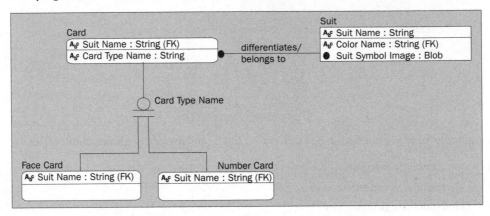

Do you think that you need the suit to identify a card? Is Queen or 9 enough to identify one? No. Suit is definitely an identifying relationship, so the model stands as is.

Card Analysis

We move on to look at `Card`, beginning with a definition of the appropriate attributes.

Card Attributes

We previously pulled out `Face Card` and `Number Card` as types, since they look different and act different. Keep in mind that all attributes in the supertype 'Card' apply to all instances of both Face Card and Number Card, but the attributes in the subtypes 'Face Card' or 'Number Card' only apply to the instances in Card that match them based on the discriminator. What do we know about Cards? They have names. That gives us:

❏ Card Name – The textual label identifying one of 13 Cards. Examples are King, Queen, Eight, Ace

So we add that in.

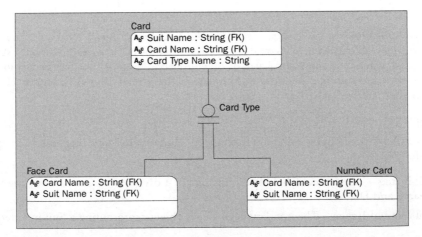

Ordering seems to be an important aspect of Cards. In the case of Number Cards we know how to put them in order, since they run sequentially by number. Face Cards are a little trickier. We need to know the name of the Card that each one precedes. What would examples of that look like? Let's make sure that we understand the data before we model it.

Card Type	Card Name	Precedes Card
Face	King	Queen
Face	Queen	Jack
Face	Jack	Ten
Number	Ten	Nine
Number	Nine	Eight
Number	Eight	Seven
Number	Seven	Six
Number	Six	Five
Number	Five	Four
Number	Four	Three
Number	Three	Two
Number	Two	Ace
Number	Ace	

It looks like Ace precedes no other cards. Face and Number Card precede both Face and Number Cards. So sequencing isn't so simple after all, but there is definitely a sequential relationship between Cards that we need to model. This relationship between the cards is a recursive one, since Card, as an entity, is related to itself.

You can read more about recursive relationships in Chapter 2.

The business rule in this case is:

❑ Each Card may precede one and only one Card.

Not only is this a single parent hierarchy, but it is also a single child hierarchy, so the dot will have a Z next to it to qualify the daisy chain of Cards, as shown overleaf:

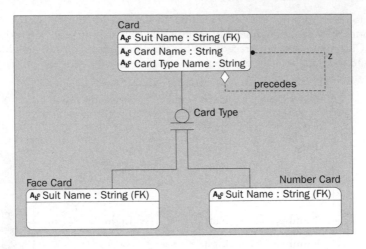

So all cards have a Card Name, Suit Name, and Card Type.

Card Key

We have already decided that Suit Name is part of the key. It does seem as though Card Name is also part of a composite key needed to make up a unique Card. Do we also need Card Type? No. The Cards are unique with a Card Name and a Suit Name.

See why definitions are so important? If we had defined Card as having 52 different names with an example of the Queen of Hearts (which is truly a legitimate name even if it does combine data elements), Card Name could have been a candidate key. As it is we need both Card Name and Suit Name to make a composite key for uniqueness. In other words, you need both pieces of information to identify one of the 52 members of the set Cards.

> *Take special notice of how every decision we are making is impacting places other than the single entity we are changing. There can be very large ripple effects in your model by changing one primary key.*

And that leads us to a special kind of attribute, that of role names.

Card Role Naming

When we added the recursive relationship, we still needed an attribute to find the preceding card. Now that we have defined the primary key of Card we ended up with two attributes named Card Name and Suit Name in the entity Card. If you were using a modeling tool then you probably wondered why it didn't show up. It is illegal in most modeling tools for the same attribute to show up twice in the same entity. If it has the same name, the software assumes that it is the same attribute. This isn't accidental or a feature; it's an IDEF1X rule that two attributes can't have the same name.

You may sometimes wish to combine migrating attributes in instances where two or more parents of a child entity share an attribute in their primary key. The same attribute migrates multiple times. Only one of the attributes shows up in a process called **unifying**. On the other hand, we may truly want the migrating foreign keys to show up. In this case we want to role name the second set of Card Name and Suit Name as the Before Card Name and Before Suit Name.

Role naming is actually a renaming of the attribute names to something descriptive of the data element. For instance, let's consider an Employee with a manager. Employee ID migrates as a foreign key to Employee, because a Manager is also an Employee. Every Employee has a Manager ID. Every Employee also has an Annual Reviewer, the person they were Hired by, and possibly an Administrative Assistant (who are also Employees). So the entity Employee also has recursive relationships resulting in role-named foreign keys of Manager ID: Hired by ID, Reviewed by ID, and Administrative Assistant ID. They all link back to Employee ID.

In our case the second `Card Name` and `Suit Name` are only there to show the order of the cards. We need to change the name of the attributes to note their role. A good verb phrase for the relationship can give a clue. Let's go with `Before Card Name` and `Before Suit Name` for now. With some software tools you can even ask it to make the renamed attribute visible.

Our model now looks like this:

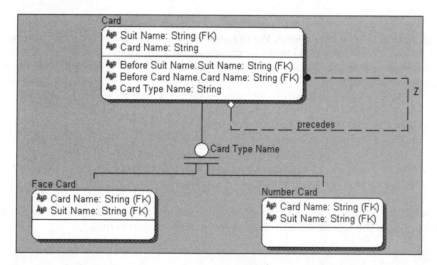

Now for the definitions:

❑ Before Card Name – The textual label noting the name of the Card that a Card comes after in a sequence of cards. This is the name of the card that precedes it

❑ Before Suit Name – The textual label noting the Suit of the Card that a Card comes after in a sequence of cards. This is the suit of the card that precedes it

If you are using modeling software, the data domain will migrate to the new attribute. If you are working this model by hand, you need to make *absolutely* sure that the data domain is exactly the same as the source attribute.

Card Relationship Check

Did we find any attributes unique to `Face Card` or `Number Card` during our attribute discovery step? No? Then we may want to remove them, since they don't seem useful at this point. Leave `Card Type Name` so that we can still differentiate face and number cards.

Now we need to verify whether we really need to know Suit to know sequencing of the Cards. Remember the rules about moves.

❑ The Discard piles are populated in ascending order according to Suit (two to King)

❑ Cards move to another Card in decreasing order in the Processing Piles (King to two)

❑ Cards that are Red move to Black Cards and visa versa in the Processing Piles

So we need to follow the order by suit in the Discard Pile, while in the Processing Pile we are only concerned about the color of the suit. But, since the ordering of the Cards during play is always the same regardless of Suit, we need to connect Card Name to Card Name without regard to a Suit. At this point we realize that we don't have an entity that contains the set of non-suited Cards, and yet we apparently have business rules that pertain to Cards regardless of their Suit affiliation. Therefore we had better create one and move the relationship that manages sequencing to it.

> **This is how data modeling works. We suggest an attribute and the rules that apply. Then we start trying out everything we know (or think we know) about the set members to see if it fits. When something doesn't totally pass the test, we back up and recheck our assumptions.**

Let's go back and see what we need to do to create an entity dealing with the set of unique face values that, when combined with Suit, makes a Card as we generally see it. In fact, let's call it Card Face.

❑ Card Face – One of 13 Cards. Examples are King, Queen, Eight, Ace. Together they make the full complement of cards defined as a Suit of Cards.

Card is actually the intersection (association) between Card Face and Suit. So our model now looks like this (I turned on the role name so you can see the renaming in action):

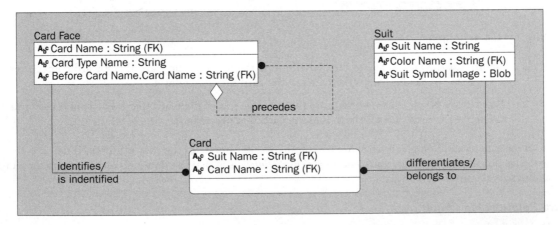

Deck and Back Design Analysis

Now let's look at the attributes for Back Design. We keep our customers in mind and check with them about the necessity for this entity. They think they might want to see if the colors or images on the back have interest in their study. So they will want to know what back design was on the cards during a game (I suppose the palm tree ones might be viewed as an escapist image from work). As far as attributes go I can only think of a Name and an Image. Let's name them and define them.

- ❑ Back Design Name – The textual label identifying a single pattern used to decorate the reverse side of a deck of cards. For example Solid Blue with white border, Exotic Flowers, Plaid, and Logo.

- ❑ Back Design Image – The non-written visual pattern used to decorate the reverse side of a deck of cards.

What identifies a Back Design? Back Design Name will work as the primary key. Back Design Image is unique, so we'll make it the alternate key.

Now what are the attributes of Deck? In the software Deck is a single instance, and doesn't have names, dates, numbers, or IDs. What identifies a Deck of Cards? Even in real life, I can't think of anything that makes one Deck of Cards unique from another one. If the Back Design is the same you can combine them without an issue. Afterwards you would probably be unable to separate them. At least you couldn't make sure what deck they came from without coffee stains, age differences, or torn corners. Look back at the model. Is Deck important? It is the path for a Card to Back Design. We said the software has multiple Back Designs. Do we think the clients will find them important? Maybe yes, maybe not. This may be a case where you want to note Deck as not being valid for this model. We have to validate with the clients after our first pass at getting the attributes together anyway.

> You will find logical entities that have no attributes. They may be important for future data development but they often fall off the logical model as interesting but unused. If they are needed in the next phase then the clients may need to review their business processes to create new data for this section of the model.

So, at this stage, let's say that there is no data of interest about a Deck, with the exception that there has to be a Deck to play a game.

Shadow Entities

A **shadow entity** is an entity included in a model as important, but not fully analyzed. They are often placeholders or interface points with other systems, or entities which may become important in future. The details of their structure are out of scope for the model in question. Shadow entities serve a couple of purposes. When you are creating your logical model and you are suddenly faced with an entity that you can't seem to find anything specific to note about, though it still seems important, then you may have a shadow entity. For instance, a logical model of a hotel booking service may include shadow entities to transportation type entities like airlines, trains, buses, or taxis. They may want to explore the relationships of the scheduled arrival / departure times to their check in / check out schedules at a later date. Having the shadow entities on their model reminds everyone of a potential link in the future. You could also have a shadow entity if it is easily recognizable as being owned by a different project team, and you just need to put a placeholder in your model until they are through with their analysis.

You will even find Shadow Tables on the physical model. They are tables that are integrated in some fashion but are not built or owned by the project. You may need to document relationships to them and ultimately build physical constraints, but you will never create them from the DDL generated from that model.

Don't be afraid to document them on your model. They give the clients a comfortable feeling that you haven't left something out and that you know about things beyond the current scope of the project.

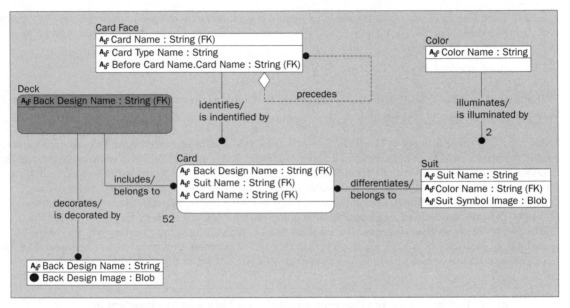

So this is what our subject area of Card now looks like. In reality you hardly ever have entities float down from the conceptual model to a subject area like Card did in this case. However, using the conceptual model from the previous chapter has helped us focus enough to complete one portion of the analysis of the Solitaire logical model.

When you have completed the first draft of a subject area you may want to set up another couple of reviews. Subject areas often align themselves to experts in that portion of the model. Subject Matter Experts (SME) often have limited time and appreciate not having to review everything you are analyzing. Check everything out one last time:

- ❑ Does every entity and attribute have a good name? Class word? Definition?
- ❑ Does every relationship have a strong verb phrase?
- ❑ Have you really thought about Cardinality? Optionality? Identifying vs. not?
- ❑ Does every entity have a Primary Key defined? Alternate Key?
- ❑ Is every attribute duplicated in an entity Role Named? Do they have new definitions to clarify their role?
- ❑ Do you have a Title for the Subject Area? Date? Notes?
- ❑ Is the picture as clear and clean and easy to follow as you can make it?

We can answer these questions for Card, so we can move on to the Card Movement subject area.

Modeling 'Card Movement' Subject Area

Review the subject area scope by reading the definitions of the conceptual entities and referring to the relationships currently modeled.

❏ Play – A Play is completed when the entire set of Available Cards are assessed resulting in a Move or Pass during a game of Solitaire

❏ Card Pile – A temporary and changeable area used to process a collection of cards, which behave differently in the game of Solitaire. A Card Pile does not have to have a Card in it to exist. Example: Draw Pile, Discard Pile, Processing Pile

Card Movement Entity Analysis

This time we have two conceptual entities to analyze.

Card Pile Entities

Here is a picture of card piles for you to look over. Make a list of the things you find. You might find the following:

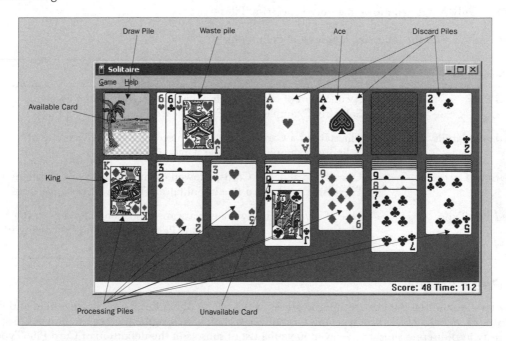

❏ Discard Pile

❏ Draw Pile

❏ Waste Pile

❏ Processing Pile

- ❑ Available Card

- ❑ Unavailable Card

- ❑ King

- ❑ Ace

Note that you need to get used to the jargon of your clients, while you are also modeling for a larger audience. I have used the general term Discard Pile here, also described as Foundation Pile in the book 'Official Rules of Card Games' 74th edition, International Playing Card Company, Limited 1991. You need to balance client jargon against wider readability of your model.

I see a lot of repetition in these titles. Pile is there four times. Card is there twice but kind of as a state of being. Kings and Aces seem to be there because they are special cards that can begin a Processing Pile and a Discard Pile, and are just values for cards too. I chose them because we discovered they were special when we looked at the rules of the game. Not all rules are discovered at the beginning of your analysis. They are often discovered over time. We made a list earlier though and so know that Aces and Kings are special:

- ❑ Only Aces can move to empty Discard Piles

- ❑ Only Kings can move to empty Processing Piles

So let's begin with the following entities and definitions:

Object Name	Definition
Card Pile	A collection of cards, which behave differently in the game of Solitaire. Example: Draw Pile, Discard Pile, Processing Pile.
Card Availability Status	The state of a Card's ability to be used in a move of a game of Solitaire. Example: Available, Unavailable.
Pile Start Card	One of two styles of Cards, allowed to change positions to an empty Processing or Discard Pile in Solitaire. These are Aces and Kings.
Card Pile Type	One of several activity areas that card processing happens in the game of Solitaire. Example: Draw Pile, Discard Pile, Processing Pile, Waste Pile.

Card Pile Category

Now let's look to see if there are any categories in this group of entities, by reviewing them and their definitions. See the clue word 'type' in our entities? It should be a signal that we might need to split up an entity into discrete subsets. We even have the list of subsets in the definition of Card Pile Type, namely Discard, Draw, Waste, and Processing. Do they follow the rules for needing a category?

- ❑ They behave very similarly

- ❑ They behave slightly different

- ❑ They share some attributes

- ❑ They have some different attributes
- ❑ The clients expect to see them grouped together

They seem to all have different rules at least, so we will consider these pile types to be a potential category as we continue our analysis. If they are going to be entities we need to define them so we know what they are (especially since I changed their technical names):

- ❑ Draw Pile – The location in Solitaire where a Card is stored until such time as it is moved to the Waste Pile for processing
- ❑ Waste Pile – The location of activity in Solitaire where a Card is made available for play in a cyclic manner until they have all been processed. A card may return to the Draw pile when the Draw pile has been completely moved to the Waste pile, but not all the Waste pile cards have been processed
- ❑ Discard Pile – The location of the activity in Solitaire where a Card is removed completely from play. Only an Ace can begin a Discard Pile
- ❑ Processing Pile – The location of the activity in Solitaire where cards are matched from the Draw pile according to playing rules. All processing piles are originally set up through the layout of a game. If during the processing of the card, a pile is emptied, then a King may be moved to the pile position and used to process more cards

Since, from what we know at the moment, there are no other pile types the category is complete. The entities and category relationship leave us without a need for the `Card Pile Type` entity, since it has been replaced with the discriminator of the category structure for `Card Pile`. You can delete it from the entity list.

Card Pile Relationships

Now let's analyze how these entities might relate to each other.

Card Pile To Pile Start Card

Review the definitions:

- ❑ Card Pile – A collection of cards, which behave differently in the game of Solitaire. Example: Draw Pile, Discard Pile, Processing Pile
- ❑ Pile Start Card – One of two styles of Cards, allowed to change positions to an empty Processing or Discard Pile in Solitaire. These are Aces and Kings

It seems that some of the Card Piles have very specific rules about what card can start them, so there must be some kind of relationship between the piles and a specific Start Card. Go back to the rules if you need to and refresh your memory. Pile Start Cards are Kings and Aces. Do they relate to `Card Pile` always in exactly the same manner? (In other words is the relationship from the `Card Pile` entity or one of the subtypes?) No, Aces begin Discard Piles and Kings sometimes begin Processing Piles. Since these members of the set `Pile Start Card` also behave slightly differently in the business world this makes them another category.

I know these look like single values. But if you need to show detail relationships like this for your audience then you have to break them out. Sometimes you have to go all the way down to this level of detail in the logical design. You only need one member to be a set. Create a category out of Ace, King, and Pile Start Card. Now set up the relationships:

- ❑ Each Ace must begin one and only one Discard Pile
- ❑ Each Discard Pile must be started by one and only one Ace
- ❑ Each King may begin zero or one Processing Pile
- ❑ Each Processing Pile may be started by zero or one King

These are relationships to a subtype, and are non-identifying, because a subset cannot be identified differently than the set it belongs to.

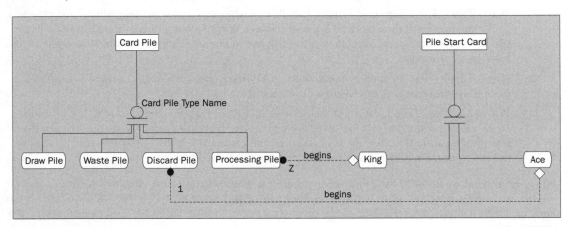

Card Relationship Optionality

Let's pause to consider the 'may' portion of the sentence in the King to Processing Pile business rule. Optionality is the 'May or Must' part of the business rule. It is always concerned with the parent side of the relationship where the foreign key originates, and notes the mandatory or non-mandatory rule for the migration of the source data. The optionality rules are as follows:

- ❑ Identifying relationship – This is always mandatory. The PK from the parent entity migrates as an FK to the PK area of the child entity. The FK is NOT NULL and the child is dependent upon the parent for *both* its *identification* and *existence.*

- ❑ Non-Identifying/mandatory relationship – The PK of the parent entity migrates as an FK to the non-key area of the child entity. The FK is NOT NULL and the child is dependent upon the parent for its *existence only.*

- ❑ Non-Identifying/optional relationship – The PK of the parent entity migrates as an FK to the non-key area of the child entity. The FK can be NULL and there is *no* child *dependency* at all.

Most modeling software will default to either mandatory or non-mandatory relationships from the source. Be wary of defaulting. If you aren't careful you will forget to change it to what you mean it to be.

Card Pile To Card Availability Status

- ❑ Card Pile – A collection of cards, which behave differently in the game of Solitaire. Example: Draw Pile, Discard Pile, Processing Pile
- ❑ Card Availability Status – The state of a Card's ability to be used in a move of a game of Solitaire. Example: Available, Unavailable

What is the relationship of Card Pile to Card Availability Status? Card Availability Status means whether or not a card is available to play during a game. Can you attach Card Status to Card Pile then? Is a card available or unavailable depending on the Card Pile it is in? Of course not. You need to status a card in one of the many positions it will be in during the course of a game. For instance a Card is available when it is the top or bottom of a Processing Pile, it is the third from the top of the Draw Pile, or it is on top in a Discard Pile. Since we don't have an entity to capture the notion of a position of a card in a pile we'll need to make one. It's time to ask questions again.

Is a Pile Position noted as always available, or is it conditional on something else? I think they are always available during a move. They do not lose availability by having a specific card in them, nor by the passage of plays. Let's capture our thoughts in a definition for a Pile Position.

- ❑ Pile Position – An especially notable location that can, when populated by a Card within a Card Pile during the course of a game, become available to move if other rules relating to the card itself are satisfied. Example: the Top (closest to the player), Bottom (closest to the table), 3rd from the Top

Now how might it relate to a Card Pile?

- ❑ Each Card Pile must be changed through the access of zero, one or many Pile Positions
- ❑ Each Pile Position must be a game rule focal point of zero, one or many Card Piles

We have a many-to-many relationship here between Card Pile and Pile Position, so we need an intersection (associative entity). The Top position is certainly valid for all the Card Piles, so we need to combine forces between the Card Pile and the Pile Position to know *which* Top we are talking about. Both bits of information are required for existence so both relationships are identifying, solid lines.

Name and define the new entity:

- ❑ Card Pile Position – A location within a Card Pile where a Card is made available for play.

Now build the relationship between both its parents:

- ❑ Each Card Pile must have zero, one, or many Card Pile Positions
- ❑ Each Card Pile Position must be located in one and only one Card Pile
- ❑ Each Pile Position must define zero, one, or many Card Pile Positions
- ❑ Each Card Pile Position must be defined by one and only one Pile Position

Now, return to Card Status. Where should it go? We defined Card Status as 'the state of a Card's ability to be used in a move of a game of Solitaire. Example: Available, Unavailable.' Look back at the definition of Pile Position. Basically it is the list of places a card has to be in order to be available. Since no other kinds of positions are noted Card Status isn't needed, since we have the concept covered with Card Pile Position. So here is what our analysis of Card Pile gives us:

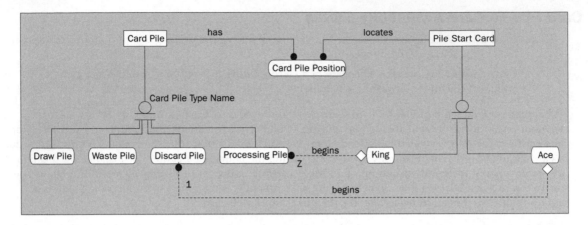

Play Entities

Now we have to do the same thing for Play. Here is the definition:

❑ Play – A Play is completed when the entire set of Available Cards are assessed resulting in a Move or Pass during a game of Solitaire

We have already analyzed and documented how to recognize if cards are available, so we can skip that and consider Play, Move, and Pass. We might also consider things involved in creating the setup of the cards such as Shuffle, Layout, and Deal. A Play seems to stand on its own as a collection of Moves, and a Move as an event of Card movement, but what is a Pass? It seems to me that a Pass is the inability or choice to not move any more cards and create a refreshed Draw Pile. Perhaps Pass would be better named Play Shuffle. Choosing to shuffle a set of cards into the Draw Pile begins a new Play and by inference ends the one before it.

Let's start the logical entity list based on the conceptual entity Play with the following entities and definitions:

Entity (Logical Element) Name	Definition
Play	A Move or series of Moves beginning with a Play Shuffle and completed when the entire set of available cards are assessed. Not all available cards may be moved even if there is a legal move available before the Player begins a new Play by choosing to refresh the Waste Pile with a new set of cards provided from a Deal of the Draw Pile.
Move	The change in location of a single Card from one Card Pile to another one.
Deal	The movement of 3 new cards from the Draw Pile to the Waste Pile.
Shuffle	A random rearrangement of all 52 cards prior to beginning a game.

Play Relationships

Let's see how these relate together.

Play To Move

Review the definitions:

- ❏ Play – A Move or series of Moves beginning with a Play Shuffle and completed when the entire set of available cards are assessed. Not all available card may be moved even if there is a legal move available before the Player begins a new Play by choosing to refresh the Waste Pile with a new set of cards provided from a Deal of the Draw Pile

- ❏ Move – The change in location of a single Card from one Card Pile to another one

This relationship almost writes itself from the definitions:

- ❏ Each Play may include zero, one, or many Moves
- ❏ Each Move must be part of one and only one Play

Play To Deal

- ❏ Play – A Move or series of Moves beginning with a Play Shuffle and completed when the entire set of available cards are assessed. Not all available cards may be moved, even if there is a legal move available before the Player begins a new Play by choosing to refresh the Waste Pile with a new set of cards from the Draw Pile

- ❏ Deal – The movement of 3 new cards from the Draw Pile to the Waste Pile

Again we see the relationship clearly defined in the definition of a Play. Good definitions are invaluable.

- ❏ Each Play must begin with one and only one Deal
- ❏ Each Deal must begin one and only one Play

Oops, a one-to-one relationship! We need to check whether this means that both entities are the same thing with a different name. Look at the definitions again. Are they the same? If I have 32 Plays in a Solitaire Game how many Deals will I have gone through? 32 right? The really important question here is actually whether or not we are interested in capturing information about a Deal? Think back to our scope. The Psychology department wants to capture information about each Game, but to what degree? Do they need every move of every card captured?

Sometimes we get so caught up in an analysis that we forget to step back and remind ourselves what the objectives are. In our scope we want to model the Game with an emphasis on its relationship to a Player, so we don't need to worry about Deal, or indeed Shuffle or Layout. If we were modeling the process of Solitaire to create a Solitaire application then that would be a different matter, where all of these would become important again. In our scope Plays and the Moves they are made up of are important, but only from the perspective of what moved and to where. The clients don't expect to be able to capture options prior to moves. They don't really care if a person is a good Solitaire player. They just want to know what cards are being played, how many moves were made in the game, and whether the Player won or lost.

Movement Combined

We had to cover more than one conceptual entity in this section so we have to look at whether there are relationships between the two sets of entities we discovered.

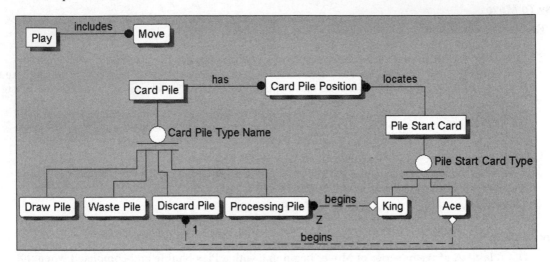

What would the relationship be between these entities? It looks to me as though we need to relate Move to the Card Pile entities. What do we know from our analysis? Moves happen in all Card Piles. Any relationship between them will be at the Card Pile level rather than any of the subtypes. Moves happen from one card pile to another. Therefore there are two relationships. Maybe something like this:

- ❑ Each Move must start at one and only one Card Pile
- ❑ Each Card Pile must begin zero, one, or many Moves
- ❑ Each Move must complete in one and only one Card Pile
- ❑ Each Card Pile must complete zero, one, or many Moves

A Move also needs a Card doesn't it? Let's go ahead and relate the Card subject area and the Movement subject area right now before we forget.

- ❑ Each Card must be used in zero, one, or many Moves
- ❑ Each Move must move one and only one Card

That brings us here:

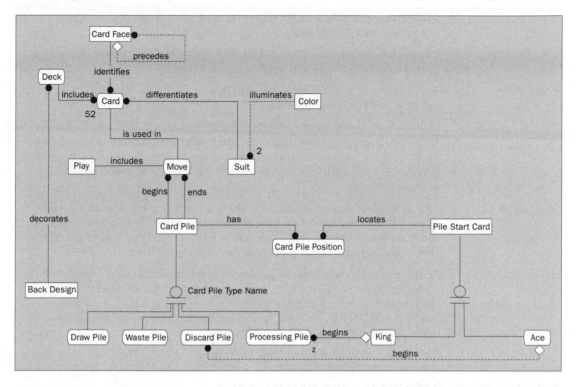

Now before we put in all the details let's look over the model again. Can we simplify it? Is anything out of scope? Are all these sets important to the process of Solitaire as it applies to the needs of our clients? Our clients don't seem to want to capture or test whether or not a Player is making correct moves or what moves are legal. In that case we don't need any logical structures relating to the rules of play, just entities about the events in a game. As a result the Card Pile Position, Pile Start Card, King, and Ace can be shadowed out, or even deleted.

You are going to hear me say this over and over. Modeling is iterative. You put things in and you take them back out. When you are going to remove several entities from your design, you may want to version a copy off in order to capture your analysis. You never know when you might want or need to bring those structures back.

Movement Entity Details

Now let's deepen the details of the Movement Subject area. Here is what our glossary looks like now. We need to find the attributes for each of the entities.

Object Name	Definition
Card Pile	A collection of cards, which behave differently in the game of Solitaire. Example: Draw Pile, Discard Pile, Processing Pile.
Discard Pile	The location of the activity in Solitaire where a Card is removed completely from play. Only an Ace can begin a Discard Pile.
Draw Pile	The location in Solitaire where a Card is stored until such time as it is moved to the Waste Pile for processing.
Processing Pile	The location of the activity in Solitaire where cards are matched from the Draw pile according to playing rules. All processing piles are originally set up through the layout of a game. If during the processing of the card, a pile is emptied, then a King may be moved to the pile position and used to process more cards.
Waste Pile	The location of activity in Solitaire where a Card is made available for play in a cyclic manner until they have all been processed. A card may return to the Draw pile when the Draw pile has been completely moved to the Waste pile, but not all the Waste pile cards have been processed.
Play	A Move or series of Moves beginning with a Play Shuffle and completed when the entire set of available cards are assessed. Not all available cards may be moved even if there is a legal move available before the Player begins a new Play by choosing to refresh the Waste Pile with a new set of cards provided from a Deal of the Draw Pile.
Move	The change in location of a single Card from one Card Pile to another one.

Attributes, Keys, Definitions, and Relationships

This time let's try to go through the process a little faster. Decide on your attributes, figure out what identifies the instances, write up good attribute definitions, and double-check the relationships to and from the entities. Refer back to the list of class words `Card Pile`. The definition example tells us that there is certainly a name and the model tells us that there is also a `Type Name`.

❑ Card Pile Name – The textual label identifying one of 13 collections of cards, which behave differently in the game of Solitaire. Example: Draw Pile, Discard Pile, Processing Pile

❑ Card Pile Type Name – The textual label identifying a collection of cards, which behave differently in the game of Solitaire. Example: Draw Pile, Discard Pile, Processing Pile.

Now we have a problem, since the attribute definitions are almost exactly the same. Here we find a case where some of the constituents of the set are actually named by the type label. The division of this category structure is at such a detailed level that the type is the same as the name. Of course, while we are dealing with pretty small sets in our example, such problems do arise in real life. For example, take the list of States and territories in the United States. The District of Columbia has different business rules about legal matters than Oregon. As do the Virgin Islands, Guam, American Samoa, and the Trust territories of the Pacific Islands (Palau Islands). If your clients are interested in specific legalities in these areas you may need to note them as a separate category, differing from the rest of the 50 states, which behave pretty much the same. However, there isn't an overall label name we can give the type. Each one is a type unto itself. Oh, you can divide normal 'State' from 'US Territory' for a first differentiation but you may need to break up Territory further where you are left with single members of each set.

There doesn't seem to be much to know about Card Piles that doesn't have to do with the rules of Solitaire. It seems to be pretty obvious that the Card Pile Name is the primary key in this case. At this point you are probably wondering why we are leaving the category at all. Since this is a logical model, I am still convinced that it will be a useful thing to document and share with our clients in the model reviews. We have options on how to design a physical table in the next chapter.

I keep telling you to simplify but there is another side to that. You must leave details in that you feel are going to be important. This is also part of the art of data modeling.

Now let's look at `Play` and `Move`. What do we know about a Play? They are a sequence of events in a Game. So there is quite likely a means of ordering them. This can be done by capturing the time of a transaction, or in this case, since we are in manual mode, we will just order them by number.

Is there anything else? We could add up the Moves to find how many happened during a Play. Unless the client is using a stopwatch it is hard to imagine capturing any time duration. Sequence Number should be unique, although I think we will need Game to make it completely unique over time. But for now, put `Play Sequence Number` in the key position.

❑   Play Sequence Number – The order in which a Play occurs in a Game

Here is where we are right now:

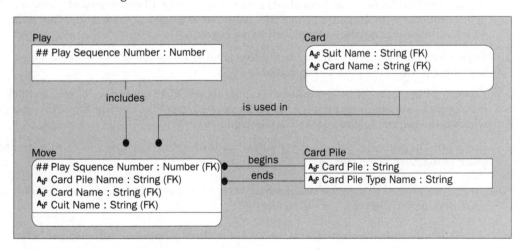

If we now consider the `Move` entity we actually already have quite a collection of attributes. We have gathered the `Play`, the `Card`, and the two `Piles` that the `Move` interacts with. Plays come in order in a Game. Moves come in order in a Play. Let's add a `Move Sequence Number`.

❑   Move Sequence Number – The order in which a Move occurs in a Play

Now let's role name the two Card Piles involved in Move to `Begin Card Pile Name` and `End Card Pile Name` so that we can see them non-unified by the software. Then review the key.

If you know the `Play` and the `Move` do you need to also know the Card Piles or Card involved to make an instance of a Move unique? Let's check and see:

Play Sequence Number	Move Sequence Number	Card Name	Suit Name	Begin Card Pile Name	End Card Pile Name
1	1	Queen	Heart	Processing	Processing
1	2	Ace	Club	Waste	Discard
1	3	9	Diamond	Processing	Processing
2	1	5	Club	Processing	Processing
2	2	5	Club	Processing	Processing

If you look at the data here it seems that we only need the `Play Sequence Number` and the `Move Sequence Number` to make a record unique, even in the last case where the player moved the 5 of Clubs twice in a row from Processing Pile to Processing Pile.

By the way, I am noticing that you can't tell which of the Processing Piles a Move is happening in. We need to add the number for the beginning and ending piles. But these attributes will be `NULL` allowed because they only apply to the Processing Piles.

❑ Begin Card Pile Name – The textual label identifying one of 13 collections of cards, which behave differently in the game of Solitaire. Example: Draw Pile, Discard Pile, Processing Pile which is the beginning place of the Card being moved

❑ Begin Card Pile Number – The number differentiating a Processing Pile which is the beginning place of the Card being moved

❑ End Card Pile Name – The textual label identifying one of 13 collections of cards, which behave differently in the game of Solitaire. Example: Draw Pile, Discard Pile, Processing Pile which is the beginning place of the Card being moved

❑ End Card Pile Number – The number differentiating a Processing Pile which is the ending place of the Card being moved

This means that we need to change the relationships of `Card Piles` and `Cards` to `Move` from identifying to non-identifying ones.

We have knocked off another subject area. Go over all the check points that we looked at before. Double-check:

❑ Names of the Entities – all singular?

❑ Names of the Attributes – descriptive even standing alone? All have class words? Role names?

❑ Definitions for both entities and attributes complete?

❑ The relationships – identifying / non-identifying? Cardinality? Optionality? Verb phrases active voice?

Here's what our model looks like now:

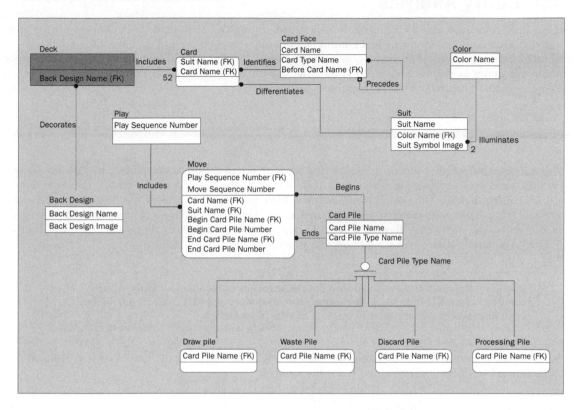

Modeling 'Event' Subject Area

We begin by reviewing the subject area.

Object Name	Definition
Event	The completed event of a single game of Solitaire including the person involved
Game	A contest played for sport or amusement (according to rules) made up of many small decisions, which affect the outcome
Playing Area	The location where a game of Solitaire is being carried out. Example: Home, Work, Park, Table, or Screen
Person	A potential participant in a study being conducted by the Psychology department

Event Entity Analysis

`Game` and `Person` should be a breeze. As you iterate through an analysis it should become easier and easier. You learn so many things that continue to be true with each cycle. You have experience with Solitaire now so instead of playing a new game you should feel comfortable drawing on your memories about the games as distinct events. What important words come to mind? I'm thinking about Game, Win, Lose, and Quit, which probably group together into:

- ❑ Game
- ❑ Ending Game State

`Person` is a little more difficult. We know that Solitaire doesn't seem to care about the Person. There is no login, and no score keeping. There is no data of interest about a Person except that there has to be a Person to play a game. Data about the Person will have to come from outside the business process we are analyzing. That means that we will have to ask our clients if they have any specific need for information. They may have forgotten to get back to us on their decisions about what they are going to need. Make sure to send them a reminder that you still need that information.

> **Don't be surprised to have to go find data elements even outside the walls of your company. Internet data use is becoming more and more popular, and Departments even buy data sets from outside vendors like the Post Office.**

So shadow out Person for the moment; we will check with the clients at the model review. Here are my definitions (I am leaving the shadows in for the moment):

Object Name	Definition
Game	A contest played for sport or amusement according to rules made up of many small decisions, which affect the outcome.
Ending Game State	The state of concluding a Game of Solitaire. Example: Win, Lose, Quit.
Person	A participant or potential participant in a study being conducted by the Psychology department.
Playing Area	The location where a game of Solitaire is being carried out. Example: Home, Work, Park, Table, or Screen.

Event Relationships

You noted that we still have some relationships left over from our conceptual model. That's because the conceptual entities didn't break down very much further. You don't have to reinvent anything that you already know.

Game To Person

What are the business rules between these guys?

- ❑ Each Person may play zero, one, or many Games
- ❑ Each Game must be played by one, and only one, Person

Game To Ending Game State

- ❑ Each Ending Game State may document zero, one, or many Games
- ❑ Each Game must conclude with one and only one Ending Game State

The only games being captured are the completed ones so every game must have an ending game state.

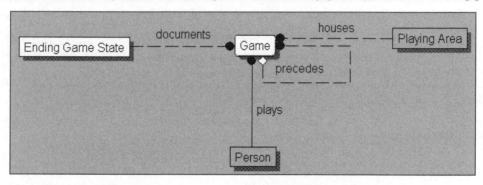

Attributes, Keys, Definitions, and Relationships

We don't know about `Person` or `Playing Area` right at the moment. So that entity could be empty until the clients tell us otherwise. I have a tendency to note an ID just to be able to speak to the FK relationships that are there logically and to test them for identification status.

- ❑ Person ID – A non-significant value uniquely identifying a Person who is a participant or potential participant in a study being conducted by the Psychology department

- ❑ Playing Area ID – A non-significant value uniquely identifying a Playing Area which is the location where a game of Solitaire is being carried out. Example: Home, Work, Park, Table, or Screen

As they are the only attributes in their entities let's make them the primary key.

Game seems really important to me, but it sure doesn't seem to have an identifier. Perhaps there are interesting things to know concerning Date/Time?

- ❑ Game Start Date – The Month, Day, Year when the game began
- ❑ Game Start Time – The 24 hour clock Hour, Minute, Second of the day when the game began
- ❑ Game End Date – The Month, Day, Year when the game completed
- ❑ Game End Time – The 24 hour clock Hour, Minute, Second of the day when the game completed

Out of these attributes what could act as the identifier? The `Start` attributes might work. But I am beginning to think that you might want the `Person` to help identify the `Game`. What about `Person ID` and Start Date/Time? I can't imagine being able to begin two games of Solitaire at exactly the same time. Leave the relationship of `Person` to `Game` as an identifying one (a solid line).

Many times you will see date and time noted as a single attribute. This is perfectly valid, although I usually don't do this anymore when I am logically modeling, as it reduces our scope for analysis with data warehousing. So why not just keep them separate until you know better when you transform your logical model to a physical one? Then at least you think about the options. On the other hand, you may want to simplify the attributes as much as possible for your clients. Like I said before, this is your judgment call.

`Ending Game State` should have at least a name. States or Statuses in general should also always have a description to document the meaning of the Status.

- ❑ Ending Game State Name – A textual label uniquely identifying the concluding state of a game.

- ❑ Ending Game State Description – A non-structured textual account of the concluding state of a game

Double-check everything. I would have reminded you that we need a role name here for the recursive relationship, but I think we have just made it redundant. If the person, date, and time identify a game, then we can derive what preceded what without a relationship. It is still a valid relationship however for the conceptual model, which has no attributes.

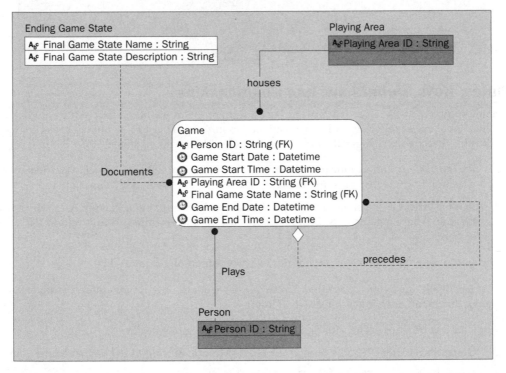

Put It All Together: The Full Picture

Here is where we are from an entity perspective. You can see our three subject areas (Card, Movement, and Event) on one model. Card/Movement and Event are floating loosely together in space like subassemblies in manufacturing. It is really beginning to look like a data model.

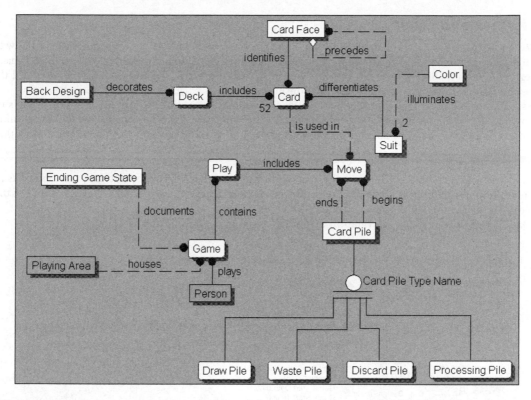

Now you need to return to the conceptual model for a moment to remind yourself of where we thought the connections lay. Go through the relationships on the conceptual model one by one. I think you will find that we have either deliberately deleted relationships, or we have taken care of them all in the logical model except one. The only one left to work out is Game to Play.

Game To Play

What are the definitions of the entities?

❑ Game – A contest played for sport or amusement (according to rules) made up of many small decisions, which affect the outcome

❑ Play – A Move or series of Moves beginning with a Play Shuffle and completed when the entire set of available cards are assessed. Not all available cards may be moved even if there is a legal move available before the Player begins a new Play by choosing to refresh the Waste Pile with a new set of cards provided from a Deal of the Draw Pile

It seems to be as simple as:

❑ Each Game must be made up of one or more Plays
❑ Each Play must be part of one and only one Game

Now I want to revisit an entity structure that just doesn't work for me.

Back Design to Game

We know that decks include cards, and that a deck is decorated with a back design. We also know that cards are used in moves, which are part of plays contained in a game. So Back Design for a Game is derivable or deducible. However, Deck is currently shadowed and may never be implemented. I think we should delete Deck and move the relationship of Back Design to the Game. It makes a few assumptions, like the deck you start with is the one you end with. But I think this is almost always true. It wouldn't be true for games that combine decks, and changing this relationship would restrict future use for three Pack Canasta which uses three decks including six Jokers, but for this application I think we are safe.

I know that Cards are the objects in the real world that have Back Designs, but data modeling has an element of reasonability to take into account. In this case, if you know the Back Design of one of the Cards in the Game, you know all of them. Move Back Design to Game in a non-identifying relationship since it is just information about the Game. Our model will now look like this:

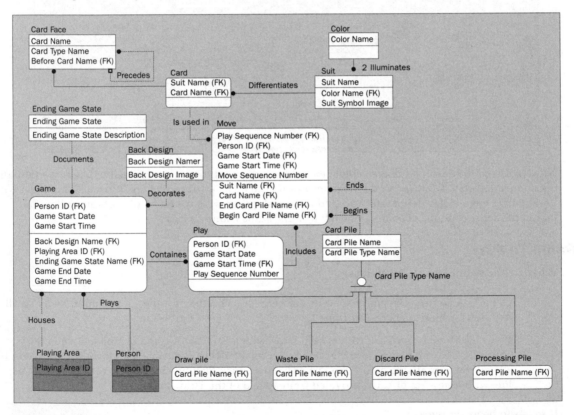

Now you need to revisit the keys that you impacted by changing the relationships. Adding the identifying relationship of Game to Play impacted every identifying relationship from Play to all its children in a cascade effect. Fortunately for us that only went one level, but that isn't always the case. You could impact quite a string of entities (the voice of experience here). You need to double check before you consider yourself done.

`Play` now needs `Person ID`, `Game Start Date`, `Game Start Time`, and `Play Sequence Number` to create a unique instance. Let's use an instance table to see if that still makes sense:

Person ID	Game Start Date	Game Start Time	Play Sequence Number
1234	1-1-02	1:00	1
1234	1-1-02	1:00	2
1234	1-1-02	1:00	3
456	1-1-02	1:00	1
456	1-1-02	1:00	2
456	1-1-02	1:00	3

That looks to be true. You need all that information to make an instance unique. What about `Move`? `Move` needs one more piece of information, the `Move Sequence Number`, to make it unique; so although the keys look rather complex, they are true.

Quality Assurance Checks

Before we deliver the model to our customers and do a model walk-through, we need to do some quality checking. You should consider the model as a prototype, which you need to subject to further review over time.

Normal Forms – 1-BCNF

Some of you must be wondering how we could have gotten all the way to here without really talking about the Normal forms as they apply to our structure. It seems to me that if you get it in your head that every entity represents a set of things, then you will generally be able to fulfil the requirements of Normal forms as you work on your model. Remember however, that this is a working definition, and that Normal Forms are the cornerstone of what we do. We are gathering the data and grouping it into sets that meet these rules of conduct. Look them over once more to see if we are on target. We built the logical model without explicitly using the Normal Form yardstick. Now let's try to break the structure by comparing it to the business rules, which in this case are the rules of the game. And, trust me; if you stick to them you will stay out of sooooo much trouble in the physicalization stage.

> *If you need to refresh your memory then go back to Chapter 3 for a more detailed discussion about Normal forms.*

Let's beat up on Game and see how it stands up:

```
Game
Person ID (FK)
Game Start Date
Game Start Time
Back Design Name (FK)
Playing Area ID (FK)
Ending Game State Name (FK)
Game End Date
Game End Time
```

First Normal Form (1NF) demands that every member of the set:

❑ depends on the *key*

❑ is unique and uniquely identified

❑ can be identified forever by the same values of the same set/s of attributes

❑ Has no repeaters of anything either internally to an attribute or by having multple attribute groups

It also means that if we use a surrogate key, which acts as a unique identifier, it can't mask the fact that the Jack of Spades is in the Card entity 15 times. That misses the point and is illegal. The goal is to store a member of the set one time and one time only, not to make the row in a table unique. As for repeaters, text blocks that allow 'value A, value B, value C' are just as illegal as attributes named Pile Position 1, Pile Position 2, Pile Position 3 would have been in the `Card Pile` entity. Looking over `Game`, it seems that we have satisfied 1NF, although I would add that we could probably include the `Person ID`, `Game End Date`, and `Game End Time` as an alternate key:

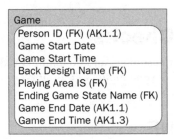

Look over every entity. Can you find a single attribute or group of attributes of each entity that can act as a unique identifier? (Yes, I still hate the Primary Key of Person and Playing Area, but I think they qualifiy.) Remember the normal forms are cumulative. 2NF depends on 1NF being true as well.

Second Normal Form (2NF) demands that every aspect of every member of the set depends on the *whole key*. All of the extra information (attributes) in an entity must be dependent on the entire key. Again surrogate keys are a problem here unless you identified the natural key to check against. For example, if we'd left the following relationships in place we would have broken 2NF:

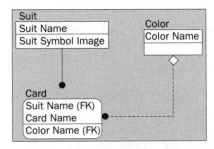

Although cards do have Color, it is dependent on the `Suit Name` only and not the `Card Name`. All Spades are Black and all Hearts are Red. The 'ownership' of the attribute belongs to `Suit`.

Third Normal Form (3NF) demands that every attribute of every member of the set depends on nothing but the key. Here again I'll break the rule.

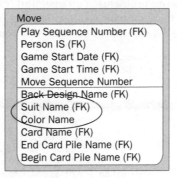

These are simple enough to do when you are pounding away at a large model. That's one of the reasons why I tried to get you to think about designing the model the way I did. Sometimes you are working with a list of attributes and just trying to find the right entity to take ownership of them. In this one I moved `Color Name` again. It breaks 3NF if it depends not on an attribute in the key but an attribute in a non-key position.

Boyce Codd Normal Form (BCNF) demands that every attribute must:

❑ be a fact about a key

❑ all keys are identified

BCNF kind of tells you what to do when you find issues in 2NF and 3NF. Dependencies between attributes in an entity require another entity to solve the problem. The attributes in question either become foreign keys from their own home base entity or they are derivable from the primary key migration of the new entities. We solve our dilemma by moving `Color Name` to the correct ownership (`Suit`). We still know the color of the `Card` in the `Move` but we have to find it by following the foreign keys back to `Suit`. BCNF also says that all attributes must be an 'Entity Owned Fact'. It is the reason we broke `Color` out into its own entity. `Color` in our model is a very small set. But `Color` has its own definition that had nothing to do with `Suit`. `Suit` is not the correct origin for `Color Name`, `Color` is.

Too Many/Too Few Attributes

If you are seeing one really huge entity, with over 15 attributes (and I have seen some with as many as several hundred), you quite likely haven't satisfied all the Normal form rules yet. Look at it again! On the other hand if you don't have any owned attributes, double-check to make sure that the entity is really necessary. We have a few in our model that might need to be looked at.

Too many entities may indicate that you have strayed out of scope. If your model is bulging at the seams with boxes and you thought that you had a small project, you should look over the entities again carefully. You may need to review what you discovered with your project lead. Too few entities may indicate that you have a hole somewhere in your analysis. (Ours is small on purpose; look how long it took for us to get here!) The project either deals with very few data elements in a very complicated fashion or you are missing something. Again review the scope and check with your project lead.

Unnecessary Relationships

Sometimes the relationships point out problems. You may find (especially in larger models where there are too many lines to see clearly) that you have one relationship pointing to an entity that either points back the way it came from or gets the same attribute from two sources. Like this:

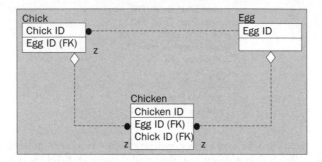

- ❏ Each Chicken comes from one Egg
- ❏ Every Chick comes from one Egg
- ❏ Every Chicken comes from one Chick

All of the above are true. And it's not that there aren't any times when this makes sense; it's just that it is suspect. In this case you don't need the relationship from the Egg to the Chicken. You can find the Egg through the relationship of the Chick to the Chicken. For the curious:

- ❏ We buy some of our chickens so the relationships of Chick and Egg to Chicken is `Null` allowed
- ❏ However, any Chicks around come from Eggs. We don't buy Chicks so Chick to Egg is a mandatory relationship
- ❏ None of our Eggs ever have twin Chicks
- ❏ And none of our Chicks are cloned! Our farm has no Doppelganger chickens

And I am only pointing this out because even this little model has many business rules captured and implied in it.

Accurate Role Names

It is so easy to lose track of role names in a working model. The modeling tools don't help you much and there isn't a good way to see them, although some software does have an option allowing you to turn on role naming in order to see what attributes you renamed. You should trace every relationship once, and verify that the primary key from the parent entity is in the child entity. If there are multiple relationships, then you should have that many foreign keys, unless you are unifying them on purpose.

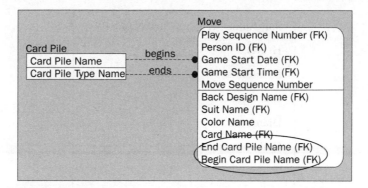

Remember this one? There are two relationships from Card Pile to Move. There need to be two attributes in Move that can be traced back to Card Pile. Be especially sensitive to this type and also recursive relationships.

Instance Tables

Don't knock just plain looking at the data. We keep talking about the fact that entities are sets of things. I generally describe this as spreadsheet analysis for the clients. Write some out and play with the data. See what becomes visible.

COLOR

Color Name PK
Red
Black

SUIT

Suit Name PK	Color Name	Suit Symbol Image AK
Hearts	Red	M
Diamonds	Red	L
Clubs	Black	K
Spades	Black	N

CARD

Suit Name PK	Card Name PK
Hearts	Ace
Hearts	Two

Table continued on following page

Suit Name PK	Card Name PK
Hearts	Three
Diamonds	Ace
Diamonds	Two
Diamonds	Three
Clubs	Ace
Clubs	Two
Clubs	Three
Spades	Ace
Spades	Two
Spades	Three
...	

Can you see how easy it is to double-check your key designations? In the case of Card, for instance, we could easily have missed the Suit Name as being part of the key. Look how simple it is to see the repeating values. With more complicated data Excel can help you sift and sort through for eyeball QA checking. For extremely serious data analysis you may need to set up test tables and check using SQL SELECT statements. Don't deliver your model until you are pretty sure you have it. I worked with a team once that had to de-scope a part of the project, because it took several months to figure out that it took seven attributes combined to make every member of the set unique!

Subject Matter Experts

Quite frequently a data model will use data from a department or source that is outside the project clients' world. In this case we have Psychology majors who may or may not know anything about playing cards. So they are going to have a difficult time verifying the work we did on Cards. Try to make time for a Subject Matter Expert (SME) review if there is a piece of the model that the review team probably can't help you with. Usually these areas are easily scoped out of the model for individual review.

Take a field trip to a game shop or a Casino and see if you have the rules right about Cards. In the real world, try to get a Postal worker to talk to you about how Zip Codes work, go out to the shop floor and talk to someone about the UPC symbol data and how they use it, talk to the Receptionist about extension numbers, or the security people about parking stickers. Use the web if you can. Most people who are SMEs love to be asked about their area of expertise. You will get more information than you might have actually wanted, but you may stumble on something that just never crossed your mind. Be very specific about your need for information and don't waste their time. Always write up interview notes that document the rules you discover this way. You may be asked to defend your analysis by being able to provide the source for the information. This is a really sensitive area. Many clients just want it 'their way'. You may have to gently encourage them to see their data as an enterprise asset that needs to be able to support a larger world.

Peer Model Walk Through

This is another way to make sure that the logical model is quality work. Let another modeler look it over and give you feedback. This is the most valuable method of gaining experience that I know of. We don't do it, or offer to do it, for each other nearly enough. Hopefully your group will have lots of wonderful suggestions that will make your model look and feel more standard to the department charter. They will hopefully help you to keep your spirits up. And they will truthfully tell you when your entity and attribute names are dreadful, before you expose them to the clients.

Finishing Touches

- ❏ Make sure that you add your name, extension, date, and time to all your documentation

- ❏ Page numbers are nice on the longer documents (I always seem to forget to add them)

- ❏ File path addresses are great if you are handing out hard copies of documents that are being stored on a shared server

- ❏ Add the project name and stage of development, especially if this is going to be a long project (over 3 months)

- ❏ Always add a glossary to documentation that is full of acronyms or words that might be out of the realm of the readers

- ❏ Print out a copy and put it on the wall...looking at it every day will help (and it will be a good reference for when you need to talk about the model)

If you need to iterate your documents and models, use some kind of versioning technique. Numbers and dates are great, but try to help out with visual clues, such as stickers or a color band, if you can. It is so much easier to see the blue stripe, or the Panda sticker, on your desk than it is to see V 2.15 in the footer of a document. Use some color in the model and documentation to highlight things that are important. You may, for example, want to change the background color of the entities to show the difference between the fairly quiet entities, like Color, versus the volatile entities, like Game Move. But if you do use color for something, be sure to add a color key to the model so that you never forget what that notation meant.

At this point you are ready for a model walkthrough with your project team, and then with the clients. Get a business rules report ready and do the true/false test. Polish up your Glossary for delivery. Do a spell check on everything. And be prepared to come back to the model with changes.

Summary

Our logical model developed in this chapter looks as follows:

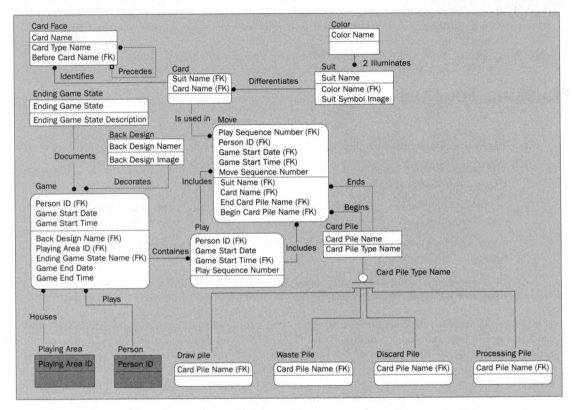

We have seen the iterative nature of the process by which we've drawn up this model, poring over each entity and its attributes, to ensure that the definitions and relationships we have are accurate and make sense. The key steps in the creation of a logical model are:

- ❑ Reinforcing the scope of your analysis often
- ❑ Determining the entities from your conceptual entities
- ❑ Defining attributes for your entities
- ❑ Discovering primary keys
- ❑ Verifying the relationships between entities
- ❑ Double-checking all that you have done in light of your business rules and Normal forms
- ❑ Validating you work against as many sources as possible, such as Instance Tables, SMEs, and Model reviews

- Project Status
- Logical to Physical
- Physicalizing Names
- Creating Tables From Categories
- Shadow Entity Examination
- Decide on the Primary Keys
- Quality Checks and Extra Value
- Other Potential Issues
- Summary

Transformation – Logical To Physical

This chapter looks into the process of transforming the logical model into a physical design. Fortunately the process is pretty straightforward, *provided you have a good Logical model to work from.* When we are finished with this chapter we will have a solid design that could be either deployed or enhanced by continued tuning.

We will look at these steps:

- ❑ Shorter names for tables and columns so as to avoid DBMS naming issues
- ❑ Decisions about the categories
- ❑ Status of any Shadow entities
- ❑ Chosen primary keys for the tables
- ❑ Review of the foreign keys names
- ❑ Defined data type and size information
- ❑ Quality tests for:
    - ❑ Data form, fit, and function
    - ❑ Naming Standards
    - ❑ Requirements satisfaction
    - ❑ Stewardship
    - ❑ Integration and interfaces
- ❑ Create scripts for the tables (DDL)

Project Status

Data modeling is generally being done in parallel with all sorts of other Project tasks. If all is going well by the time you are ready to transform your Logical model into the initial Physical design, the team will have signed off the following:

- ❑ Business Requirements
- ❑ Process analysis (often flow diagrams and use cases) and definitions
- ❑ Logical model
  - ❑ Definitions
  - ❑ Entities
  - ❑ Attributes
  - ❑ Relationships

This is not to say that there are not some outstanding items that are still being worked on, but it's important to have as stable and comprehensive an understanding as possible *before* beginning the physical design.

Next Steps

What is the team doing while you are beginning the physical design? They are beginning to explore the technical implementation issues. In fact one of the first decisions that is going to be made, is whether or not an automated solution is still justified based on what the team now knows. They will look at significant improvements in areas like time saving, decision-making ability, and genuine process improvements. All of the team's efforts, including the creation of the logical model, are part of that decision-making process. They would have brought us to this point.

In some companies the process of going from logical to physical involves a complete change in task owner. The skill sets involved in logical and physical modeling are very different. It may be that the logical modeler simply hands over the signed off logical model to a DBA for physicalization.

The decisions that have to be made about the design at this point are based on an intimate working knowledge of the platform/s that the tables are targeted for, the requirements of the screens/forms, interfaces, processing, security, and other hardware/software/infrastructure issues. We are going to take this example through to a good test environment design using Oracle as our target DBMS. But I don't claim to be a DBA or tuning wizard. If you would really like to pursue that aspect of logical to physical transformation deeper you can read more about it in *'Professional SQL Server 2000 Database Design'* (Wrox Press, ISBN 1-861-004-761).

Logical To Physical

Transforming the logical to the physical is another period of discovery; only this time the focus is on how to build the data repository. This task is a critical juncture for an application development project team. This is where they say 'the rubber hits the road'. A poor physical design will result in a poorly performing application. Changes to the physical data structures impact all code that uses it. This impact becomes broader, more difficult to locate and fix, and more expensive to implement, the further into a project you get. Granted we are only going to the first pass at physicalizing, but you must be extremely diligent with this version. It is the starting place for the DBA and programmers to begin the process of tuning and enhancing to support the application. Once the DBA builds it, the repercussions of changing something as little as a misspelled column name can be extremely costly. We sometimes refer to the cascading impact as a ripple, but sometimes it feels like a tidal wave.

Physicalizing Names

When we ended our logical design it included the entities and attributes named in full word descriptive titles. The first task is to shorten those names for simplicity, and to ensure that we don't run into any table and column name length issues when implementing the physical model. Always bear in mind that DBMSs have Table and Column name length restrictions, which you need to be aware of. Our target is Oracle 8, which only allows 30 characters for table and column names.

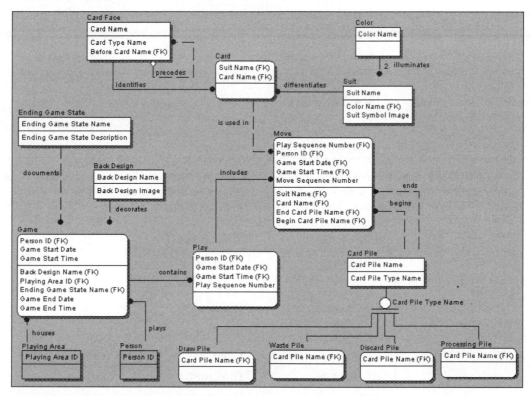

Consistency is more important than almost anything in naming and most especially in the art of abbreviation. Remember our attribute type list from Chapter 2? Each type should have a standard abbreviation. Your DBAs or Data Management group might already have a standard abbreviation list for you. Ensure that the abbreviations you use are documented in the model so that nobody will be confused in situations where different projects use different abbreviations.

Class Word	Abbr	Meaning	Data Domain
Amount	Amt	A monetary number	Number
Code	Cd	An alpha-numeric meaningful abbreviation	Text
Date	Dt	A calendar date – month, day, year	Date
Description	Dsc	A textual account or portrayal	Text

Table continued on following page

Class Word	Abbr	Meaning	Data Domain
Flag	Flg	A one letter or number Boolean set	Text
Identifier	ID	A unique recognition tag – character and/or number or system generated or a GUID – sometimes nonsensical and insignificant to the data user / sometimes process driven	Text
Image	Img	A non-language visual object	Blob
Name	Nm	A textual label	Text
Number	Nb	A place in a sequence	Number
Quantity	Qty	A number totaling a measurement by a unit	Number
Sound	Snd	A non-language aural object	Blob
Text	Txt	An unformatted language segment	Text
Time	Tm	A moment – hour, minute, second, etc.	Time

Note that DBMS hate spaces, so we need to remove them either through the use of underscores, or Pascal notation (letting the first letter capital note the next word in the name). We will use Pascal notation in this case. So to begin with this is a simple case of renaming.

Entity Name	Table Name
Back Design	BackDesign
Card	Card
Card Face	CardFace
Card Pile	CardPile
Color	Color
Discard Pile	DiscardPile
Draw Pile	DrawPile
Ending Game State	EndGameState
Game	Game
Move	Move
Person	Person
Play	Play
Playing Area	PlayArea
Processing Pile	ProcessPile
Suit	Suit
Waste Pile	WastePile

Notice we removed the 'ing' from some of the names. We tend to use as simple a name for tables as possible.

Table Name	Attribute Name	Column Name
BackDesign	Back_Design_Name	BackDesignNm
BackDesign	Back_Design_Image	BackDesignImg
Card	Suit_Name	SuitNm
Card	Card_Name	CardNm
CardFace	Card_Type_Name	CardTypeNm
CardFace	Before_Card_Name	BeforeCardNm
CardFace	Card_Name	CardNm
CardPile	Card_Pile_Name	CardPileNm
CardPile	Card_Pile_Type_Name	CardPileTypeNm
Color	Color_Name	ColorNm
DiscardPile	Card_Pile_Name	CardPileNm
DrawPile	Card_Pile_Name	CardPileNm
EndGameState	Ending_Game_State_Name	EndGameStateNm
EndGameState	Ending_Game_State_Description	EndGameStateDesc
Game	Person_ID	PersonId
Game	Game_Start_Date	GameStartDt
Game	Game_Start_Time	GameStartTm
Game	Back_Design_Name	BackDesignNm
Game	Playing_Area_ID	PlayAreaId
Game	Ending_Game_State_Name	EndGameStateNm
Game	Game_End_Date	GameEndDt
Game	Game_End_Time	GameEndTm
Move	Suit_Name	SuitNm
Move	Move_Sequence_Number	MoveSeqNb
Move	Card_Name	CardNm
Move	End_Card_Pile_Name	EndCardPileNm
Move	Begin_Card_Pile_Name	BeginCardPileNm

Table continued on following page

Table Name	Attribute Name	Column Name
Move	Play_Sequence_Number	PlaySeqNb
Move	Game_Start_Time	GameStartTm
Move	Person_ID	PersonId
Move	Game_Start_Date	GameStartDt
Person	Person_ID	PersonId
Play	Game_Start_Time	GameStartTm
Play	Play_Sequence_Number	PlaySeqNb
Play	Game_Start_Date	GameStartDt
Play	Person_ID	PersonId
PlayArea	Playing_Area_ID	PlayAreaId
ProcessPile	Card_Pile_Name	CardPileNm
Suit	Suit_Name	SuitNm
Suit	Color_Name	ColorNm
Suit	Suit_Symbol_Image	SuitSymbolImg
WastePile	Card_Pile_Name	CardPileNm

We only had to abbreviate one non-attribute type word; Sequence turned into Seq. You want to maintain an 'Abbreviation' key on the physical model so that anyone unfamiliar with the project standards can still feel fairly confident that they are looking at a Company Name rather than a Component Name when they are looking at CoNm in a Parts table.

Try to use the same abbreviation for a word throughout at least the entire model. Some companies manage abbreviating at the Enterprise level and manage a Standard Abbreviation list for projects.

Now it looks like this. I know this seems like a simple step, but it is fundamentally important so take special care.

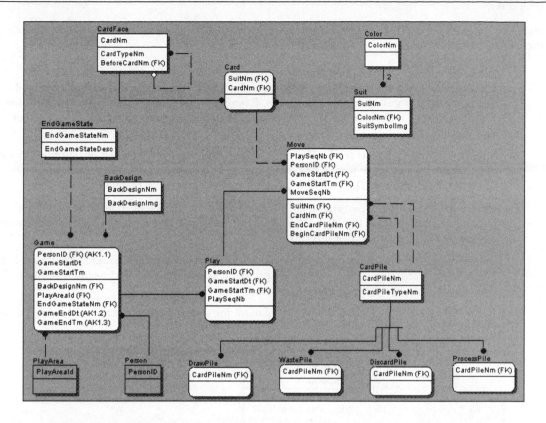

Look At Other Applications

Now you have a good list of potential tables. You need to use that list to see if you have data structures already in place that will allow you to share data rather than having to spend more time designing a table for it.

Ask around. You know what you have. Now check other tables and columns in other applications in the server. You would not believe how many Calendar tables exist in some mainframe environments. Besides if you find a source to share, and get the appropriate authorization to use it, then you can shadow out those tables and reduce the programming tasks. You could be a hero to the whole team.

Unfortunately in this case we don't have any outside sources. We have to work with the whole scope.

Creating Tables From Categories

One of the next steps in transforming the logical to the physical involves deciding the physical structure of categories. The only one we have to work with in our tutorial is the Card Pile category, and because it is too simple to really give you a feel for the thought process of choosing a category implementation, I will give you another category to work with, allowing us to look at the ultimate differences in data storage.

Here is a category from a Hospital billing system dealing with the charges made to patients dealing with their medical treatments:

❑ MedicalExpense – An assigned facility, professional time, medical procedure, or supply provided to a patient. The billing arrangement for these depends on the patient's medical insurance and/or government support type. Example: Emergency room visit, Anesthesiologist, Cut Down Tray, and Bone Set Simple Fracture. Does not include: Late fees, TV rental, or Flowers.

❑ Supply – A material provided by Central Service. This may be consumed during the process of supporting a patient or it may be reused after sterilization and repackaging. Examples: Crutches, High Forceps Delivery Tray, Admitting Set Up, or 4x4 Bandage.

❑ Procedure – An activity performed by members of the hospital staff to provide care for a patient. Example: Blood drawing, Chest X-ray, Complete Blood Count. This does not include housekeeping or maintenance services.

❑ StaffSupport – The professional services used to support at patient. Example: Anesthesiologist, Radiologist, Cardiologist. Support will be provided as either direct or consultant support. This does not include hospital operations staff support.

❑ Bed – An assigned location provided to a patient for a period of time. Example: Semi-Private, Private, Maternity, Emergency Room, Recovery Room.

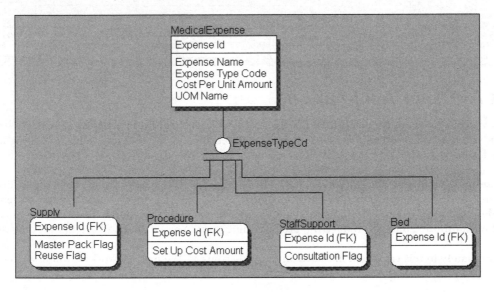

This category separates things charged to a patient on a hospital bill. Three of the types of medical expenses have some attributes that refer only to them. Some of the subtypes have special relationships. The hospital buys Supplies and contracts for certain types of StaffSupport. Each Bed expense must be an actual room in the facility (although configurations change).

You have three basic options when transforming categories, and we'll look at each in turn. I have pointed out the special features of each choice. Decide what is most important by reviewing the logical model and thinking about your team/application/client needs.

Rolled Up Categories

The first choice takes all of the extra attributes of the children and merges them into the supertype of the category. This merges together all of the attributes of the supertype and all subtyped into one table. It will transform our category so that it looks like this:

That would create a storage area for data that looks like this. Notice how many `Nulls` have to be allowed because each column is only valid for certain types of the category. Many rules need to be coded to prevent incorrect data from being created.

Id	Name	Type	Cost	UOM	Master	ReUse	Disposal	SetUp	Cons
72	Alcohol Swab	Supply	2.50	Each	N	N	N		
2	Dressing	Supply	25.00	Each	N	N	N		
821	10 Suture kit	Supply	56.00	Each	Y	N	Y		
309	Suture	Proc	60.00	Event				Y	
81	Doctor	Staff	250.00	Visit					N
56	Emerg-ency Room	Bed	150.00	Visit					

Here is an example of how the relationships change:

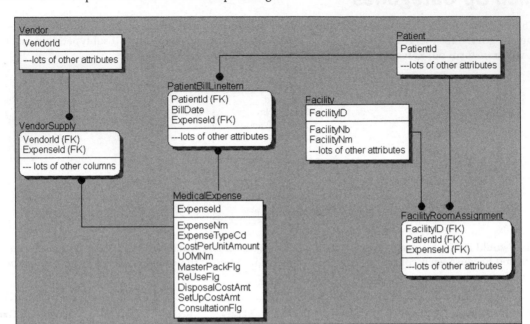

Notice that now the set of records relating to `FacilityRoomAssignment` and `VendorSupply` must be programmatically tested for by type. We didn't create a separate set of records in a table of the subtype to enforce the integrity rule.

When considering using this style you need to remember that:

❑ This gives you the least tables

❑ You keep a single source for FK migrations of the master category

❑ Business rules/Relationships based on the subtype will need to have identification logic hard coded instead of being found through subtype record segregation

❑ All the attributes of the subtypes need to be `NULL` allowed

In this choice, Master and Subcategories have no independence from each other whatsoever. We generally use this structure when the subtypes look and behave very similarly. We try to avoid this choice if there are relationships unique to the subtypes, but it can be done if other considerations are more important and you take the proper care to ensure data integrity.

Rolled Down Categories

This style takes all the attributes of the supertype and transfers them to each of the subtypes. You don't actually need the type code anymore since each subcategory is completely distinct. Notice that each table has exactly the same structure except for a few special columns (bolded for clarity):

Supply	Procedure	StaffSupport	Bed
Expenseld	Expenseld	Expenseld	Expenseld
MasterPackFlg	**SetUpCostAmt**	**ConsultationFlg**	ExpenseNm
ReUseFlg	ExpenseNm	ExpenseNm	CostPerUnitAmount
DisposalCostAmt	CostPerUnitAmount	CostPerUnitAmount	UOMNm
ExpenseNm	UOMNm	UOMNm	
CostPerUnitAmount			
UOMNm			

That would give you data stored like this:

Supply

Id	Name	Cost	UOM	Master	ReUse	Disposal
72	Alcohol Swab	2.50	Each	N	N	N
2	Dressing	25.00	Each	N	N	N
821	10 Suture kit	56.00	Each	Y	N	Y

Procedure

Id	Name	Cost	UOM	SetUp
309	Suture	60.00	Event	Y

StaffSupport

Id	Name	Cost	UOM	Cons
81	Doctor	250.00	Visit	N

Bed

Id	Name	Cost	UOM
56	Emergency Room	150.00	Visit

This changes the relationships. Now the subtypes with separate relationships can support them, but where you need a supertype table, you have to work with a unification column to combine the foreign keys, as you can see overleaf in `PatientBillLineItem`.

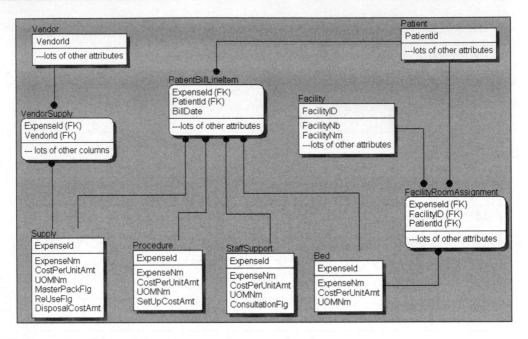

When considering using this style you need to remember that:

❑ You lose a single source for FK migrations of the master category and may have to use a unification process to note the multiple sources

❑ Common attribute reporting must be combined or united to make one list, like ExpenseNm and CostPerUnitAmount (uniting can have a large performance impact).

❑ Attributes of the subtypes should be NOT NULL

❑ If you want the combined sets of primary keys of all of the subtypes to still be united, you will need to add programming rules to manage each subtype record creation to check for uniqueness across each other.

With this choice subtypes are very independent but there is no master or supertype category. We tend to use this structure when the supertype has very little reason to exist as a table unto itself. It is also very appropriate when each subtype needs different processes to maintain them: security, ownership, screens, complex interfaces. It may just make more sense to physically deploy the logical category as completely separate physical tables.

The Expansive Category

Finally there is the choice of creating a table for the supertype and subtypes. This is the default for most modeling software. Our example in this case would look as follows:

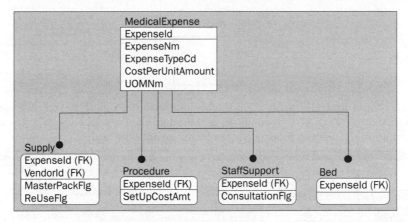

MedicalExpense

Id	Name	Type	Cost	UOM
72	Alcohol Swab	Supply	2.50	Each
2	Dressing	Supply	25.00	Each
821	10 Suture kit	Supply	56.00	Each
309	Suture	Proc	60.00	Event
81	Doctor	Staff	250.00	Visit
56	Emergency Room	Bed	150.00	Visit

Supply

Id	Master	ReUse	Disposal
72	N	N	N
2	N	N	N
821	Y	N	Y

Procedure

Id	SetUp
309	Y

StaffSupport

Id	Cons
81	N

Bed
Id
56

This style of category physical structure builds tables for both the supertype and subtypes. They maintain connectivity to each other through an identifying relationship. Now columns and relationships can be maintained in the most appropriate place (super-or subtype tables).

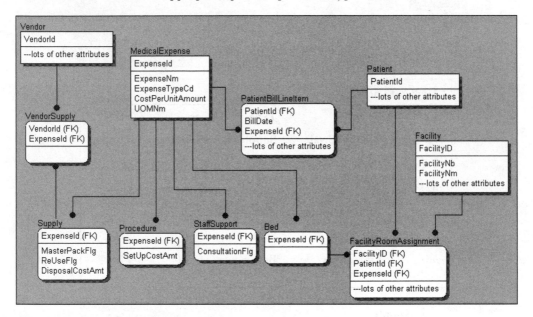

When considering using this style you need to remember that:

❑   This gives you the most tables

❑   You keep a single source for FK migrations of the supertype

❑   Almost any request for reporting data about a subcategory will require a join to the Master

This choice offers the most structural flexibility and growth potential, but is generally the most complicated. This design also keeps as many of the rules of integrity at the database level as possible. We generally use this structure design when there is a fairly complex category needing to manage many categories with unique attributes and relationships.

In this example this design would be my first choice.

The Solitaire Example

Refer back to the Solitaire model. Let's pick a physical design for the CardPile category. Review the relationships to other entities. Right now, all of the relationships are at the supertype level.

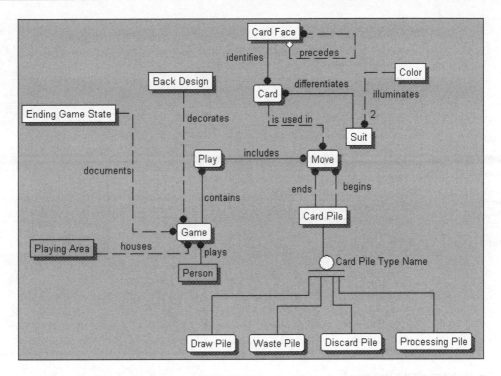

Then review the attributes. This is a pretty dull category. The subtypes have no specific attributes. Remember we found out from the clients that the scope didn't include rules pertaining to Solitaire. They are interested in capturing a player's moves, not the allowed moves. We ended up with the logical model losing some of the special relationships and owned attributes of the CardPile category.

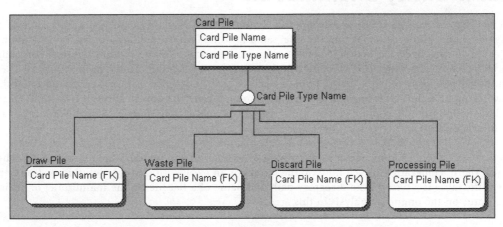

Under these circumstances I would propose a rolled up structure and would actually drop the Card Pile Type Name as being unnecessary at this point. That would change our evolving physical design to look like this:

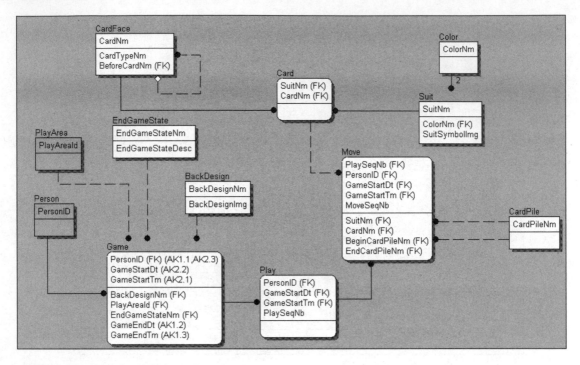

And finally what about this one?

Shadow Entity Examination

The fact that `Person` and `PlayArea` are still shadowed should glare out at you at this stage of our transformation. They are tables that are integrated in some fashion, but are not built or owned by the project. You may need to document relationships to them and ultimately build physical constraints, but you will never create them from the DDL generated from that model. This requires another discussion with the clients. They tell you that they have decided that `PlayArea` is out of scope, and that they are still working on a Survey form with the information they want to capture about the Person. You will need to remind them that there is increasing risk of being unable to deliver the software if they don't get you the specs soon.

When you examine shadow entities on a physical design, you will want to document exactly why they are still there. Generally this is a note on the model or an explanation in the definitions. It may note the system the table is a part of, the directory path and name of a flat file on the mainframe, or, as in this case, status on the ongoing analysis in this area.

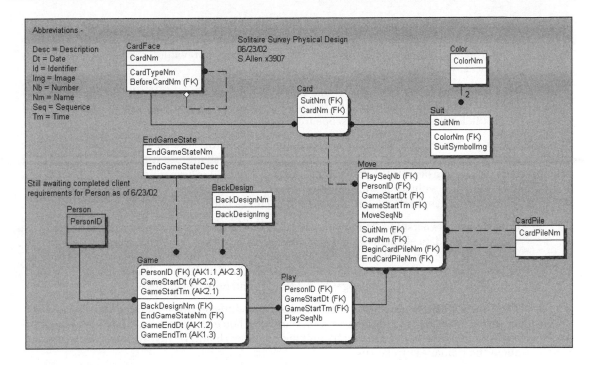

Decide On the Primary Keys

Now that we have chosen a structure for the categories and determined what to do with the shadow entities, it is time to look at the choices for the physical primary key. Remember that we are now talking about table designs rather than information designs. The analysis that we did to build the logical design was an attempt to find out and document as much as possible about pure data and the rules that govern its behavior, including what made each member unique and identifiable. The knowledge we discovered is still applicable, but we have several options in generating its physical manifestation. Choosing a primary key for a table has several goals. They are prioritized according to your Information Management charter, project requirements, DBMS strengths and weaknesses, and future needs. The considerations for the choices are:

❑ **Integrity** – Integrity emphasizes the necessary uniqueness of a data set. We need to ensure quality in the data by preventing any duplication of data records thereby causing anomalies in relating the data together. Having two or more records that seem to be the same leaves a data user wondering which one to pick (I have seen programmers literally have to code for this problem by just picking the first one).

❑ **Performance** – We also emphasize inserting, updating, deleting, and selecting the correct data as quickly as possible. Some designs that impact performance occur in multi-column, slower-to-match data types, like large textual or date/times, and any column that might need to be updated.

❑ **Integration** – We try to be sensitive to the fact that other systems might want to use the tables we are building. Sometimes we look over the choices of primary key with an eye to the enterprise needs, rather than just the system being worked on.

❑ **Data Readability** – Since primary keys are the bit of data that migrates, sometimes we give consideration to migrating simple/stable names rather than having to join back to get a piece of information. For instance, migrating a State Name or abbreviation can remove quite a few joins, because enough of the data is there for simple use.

❑ **Maintainability** – Someone has to take care of the system after you deploy it. We try to think about how difficult it is going to be to add in new structures, audit and fix anomalies, or deal with bulk load increases in data scope from time to time.

❑ **Security** – Sometimes instead of worrying about making the foreign keys understandable, we try to do just the opposite. Using pseudo-keys can mask significant information. Using ID numbers for sensitive lists like Bank Accounts or Personal information can allow foreign key data migration without providing information to the target table. The privileges have to be granted to join and select from the parent table to decode the foreign key.

❑ **Data element ownership** – Sometimes we take into consideration who actually owns, manages, and issues the data elements we are considering for a primary key. Data elements whose size, content, or type can be altered by an influence outside your enterprise, like the government, phone company, or post office should be considered a risky choice. What will we do when Zip codes and Phone numbers change their size and content in the future?

❑ **The DBA** – There is also the fact that the database administrator may have knowledge and experience that leads them to favor a primary key choice above others. They know the environment the application will be running on. They should be involved in the discussions about the primary key choices.

Primary Key Review

Each table should be reviewed *individually* before you commit to a choice for its primary key. The default choice made by the modeling software is the primay key you chose during the Logical model development. That doesn't necessarily make it the best choice for the physical design. However it is always good to remember what you discovered as candidate keys by noting them as alternate keys, even if you don't choose to use them.

Natural Key

Let's go back and look at the logical model. What primary key for Color is more appropriate than ColorNm in this physical design? What do you gain by putting an ID or Code in its place? In this case, absolutely nothing. There are only two very short values; you aren't going to get any discernable speed out of making a non-significant number take the task of primary key on its shoulders. We have no other systems on the horizon to integrate with (although checking with the users is always a good idea). Red and Black are much more useful in the Suit table than a system-generated ID value1 and 2. ColorNm is already simple and understandable. And, finally, no one has mentioned a need to encode this data for security sake.

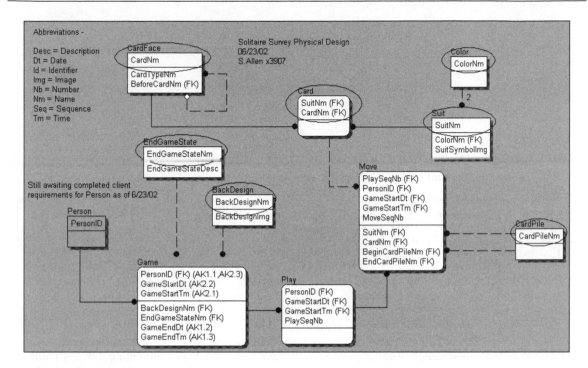

The `Suit`, `Card`, `CardFace`, `EndGameState`, `BackDesign`, and `CardPile` tables are the same. They all have simple, solid, useable primary keys already defined. So go ahead and use them. That leaves us with `Game`, `Play`, and `Move`. Their primary keys have some aspects that make it important to take a little extra time and care with them. The current primary keys:

❑   Include more than two columns

❑   Have Date and Time datatypes in some columns

❑   Are the major tables (potential record quantity, highest usage)

What are the alternatives if one doesn't use a natural (primary or alternate) key? I know of three that I have come across, but the world is changing rapidly and the creativity of our associates never fails to delight and surprise me. Let's look at them now.

Surrogate Keys

These types of keys are almost never defined in the logical model. They either don't map to real data elements or they are derivable both of which we avoid in logical modeling. That means that until the physical transformation stage we never took these into consideration as another type of candidate key. There are three surrogate key alternatives:

❑   **Concatenated** – compressed multi-column data strings

❑   **Semi-Surrogate** – replacing a portion of a multi-column key with a system-generated number

❑   **Surrogate** – system generated

Let's look at `Game` and review the choices:

```
Game
PersonID
GameStartDt
GameStartTm
BackDesignNm
EndGameStateNm
GameEndDt
GameEndTm
```

What does an instance table about `Game` look like?

Person Id	GameStart Dt	GameStart Tm	BackDesign Nm	EndGame StateNm	GameEnd Dt	GameEnd Tm
1	1/6/02	1824	Palm Trees	Win	1/06/02	1852
1	1/6/02	1853	Palm Trees	Lose	1/06/02	1910

These rows tell us that Person 1 has documented playing 2 games; they won one and lost one. Sometimes looking at sample data helps find more options than the logical modeling did. But I still don't see any natural keys other than the one we already found. However, my experience has told me that having dates and times in a primary key should be avoided if possible. This is mostly because of the way DBMSs want to format Date and Time data for you. It can be extremely complicated, which makes using it programmatically awkward. So let's decisively rule out the natural key.

Concatenated

How about a concatenated key choice? Concatenating would compress the three columns (`GameStartDt`, `GameStartTm`, and `PersonId`) into one value. For example: 01060218241, 01060218531, and 01060219121. This is called a **smart key** although it is *not* always a smart choice. This type of key is used quite frequently in manufacturing systems for part numbers. The clients can read this kind of key the way librarians read the Dewey Decimal numbers for a book to get an overview about the books' subject matter (000 is the Computers, Information, and General Reference category, 500 is the Science category, 600 is the Technology category, and so on). In fact, clients love these kinds of keys, in terms of their human readability (by the way, you can build a derivable column like this without using it for a key).

If we choose to use a concatenated key, then we move the current attributes below the line, identify them as an alternate unique key, and create a new GameID attribute. Don't forget to note the natural key when you move them as alternates. Just remember that one of the rules of a primary key should be that it can't be updated. For this reason concatenated keys can be a bit of trouble; they have to follow the same rule as other primary keys, but now you also cannot update the alternate key, since it is the foundation data for the derivable concatenated key.

The table and data now look like this:

```
Game
GameId
GameStartTm (AK2.1)
GameStartDt (Ak2.2)
PersonID (AK1.1,AK2.3)
BackDesignNm
EndGameStateNm
GameEndDt (AK1.2)
GameEndTm (AK1.3)
```

Game ID	Person Id	Game StartDt	Game StartTm	BackDesign Nm	EndGame StateNm	Game EndDt	Game EndTm
010602 18241	1	1/6/02	1824	Palm Trees	Win	1/06/02	1852
010602 18531	1	1/6/02	1853	Palm Trees	Lose	1/06/02	1910

The biggest risk for this type of key actually comes from the clients (especially power clients who are doing some of their own *ad hoc* reporting) who will request adding a certain special code to the key to make reporting easier. Try to make their lives easier but don't ever allow a portion of a concatenated key to be anything other than the immortal, never changing, natural key attributes. A primary key must be stable; otherwise you have the challenge of cascading a primary key change. Not a good thing.

> **A concatenated key should only ever be made up of the elements of the natural key to preserve the mapping back to the significant data elements that are being referenced.**

Semi-Surrogate

Semi-Surrogate keys have the interesting aspect of preserving some of the natural key, while replacing other parts. In this case, from a data usefulness perspective, migrating the PlayerID to the GameMove may make a lot of sense, while migrating the Start Date and Time isn't all that important.

Remember primary keys have several roles to play, uniqueness being the most important, but not the only role. Your choice impacts more than the table you are looking at; it impacts all of the places that the foreign key migrates to. We could replace the Start Date and Time of the Game with a number identifying one of the Games a Player has played. (You would almost be tempted to call it a sequence number. Don't. If you ever had a problem loading the data to the table out of order, your sequence generator would be out of step with the Start Date and Time.)

So you have Person 1 – Game 1, Person 1 – Game 2, and so on. In order to try this one you need to drop the GameStartDate and GameStartTime under the line as follows:

```
Game
PersonGameId
PersonID (AK1.1, Ak2.3)
GameStartTm (AK2.1)
GameStartDt (AK2.2)
BackDesignNm
EndGameStateNm
GameEndDt (AK1.2)
GameEndTm (AK1.3)
```

Note that we didn't use `GameID` for the name of the column here, because it isn't the whole identifier of the `Game`. It is only an identifier of one of a single player's games. The data now looks like this:

Person GameId	Person Id	Game StartDt	Game StartTm	Back DesignNm	EndGame StateNm	Game EndDt	Game End Tm
1	1	1/6/02	1824	Palm Trees	Win	1/06/02	1852
2	1	1/6/02	1853	Palm Trees	Lose	1/06/02	1910

Semi-Surrogate keys must be managed with an eye to both natural data element issues and system-generated identifier issues. The primary key of a `Person` can't change. The relationship of a specific `Person` record to a `Game` cannot be changed. And finally there would have to be a test for uniqueness of the `PlayerGameId` for each `Person`.

Surrogate

Finally there is the tried and true surrogate key. Have the system generate a number each time a record is inserted into the table and let that migrate. Just remember to put a unique index on the natural key values to prevent inadvertent duplication of rows. These keys are a fabulous addition to our design arsenal. They are a great choice if you need to set up a large table that has speed issues, since numbers are much speedier to sort and locate than text. But they should never be applied as the default key of a design.

> **Surrogate keys are often defaulted as the primary key of everything, without a single thought about what other choices might be made. This can promote a kind of narrow view of the design and lack of concern about the quality of the data.**

Surrogate keys have issues, the same way that concatenated and semi-surrogate did. None of these primary keys *mean anything* to anybody. In order to fulfill all of the role of a primary key to at least one of the natural keys must be given a unique index in order, maintain the data set member. The good news is that they are fast, simple, and small. The design looks exactly like the concatenated choice. However, the data looks a little different.

```
Game
GameId
GameStartTm (AK2.1)
GameStartDt (AK2.2)
PersonID (AK1.1, Ak2.3)
BackDesignNm
EndGameStateNm
GameEndDt (AK1.2)
GameEndTm (AK1.3)
```

Game ID	Person Id	Game StartDt	Game StartTm	Back DesignNm	EndGame StateNm	Game EndDt	Game EndTm
15	1	1/6/02	1824	Palm Trees	Win	1/06/02	1852
49	1	1/6/02	1853	Palm Trees	Lose	1/06/02	1910

How To Choose

All of these options have pros and cons: Go through a checklist of the necessary functions and characteristics of the primary key:

Factor	Natural	Concatenated	Semi-Surrogate	Surrogate
Integrity maintained	Yes	Yes	Yes	Yes
Performance	Not Good Date and Time datatypes and 3 Columns	Better but still a long number	Better still Small numbers 2 Columns	Best 1 Small number
Integration	None on the horizon	None on the horizon	None on the horizon	None on the horizon
Data Readability	The best – readable elements with the exception of Person Id	OK – those familiar with the data will be able to recognize it	Compromise – distinctive person and game differentiation but no real data	None
Maintainability	Dates and Times can be awkward to join to	Won't be able to use this for individual data elements. The join will have to be to individual columns	Fairly simple for future use – will have to join to get real data elements	Fairly simple for future use – will have to join to get real data elements

Table continued on following page

253

Factor	Natural	Concatenated	Semi-Surrogate	Surrogate
Security	Almost none – all the data is right there to read	Almost none – all the data is right there to read	Better – Game dates and times have been substituted for an ID	Best – Cannot read any Person or Game columns without a join
Data Element Ownership	Client owns all data elements	Client owns all data elements	Client owns all data elements	Client owns all data elements
DBA	Might want to use a single ID – will check	Might want to use a single ID – will check	Might want to use a single ID – will check	Might want to use a single ID – will check

So we can see that:

❑ The natural key from the logical model is three columns long and has `Date` and `Time` elements. However, it is true to the world and in a drop-down list of choices is highly defining

❑ The concatenated key is awkward if you are looking for `Game Moves` for Player 1 and you don't want to join back to `Game` to find the IDs for Player 1, but is informational from a shortcut perspective

❑ The semi-surrogate key has problems with a potential misunderstanding of the number (it's non-significant by itself and not necessarily a sequence of the games), and yet it has some information which may be valuable to the client

❑ And finally `GameID` only migrates nonsense numbers with no information value at all, but it does do the job very simply. This choice has the highest performance potential

What would you pick? Remember that you have to consider the needs of not only the client, but also the programmers and DBAs at this point. For this one I would probably lean toward the semi-surrogate key. I like being able to have the PlayerID in the GameMove. But this one would definitely be up for discussion. Now see how changing the primary key of `Game` changed `Play` and `Move`:

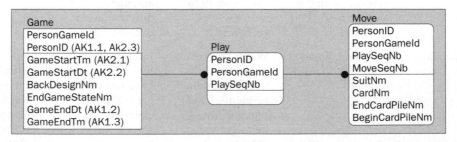

What does an instance table for `Play` look like?

PersonId	PersonGameId	PlaySeqNb
1	1	1
1	1	2
1	1	3
1	2	1
1	2	2
1	2	3
1	2	4

We read here that Person 1 in Game 1 had 3 Plays and 4 Plays in Game 2. Go through a short survey of the key design:

❑ Integrity maintained – Yes

❑ Performance – Number datatypes but three columns

❑ Integration – None on the horizon

❑ Data Usefulness – Not very except for `PlaySeqNb`

❑ Maintainability – Don't foresee any problems

❑ Security – Actually are masking the identity of the `Player` and what `Game` with surrogate keys

❑ Data Element Ownership – The clients own these data elements

❑ DBA – Might want to use a single ID – will check

Now look at an instance table for `Move`:

PersonId	Person Game ID	PlaySeq Nb	MoveSeq Nb	Suit Nm	Card Nm	EndCard PileName	BeginCard PileName
1	1	1	1	Clubs	King	Waste	Draw
1	1	2	1	Hearts	Two	Processing	Draw
1	1	2	2	Clubs	Jack	Processing	Processing

Here we read that Player 1 in Game 1, on the first Move of the first Play, put the King of Clubs on the Waste pile, which ended Play 1. On Play2, Person1 was able to Move the Two of Hearts out of the Draw Pile to a Processing Pile, and the Jack of Clubs from one Processing Pile to another.

So is there any reason to not choose the current key for `Move`, now that we have taken the date and time elements out of it? They are all short number columns but there are four of them. The key doesn't migrate anywhere in this application. There is no security issue suggesting that we would be better served with a surrogate key. I would leave it and expect to have a discussion about it with the DBA.

Now let's review each of the foreign keys for name appropriateness and definitions.

Foreign Key Naming/Definitions

First make a list of all foreign keys and their sources. When a primary key migrates from one table to the next, it often means something subtly different in its new location. This is one case where having software migrate the definition along with the foreign key column for you may actually contribute to a poorer quality product in the long run. Modeling software generally takes all the values (names, definitions, datatypes) from the parent table and applies it to the child table. If you are doing this process manually you may think about what is happening a bit more. We have to remember to review those automatically generated or migrated default definitions one last time before the names and definitions are committed to the design of a database.

How does the data migrate now? I added the verb phrase to remind you of *why* they were migrating. Pay special attention to the highlighted role names. Even if none of the other definitions change in migrating, these will, due to their roles.

Parent table	Verb phrase	Child table	Parent PK	Child FK
BackDesign	decorates	Game	BackDesignNm	BackDesignNm
Card	is_used_in	Move	CardNm	CardNm
Card	is_used_in	Move	SuitNm	SuitNm
CardFace	precedes	CardFace	CardNm	BeforeCardNm
CardPile	ends	Move	CardPileNm	**EndCardPileNm**
CardPile	ends	Move	CardPileNm	**BeginCardPileNm**
Color	illuminates	Suit	ColorNm	SuitNm
EndGameState	documents	Game	EndGameStateNm	EndGameStateNm
Game	contains	Play	PersonGameId	PersonGameId
Game	contains	Play	PersonId	PersonId
Person	plays	Game	PersonId	PersonId
Play	includes	Move	PersonGameId	PersonGameId
Play	includes	Move	PlaySeqNb	PlaySeqNb
Play	includes	Move	PersonId	PersonId
Suit	differentiates	Card	SuitNm	SuitNm

Let's remind ourselves of our original source tables (independent tables where the data originates before it becomes a foreign key) and columns, and their definitions (the source table is listed together with the source column, separated with a forward slash):

Source Table and Column	Definition
BackDesign/BackDesignNm	The textual label identifying a single pattern used to decorate the reverse side of a deck of cards. Example: Exotic Flowers, Plaid, and Logo.
CardFace/CardNm	The textual label identifying one of thirteen Cards. Example: King, Queen, Eight, and Ace.
CardPile/CardPileNm	The textual label identifying a collection of cards, which are the locations of a play in the game of Solitaire. Example: Draw Pile, Discard Pile, Processing Pile.
Color/ColorNm	The textual label identifying one of two hues used in the creation of the suit of a Card. They are Red and Black.
EndGameState/EndGameStateNm	The textual label identifying the outcome of a completed Game. Example: Win, Lose, Quit.
Person/PersonId	Λ non-significant value uniquely identifying a Person who is a participant, or potential participant, in a study being conducted by the Psychology department.
Game/PersonGameId	A non-significant number uniquely identifying a single game played by a person.
Play/PlaySeqNb	An ordered number identifying a single Play in a single Game and noting the order in which it happened.
Move/MoveSeqNb	An ordered number identifying a single Move in a single Play in a single Game and noting the order in which it happened.
Suit/SuitNm	The textual label identifying one of four divisions of Cards. They are Clubs, Spades, Hearts, and Diamonds.

Now let's consider the target table and column names and definitions (listed in the same order as the source tables and columns). I have highlighted changes that have been suggested.

Target Table and Column	Definition
Game/BackDesignNm	The textual label identifying a single pattern used to decorate the reverse side of a deck of cards. Example: Exotic Flowers, Plaid, and Logo.
CardFace/BeforeCardNm	The textual label identifying **the card preceding** one of thirteen Cards. **Example: null before King, King before Queen, Nine before Eight, and Two before Ace.**
Move/CardNm	The textual label identifying one of thirteen Cards **that is being used in a Move during a Play of a Game of Solitaire.** Example: King, Queen, Eight, and Ace.

Table continued on following page

Target Table and Column	Definition
Move/SuitNm	The textual label identifying one of four divisions of Cards **that is being used in a Move during a Play of a Game of Solitaire.** They are Clubs, Spades, Hearts, and Diamonds.
Move/BeginCardPileNm	The textual label identifying **the originating** collection of cards, which is a location of a Play in the Game of Solitaire. Example: Draw Pile, Discard Pile, Processing Pile.
Move/EndCardPileNm	The textual label identifying **the concluding** collection of cards, which is a location of a Play in the Game of Solitaire. Example: Draw Pile, Discard Pile, Processing Pile.
Suit/ColorNm	The textual label identifying one of two hues used in the creation of the suit of a Card. They are Red and Black.
Game/EndGameStateNm	The textual label identifying the outcome of a completed Game. Example: Win, Lose, Quit.
Game/PersonId	A non-significant value uniquely identifying a Person who is a participant in *<remove potential – now they are playing>* a study being conducted by the Psychology department **who is the Player of the Game.**
Play/PersonId	A non-significant value uniquely identifying a Person who is a participant in a study being conducted by the Psychology department, **who is the Player of the Game conducting the Play.**
Move/PersonId	A non-significant value uniquely identifying a Person who is a participant in a study being conducted by the Psychology department, **who is the Player of the Game conducting the Play and determining the Move.**
Play/PersonGameId	A non-significant number uniquely identifying a single game played by a person **of which this Play is an event.**
Move/PersonGameId	A non-significant number uniquely identifying a single game played by a person, **of which this Move as part of the Play is an occurrence.**
Move/PlaySeqNb	A ordered number identifying a single Play in a single Game and noting the order in which it happened **of which this Move is an occurrence.**
Card/SuitNm	The textual label identifying one of four divisions of Cards. They are Clubs, Spades, Hearts, and Diamonds.

Now we go back over the data dictionary and double check it. Do you think that when `ColorNm` migrated from `Color` to `Suit` that the definition remained *exactly* the same? Is it made up of the same set of values (no reductions, no exceptions)? It looks the same to me too therefore both the names and definitions remain the same in both locations.

What about SuitNm for Suit and Card? That seems OK too. How about CardNm in CardFace? We already had to role name the foreign key to BeforeCardNm. However we missed changing the definition didn't we? Now is the time to clear that up. Usually all you need is a modifying clause to explain why this column is different.

❑   Was – The textual label identifying one of thirteen Cards. Examples are King, Queen, Eight, Ace

❑   Should be – The textual label identifying **the card preceding** one of thirteen Cards. **Examples are null before King, King before Queen, Nine before Eight, and Two before Ace**

If you have a definition that reads exactly the same for two differently named attributes, then either your name or definition is wrong. The attributes are either different or identical; they can't be both. A column with the same name in different tables should always be reviewed for complete consistency (some DBMSs won't allow this anyway).

Go over the changes I made and see if they help build a clearer definition of not only the data element in that table, but the role it plays once it gets there. It can be very confusing to find the same column has migrated to 20 places but it always has the same definition. For instance, PersonId in the Game table is the person who played the game, but in the Move table it is the person who made the move. Solitaire allows only one player, but that wouldn't be the case for Gin Rummy.

Have you ever looked at different reports that all have Date on them somewhere and no label explaining exactly what that date is? And reports are not the worst places. I have looked over database designs with hundreds of tables and tried to find specific data elements only to be completely frustrated by the lack of specifics in the names of columns.

> **Do the physical design with future analysts in mind. Help them out. Be as specific and descriptive as possible in your column names and then back them up with good definitions. Only use the same column name for exactly the same data element.**

Adding Data Types and Sizing

Now you need another table to look at your handiwork. This time let's concentrate on the physical details of the columns. When we first decided on the class word for each of our columns, we determined the general direction of the data type. Unfortunately data types are completely dependent on the DBMS you are targeting, so you need to know what data types are specific to the database you are working with, in order to go very much further with the design.

You can however document a generic kind of hint for the DBA and programmer from your analysis. These columns will ultimately be the care and concern of the clients. They will know better than anyone how big they think they need things to be. Having sample data and a review with them here is a big help. Some data types such as Images, Dates, Binary, and Integers, all have a built-in size. Text and numbers are your biggest concern. Remember that textual data types allow numbers but numeric data types don't allow alphabetical or special characters (except a few numeric notations like minus or decimal).

Clients often give you really generic requirements for text fields, and I have put my general use guess next to the target size. These are not platform-specific datatypes yet. They are just estimated sizes:

- ❏ Tiny – flags or a single character for small codes
- ❏ Small – 3-6 for abbreviations
- ❏ Medium – 20-40 for names
- ❏ Large – 40-2000 for descriptions and paragraph text blocks
- ❏ Really Large – 2000+ sometimes called Long for almost unlimited text space

Numbers generally come in the following:

- ❏ Tiny – 1-9
- ❏ Monetary – will generally need at least 2 decimal places
- ❏ ID – whole numbers with lots of space for growth – usually a system-generated number
- ❏ Hundreds – 3 spaces up to 999
- ❏ Thousands – 4 spaces up to 9,999
- ❏ And so on

There may be a Data Management sizing standard that you should refer to as well. Use the generalities above and apply the first cut. Varchar2 is the most flexible text type in Oracle. I am using it as an example.

Remember all the foreign key data types and sizes MUST match their source column exactly.

Table Name	Table Column Name	Table Column Datatype	Table Column Null Option
BackDesign	BackDesignNm	VARCHAR2(20)	NOT NULL
BackDesign	BackDesignImg	BLOB	NULL
Card	CardNm	VARCHAR2(10)	NOT NULL
Card	SuitNm	VARCHAR2(10)	NOT NULL
CardFace	CardNm	VARCHAR2(10)	NOT NULL
CardFace	CardTypeNm	VARCHAR2(10)	NOT NULL
CardFace	BeforeCardNm	VARCHAR2(10)	NULL
CardPile	CardPileNm	VARCHAR2(15)	NOT NULL
Color	ColorNm	VARCHAR2(10)	NOT NULL
EndGameState	EndGameStateNm	VARCHAR2(20)	NOT NULL
EndGameState	EndGameStateDesc	VARCHAR2(60)	NOT NULL

Table Name	Table Column Name	Table Column Datatype	Table Column Null Option
Game	EndGameStateNm	VARCHAR2(20)	NOT NULL
Game	BackDesignNm	VARCHAR2(20)	NOT NULL
Game	GameEndDt	DATE	NULL
Game	GameEndTm	NUMBER(5)	NULL
Game	PersonGameId	NUMBER(5)	NOT NULL
Game	GameStartDt	DATE	NOT NULL
Game	PersonID	NUMBER(5)	NOT NULL
Game	GameStartTm	NUMBER(5)	NOT NULL
Move	CardNm	VARCHAR2(10)	NOT NULL
Move	SuitNm	VARCHAR2(10)	NOT NULL
Move	CardPileNm	VARCHAR2(15)	NOT NULL
Move	CardPileNm	VARCHAR2(15)	NOT NULL
Move	PersonID	NUMBER(5)	NOT NULL
Move	MoveSeqNb	NUMBER(3)	NOT NULL
Move	PersonGameId	NUMBER(5)	NOT NULL
Move	PlaySeqNb	NUMBER(3)	NOT NULL
Person	PersonID	NUMBER(5)	NOT NULL
Play	PersonID	NUMBER(5)	NOT NULL
Play	PersonGameId	NUMBER(5)	NOT NULL
Play	PlaySeqNb	NUMBER(3)	NOT NULL
Suit	SuitNm	VARCHAR2(10)	NOT NULL
Suit	ColorNm	VARCHAR2(10)	NOT NULL
Suit	SuitSymbolImg	BLOB	NULL

Double-check the nullability one more time and look at the results:

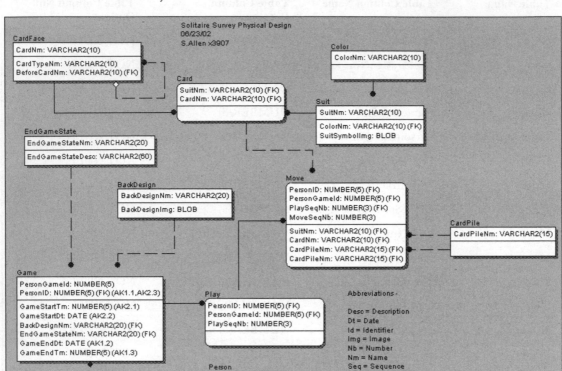

Now you have something that is really looking like a physical design. Remember that even though it looks good enough to deploy this is only a first pass. We are still lacking many reviews by the DBA and programmers. We could consider it the 1.0 version that is beginning the review cycles.

Quality Checks and Extra Value

We have gone through the simplified steps to take a logical design to a physical one. Is there anything else to do to make sure it is right before we deliver it? Yes.

Instance Tables

Do an instance table of each of the tables, and try to walk through all the screen and report requirements. Try to deliberately break what you have, by putting strain on the sizes and nullability. Then set them side-by-side and try to find answers to questions. In the case of our Solitaire model, we can ask questions such as:

- ❏ What are the red Suits?
- ❏ How many Games are Won?
- ❏ How many Games are Lost?
- ❏ What is the ratio of Won to total Games?

Get the clients to help you make up questions they will want answers to.

Names and Definitions

Double-check the names and definitions of the tables and columns one more time. I can't emphasize enough how dreadful it is after three weeks of programming effort to find that you typed a name incorrectly. And I can't tell you how many times I had to let an incorrect name go on to production because it would have been too costly to fix. While imperfections will always appear at some stage, try to minimize your naming errors as much as possible.

Requirements Review

A functionality review of the data requirements is another good check. Your development team should have a good version of the development requirements by now. Compare your model with them, and carefully document any extraneous or missing data elements. Spotting any missing data elements is the harder, but crucial, task.

Telling the Story

Sit down and verbalize the activity being captured by the data elements. The Psychology department is collecting data about people playing Solitaire.

- ❏ Can they differentiate players? Yes
- ❏ Can they differentiate games? Yes
- ❏ Can they differentiate moves in a game for a player? Yes
- ❏ Can they tell the optional moves for a player in order to see which choice they made? No (But they told us they didn't want to)

These are just a few of the questions we need to ask here in order to test the scope boundaries one last time for appropriateness.

Identify the Data Stewards

Data stewardship means someone takes some responsibility for the correctness of a data set. It doesn't necessarily mean they 'own' it. Who would 'own' ColorNm after all? However, you should be able to find someone willing to look at the data set from time to time and verify the correctness of the records. It should send up a red flag to the team if you can't find anyone to do this, since it may well suggest that the data is out of scope or needs to be integrated from a different system where data stewardship is already established.

After all the care and concern you have put into the models and designs, many people may come to believe that you are the data *steward*. It is hard to explain that while you may be considered the data structure steward, you don't watch over their data on a day-to-day basis. Someday I hope to see quality checking in the form of random 'Verify this data record' functionality incorporated into applications, along with the Application Administration and Help functions.

Build Test DDL

Let's look at some sample DDL generated from the model. It is a great check to do; if you can't build it then you have missed something. Here is sample coding for Color, Suit, and Card just as an example.

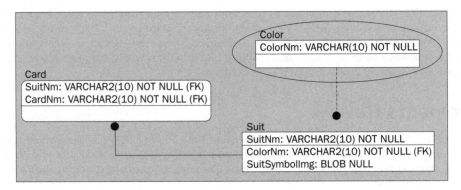

You should be able to follow every detail of the DDL from the model. Here are the names that we chose for table and columns, plus the sizes and whether they were Null.

```
CREATE TABLE Color (
    ColorNm        VARCHAR2(10) NOT NULL
);
```

Here are the definitions we slaved over to add to the DBMS library files where they will never get lost. (Oracle lets you do this but not all DBMSs do):

```
COMMENT ON TABLE Color IS 'One of 2 hues used in the creation of the suit of a
Card. Red, Black';
COMMENT ON COLUMN Color.ColorNm IS 'The textual label identifying one of 2 hues
used in the creation of the suit of a Card. They are Red and Black.';
```

Here is the primary key we chose after much thought to identify a record in the Color table:

```
ALTER TABLE Color
    ADD ( PRIMARY KEY (ColorNm) ) ;
```

Let's now consider Suit. You can follow every choice we made here too:

```
CREATE TABLE Suit (
    SuitNm          VARCHAR2(10) NOT NULL,
    ColorNm         VARCHAR2(10) NOT NULL,
    SuitSymbolImg    BLOB NULL
);

COMMENT ON TABLE Suit IS 'One of 4 divisions of Cards. Clubs, Spades, Hearts,
Diamonds.';
COMMENT ON COLUMN Suit.SuitNm IS 'The textual label identifying one of 4 divisions
of Cards. They are Clubs, Spades, Hearts, Diamonds.';
COMMENT ON COLUMN Suit.ColorNm IS 'The textual label identifying one of 2 hues
used in the creation of the suit of a Card. They are Red and Black.';
COMMENT ON COLUMN Suit.SuitSymbolImg IS 'The non-language visual object
representing a Suit in a deck of cards.';

ALTER TABLE Suit
    ADD ( PRIMARY KEY (SuitNm) ) ;
```

And finally let's consider `Card`:

```
CREATE TABLE Card (
    SuitNm          VARCHAR2(20) NOT NULL,
    CardNm          VARCHAR2(20) NOT NULL
);

COMMENT ON TABLE Card IS 'One of 52 unique game pieces used in playing games
bearing pictures of figures or numbers organized by suit. Example: Queen of Clubs,
2 of Diamonds';
COMMENT ON COLUMN Card.SuitNm IS 'The textual label identifying one of 4 divisions
of Cards. They are Clubs, Spades, Hearts, Diamonds.';
COMMENT ON COLUMN Card.CardNm IS 'The textual label identifying one of 13 Cards
which precedes the Card noted in the record ordered from King to Ace. Examples are
King for the Queen, Eight for the Seven, and Two for the Ace';
```

```
ALTER TABLE Card
    ADD ( PRIMARY KEY (SuitNm, CardNm) ) ;
```

If we now consider the relationship between the Color and Suit tables, we can see the relational integrity constraint requiring that a `Color` name exist in the `Color` table before it can be inserted into the `Suit` table:

```
ALTER TABLE Suit
    ADD ( FOREIGN KEY (ColorNm)
            REFERENCES Color ) ;
```

As for the relationship between Suit and Card, we can see the one making sure that all Suit names appear in the Suit set before it can be used in the definition of a Card.

```
ALTER TABLE Card
    ADD ( FOREIGN KEY (SuitNm)
                REFERENCES Suit) ;
```

Every symbol and nit-picky little detail ends up in the DDL. Every choice you made from the beginning of our tutorial has become part of the foundation for the physical model of the Solitaire Survey application for our clients.

Other Potential Issues

Now that you have a physical model in your hands, there are a number of further modifications you may need to do.

Operational Additions

You may be asked to add columns to the tables that have nothing to do with the client's needs. The DBA may have a set that they like to add for table/data/process management. I call these operational tables, referring to the process of managing the operations involved in creating and managing the data itself. These come in very handy when someone is trying to troubleshoot or audit the database.

Usually they are something like these:

❑   CreateID – user or process

❑   CreateTimeDt

❑   CreateTerminalID

❑   LastModifiedByID – user or process

❑   LastModifiedDt

❑   LastModifiedByTerminalID

These are generally the last additions before the test environment is built, only because they make the model so much bigger. In our model, the operational columns would outnumber the actual data columns and make them harder to concentrate on. Sometimes you will even need to add extra tables that have to do with operational management of the application. It's all part of the physical model.

These tables and columns will generally not show up on the logical model. They won't be elements that map logical to physical. In fact sometimes these elements aren't even put in place by the data modeler. The model may be given to other members of the team to hone and polish the physical design for greater performance.

Population Documentation

One of the things that the DBA needs in order to continue the process of physicalizing, is an estimate of the quantity of rows and growth rate (this is technically referred to as volumetrics). The clients are going to have to help you with growth rate, but from your analysis you should be able to come up with some insights about the number of rows. Keep it simple, and use a rule of thumb (which you and the team will decide on) such as:

❏   Small – less than 100 records

❏   Medium – less than 1,000 records

❏   Large – over 1,000

Color-code the model and add notes next to the table name. Be aware that you may still have to come up with a guess on actual quantity For example:

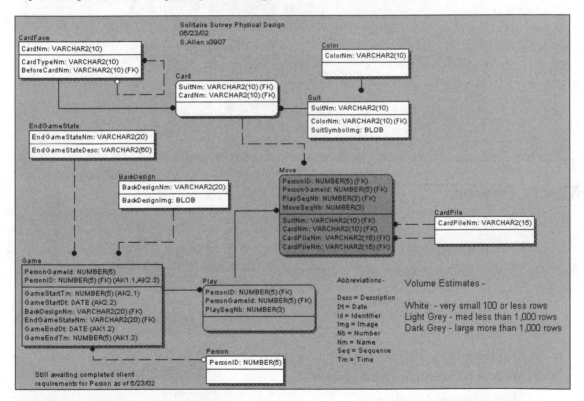

Activity Documentation

Another thing that could be very useful is an overview of how much INSERT, UPDATE, and DELETE activity is expected per table, using a scale such as Static, Mildly Active, and Very Active.

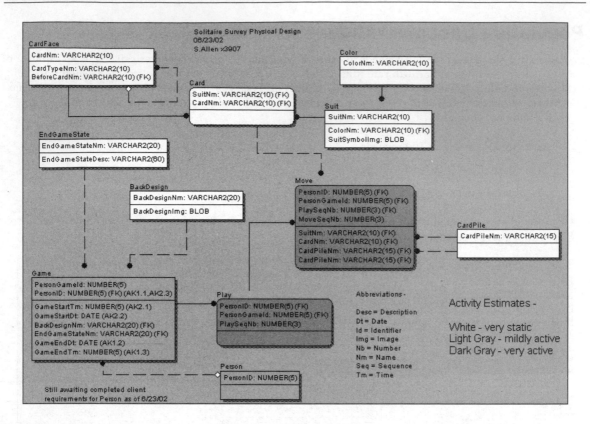

Model Power

You can use the model now to identify other aspects like:

- ❑ Frequent query path
- ❑ Targeted integration points
- ❑ Special security sensitivity
- ❑ Criticality of quality
- ❑ Known required speed requirements
- ❑ Expected data use statistics in screens and reports
- ❑ Pedigree information for data sources
- ❑ Stewardship of data elements

There are numerous concerns that are going to be covered while the model matures towards the final design. Keep the model up to date and useable for everyone. Adding other information about data to the physical model helps with the next set of decisions to be made, dealing with denormalization. The more the team knows about the use of the data at this point, then the more informed the next decisions will be. For example, the more records, or the more active the table that is being targeted for a denormalization decision, then the greater the risk.

Now you are ready for a walkthrough with the rest of the team. You have some marvelous documentation to help move the team on to the next steps. Don't expect it to be perfect however; there are always further changes to these models as they are reviewed.

Summary

In this chapter we have taken our logical model and transformed it into a transactional physical fully attributed model. In creating this physical model the basic steps we have taken are:

- ❑ Breaking down the categories in our logical model in terms of tables in our physical model
- ❑ Identifying suitable primary keys for each table
- ❑ Defining and naming foreign keys
- ❑ Testing the accuracy of the physical model

We have seen how several iterations are required in looking over the model created, and double-checked that it makes sense. It is crucial to get this physical model as accurate as possible, since it is the basis for both programmers and DBAs to get to work. Mistakes at this stage can prove very costly, and all members of the team should be involved in developing the physical model.

While the physical model in its completed state should be ready to implement, it is important to realize that each system will require a tradeoff between the process of physicalization and denormalization.

And just to remind you, although we have gotten through the transformation of logical to physical, our clients have left the Person data outstanding yet. We will have to deal with that in the next chapter.

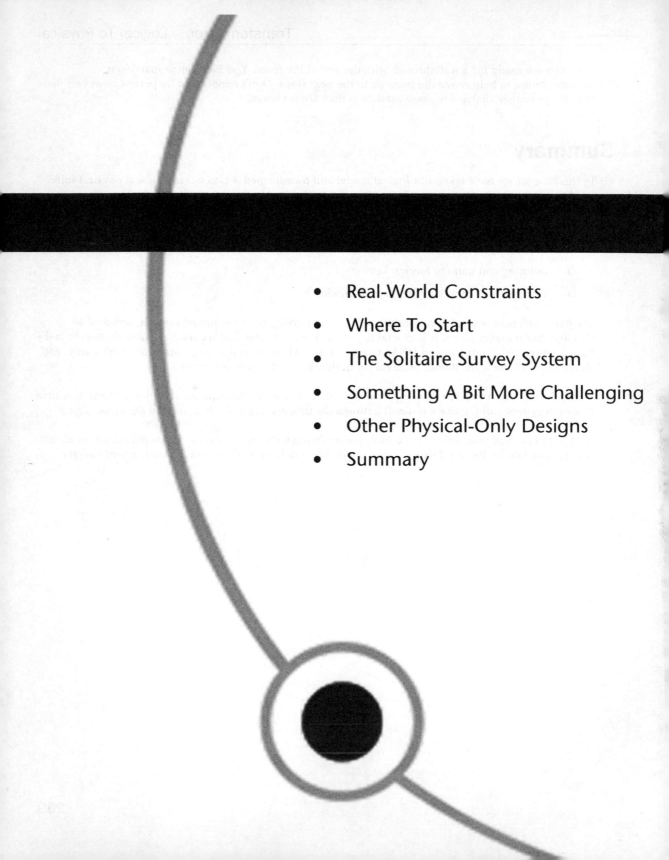

- Real-World Constraints
- Where To Start
- The Solitaire Survey System
- Something A Bit More Challenging
- Other Physical-Only Designs
- Summary

Designing Only a Physical Model

This chapter is going to look at the process of building a physical data model without going through the expected steps of creating a conceptual model to guide the analysis to build a logical model which is then transformed into a physical model. You only exercise this method when the alternative is no data modeling involvement with the design at all. It is an emergency technique.

We are going to continue our tutorial of Solitaire and flesh out the Player portion of the physical design along with adding a brand new requirement tossed in by the clients. This covers a 'Bottoms Up' approach to data modeling.

Real-World Constraints

Why would you create a physical model without going through the traditional, disciplined, industry-approved approach of conceptual – logical – physical design stages? In an ideal scenario there is sufficient project time given to the development, and review, of each of the models we have discussed throughout this book. However, in the real world of business, projects get behind in schedule, resources, and/or budget. The business may not be able to afford the time and effort it takes to carry out the full analysis cycle on smaller projects. Team members are asked to accomplish project goals without the ideal skills, analytical tools, time, or access. They find themselves sideswiped with unexpected requirements that need to be incorporated long after the conceptual and logical phases have been completed. Also, believe it or not, this kind of modeling is frequently the chosen methodology used in software maintenance. Assumed 'quick fixes' to existing systems are often constrained to working with the narrowed vision of the physical model with no thought given to a logical or conceptual one. It takes a highly developed and strategically aligned data management group to be able to funnel software change requests through the full data modeling process without developing the perception of being a bottleneck.

In these sorts of scenarios, it is a question of being pragmatic, and doing the best that you can, given the constraints that you are under. This is when some analysis is better than no data management involvement in the solution at all. While speed is generally of the essence in these situations, this doesn't mean that you can't apply the data management requirements of standardization, normalization, and quality in order to develop a solution, which has some level of flexibility and possibility to support future growth. Without some data management oversight, this kind of database design will generate table structures much less optimal than those carefully chosen under calmer circumstances.

> **The key point here is that this is not to be recommended as the normal choice, but as a 'better than no model' under certain circumstances approach.**

There are some times when we really dig in our heels and strongly protest this approach.

❑ Mission Critical Data elements – the whole enterprise is going to need this data

❑ Long life expectancy – this has to last for a while to be a cost-effective solution

❑ Shared environment impacts – bad table design and poor performance could seriously impact other users on the same servers

Sometimes it is worth putting up a fight. However, in our case we know this is intended to be a 'Standalone', single semester project, running on a single department machine so no one else should be impacted.

Where To Start

The only good thing about getting the kind of pressure that results in you doing data modeling this way, is that you usually have a very defined set of data elements that need to be physically designed. It's usually a form or a report that needs to be added to an existing table design. The key points at the outset of this work are:

❑ Identify as complete a set of data element requirements as possible. Get copies of all the forms or reports relevant to the task in hand. Talk to the clients to establish exactly what they want

❑ You begin with a physical table design. Start with a table design that looks exactly like what you have been given. Capture every data element 'as-is' from the sources. You may be working from a complicated set of Excel files, forms, or documents. Try to start with a simple, single flat table. By 'flat' I mean that there are no relationships to other data sets. It is all in one list form

❑ Look for data sets by using the rules of normalization for review or by looking for natural restricted values and repeating groups

❑ Draw up your table and column definitions once more. The original naming of the columns will have more to do with the labels of analysis sources than your deep understanding of the data. That means that the names will be much narrower, and in danger of being misunderstood in the future. Definitions are an absolute must here

❑ Look over each data element and consider whether it can be broken down further. Focus particularly on text information in forms and reports. Look back over the client requirements and consider what information they really need to be immediately available to them. Remember that this physical model is going to be used in actually implementing the application, so reporting requirements are a factor in the model here

❑ Consider what elements lend themselves to be used as primary keys. Draw up and verify relationships between data elements, and apply the requirements of the various Normal forms

❑ Look back at the client requirements, and try to plan for future growth of the system

With this checklist in mind let's take a look at our new requirements for the Solitaire Survey system, as our first example.

The Solitaire Survey System

In the case of our Solitaire model, the clients have finally given you a copy of the form they intend to use to register the Solitaire players who have volunteered to allow their games to be analyzed. It's late in the project and the budget doesn't allow the team to keep the programmer much longer. You are being asked to add the new requirements to the existing table design in as short a time as possible.

So that's where you start, with as complete a set of data element requirements as you can get your hands on. You will want examples of completed forms as well as blank ones to help you understand the data rules. Here is the form:

Solitaire Player Survey   For Internal Use Only _____
For use by the Psychology department

Gender (circle one):   M   F

Marriage Status (check one):   single _____ married _____ divorced

Age Range: 15-18 _____ 19-24 _____ 25-35 _____ 36-45 _____ 46-55 _____ 56-65

Highest Education Level Completed (check only one):

Did not complete HS _____ HS _____ AA _____ BA/S _____ MA   PHD

General Occupation:
(example: sales person) _____

Hobbies/Interests (check all that apply)

_____ Outdoor Sports
_____ Video Games
_____ Board Games
_____ Card Games
_____ Movies
_____ Books
_____ Other

Model Exactly What You See

The table we are building to begin with is `Player`, using a definition that looks something like this:

❑   Player – Information about a Solitaire Player as captured by the Psychology department registration form

Start with Labels

One of the best ways to begin is to make a list of all the labels you find on the form. We have so much flexibility today in handling data with dynamic screen creation and looping queries, that we have almost forgotten the old days of simple, fill-in-the-blank-style data gathering. A form doesn't offer much flexibility (in fact it is frowned upon). So at the beginning, go with the notion that the data elements are singular, stable columns supporting a form. It doesn't have to have any more sophisticated a structure than the form itself.

Reports can be a little more complicated in that they already have one-to-many relationships in the data display. Don't force everything into one table if that doesn't make sense. Start with what is easy to understand and build from there.

Generally a single form can begin as a single table. Simply taking all the headings from the form above will give us a beginning place as a flat table that looks the one on the left of the diagram below. You will find many, many tables in production-deployed applications that look a lot like this. Forms that have been simply made into database tables without any thought to the future.

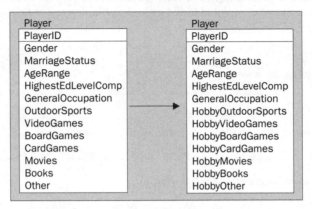

At this point we need to review these names and consider how descriptive they really are. The last six columns are actually to do with Hobbies, so we should alter the column names to reflect this. The resulting table is shown on the right-hand side of the previous diagram. One of the things you are going to look for right away, are the columns that seem to repeat. Without the hint in the names you can easily miss them.

Apply Naming Standards

No matter which one of these table structures you start with don't let it go one step further like this. Even when you are pressed against a wall, get the column names set up for future analysis. When you revisit this table in the future, you will at least have names that help you out. In other words get your attribute types in place. Every column must be one of these (or the ones defined by your data management group) and the attribute type should be at the end of the column name no matter where they are in the source names. Look back to the previous chapter if you need a reminder of what attribute types are available to us.

While you are looking at the column names, make sure that they are complete enough to stand on their own. Add extra modifiers if you think there may be confusion in the future.

> **Remember table and column names are almost always permanent once they are built for an application. Even if we get to enhance the structure in the future we rarely get the opportunity to change table and column names.**

The best you can do is make sure that you aren't responsible for another table filled with columns named Column1, Column2, Date, Name, Description, and so on, being brought into the world.

First Version Column Name	New Column Name
PlayerID	PlayerID
Gender	GenderFlg
MarriageStatus	MarriageStatusNm
AgeRange	AgeRangeNm
HighestEdLevelComp	HighestEdLevelCompCd
GeneralOccupation	GeneralOccupationTxt
HobbyOutdoorSports	HobbyOutdoorSportsFlg
HobbyVideoGames	HobbyVideoGamesFlg
HobbyBoardGames	HobbyBoardGamesFlg
HobbyCardGames	HobbyCardGamesFlg
HobbyMovies	HobbyMoviesFlg
HobbyBooks	HobbyBooksFlg
HobbyOther	HobbyOtherFlg

Introducing our class words to the second table structure we developed originally leaves us with the following structure:

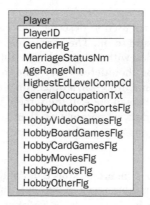

It's not 3NF and it's not flexible. You would need to alter the structure to add in a new hobby. Any deviation from codes that are expected could cause reporting anomalies because there is no way to know what they mean. GeneralOccupation might as well be named Stuff because there is no way to add any integrity check to it.

It's not pretty, but it works. At least you have standardized the names and created definitions for everything. You could take this table and add it to the design we concluded with in the last chapter since it supports the data requirements of the clients (today).

Really, in a requirement as small as this (especially since a logical model already exists), you should be able to do a quick and dirty logical design first. Please look at this as just an emergency contingency measure. Most modelers would say that stopping here is a waste of time. Again, it breaks our hearts to do this, but it happens. So let's take it at least one step further. There are some easy things we can do to give it just a bit more quality and flexibility. Let's look at them now.

Create Lookup Tables

You know that the form, as it was given to you, has a restricted list of values for three columns: `MarriageStausNm`, `AgeRangeNm`, and `HighestEdLevelCompCd`. Try to assume that you are dealing with what is probably the first version of the form and that someone is going to realize they left off the 'Widow/er' from Marriage status, '12-14 year olds' from the Age Range, and the 'GED' from the Education level. At least if the list of values live in a table, a new value can be added without a database structure or programming change to add those values to the hard-coded list that is being managed in a check constraint like this:

```
CREATE TABLE Player (
    GenderFlg Varchar2(1) NULL
        CHECK (GenderFlg IN ('M', 'F'),
    MarriageStatusNm Varchar2(10) NULL
        CHECK (MarriageStatusNm IN
        ('Single','Married','Divorced')
    AgeRangeNm Varchar2(5) NULL
        CHECK (Age IN ('15-18', '19-24', '25-35',
        '36-45', '46-55', '56-65'))
...
```

Hard coded (or 'Nailed Up') is the term used to describe data values explicitly stored in screens, procedures, triggers, views, HTML, and so on. They are values that are not dynamically selected out of a set. Frequently values are hard coded without enough thought being given to the maintenance steps (and therefore dollars) that have to be shouldered every time the list changes in the smallest way. For example, if the set of values is kept in a drop-down object on a screen, every time the list is changed you need to deploy a new version of the screen code. If the screen, trigger, procedure, or view code uses hard-coded filters and 'IF ... THEN' data set parameters, then you must know what programming code needs revising and change *all* of it *appropriately* when a business rule changes.

> **Rule of Thumb** – All data values should be stored in database tables. All business restrictions of data values should be stored in database tables.

Give the data some room to grow. Look to break out some of the columns in the current table design into new tables. In this case we can break out `MarriageStatus`, `EducationLevel`, and `AgeRange`. The relationships between these tables and the main table are non-identifying. At this stage we'll use a cardinality of zero, one, or many. Our table design would now look like this:

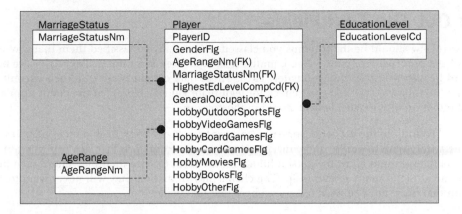

Look Again for Important Data Sets

At this point we need to look again and determine whether we really have the data sets that we need. Look at the form again. The reason we have a pile of Hobby flags is that the form presented the data set as options that allowed multiples. Currently each option is a 'True/False' or 'Yes/No' data value. If you analyze the data without the business rules you might be lead to believe that 'Yes/No' is the data set we are looking at here.

> **Not all the data sets are found in the fields of a form. Sometimes they are in the labels themselves.**

What we really want to capture here is Hobby. Right now it has seven members of the set defined. Pull `Hobby` out as a separate table. Can more than one Player enjoy a Hobby? Yes, that's why we had all those flags. It is also obvious that one Player can enjoy more than one Hobby. So we have a many-to-many relationship between the set of Hobbies and the set of Players. At this point we need to create an intersection (associative) table and remove all the Hobby flags from `Player`.

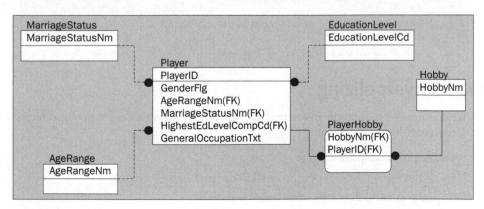

Check Out The Text Fields

The next review should be the columns you classed as 'Text'. You classified them that way because they seem to have unformatted, multi-valued, multi-element, or free form notes. Text fields are basically just 'stuff' and I assure you they do legitimately exist. These data elements can't (in their current form) be disciplined to follow rules. You can't check for legitimate values or prevent the client from altering the original intention of the data element stored in the column.

The '…Txt' column in the model is `GeneralOccupationTxt`. Look back over your notes from the initial discussion with the client and consider what sort of information they are expecting to document. If they feel they want to allow the person filling out the form to note multiple values, then break out the column into a one-to-many relationship. The clients may think that they will never want to report or search on that field, but you need to assume here that they will.

I have seen text blocks take on such a life force that you would be stunned. Suddenly a poor programmer is parsing for dates, asterisks, and pound signs to identify different data elements and then forcing an application response due to the findings. At best if you build a physical design to encourage single entries, you will have built a structure for the development of one or many data sets. It will provide a place for the expansion of importance of new data elements. At worst you designed an extra table.

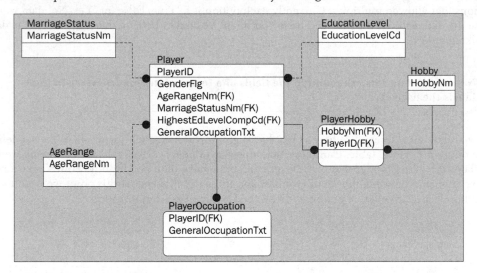

Continue Physicalizing

Everything that needed to be done in the previous chapter to polish a design needs to happen here as well. As a reminder here we need to:

- ❑ Select appropriate primary keys
- ❑ Review the foreign keys for correct definitions and names
- ❑ Give some generic data type and size information
- ❑ Double-check naming conventions, and re-evaluate the model
- ❑ Add in details which may be pertinent to the rest of the team

Primary Key Choice

Look closely at the current key choices. Every column that is a longish text field should be thought about, since Text data elements almost never stay as the first primary key choice. They are just too undisciplined. Since `GeneralOccupationTxt` is going to be far too general to use as a primary key, let's move it below the line in the `PlayerOccupation` table and create an ID column instead. While it is possible at this stage to move `PlayerID` out of the PK (since IDs can be fully unique), we'll keep it in for now, since I like to keep as much of the natural key intact as possible.

Now look at the Name columns. Most Name type data elements that end up in a primary key position can easily be replaced by a code to shorten the migrating value. The only issue here is that you would need to ask the clients if they want to take responsibility for a new data element. Right now all the data elements they want are on the form. You are proposing a new one. IDs are different. They are used for performance tuning and are never displayed to the clients. At this point you should make a note to discuss this with the client at the review meeting scheduled for when you have your design to present to them. It's important that you ensure that the client is fully aware of any implications your design may have on their system, and its maintenance.

Most clients seem to like codes when they have to type. They want to use 'S' instead of 'Single', 'VG' instead of 'Video Games'. But they generally want it the other way around on reports. They want the full name. The important point here is to help them do both. Give them long names if they only have codes, and use long names to build codes that are as intuitive as possible. Document your coding alongside your model to ensure the minimum of confusion. If the client agrees that your coding convention is suitable for the system then the new model looks like this:

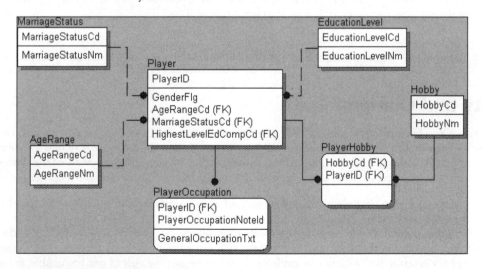

Physical Detail Characteristics

Now you need to estimate data types, sizes, `nulls`, and population statistics to give a completed model to the DBA. Highlight the level of precision that you have provided, and in particular note areas where your estimate is very general. This will aid the DBA in assessing the physical requirements they will have of the system. You may need to add the default operational data columns to the tables as well. Go back to the design standards and make sure that even this fast form of analysis has followed as many of the rules as possible.

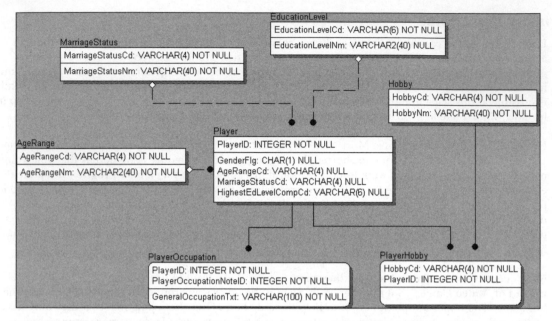

Often you will allow much less restrictive choices for the details in this type of modeling than when we can do a more thorough analysis of the data elements. Make things a little larger than you see on the form. You need to assign physical characteristics that will support the broad spectrum of data values in the future without having much of a clue as to what that will be.

> **Most non-key columns should be NULL allowed unless it states otherwise on the form.**

Quality and Compromise

What now? You are probably going to cut some of your walkthroughs out but you do need to re-evaluate and justify your design before it goes to the DBA to be built in test. In the same way that we went backward on this kind of modeling, so you will probably go backward on the review of the design. This time around the team gets to look at it first, since the design has to fit into their development schedule.

You now have eighteen data elements and seven tables, in comparison to the thirteen data elements and single table we started with. Not a huge difference in object quantities, but a huge difference in quality, integrity, and expandability for the data elements themselves. Are seven tables harder to code for than one? Oh yes. So why in the world is this a better design that the nice single table we had at the beginning? It certainly isn't quicker to implement and increases the risk of not being able to meet the deadlines that weren't changed when the new requirements came in.

The key question here is, what do you do if next week you are asked to put a new field in the database describing the probability for game success as a factor of a hobby for a Player? Would it fit in our nice single table? Sure, as seven separate new columns. Each one of the Hobby columns would have to have a corresponding probability factor column. And if there were three or four more interesting pieces of information dealing with hobbies, then the table column quantity sky-rockets, and the application impacts become bigger and bigger.

You see that kind of column growth quite frequently in applications that didn't recognize and remove buried lists, or chose to denormalize on purpose. They have repeating groups that go on and on. Not only that but, having implemented that design, it is extremely difficult to revise the design and physical implementation, without incurring considerable cost (and downtime for the application).

What do those flat table column additions do to the front-end and the reports? Can you see the simple input screen becoming more and more cluttered? Do you see blocks of code managing those repeating groups replicating over and over? Do you see the danger of missing a maintenance point if the code needs to be altered?

Now, think about querying that kind of data. How do you find out how many hobbies players list on average? Instead of a nice coded AVG(COUNT ... GROUP BY PlayerID) query, you have to do loop analysis to get a quantity on hobbies. The same goes for any hobby owned column that shows up in the future. Reporting becomes increasingly difficult, since it has to combine large numbers of disparate values. The bottom line is that adding new data elements in the future will be a much larger task if we leave normalization until later.

On the other hand, it is best to acknowledge up front that project teams have to pick and choose between physical designs the way a family has to pick between houses to buy. How much can you afford up front when compared against the available budget and prioritized requirements? Just remind everyone that whatever is chosen has a huge probability of being around for a long, long time. A poor choice at this stage will be around for some time to come (though the person making the decision might not be).

The structure we have now lends itself to enhancement and future needs. What have we gained?

❑ We have isolated as many of the data sets as we could find

❑ We can now expand their owned data elements easily over time

❑ We can now set up new relationships to simple data sets

❑ We have simplified future integration with other systems because we have reduced the parochial combinations as much as possible

The new model presents a fertile environment for growth. Build for the future if you can afford it. If you have to let it go forward with the flat table, at least you applied naming standards and documented what the business rules really are that will be buried in it.

That's as far as this one can go for now. We have taken a tiny little form and made what is actually a very normalized data structure for it. Try out the Normal form questions on it and prove it to yourself.

At this stage you could continue with a further backward step and pull the logical design out of it, though we won't consider that here. It is also possible to add this new section into the larger project model. It would slip in very easily, although right now we have a shadow entity called Person with a PersonId. We would have to change either our table here to Person, or modify the foreign keys to be valid for relationships with Player.

This is about 6-8 hours of work when you include the definitions, quality checking, and report generation. Almost any team will give you a day, and it will be worth it both to the application and the clients in the future. This 6-8 hours spent up front developing a normalized design could be worth hundreds of hours of maintenance in the future.

Now let's try an exercise that has a more complicated set of data rules embedded in it.

Something a Bit More Challenging

The Psychology department has decided that they also want to keep track of the students who help them with the research project. They need to keep certain information about them for tax purposes and want to add it to their project.

Firstly I would hope that your project manager would push back such a huge addition to the requirements at such a late date. Sometimes your ability to provide a 'quick and dirty' model for them gives the project manager the ammunition they need to explain how large a task actually is. However, we'll take the 'worst case' scenario here, and assume that we are still up against a hard deadline as before. Once again it is 'emergency' data modeling we're performing here. Let's begin by taking a look at the registration form:

Student Employment Registration
For use by the Psychology department   Date of Registration _____

Person Info:

Name: Last _____ First _____ Middle _____

Nickname: _____

Date of Birth: _____ Social Security Number _____

Place of Birth: City _____ State _____ Country _____

Phone Number: Day _____ Evening _____

Email Address: _____

Mailing Address: Street _____ City _____ State _____ Country _____

Education History

Type	Name of School	City, State, Country	Graduation Year	GPA	Degree or Cert
High School					
College					
Graduate School					

Previous Employment Info:

Company Name: _____

Company Address: Street _____ City _____ State _____ Country _____

Occupation Name: _____

Applying the same general principles that we outlined earlier in the chapter, we begin by noting down exactly what we see, and create one large preliminary list of data elements that could resemble a flat table. We do this so that we don't lose anything during our analysis and you can see how easy it would be to lose something in this long set:

I repeated section labels in names if they applied to multiple fields like those after the heading 'Name:' or in the Education history table. This prevents duplication of column names in the first pass when the form labels have been simplified.

This table doesn't currently have a primary key, because we have no idea what is going to make the record unique at this stage. But we need something to use as a bookmark for a key. Some would elevate Social Security Number as a unique identifier to the primary key, but only a certain set of the student body will have these numbers. Resist the temptation to use Social Security Numbers for much of anything. This is sensitive information, which in many cases may well need to be encrypted to meet data protection act requirements.

When in doubt and in a hurry, create a surrogate key ID field to act as the primary key.

Classification of the Data Elements

Organize and rename the data elements by class word. Here is what you are starting with versus a list of renamed columns:

First Version Column Name	New Column Name
CollegeCityStateCountry	CollegeCityStateCountryTxt
CollegeDegree	CollegeDegreeCd
CollegeGPA	CollegeGPANb
CollegeGraduationYear	CollegeGraduationYearNb
CollegeName	CollegeNm
CompanyAddressCity	CompanyAddressCityNm
CompanyAddressCountry	CompanyAddressCountryCd
CompanyAddressState	CompanyAddressStateCd
CompanyAddressStreet	CompanyAddressStreetTxt
CompanyName	EmpCurrentCompanyNm
DateOfBirth	EmpBirthDt
DateOfRegistration	EmpRegistrationDt
EmailAddress	EmpEmailAddressTxt
GraduateSchoolCityStateCountry	GradSchoolCityStateCountryTxt
GraduateSchoolDegree	GradSchoolDegreeCd
GraduateSchoolGPA	GradSchoolGPANb
GraduateSchoolGraduationYear	GradSchoolGraduationYearNb
GraduateSchoolName	GradSchoolNm
HighSchoolCityStateCountry	HighSchoolCityStateCountryTxt
HighSchoolDegree	HighSchoolDegreeCd
HighSchoolGPA	HighSchoolGPANb
HighSchoolGraduationYear	HighSchoolGraduationYearNb
HighSchoolName	HighSchoolNm
MailingAddressCity	EmpMailingAddressCityNm
MailingAddressCountry	EmpMailingAddressCountryCd
MailingAddressState	EmpMailingAddressStateCd
MailingAddressStreet	EmpMailingAddressStreetTxt
NameFirst	EmpFirstNm
NameLast	EmpLastNm
NameMiddle	EmpMiddleNm
Nickname	EmpNicknameTxt

First Version Column Name	New Column Name
OccupationName	EmpOccupationTxt
PhoneNumberDay	EmpDayPhoneNb
PhoneNumberEvening	EmpEveningPhoneNb
PlaceOfBirthCity	EmpPlaceOfBirthCityNm
PlaceOfBirthCountry	EmpPlaceOfBirthCountryCd
PlaceOfBirthState	EmpPlaceOfBirthStateCd
SocialSecurityNumber	EmpSocialSecurityNb

If this is as far as you can go with the physical table design, you need to look at abbreviating some of the more lengthy names.

This will leave our flat file looking like this:

```
Employee
EmpID
EmpRegistrationDt
EmpLastNm
EmpFirstNm
EmpMiddleNm
EmpNickNameTxt
EmpBirthDt
EmpSocialSecurityNb
EmpPlaceOfBirthCityNm
EmpPlaceOfBirthStateCd
EmpPlaceOfBirthCountryCd
EmpDayPhoneNb
EmpEveningPhoneNb
EmpEmailAddressTxt
EmpMailingAddressStreetTxt
EmpMailingAddressCityNm
EmpMailingAddressStateCd
MailingAddressCountryCd
HighSchoolNm
HighSchoolCityStateCountryTxt
HighSchoolGraduationYearNb
HighSchoolGPANb
HighSchoolDegreeCd
CollegeNm
CollegeCityStateCountryTxt
CollegeGraduationYearNb
CollegeGPANb
CollegeDegreeCd
GraduateSchoolNm
GraduateSchoolCityStateCountryTxt
GraduateSchoolGraduationYearNb
GraduateSchoolGPANb
GraduateSchoolDegreeCd
CompanyNm
CompanyAddressStreetTxt
CompanyAddressCityNm
CompanyAddressStateCd
CompanyAddressCountryCd
EmpOccupationTxt
```

Now we need to look over the text data again, and look for any other useful information we need to include in our design.

Text Fields

We need to examine the text data fields in our model, to determine any important data elements that are currently obscured within them. In this case the relevant fields are:

- ❏ CollegeCityStateCountryTxt
- ❏ GradSchoolCityStateCountryTxt
- ❏ HighSchoolCityStateCountryTxt
- ❏ CompanyAddressStreetTxt
- ❏ EmpEmailAddressTxt
- ❏ EmpMailingAddressStreetTxt
- ❏ EmpNicknameTxt
- ❏ EmpOccupationTxt

To aid us in this task we should speak to the client to determine any expected patterns or rules regarding the data collected in these text fields. Get the clients to give you sample data for these. If they have already received completed forms, take a look over them to aid your understanding of the data collected. You need to know what they are expecting (not what you are expecting) before you can analyze them with any confidence. If for instance, the client is expecting values like 'William Cody, Buffalo Bill' in the EmpNicknameTxt column, it should be reviewed as a possible repeating value as you go forth into the Normal form rule analysis. You won't know until you ask.

Street addresses are usually left as text, since there is generally little value (except for the Post Office) in splitting out the number of the building, street or route name, PO Box number, and apartment number. Remember though, that there are many real and distinct data elements buried in address text fields. If it became important, for example, to find everyone living on the 1000 block of 'Main' street, a programmer would have a hard time parsing for the values.

You probably already wondered why I left the …CityStateCountry… multi-element columns together. You almost instinctively pull such labels apart. However, my rule of thumb is that the first pass should document what you are given as closely as possible. The form designer didn't create separate fields for different data elements so maybe you shouldn't either. Starting with what you see gives you a starting place for data element discussions referring to things that should be familiar to the client.

There may be reasons unknown to you regarding why the form was created that way. If the clients don't care about the distinct data elements that make up Address then they may not care (other than for information) what is being put in the combined '…CityStateCountryTxt' columns either. Especially as those data elements are treated differently in different parts of the form. Just make sure that you classify them as Txt so that you and the programmers will know in the future that the data here is extremely undisciplined.

It is easy to assume a level of detail that isn't necessary. If you hadn't looked at it as a modeler, it is likely that no one would have thought to pull those data elements apart at all. A lot of forms are put into databases on a 'One Blank – One Column' rule.

When you encounter no desire for true data integrity, you may want to compress several fields on the form together and simplify the data. Why not offer a `FullAddressBlockTxt` of `VARCHAR(2000)`? They probably have separate lines for address just because it doesn't fit otherwise on paper. On checking with the clients, they tell us that in this case all of the addresses are basically informational. They don't expect to report on it.

> **Try not to add extra detail because you know it exists in the real world. Unless you are building with corporate standards in mind, then the customer knows best, and you should implement their requirements.**

Send the fields that you think are unclear or uncontrolled to the clients for clarification and then respond in the model appropriately.

Now let's look at the rest of what we are dealing with. This time, let's use normalization to see if we can quickly find some of the simple data sets buried in this flat table.

First Normal Form (1NF)

Look at the list of columns in our table. Remember 1NF requires every column of the table to depend on the *key* exclusively. What do you make of these columns?

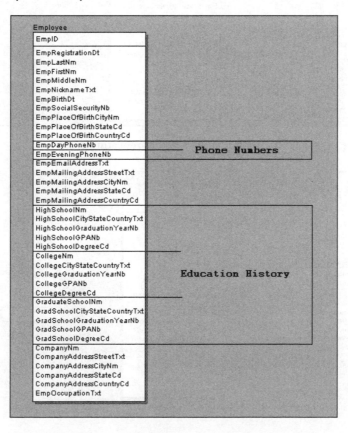

One of the industry standard phrases we use about 1NF is 'Remove repeating groups'. Data elements that repeat can't possibly depend entirely on the key. `PhoneNumber` occurs twice. A phone number for an Employee is dependent on two pieces of information, namely the Employee and the Type of phone number. There is a one-to-two relationship between `Employee` and `Employee Phone` at the moment.

When you look for repeating groups, concentrate on the back part of the column name and clumps of columns that seem to be grouped in repeating patterns. In this case 'Name, Text, Number, Number, Code' happens three times in a row for school information. That is another set of repeaters, even more dramatic than the single columns for phone numbers. Each type of education history for an Employee has a whole set of informative columns. The data about one level of education for an Employee depends on the Employee and the Level of education involved. Here there is a 'one-to-three' relationship at the moment. These columns are easily broken out from the current flat table to be made more relational, as follows:

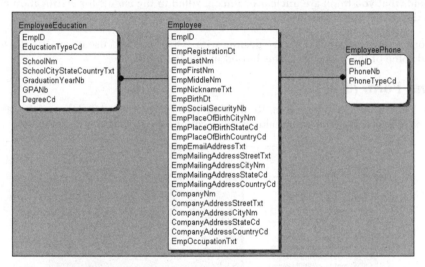

Let's now consider the Address elements with regard to repeating groups:

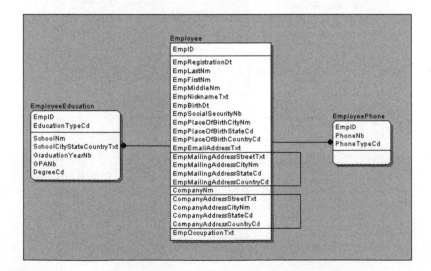

Repeating values have to do with multiple instances of the same data elements allowed for a member of a set, like the three education information instances that we just removed. So you need to be careful with this one. These addresses aren't both about Employee are they?

Company address does not depend on Employee, rather on the set of Companies. Pull out just the Company information leaving the Employee address behind and create a Company table. Then relate it back to Employee. Note that Company information in the Employee table is really a violation of 3NF. Even though we are resolving 1NF violations, we have suddenly resolved a 3NF violation. Resolving NF violations is not always a sequential process.

The fact is that this set of data elements, repeated, helped you locate a problem, but it won't be handled the same way we handled `Education`. You need to be aware of *why* columns are repeating. Like this:

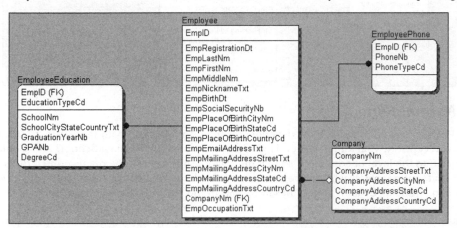

Do you see how far we have come, and rather quickly at that? Don't think that because you are being pressed to complete a fast solution, you can't bring value to the design quickly. Granted, even repeating groups are not always easy to recognize, but there is always the notion of going for 'low hanging fruit'.

Our clients may not want us to go any further than this. Believe it or not, sometimes rules get in their way. It is quite likely that they will appreciate the new expanded flexibility of `EmployeePhone` and `EmployeeEducation`. The new `Company` table provides them with the means to analyze the Company an employee worked for, something which was not possible using the previous design. However, remember that we should always be sensitive to the clients' needs here. We need to consider questions such as whether this is an Enterprise-critical development project, where the structure may need to integrate with other applications, or a department-specific project. Keep in mind that even the department-level development projects (especially if they are successful) have the potential of becoming Enterprise-critical in the future. If the checks for these student employees ever need to be cut by the Payroll department, then you may need to be much more sensitive to what is happening here and maybe even suggest a different business solution than expanding this application.

We are beginning to see more of a relational design growing from our single registration form. Just a small reminder here that at every breakout, you need to return to the question of Normal forms and ensure that your design conforms to them. Look, for example, at `EmployeeEducation`, which we just created. What does the `SchoolCityStateCountry` have to do with the `EmpID` or `EducationTypeCd`? School location information is actually dependent on the school, rather than the employee or the degree, so we should create a `School` table, in order to comply with first normal form.

Our modified design now looks as follows:

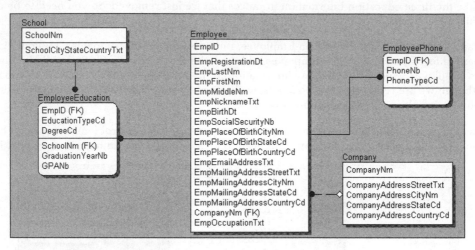

Second Normal Form (2NF)

Look at `EmployeeEducation`. How dependent is the `DegreeCd` on both the `PlayerID` and the `EducationTypeCd`? Can a Player get a High School diploma in Graduate School? No. Choices of degree are restricted to the level of education, so that the relationship needs to be managed in a different table. Not only that, but no matter what the registration form tells us, you can get both your Master's and your Doctorate in Graduate School. Degree has to be part of the key of `EmployeeEducation`.

Make sure that when you discover something that would change the rules of the paper form, you review your findings with the client. Usually they tell you that they forgot about that or have allowed people to write on the back under those circumstances. If they do, then press them slightly and find out what else people write on the backs of forms.

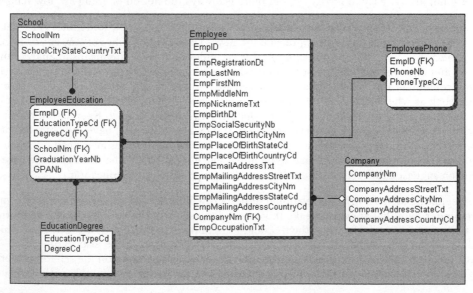

Third Normal Form (3NF)

Here in 3NF we try to ensure that every attribute of every member of every set depends on *nothing but the key*. How about all of the geographical data elements in this model? What do you make of the City, State, and Country attributes? Can the value of a State 'Quebec' be a state of the country 'Mexico'? Should we pull out the data sets and try to find the relationships in this kind of data modeling?

Well, the nice thing about doing the analysis this way is that you can save every level of breakout for the client/team/DBA/programmer to look over. In effect you have a set of denormalization options that can easily be put back in. However, if you don't get as much of the analysis as possible documented, nobody knows the options.

Let's take the geography sets out and consider the relationships. For example, if you pull out an atlas, you'll find that there is a city named Newport in the states of Washington, Oregon, Arizona, Nebraska, Minnesota, Missouri, Indiana, Ohio, Kentucky, Tennessee, North Carolina, Virginia, Pennsylvania, New York, New Jersey, Vermont, Maine, Rhode Island, and New Hampshire (Wow!). As a result, the entities City and State will have a many-to-many relationship that needs to be resolved with an intersection table, as we've seen in the previous three chapters. Double-check the role names for the two relationships from StateCity to Employee. A modeling tool will just migrate one set in unless you role name them. It would look like this:

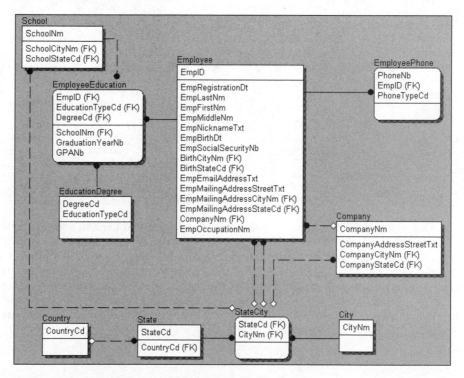

Boyce–Codd Normal Form (BCNF)

Here is where the restricted lists are born. The Boyce-Codd Normal form is the reason for creating separate tables to control what are often tiny sets of reused data, in the form of drop-down or pick lists. BCNF says that every attribute must be identified by a key. The unique list must be part of a set.

Is the list of `EducationTypeCds` managed anywhere? No. Is it a unique data set? Yes, certainly. How about `PhoneTypeCds`? I can easily see them as lists being managed by the clients. Let's separate them out, giving the client the option of allowing the codes full names if required. Now the model looks like this:

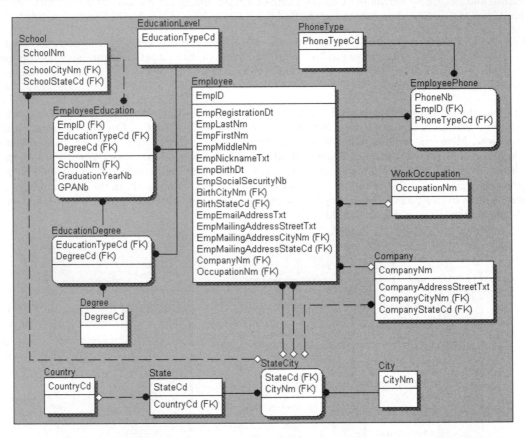

This is where we will stop for this one. To polish the model we would need to add all the definitions, revisit the primary keys, and determine the data types, lengths, precisions, and NULLs. Review your design again, look back at the original client requirements, and document your analysis to ensure that you present the team with the highest quality data analysis you can under the existing constraints. Take time to scan for known weaknesses and identify the things you perceive as trouble spots. You may need to justify some of your key decisions. You may want to document your analysis in layers the way we built it. It provides a good way of walking through your analysis, reminding you of what was gained with each step.

Something like this:

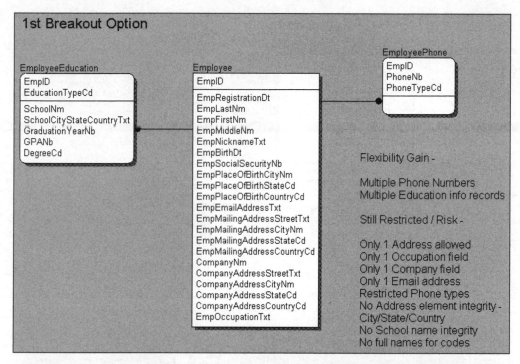

1st Breakout Option

EmployeeEducation
- EmpID
- EducationTypeCd

- SchoolNm
- SchoolCityStateCountryTxt
- GraduationYearNb
- GPANb
- DegreeCd

Employee
- EmpID

- EmpRegistrationDt
- EmpLastNm
- EmpFirstNm
- EmpMiddleNm
- EmpNicknameTxt
- EmpBirthDt
- EmpSocialSecurityNb
- EmpPlaceOfBirthCityNm
- EmpPlaceOfBirthStateCd
- EmpPlaceOfBirthCountryCd
- EmpEmailAddressTxt
- EmpMailingAddressStreetTxt
- EmpMailingAddressCityNm
- EmpMailingAddressStateCd
- EmpMailingAddressCountryCd
- CompanyNm
- CompanyAddressStreetTxt
- CompanyAddressCityNm
- CompanyAddressStateCd
- CompanyAddressCountryCd
- EmpOccupationTxt

EmployeePhone
- EmpID
- PhoneNb
- PhoneTypeCd

Flexibility Gain -

Multiple Phone Numbers
Multiple Education info records

Still Restricted / Risk -

Only 1 Address allowed
Only 1 Occupation field
Only 1 Company field
Only 1 Email address
Restricted Phone types
No Address element integrity -
City/State/Country
No School name integrity
No full names for codes

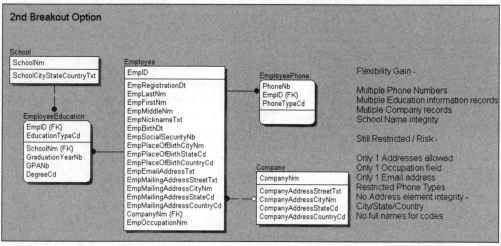

2nd Breakout Option

School
- SchoolNm
- SchoolCityStateCountryTxt

EmployeeEducation
- EmpID (FK)
- EducationTypeCd

- SchoolNm (FK)
- GraduationYearNb
- GPANb
- DegreeCd

Employee
- EmpID

- EmpRegistrationDt
- EmpLastNm
- EmpFirstNm
- EmpMiddleNm
- EmpNicknameTxt
- EmpBirthDt
- EmpSocialSecurityNb
- EmpPlaceOfBirthCityNm
- EmpPlaceOfBirthStateCd
- EmpPlaceOfBirthCountryCd
- EmpEmailAddressTxt
- EmpMailingAddressStreetTxt
- EmpMailingAddressCityNm
- EmpMailingAddressStateCd
- EmpMailingAddressCountryCd
- CompanyNm (FK)
- EmpOccupationNm

EmployeePhone
- PhoneNb
- EmpID (FK)
- PhoneTypeCd

Company
- CompanyNm

- CompanyAddressStreetTxt
- CompanyAddressCityNm
- CompanyAddressStateCd
- CompanyAddressCountryCd

Flexibility Gain -

Multiple Phone Numbers
Multiple Education information records
Mutiple Company records
School Name integrity

Still Restricted / Risk -

Only 1 Addresses allowed
Only 1 Occupation field
Only 1 Email address
Restricted Phone Types
No Address element integrity -
City/State/Country
No full names for codes

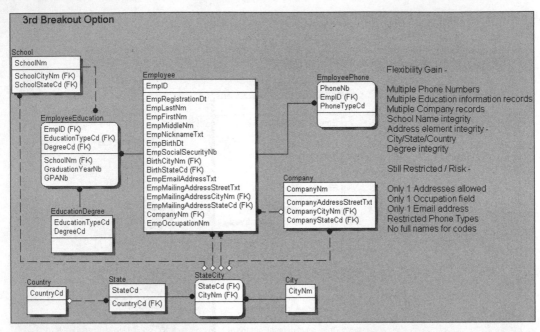

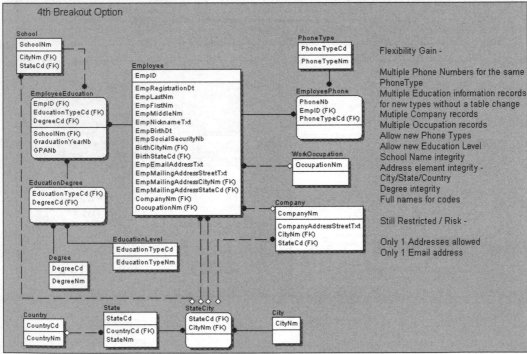

It would be a small task to upgrade this to a logical design. If they choose to take this scope forward to development, then you may want to bring the data elements all the way back to the logical data model at your leisure.

Remember that, if you integrate models that you designed separately, then you need to look for integration points. Find the data sets that are really the same even if they are treated or named slightly differently. For example, there is a similarity between the `WorkOccupation` table in this model and the `GeneralOccupation` text in the `Player` model. We would want to find out what, if any, difference there was between the set of `Employees` and `Players`. Do they share any attributes as they are both types of people? What difference is there between `HighestEdLevelCompCd` and `Degrees`?

If our clients require that the model we have developed should be integrated with Player and Solitaire, then we would list this as a design requirement in our initial scope development phase. This would ensure that we avoided building a similar structure twice.

Other Physical-Only Designs

There are other kinds of table that we might run across from time to time that are 100% physical. These are the tables used to manage the working application, and will not be found in a logical design (except maybe in a meta data model). DBAs and programmers generally design them for database maintenance, but if we manage the models then they may become part of our documentation if so requested. They are not modeled in the purest form of the word in that they do not support the client business process, and never go from Conceptual to Logical to Physical. However, it is worth being aware of them.

They generally fall into three categories:

- ❑   Operational
- ❑   Staging
- ❑   Archive

Operational Tables

Sometimes, at the application management level, data needs to be kept that you would never have modeled. You might find tables that hold filenames, dates, and status from downloads that happen to synchronize one table with another one. You might see operational tables that manage partitioning of data by value for certain login names. For instance Login X is able to see Florida Employee data. All of the Employee data is in one table, but a view is dynamically built that partitions it based on an Operational Security table.

Operational data doesn't have to be in separate tables, and is quite frequently tacked onto the end of your data tables in the form of Create dates, User IDs, or Security flags at the record level. This kind of operational data is still dealing with the members of the data sets. There are tables that manage sequence number generation in some databases. They include LastNumberAssigned. You may see operational tables managing statistics on the activity of the application. There are lots of reasons for them to be hanging around.

Operational tables are often seen floating around the edges of physical designs with no relationships to anything. They are there to hold bits of information that the application needs to remember to perform some of its functions correctly. They deal with timing, security, and business rules based on value. The DBA adds these tables to the database, and you end up adding the tables to the model as you get deeper in the project development and closer to full scale system testing.

Staging Tables

Staging tables are usually completely segregated from the application data. They are used for the conversion of data from one system to another, in a one-time or periodic load process. For the most part, staging table design will be handed to you by the programmers who design the conversion technical requirements.

You can see here that the Employee data is coming in from an outside source. The programmers are going to have to find a way to parse out the Last/First/Middle name because the data coming in concatenates it all together. They also have to try to figure out the Address data elements and translate the Dun and Bradstreet company number into a Company name.

The Staging table also includes a Source name, Load date, and Error code, probably for feedback to the source system that a record was unloadable for some reason.

Staging tables are notorious for not having primary keys. They need to be large and flexible in order to transfer data that may not have the same stringent quality rules embedded in it that the target system has. Programmers need a 'Sandbox' working area to catch and clean the data before it can move to its new home. This is often called ETL effort (Extraction/Transformation/Loading). A Transactional system may only need these types of table to support the initial load. Data Warehouse applications may need them to permanently support this type of data loading.

Archive Tables

The last kind of physical-only table you may see is the archive table. Generally these look almost exactly like some other table in the database, both in structure and in name. They are used as a form of 'Nearest Line Storage' for large active data tables like the one below for inactive employees who are removed from the Employee table following specific business rules:

Employee	InactiveEmployeeHistory
EmpID	EmpID
EmpRegistrationDt	EmpRegistrationDt
EmpLastNm	EmpLastNm
EmpFirstNm	EmpFirstNm
EmpMiddleNm	EmpMiddleNm
EmpNickNameTxt	EmpNickNameTxt
EmpBirthDt	EmpBirthDt
EmpSocialSecurityNb	EmpSocialSecurityNb
BirthCityNm	BirthCityNm
BirthStateCd	BirthStateCd
EmpEmailAddressTxt	EmpEmailAddressTxt
EmpMailingAddressStreetTxt	EmpMailingAddressStreetTxt
EmpMailingAddressCityNm	EmpMailingAddressCityNm
EmpMailingAddressStateCd	EmpMailingAddressStateCd
CompanyNm	CompanyNm
OccupationNm	OccupationNm

There is also the kind of history table that exists for audit purposes. You may only want to keep the most current version of a record in a data table. But you may need to be able to see the history of all the updates and 'Whodunits' for research purposes. Again you almost never model these kinds of requirements, the DBA simply adds a physical table to take the primary key of each record, and adds a timestamp to separate versions by creation time.

Summary

This chapter has considered good practice in the event of having to leap straight into a physical-only model. This is often the case when there is insufficient project time and/or money to follow a rigorous conceptual/logical/physical modeling methodology. We have looked at what can be done to improve upon existing physical models, prior to their implementation, in order to ensure that the application being developed not only runs smoothly, but also has scope for expansion to meet future requirements. In particular we have noted the need to:

❑ Document client requirements accurately

❑ Review as much data as possible to aid your design

❑ Meet the requirements of Normal form in your design

❑ Verify overlap with existing models and projects, to avoid unnecessary repetition of analysis.

It only remains to emphasize that these steps are to be taken only when time or budget constraints don't allow for a more rigorous analysis. For the most accurate data models for physical implementation, we should always carry out the conceptual/logical/physical methodology outlined throughout the second half of this book. Don't be tempted to rush straight to the physical model; it will always be a 'make do' approach to data modeling.

- Dimensional Model Basics
- The Solitaire Survey Model
  - *Targeting the Facts*
  - *The Game Data Mart*
  - *GameMove Data Mart*
  - *Finish Up*
- Summary

Dimensional Data Modeling

Dimensional data modeling is a technique used to create tables designed to store data in data warehouses or data marts. It is a disciplined denormalization technique that tunes data for fast query results in the case of huge quantities of table rows. Such systems are termed OLAP (Online Analytical Processing) systems, since they are used in business analysis and decision support work to develop reports and historical trends, such as sales figures. These systems are organized in such a way so as to optimize querying of data, with fast retrieval of data the key design aim.

This method of design is very different from what we learned about in the previous two chapters, where we practiced the style of physical design that followed rules discovered by searching for and applying Normal forms to the data. We created a table design disciplined to manage single, atomic data sets in their purest form. It is designed, and subsequently tuned, for insert, update, and deletion of those singular data elements. These databases are termed OLTP (Online Transaction Processes) systems, since they involve a large number of transactions, usually from a large number of users, with constant manipulation of the data. They are tuned with user transactions in mind, rather than data retrieval and analysis. While strictly normalized structures ensure absolute data integrity, they are generally inefficient in allowing fast querying of data. Data warehouses on the other hand are designed specifically for reporting needs, providing data combinations and knowledge sets for analysis and aggregation. It builds an easy-to-use but powerful information analysis structure that we will explain in more detail later in the chapter.

In this chapter, we will create dimensional modeling schemas using our Solitaire example to build two data marts. In the course of creating these two schemas we'll cover:

- ❑ The nature of data warehouses and data marts
- ❑ What dimensional modeling is, and why we need it
- ❑ Star Schemas, fact tables, and dimensional tables

Dimensional Model Basics

Before we begin to look at our schemas we need to consider what system we are actually attempting to model. A data warehouse is a database designed to hold data collected in a business's operations. It often integrates data from a variety of sources, generally OLTP applications, and organizes it with analytical processing needs in mind. The data is generally stored as a 'snapshot' of the business at a given time, and as such is not subject to change.

One description found in *'The Data Warehouse Lifecycle Toolkit: Expert Methods for Designing, Developing, and Deploying Data Warehouses'* (John Wiley & Sons; ISBN 0471255475) is: '**The queryable source of data in the Enterprise. The data warehouse is nothing more than the union of all the constituent data marts.**'

Dimensional modeling is often used to create a presentation layer of the data warehouse. Some data warehouses include many different types of table design (normalized and dimensional) in different layers (Staging, Core, and Presentation) to support all the processes involved in managing Enterprise data.

Data marts are smaller versions of the Enterprise-wide data warehouses, tailored for the needs of a particular department or team. They can be defined from the same source as follows: '...**the data mart is defined as a flexible set of data, often based on the most atomic (granular) data possible to extract from an original source, and presented in a symmetric (dimensional) model that is most resilient when faced with unexpected user queries. Data marts can be tied together using drill-across techniques when their dimensions are conformed.**'

In addition, data marts often use pre-aggregation or summarization structures to enhance query performance. However, it is important to maintain the ability to access the underlying base data to enable drill-down analysis as necessary.

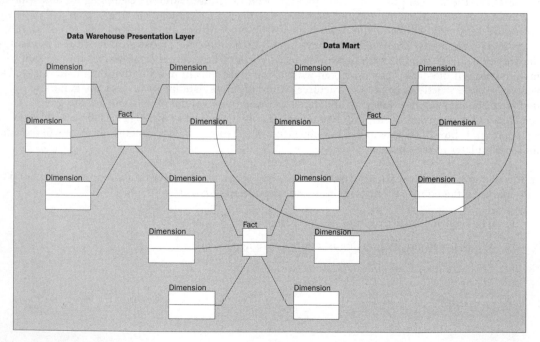

So what is Dimensional modeling? The definition is: **A methodology for modeling data that starts from a set of base measurement events and constructs a table called the fact table, generally with one record for each discrete measurement. This fact table is then surrounded by a set of dimension tables, describing precisely what is known in the context of each measurement record. Because of the characteristic structure of a dimensional model, it's often called a star schema. Dimensional models are the logical foundation of all OLAP systems.**

Dimensional modeling, like all our modeling techniques, is a technique of data analysis and design that revolves around knowing and understanding the business requirements of the client. In building a data mart, such designs are tailored to focus on simple, understandable, and efficient retrieval of data, used In answering questions like.

- ❑ What are the quarterly Net Sales for the company by department, region, and product?
- ❑ What are the costs of transportation by product, service level, vendor, region, and time of year?
- ❑ What are the combinations of products being purchased together by store, time of day, purchase threshold, and advertising campaign?

If the question isn't completely understood yet, maybe the goal will be, and an interview with the clients will help determine what their questions will be. Such interviews help to determine the information objectives (as highlighted in bold below). They may say to you:

- ❑ **I want to know what products to cut from the inventory because they aren't performing**.
  - ❑ Q: How do you know they aren't performing?
  - ❑ A: I compare the quarterly Net Sales for the company by department, region, and product.
- ❑ **I want to know if I need to renegotiate the contracts with the transportation companies.**
  - ❑ Q: What triggers you to renegotiate the contracts?
  - ❑ A: When the contracts are within three months of expiring I start looking at the costs of transportation by product, service level, vendor, region, and time of year.
- ❑ **I want to know what products to put together in the aisles to encourage people to buy more.**
  - ❑ Q: What research do you do to decide product location?
  - ❑ A: I do market basket research by looking at the combinations of products being purchased together by store, time of day, purchase threshold, and advertising campaigns.

You start a dimensional model by knowing what sort of question the clients want to answer and how they want to be able to sort, restrict, and aggregate the answers. This is the scope of the data mart. This is generally an iterative process, since the analysis needs are likely to change over time. This is where a degree of flexibility in design is needed, in order to meet the existing requirements of the client, and allow for modification of these requirements in the future.

The Benefits of Dimensional Design

It is pretty obvious that we already have all the data stored in our normalized structures to answer all the questions that our clients might like to ask about their data. Why not just write reports off the design and be done with it?

We have been supporting clients for years with flat files that they then imported into tools like Excel and Lotus 1-2-3. Designing tables dimensionally and providing them access to their data this way is much more powerful, easy, and safe. It is a halfway point between flat files and normalized tables, offering the ability to restrict, aggregate, and combine data.

We know that some questions are very simple and some are very complex. Part of the reason a query is simple or complex is due to the design of the underlying data storage structures. Data sets in their most normalized form are disciplined compilations of a group of things. They are so atomic that they have the feel of an extremely narrow, highly specialized collection of objects such as shoelaces, radishes, and paper clips. 3NF data is isolated into tables that box up and control single members of a set. This is the most appropriate way to collect, remove, and modify members of a set. The problem with this design comes when we want to aggregate these sets in order to answer a question. Quite frequently the answer to questions put to a database needs to trace and gather data elements from 5, 10, 20, or more tables, involving a number of table joins. Performing table joins is a slow process, since the contents of each table is read before the correct and aggregated data required is returned. Larger numbers of joins (especially with additional restriction complexity) will inevitably lead to a slowing of the processing of the given query.

Most denormalization is an attempt to help solve this problem. Denormalization breaks normalization rules, so that we can store information in such a way as to reduce the need for a large number of joins. Look, for example, at how your physical design for the Solitaire exercise is organized. See how easy it is to know the color of the Queen of Diamonds? It is a single join from Card to Suit.

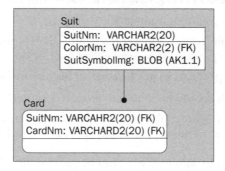

However, if you want to know the count of each color played, for all games documented, all broken out by age, occupation, and hobby name of the players then the query becomes much more complex. To return this count we need to join the Suit, Card, Move, Play, Game, Player, PlayerHobby, PlayerOccupation, AgeRange, and Hobby tables in gathering our information (I italicized the matching columns for you):

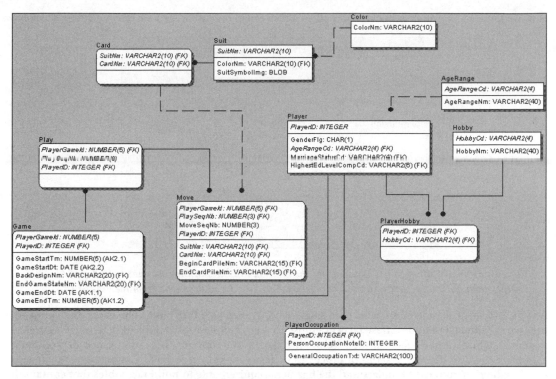

We are now facing eleven joins to get to all the information we need. If we need to do this often, we may wish to create a dimensional star schema allowing redundancy in the table, bringing all the pertinent data elements into one simple structure for simple query joins.

Our clients in the Psychology department can come back to us to supply the expertise to help them find out the answer to the question with the eleven joins. The problem here is trying to design a data structure that allows us to perform such queries more efficiently. The solution is to use star schemas, as we'll see now.

Star Schemas

Before we discuss star schemas, you need to know the following dimensional modeling vocabulary:

Dimensional Vocabulary

❑ **Fact** – A measurement, typically numeric and additive, that is stored in a fact table. a.k.a. Measure, Key Performance measure, Key Business measure

❑ **Fact Table** – The central table in a dimensional model (star join schema), characterized by a composite key, each of whose elements is a foreign key drawn from a dimension table.

❑ **Dimension** – An independent entity in the model of an organization that serves as an entry point, or as a mechanism for slicing the additive measures of the organization.

❑ **Dimension table** – A table in a dimensional model (star join schema) with a single part primary key.

❑ **ETL** – Extraction Transformation and Loading. The primary processes of the staging area leading to the loading of a data warehouse. This process uses tools from simple SQL transactions, to batch processing, to sophisticated automations tools like Informatica.

Now we know the vocabulary above, a star schema is so called because its general design pattern is as follows:

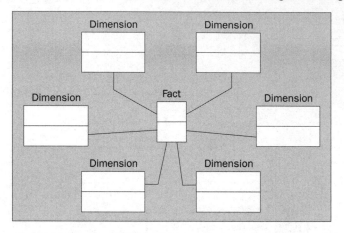

It is traditional (although not required) for the relationship lines in Star schemas to be diagonal rather than horizontal and vertical. The relationships here are always read from the outside in.

As you can see, star schemas center on a single table known as a **fact** table. This fact table is linked to a number of **dimension** tables. **Base** facts are those that are simple replications of data in the source system(s), while numeric facts formed from other data in the source system are termed **derived** facts. You have to build those in a series of processes collectively known as ETL (Extraction, Transformation, and Loading). You need to understand the business requirements to build fact tables that contain the correct **measures** of interest (such as sales amount). These measures come in various forms:

❏ Perfectly **Additive Numeric Measures** – a.k.a. Additive Facts. These are the basic numeric facts in a fact table. They can always be added together across any measure. An example would be 'Retail Price' of the InvoiceLineFact table. They offer enormous possibility for aggregation and trend determination

❏ **Semi** and **Non-Additive Numeric Measures** – These aren't quite as flexible although they do offer the client data values that could be difficult for them to compile. These are generally in the form of prederived values (such as Net versus Gross Sales and Profitability) or measures of intensity (like account balances, temperature, or inventory levels). The formula to get to these values may be difficult to nail down. Plus there will be certain measures, like Time, that they can't be added from

❏ **Textual** Facts – These aren't useful for anything other than counting them. Most of the textual information about a fact is found in a Dimension. An insurance company may add Car Color to the Accident Fact. It may not make sense to have a whole dimension for color but it may not make sense to add color to the Vehicle dimension either. It is added to the fact table just for reference

❏ **Degenerate** Facts – Degenerate facts are usually bits of data used to reference a higher-level form or aggregation, like the Bill of Lading number on a Shipped Material fact table for example. They are generally part of the identifying set of attributes of the fact table, but they are used for very little else. Research being done about a single Bill of Lading would generally happen in the operations system not in the analysis reports. These are referred to as Degenerate Dimensions, although there is no dimension table to reference back to.

The Level of Detail

The term **granularity** is used to describe the level of detail contained within a fact table in a data warehouse. A table may contain data that is highly detailed (like the separate product lines on an order), or it may contain data that has been summarized to any level required by your users (like one record for a store for a year's worth of aggregated sales facts). The use of the word grain brings to mind different kinds of wood. Soft wood has broader, looser grain whereas hardwood has narrower, tighter grain. Just like the builder's requirements for different woods to support different needs, your choice in the granularity of the fact table should be chosen with an understanding of the different functionality in the future.

Think of fact tables that refer to more aggregated types of data, such as the Invoice rather than the Invoice Line, as being more like the soft wood. It is less able to support detailed analysis. Think of fact tables that refer to the most granular data available as being more like the hardwood. It has a better chance of supporting refined data analysis and *ad hoc* data mining needs to get to the root cause of a trend in the future.

Snowflake Schemas

The star schema is the simplest representation of the business entities and their relationships in the dimensional model. However, sometimes we apply some level of normalization to the dimension tables and create a variation of the star schema known as a **snowflake** schema. This model decomposes one dimension into separate dimension tables. In this way we can define one-to-many relationships among members of the original dimension table.

The 'classic' snowflake is used to remove low cardinality attributes from one dimension table. Look at this simple design for Customer Service calls for an international company. Consider the `GeographyDim`. The columns that refer to Country only will have a 50 state to 1 country cardinality in the case of United States records. Pulling out the Country columns into a `CountryDim` reduces the redundancy of `CountryNm`, `CountryAbbrNm`, and `GrossNtlProductAmt` by a factor of 49 times. This may make sense to your team.

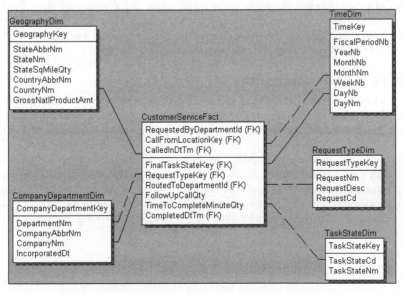

So, for example, here is a snowflake removing Country columns from the `GeographyDim` and `Company` columns removed from the `CompanyDepartmentDim`. All of the relationships are moving toward the fact table in a one-to-many cardinality.

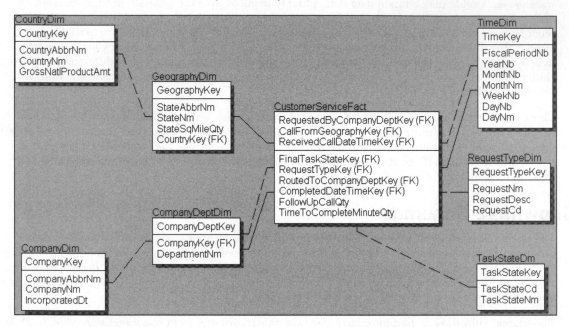

Many practitioners suggest that dimensional models should only be snowflaked if they have an excellent reason for doing so. Ralph Kimball in an article for Intelligent Enterprise called 'A Trio of Interesting Snowflakes' June 29, 2001 has this to say in warning:

> *"A classic physical snowflake design may be useful in the backroom staging area [of a data warehouse] as a way to enforce the many-to-one relationships in a dimensional table. But in the front room presentation part of your data warehouse, you have to demonstrate to me that the end users find the snowflake easier to understand and, moreover, that queries and reports run faster with the snowflake, before I am comfortable with the snowflake design."*

Base-dimension / Sub-dimension

These are cases where you are working with unevenly distributed descriptive columns in the subtypes of a category. Instead of rolling up the columns of all the subtypes into one dimension it may make more sense to design a base-dimension to hold the shared columns and separate subdimensions to hold the others.

One example Ralph uses is of Web Shoppers, broken into Visitors (of which we know very little) and Customers (of which we know quite a bit). Instead of rolling all the attributes of the logical entity `Shopper` up to one dimension, he suggests breaking the dimension in two. One dimension, `Shopper`, becomes the base dimension with a one-to-zero-or-one relationship with a `Customer` dimension that contains information about a Shopper who actually purchased something.

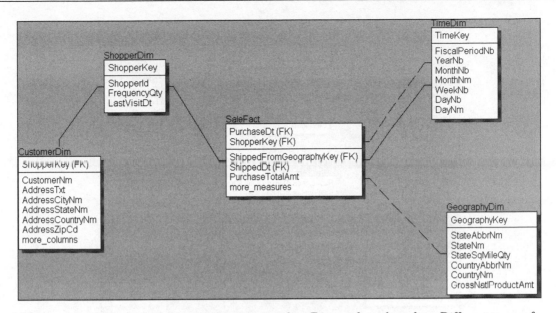

Another example deals with requirements surrounding Financial product data. Different types of financial accounts have a great variety of attributes. Combining all the different account types together into one dimension can cause you to end up with a dimension of hundreds of columns, most of which are empty for every given record. Again you may decide to build a core dimension isolating the core attributes and a set of 'context-dependent' subdimensions. The key in the base Account dimension points to the proper extended account subdimensions. This example would look a lot like the model of our shoppers, but it would have multiple relationships from ShopperDim to other children dimensions.

The final example deals with many-to-many relationships. The example deals with a multi-Enterprise calendar dimension. In this case you are working with many idiosyncratic divisions of dates into various fiscal, manufacturing, and planning calendars with parochial views of seasons and holidays. Ralph says *"Although you should make a heroic effort to reduce incompatible calendar labels, many times you want to look at the overall multi-Enterprise data through the eyes of just one of the organizations."*

This time the base table is a generic calendar table. Each subdimension will have pretty much the same set of columns with different values. Australia may denote November 1 as being part of season 'Spring' whereas Canada has November 1 in the season 'Fall'. This type of subdimension snowflake structure includes both the key of the base dimension and the organization dimension.

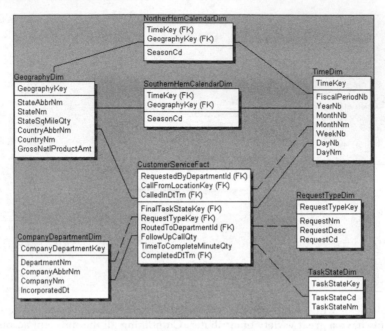

Kimball points out that you can provide a different presentation to clients using views. This precodes the joins and allows you to relabel the columns.

The Solitaire Survey Model

Having discussed the terminology we need, let's take a look at our Solitaire model as it stands following our previous analysis (this is still the physical model. I just turned off the datatypes to simplify the graphic):

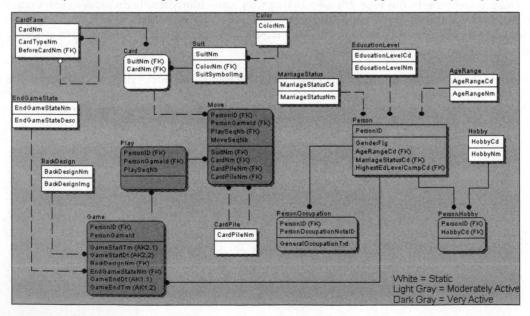

I picked this copy of the model on purpose, since it highlights the expected transaction activity. Facts have a tendency to be found where the activity is greatest. `Game`, `Play` and `Move` are the tables with the highest expected quantity, but more important they are modified with new, altered, or deleted records more frequently. These would seem to be prime candidates for our central fact table.

> **The attributes that are chosen to be in fact tables are generally found where the data activity in an Enterprise is the highest and the most focused.**

Targeting the Facts

As with our transactional system analysis, the first task is to discover the requirements of your clients. So what do our clients back at the Psychology Department want from us in this case? Their latest information need (objective) is an ability 'to analyze the moves, and wins or losses in Solitaire games, to find out if there are any trends with time of day, day of week, back design choice, age, marriage status, hobby, and education level of a Player'. When we question them further we find that they are actually interested in anything to do with the grouping of Moves into Plays. They are targeting Game and Move information only.

In general, to create a data mart (the fact and dimension tables for our schema) we need to learn:

❑   Where does the data come from?

❑   What answers are needed in the future?

❑   Is there an expected need to grouping and restricting the data?

Find out how your clients do this kind of analysis now. In our exercise, the clients probably have no analysis methods that they are used to, but you will often find that your real-world clients have 'Tried & True' processes that they count on. In fact, you may have to remind them of their new application, processes, data sources, and designs so they can brainstorm a little comparing the past and the future. It is quite likely they will be able to show you values on existing reports that are meaningful to them, or screens or spreadsheets where they build aggregations. All of these things are probably going to need to be incorporated into their data mart. You want to bring as many requirements together as possible and build a 'one stop shop' for them.

Don't restrict your research to just their goal however. They may only be looking for monthly data, for example, but you should try to take a slightly longer view allowing them to 'drill down' to a lower level of detail in future.

> **Capture at least the next lower level of detail data when possible in fact tables, even if it expands the scope of the requirements. Anticipate the needs of your client beyond their scope whenever feasible.**

It also never hurts to do a little reconnaissance to see if their fact and dimensional tables might fit into a larger vision. Departments in a business don't stand alone. If there is a requirement for a particular fact or dimension in one department, chances are that there is some other department that may benefit from having it as well. Alternatively, it may already exist in another department, and if this is so, it could substantially reduce the time needed to create your model. What do we need to provide our clients with in our data mart? In our discussion with them, their stated aim was to be able:

'to analyze the moves and wins or losses in Solitaire games to find out if there are any trends within time of day, day of week, back design choice, age, marriage status, hobby, and education level of a Player'

If you dissect this requirement into clauses, then you start to see the entity sets the way we did in the Logical modeling exercise. In this case we have:

to analyze:

- ❑   the moves
- ❑   the choices of back designs
- ❑   and wins or losses in Solitaire **Games**

to find out if there are any trends within:

- ❑   time of day
- ❑   day of week
- ❑   age
- ❑   marriage status
- ❑   hobby and
- ❑   education level of a **Player**

Dimensional modeling still has to do with organization of the data sets. This time we are looking to organize the sets into the structure of a data mart, which generally has one central fact table with a series of dimension tables linked to it, which can be used to filter the facts by. Looking at our list we seem to have two big concepts that we are working with, Games and Players. Now if we read the requirements we can surmise that the clients want to focus on, or measure, the facts about Games. They have also told us they want to be able to look for trends about those facts by various aspects of the Players and Time concepts. This gives us our first indicator that we will be looking for discrete measurable facts about Game, which will be organized into the fact table of this data mart. Meanwhile the more textual, informational data referring to Players and Time will become the dimensions.

So how do we focus on the facts?

Choose the Granularity

What grain choice do we have in this case? Look over the tables that contain the Game data elements:

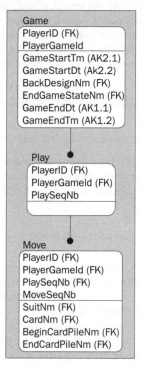

Since the clients told us they aren't interested in Plays, we will ignore it and look at the other two levels of detail:

- ❑ Details of single Games
- ❑ Details of single Moves

We can provide the data in event form at the granularity level of the Moves, or aggregated one layer up at the granularity level of Games. We would do that by adding all of the Move knowledge up to the Game it is about in summary form. Both would satisfy the requirement as it is currently stated. However, the rule of thumb is to always provide the lowest level of granularity that satisfies the requirements. The requirements look as though we need to either focus on Game and Move. We will probably be building two data marts.

The choice of granularity creates the definition of the fact table. If we are looking at a single record for each Game, the granularity is Game. If we are looking at a record for each Move in a Game, the granularity will be Game+Move. We can have granularity that aggregates like a single record for all Games that happened over a day for a Player. The granularity would be Day+Game+Player.

Choosing the right grain to support your client's requirements is very important. We are going to build two data marts. One will be at the Game level, and the other will be at the Move level. This will allow the clients to analyze Games as they requested with the ability to 'Drill Down' to details of a Game, in other words the Moves.

Choose the Facts

Facts or Measures, as we mentioned earlier, are the data elements used to do data mining or analysis. As the name suggests, they are often things you can weigh, count, time, cost, get the length, width, or height of. Designing stores of information at defined granularity makes facts or measures in their easy-to-manipulate form (simple numbers are best, although textual measures are allowable) the foundation of a data mart. Measures are all answers to the question 'How ...' or answers to calculation questions like 'What is ...' the average, the minimum, the mean, the max, the delta from, the growth rate, and so on.

We went over the types of facts they already are:

❏   **Perfectly Additive Numeric Measures** – a.k.a. Additive Facts. These are the basic numeric facts in a Fact table. They can always be added together across any measure.

❏   **Semi and Non-Additive Numeric Measures** – these are generally in the form of pre-derived values or measures of intensity and there will be certain measures – like Time – that they cannot be added from or they simply cannot be added at all.

❏   **Textual Facts** – just for reference.

❏   **Degenerate Facts** – generally part of the identifying set of attributes

We also need to be able to recognize whether this fact is an original base fact, or if it has been derived by combining two or more facts together. Noting that the TotalBilledAmt off the source system data record is a base fact, is very important if you are also providing a SummedChargeAmt which you have built from adding all the charges in the details of the Invoice together dynamically at the time of record creation. TotalBilledAmt is a static fact based on what happened. SummedChargeAmt is a derived fact based on details. This may be a very important aspect of the data mart to the clients. They may be looking for Sales persons who consistently give too large a discount to certain accounts. Base vs. Derived is very important to the ETL team as well, since one is a simple transfer, and the other may be a complicated post-process formula to build and maintain.

Start with a submodel of Solitaire focusing in on Game and Move. Take special note of the attributes you can count, measure, or add. I have removed Play by denormalizing the PlaySeqNb into Move. Also I have suppressed the datatypes on the Physical model again just so that we can concentrate on the column names:

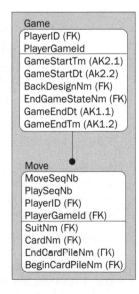

We can list the things that are simply base facts from the original tables:

- ❑ Who played the Game?
- ❑ When did the Game Start?
- ❑ When did the Game End?
- ❑ Was the Game Won or Lost?
- ❑ What Back Design was used?

And we can also begin to ask questions such as:

- ❑ How long was the Game in minutes and seconds?
- ❑ How many moves were there?
- ❑ How many red moves?
- ❑ How many black moves?
- ❑ How many Hearts moves?
- ❑ How many Clubs moves?
- ❑ How many Diamonds moves?
- ❑ How many Spades moves?
- ❑ How many moves were made from the Draw Pile?
- ❑ How many moves were made to the Discard Piles?
- ❑ How many moves were made to the Processing Piles?
- ❑ How many moves were made to the Waste Pile?
- ❑ How many moves were made from the Waste Pile?

This list will do for now. Double-check the client requirements to remind yourself of what they want to know. These quantities will be the basis for their analysis. They may ask us to add precalculated averages or other measures when they look it over.

What about measures for Move? The movement of a Card from place to place in a Game is an event. This event has no measure, other than that it happened, which equates to a value of 1 and so does not need to be stored, although you may choose to create a column to store the quantity '1' so that it may be added easily using a SUM function rather than a COUNT. The event is stored in a **factless fact table**.

You will want to very carefully document what the measures are, their definitions, expected values, quality checks, and formula. It is extremely important to the ETL team who has to load the fact table.

Fact Definitions

Question	Mapped to	Base? Derived?	Additive Factor
Who played the Game?	Game.PlayerId	Base	Textual
When did the Game Start?	GameGameStartTm, Game.GameStartDt	Base	Textual
When did the Game End?	Game.GameEndTm, Game.GameEndDt	Base	Textual
Was the Game Won or Lost?	Game.GameEndStateNm	Base	Textual
What Back Design was used?	GameBackDesignNm	Base	Textual
How long was the game in minutes and seconds?	GameGameStartTm, Game.GameStartDt, Game.GameEndTm, Game.GameEndD	Derived	Fully Additive
How many moves were there?	Game.PlayerGameID, Move.PlayerGameID	Derived	Fully Additive
How many red moves?	Game.PlayerGameID, Move.PlayerGameID, Move.SuitNm, Suit,ColorNm	Derived	Fully Additive
How many black moves?	Game.PlayerGameID, Move.PlayerGameID, Move.SuitNm, Suit,ColorNm	Derived	Fully Additive
How many Hearts moves?	Game.PlayerGameID, Move.PlayerGameID, Move.SuitNm	Derived	Fully Additive
How many Clubs moves?	Game.PlayerGameID, Move.PlayerGameID, Move.SuitNm	Derived	Fully Additive
How many Diamonds moves?	Game.PlayerGameID, Move.PlayerGameID, Move.SuitNm	Derived	Fully Additive
How many Spades moves?	Game.PlayerGameID, Move.PlayerGameID, Move.SuitNm	Derived	Fully Additive
How many moves were made from the Draw Pile?	Game.PlayerGameID, Move.PlayerGameID, Move.BeginCardPileNm	Derived	Fully Additive

Question	Mapped to	Base? Derived?	Additive Factor
How many moves were made to the Discard Piles?	Game.PlayerGameID, Move.PlayerGameID, Move.EndCardPileNm	Derived	Fully Additive
How many moves were made to the Processing Piles?	Game.PlayerGameID, Move.PlayerGameID, Move.EndCardPileNm	Derived	Fully Additive
How many moves were made to the Waste Pile?	Game.PlayerGameID, Move.PlayerGameID, Move.EndCardPileNm	Derived	Fully Additive
How many moves were made from the Waste Pile?	Game.PlayerGameID, Move.PlayerGameID, Move.BeginCardPileNm	Derived	Fully Additive

Having considered the nature of the facts or measures and granularity level we need to apply in this case, let's now begin to construct a data mart for Game.

The Game Data Mart

We start with a discussion of the Game fact table.

Game Fact Table

Begin by noting the granularity of the fact table. How do we identify one game? In our case we know the primary key of the source table Game. Remember that a Game was an event for a Player in our Solitaire solution so it took two pieces of information to uniquely identify it. The composite primary key (pair of IDs) represent a row that will have data values looking something like: PlayerGameId = 15, PlayerID = 127 (which when joined back to the Player tables resolves to knowledge that we are working with the fifteenth game of a 36-45 year old, male, married, BA/S level, librarian).

Now we add in the measures following the same naming conventions we used in our physical modeling. Every column must have a class word, Pascal notation (which we chose), and consistent abbreviations as necessary. As in every stage of modeling, make sure you have very clear names; in this case the clients may actually be using a query tool to see the tables and will be able to create SQL queries themselves so clear names will be very helpful.

```
GameFact
PlayerId
PlayerGameId
GameStartDt
GameStartTm
GameEndDt
GameEndTm
BackDesignNm
EndGameStateNm
GameDurationMinQty
MoveQty
RedMoveQty
BlackMoveQty
HeartMoveQty
ClubMoveQty
DiamondMoveQty
SpadeMoveQty
FromDrawPileMoveQty
ToDiscardPileMoveQty
ToProcessPileMoveQty
ToWastePileMoveQty
FromWastePileMoveQty
```

Dimensional Model Keys

There are a few advisory warnings about keys in dimensional models, especially those that are going to become a part of a data warehouse.

Avoid Source System Keys

By Source System, I mean the origin of the data elements that you are going to load into your data mart. One would expect that the primary keys used in the source system or source tables should be a good choice by default. Unfortunately we have learned over time that is not always true. You may want to avoid existing primary keys for a number of reasons:

❑ **New Sources** – You may need to incorporate data sources other than the one you are currently using, and the new source will quite likely use a different primary key

❑ **Data Duplication** – The IDs or natural keys from the source system lock you into not just size and datatype but *values* from the source system. You could potentially be forced to deal with duplicate IDs if you are adding in new sources that have a similar constructs and generation functions, like system-generated IDs or sequential numbers. This becomes especially true if the source application is actually installed in multiple locations and the data is expected to be compiled into this one data mart

❑ **Structure Synchronization** – Source systems change. Having a primary key that is isolated to the data mart keeps you from dealing with the pain of the ripple

❑ **History** – It may become part of your requirements to save changes to data from source systems. If you need to record both the old and new version of the record using the source system primary key then you are now faced with a problem and a primary key that will not support this need

Avoid Smart Keys

In this type of design using natural data elements may cause you problems. Keep the actual data in non-key positions.

Avoid Multi-Column Keys

One of the primary goals of this type of design is speed. You want to avoid having to use multiple columns joins. The best performance will be from a single column, numeric key. Let's create a new attribute type for the data warehouse naming standard called Key. This will be a specific form of identifier available only in this environment to use as a default identifier column for all tables. Keep the IDs for the moment. It is good to keep the identifiers in the record to map backwards in case you need to audit your data for quality checking.

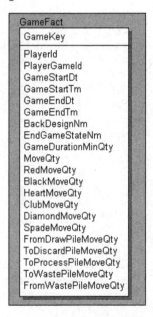

Game Dimensions

Dimensions are defined in *'Official Sybase Data Warehousing on the Internet: Accessing the Corporate Knowledge Base'* (International Thomson Publishing, 1998) as:

> ... *a physical property, such as time, location, or product, regarded as a fundamental way of accessing and presenting business information. A dimension typically acts as an index for identifying data. It is common to think of standard reports that present rows and columns as two-dimensional. A manager who evaluates budgets may look at a two-dimensional spreadsheet containing accounts in the rows and cost centers in the columns. The intersecting point between the rows and columns, a cell, contains relevant numerical information about the specific cost center and account, such as product development's salary budget*

Dimensions are more easily described in terms of 'roll-up' points or pivotal aspects of the facts. So our next step is to look at the ways the clients wanted to 'slice and dice' their Game data, in other words how they want the data presented for their analysis. Those are the dimensions we need to identify. What were the requirements?

- ❑ analysis of moves of a game
- ❑ age of a **player** in a game
- ❑ marriage status of a **player** in a game
- ❑ hobby of a **player** in a game
- ❑ education level of a **player** in a game
- ❑ **time** of day of a game
- ❑ **day** of week of a game
- ❑ win or lose **status** of a game

Group them by concept or nouns by looking for similarities. Player makes up a large share of the required reporting points. Make a subject area (a submodel including just the tables pertinent to the discussion) from the source system model of `Player` and look it over:

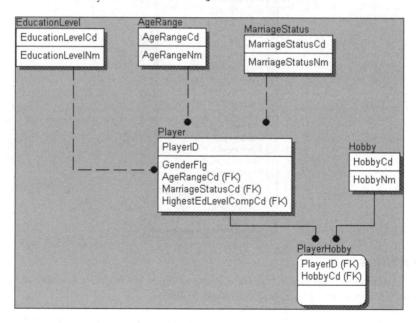

In order to build the dimension `Player` we want to gather as many of the data elements that we broke out for normalization back into `Player`. In other words we are going to denormalize to reduce the joins needed. This is relatively simple with the relationships where `Player` is a child (in this case all of the non-identifying relationships on the model (dashed lines) are relationships where `Player` is the child). Bring all the data elements from `EducationLevel`, `MarriageStatus`, and `AgeRange` into `Player`.

Dimensional designs focus strongly on the ways to provide the fastest query response time. Getting rid of as many joins as possible is a must. However, removing those tables could have an impact in quality on an ordinary system because now there is no ability to check for valid values. In order to make query response time a priority, it is generally expected that data quality checks have been made earlier in the process, either in the source OLTP system or the staging area of the data warehouse.

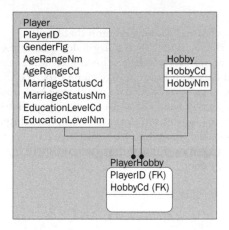

Dimension Table Structure

`PlayerHobby` has a one-to-many relationship with `Player`. It can have multiple occurrences of each `Player`. You must choose whether to snowflake or try to denormalize the data in (building a snowflake leaves it in the more normalized form). The choice is basically between a restrictive, more simplistic structure with a better performance schema, and a completely flexible, more complex structure with a potential performance impact.

Here is the more complex choice. We changed the name of the table to include Dim in compliance with a local data warehouse naming standard, moved the source system IDs below the line, and created a key column to act as the primary key. Here is what it would look like if we chose the base/subdimension snowflaking scenario:

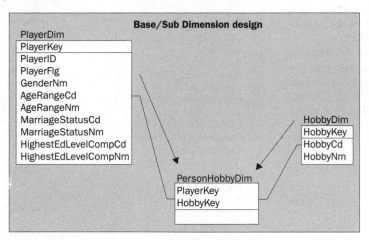

Alternatively, we can bring all the Hobby value options into `Player` as flags. This choice should be made from a couple of perspectives: the requirements of the clients, and the quantity and stability of the Hobby list of values. Our requirements don't seem to include any discussion of the simplicity of the dimensional design for client navigation. You may need to go back to the clients to discuss this as a goal. You will also want to verify the current list of hobbies completeness, and how stable the client feels they are. We will go forward with a belief that the forms are printed predetermining hobby choice, there will be no write-ins allowed, and the clients think the list is extremely stable. So we will design a very simple `PlayerDim`.

How do you denormalize the choices? Make a column that has the actual name and code of the Hobby rather than a flag field, since these are the values that will show on reports as labels. This design still goes through the steps of our local data warehouse design standards. We renamed the table `PlayerDim`, gave it a new data warehouse key, and moved the `PlayerID` out of `GameFact`. The source system key should be kept with the `Player` records for future reference and updatability. Some teams will choose to keep the mapping of `PlayerKey` to `PlayerID` in a staging area. This type of data often isn't a useful attribute for the clients to query on.

PlayerDim

PlayerKey
PlayerID
PlayerFlg
GenderNm
AgeRangeCd
AgeRangeNm
MarriageStatusCd
MarriageStatusNm
HighestEdLevelCompCd
HighestEdLevelCompNm
HobbyOutdoorSportsNm
HobbyOutdoorSportsCd
HobbyVideoGamesNm
HobbyVideoGamesCd
HobbyBoardGamesNm
HobbyBoardGamesCd
HobbyCardGamesNm
HobbyCardGamesCd
HobbyMoviesNm
HobbyMoviesCd
HobbyBooksNm
HobbyBooksCd
HobbyOtherNm
HobbyOtherCd

Relate the `PlayerDim` to the `GameFact`. The `GameKey` will make the record completely unique, so you can use a non-identifying relationship, although some modelers prefer to make the granularity of the table more apparent by creating a multi-part key. You could use an identifying relationship if you wish, to note that this fact table is at the Game/Player granularity level.

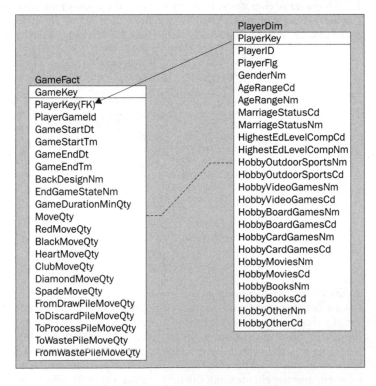

GameFact

GameKey
PlayerKey(FK)
PlayerGameId
GameStartDt
GameStartTm
GameEndDt
GameEndTm
BackDesignNm
EndGameStateNm
GameDurationMinQty
MoveQty
RedMoveQty
BlackMoveQty
HeartMoveQty
ClubMoveQty
DiamondMoveQty
SpadeMoveQty
FromDrawPileMoveQty
ToDiscardPileMoveQty
ToProcessPileMoveQty
ToWastePileMoveQty
FromWastePileMoveQty

PlayerDim

PlayerKey
PlayerID
PlayerFlg
GenderNm
AgeRangeCd
AgeRangeNm
MarriageStatusCd
MarriageStatusNm
HighestEdLevelCompCd
HighestEdLevelCompNm
HobbyOutdoorSportsNm
HobbyOutdoorSportsCd
HobbyVideoGamesNm
HobbyVideoGamesCd
HobbyBoardGamesNm
HobbyBoardGamesCd
HobbyCardGamesNm
HobbyCardGamesCd
HobbyMoviesNm
HobbyMoviesCd
HobbyBooksNm
HobbyBooksCd
HobbyOtherNm
HobbyOtherCd

Extra Dimension Attributes

The quantity of columns provided for the client's use in a dimension is often quite large. It is often advisable to add in **preformatted** columns to increase the usability of dimensional data elements. Review the attributes and make sure that each one is shown in as many useful configurations as possible. For instance, you might want to provide columns to see a day of a week in these three forms: Full Name, Abbreviated Name, Day of Week number (Sunday, Sun, 1 / Monday, Mon, 2 / Tuesday, Tues, 3 / and so on). You only need one of these values to provide day of week information. The rest are just preformatted to reduce extra processing in the future.

The client uses these values as headers on columns of their reports. This just makes it easier for them. Use standard abbreviations, IDs they are used to, full names, names in capitals, names in mixed case, or any other way they would like to see that attribute. It is important they are all built correctly and stay synchronized with each other. You ETL team will need to know which columns are really just a reformatting of another data element.

The Time Dimension

Walking down the requirements you come to time of day:

- ❑ **time** of day of a game
- ❑ **day** of week of a game
- ❑ win or lose **status** of a game

Time is the next dimension, and it relates twice to GameFact using role naming, just like we've gone over before. Unfortunately the Solitaire system isn't going to be the source for the data in this dimension. Fortunately most RDBMS have almost every attribute you ever wanted about Date and Time built in. A programmer will have to create a process to populate what isn't available as a format from the RDBMS. Find out from the client how they would like to see hours and minutes. You have lots of options:

- ❑ Local Time in 24 hour format
- ❑ Local Time in 12 hour format
- ❑ Local AM – PM notation
- ❑ Time names – Midnight, Noon
- ❑ Greenwich Standard Time in 24 (for comparison of events globally)
- ❑ Greenwich Standard Time in 12
- ❑ Local AM – PM notation
- ❑ O'Clock name
- ❑ 00:00 notation
- ❑ Running Minute number from 1 at midnight (helps sequencing)
- ❑ Day Period Name (Late Night, Early Morning, Late Afternoon, Early Evening)

> Sometimes you have to build dimensions from data sources outside your targeted sources.

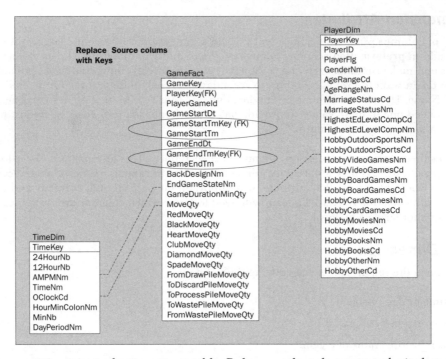

Relate the new `TimeDim` to the `GameFact` table. Role name the columns to make it clear what data they are providing. Make sure you remove the original time attributes that these are replacing. Here is where we are now:

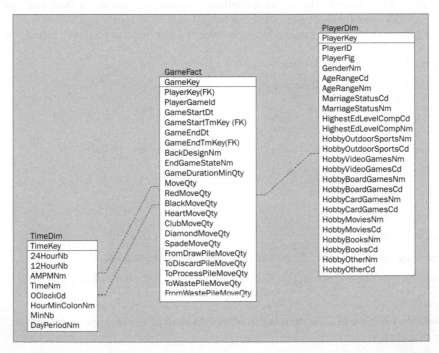

The Day Dimension

Next add the Day dimension. It also has a huge potential for interesting and decorative attributes.

- ❑ Day in Month Number
- ❑ Day in Week Name
- ❑ Day in Week Number
- ❑ Day in Week Abbreviation
- ❑ Week Number Sun – Sat
- ❑ Week Number running 7
- ❑ Month Number
- ❑ Month Name
- ❑ Month Abbreviation
- ❑ CenturyYear
- ❑ Standard Holiday Name (although Holidays are usually snowflaked with lots of added attributes)
- ❑ DDMMYY
- ❑ MMDDYYYY
- ❑ Number of Day in the year
- ❑ Season Name
- ❑ Quarter Number
- ❑ Half Year Number
- ❑ Leap Year Flag

Now relate it twice to the GameFact table, continuing to role name and removing the original source system columns:

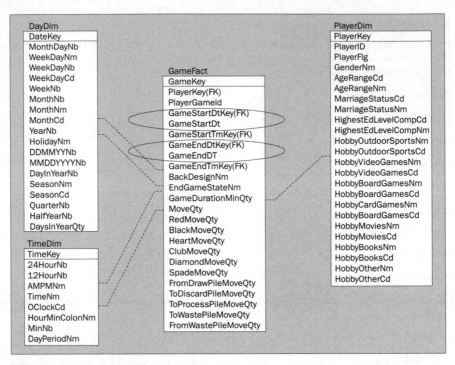

We end up here for a moment:

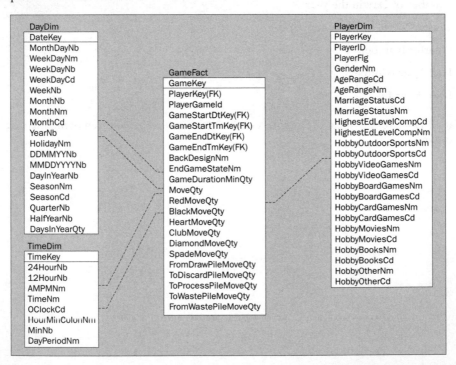

Conforming the Dimensions

We talked about the process of joining data sets together. Fact tables are data sets also, containing completely unique members of generally enormous sets of data. Clients often want to be able to combine queries of different fact tables into a single summary. The only easy way to do this is to use the same foreign keys from the same dimensional data in different fact tables. If you do that then Time has the same meaning in all circumstances, Geography is defined in the same way, and Customers have the same history and members of the set. If you don't use the same dimensions you get a bad case of 'stove piping', which is when data and data structures are built to be used in one system only, with no knowledge or forethought to what needs there could be outside the system, and with no visibility of its data to other systems. Your new fact table is basically isolated, and it takes special effort to try to leap the gap.

> **Share dimensional tables with as many projects in your company as you can. Homegrown Data marts can be prevented from becoming stove pipes if you do.**

In our case we need to look outside the Solitaire application, probably no further than the Psychology department, to find out if someone else has been doing dimensional modeling. If someone has, then you might want to look over their dimensions and see if it makes sense to conform to them. If you can conform Time and Day, for instance, then the research being done with the Solitaire data may be able to be combined with data gathered about mood swings or stress being done elsewhere.

The Back Design & Status Dimension

There are just two requirements left.

- ❑ The back design choice
- ❑ Win or lose **status** of a game

Go back to the source system and see what data elements exist for them.

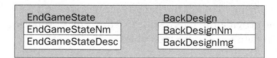

There is a name, and a description. Quite frequently in dimensional modeling, you avoid anything that would be too long or bulky to display easily on a report. Check with the clients first of course, but it is a good bet that you can safely remove `GameStatusDesc` and `BackDesignImg` from the dimensions. Move the source system key beneath the line and add the data warehouse-specific keys. Relate it to `GameFact`. Here it is in the first draft to satisfy the requirements at the `Game` granularity.

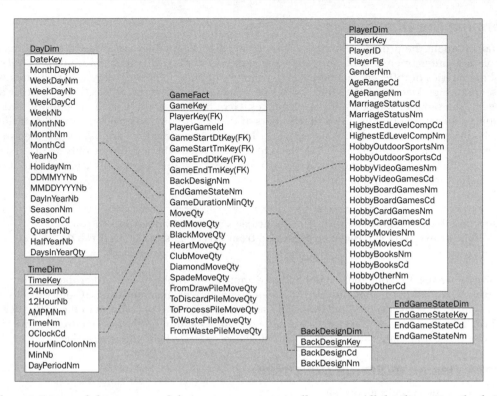

Add your sizing and datatypes, and determine your NULL allowances. All the dimensional relationships are generally required. Often a record is placed in the dimension for Unknown, rather than using a NULL. That prevents different summations of the fact when a dimension attribute is used on the report without having to explain outer joins to the client.

Different requirements will cause different choices at this level of analysis. The requirement may be to allow incomplete data records in the fact table to match the source system. However, it may also be that a transformation happens during loading, to change empty space into zero for number fields, or empty text into 'Not in Source' to provide the client with a better way of reporting on the immense number of records generally stored in data warehouse fact tables.

Slowly Changing Dimensions

Now that you have a first draft dimensional model, you need to review the dimensions again with the client to determine the history requirements. Data changes. It changes because of errors being fixed in the source system. Groups reorganize, dates are classified into different fiscal reporting periods, and roads get different names. Data is cleaned, matured, mutated, and enhanced all through the source systems.

You need to ask the clients:

❑   Will the data records be loaded once or updated?

❑   Do you care about knowing that records changed?

❑   If you care, do you want to know what the previous values were?

❑   How many changes do you want to be able to see?

In our Solitaire example there is no history. The data gathered about the Players was a one-time registration that will not be updated. In fact it can't be, because there is no information in the Player data that would connect a person to their registration record. All the attributes allow for data fixing, like an update to the `AgeRangeCd` in case of a mistaken entry. But obviously that is not the case for most data in the business world.

Each column in each dimension needs to be looked at to see how you want to manage a data value change. Do you want to overwrite the value, keep the old and new value, or keep the last value and the new value? The dimensions need to be structured correctly to support these changes. Is it OK to overwrite `MarriageStatusCd` or do you need to know that it was updated? How about `AgeRangeCd`, or `HighestEdLevelCompCd`? They may all need to be treated differently. For some columns, a simple overwrite is fine, whereas in others it is critical to keep a full history of change. What I am trying to emphasize is that change control isn't at the table level; it is at the column level, and the choices made change the design of the table to accommodate the requirements.

Let's look at what change value types are available to us (as found in *The Data Warehouse Lifecycle Toolkit: Expert Methods for Designing, Developing, and Deploying Data Warehouses* (John Wiley & Sons; ISBN 0471255475):

Type 1

Type 1 is a simple overwrite. There is no record of the old one left in the data mart. In fact there is no way to know that anything changed from a moment ago. This is the simplest type of change, but it gives the least ability to track changes as well.

- ❏ Fixes incorrect data
- ❏ Doesn't care what it used to be
- ❏ No change to the dimension structure
- ❏ No new records

Type 2

Type 2 changes add a whole new record every time something changes that you want to track. So for example, a Company with `CompanyNumber` of 123, changed `CompanyName` from 'Jones Ltd' to 'Jones & Harry Inc'. You would have two records for this company. Selecting sales for `CompanyNumber` 123 would give you all their sales, while selecting `CompanyName` 'Jones & Harry Inc.' would restrict the sales to those after the name change. This allows you to 'perfectly partition history' so that you always use the records that were valid for a point in time.

- ❏ Track all changes you are interested in – permanent memory
- ❏ Perfectly partitions history
- ❏ Adds date span to note when the record was valid
- ❏ Adds a new record to the dimension for every change

Type 3

Type three takes two subtly different forms:

- ❏ Compares original record to current record
- ❏ Adds an 'Original<ColumnName>' attribute to the dimension structure

❑ Modifies the existing record by moving an attribute value to the 'Original<ColumnName>' column if it is the first one, while updating the record with the new value. After the original, it simply updates the 'Current' column

Or

❑ Tracks one change back

❑ Adds a 'Used to be<ColumnName>' attribute to the dimension structure

❑ Modifies the existing record by moving an attribute value to the 'Used to be<ColumnName>' column, while updating the record with the new value

Type 3 adds an addendum to the record of either the original or the previous value. This type of change doesn't allow for the ability to perfectly partition history.

> **Every dimension could have attributes managed by Type 1, 2, or 3 for history management. You generally have a combination of rules for different attributes within the dimension.**

So just as an example, let's look at the `PlayerDim` and how the structure would look with the different options. I have added the new columns needed to support the change control at the bottom of the tables and italicized them.

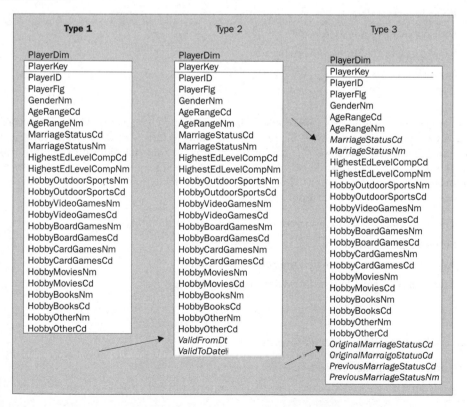

I put in the 2 options of Type 3 at the bottom of the example. You would probably pick just one of these to keep (although I don't see any reason you couldn't keep the Original, which is only updated once, as well as a Previous, which would be updated as many times as the MarriageCd was updated).

Instance Table Example

Let's assume that the only data element we are talking about is marriage status. In the case of Type 1 data, yesterday's entry looked like this:

PlayerKey	PlayerID	...	MarriageStatusCd	MarriageStatusNm
1875	398	...	S	Single

While today, with a simple update to MarriageStatusCd and MarriageStatusNm, it looks like this:

PlayerKey	PlayerID	...	MarriageStatusCd	MarriageStatusNm
1875	398	...	M	Married

In the case of Type 2 data our example looked like this yesterday:

Player Key	PlayerID	...	MarriageStatus Cd	MarriageStatus Nm	ValidFrom Dt	Valid ToDt
1875	398	...	S	Single	1/1/02	

While today it looks like this:

Player Key	PlayerID	...	MarriageStatus Cd	MarriageStatus Nm	ValidFrom Dt	ValidTo Dt
1875	398	...	S	Single	1/1/02	6/1/02
8769	398	...	M	Married	6/1/02	

And finally, our Type 3 data example yesterday looked like this (we are choosing to keep just the Original value instead of the Previous one):

Player Key	PlayerID	...	MarriageStatus Cd	MarriageStatus Nm	Original Cd	Original Nm
1875	398	...	S	Single		

While today it looks like this:

Player Key	PlayerID	...	MarriageStatus Cd	MarriageStatus Nm	Original Cd	Original Nm
1875	398	...	M	Married	S	Single

> This type of data value management for the clients is really important. Frequently the data mart or data warehouse that the mart is built on is the only way for them to see this type of history.

Data Element Definitions

Here we go again. Have I told you yet that definitions are important? Or that the creation of a record of your analysis is the basis for quality data management? It is even more important here. You need to document so much more than the description of what a data element means for dimensional modeling. Here is just a draft of what will probably be needed. Some of it the modeler just notes from their analysis, while the ETL team and DBAs create a more complete definitions document later.

What you might need to capture	Definition
Server Location	Test, Quality Control, or Production Location if you know it
Server Database Name	For the source data (if you know it)
Data Mart Name	What do you refer to this collection of tables as?
Table Name	Table Name
Table Type	Fact or Dimension
Table Description	A complete sentence or paragraph describing what this Fact or Dimension covers. The granularity would be good to note
Column Name	Column Name
Column Data Type	Number or Text; make it specific to the deployed structure
Column Size	The allowed size of a data value
Column Definition	A complete sentence or paragraph describing what the client means by all their data elements (like profitability increase percent for example)
Column Type	Base or Derived
Staging steps	A brief textual description of your understanding of the expected steps needed to acquire the data from the source system and transform it into the target value – will need:
	Source System Location
	Source Table Name/s
	Source Column Name/s
	Derivation / Formula / Transformation requirements

What you might need to capture	Definition
Formula	Need to document the client's formula to create this data value
Value change management	Type 1, 2, 3
Additive rules	Additive, Semi, Non
Business owner	The client to whom feedback is sent and communication is due
IT owner	Programmer or team in charge of maintenance
Accuracy need	Are there 'sanity' checks for data quality checks?
Criticality need	Is this data element mission-critical to the Enterprise?
Security or Sensitivity requirements	Who can or can't see it? Why?

This concludes the first exercise we are going to do of dimensional modeling. We built a fairly typical star schema of a fact at the granularity of a single Game. You should now have a good idea of how to approach dimensional modeling. What did we do?

❑   Gathered requirements and determined the goal of the fact

❑   Chose the granularity and measures

❑   Determined the dimensions and chose whether or not to use a snowflake design for them

❑   Related the dimensions to the fact and determined the history requirements of all dimensional data elements

❑   Validated general design decisions with actual data

❑   Detailed out all physical design needs for table creation

❑   Documented all data analysis definitions for team reference

Like relational modeling, dimensional modeling takes practice. If you can, solicit feedback from someone with experience in it. If you have experienced ETL people, get some idea of how different choices in the star schema affect how the ETL gets implemented. There are websites and bulletin boards out there to network on so use them.

GameMove Data Mart

Let's try one more exercise and build a data mart for Move. It should be much easier this time. Look at the requirements again. We need to analyze:

❑   the moves

❑   and wins or losses in Solitaire **Games**

to find out if there are any trends within:

- ❑ time of day
- ❑ day of week
- ❑ age
- ❑ marriage status
- ❑ hobby and
- ❑ education level of a **Player**

Grain and Measures for GameMove

Just like before, we begin with the granularity. This time it is one move for one play for one game for one player.

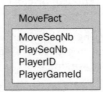

Next we try to discover the measures. Game moves are events. Look at the current columns in the source system table. Is there anything here we can measure or count in any way?

A `Move` doesn't do much other than occur (like hits on a web site). There is a numeric measure `GameMoveQty`, but it is always quantity 1. You make this little measure to give the clients a number to sum and average rather than count in code. It also provides a column to select and apply SUM functionality to, rather than requiring the report designer to a derived column in the report. Add the measure to the design:

Dimensions for GameMove

Now find the dimensions. We know that a GameMove is made up of one card moving from one card pile to another one. So we need Cards and Card Piles. Make a subject area for Cards and look over the attributes available.

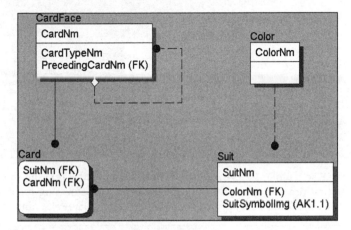

We will look over the data elements and use as much as we can. The images are probably not useful for the type of analytical reporting done in dimensional modeling, but all the rest of the attributes probably are. Denormalize them into Card to create a CardDim.

Create the new data warehouse key to reduce the risks of using current system keys that we talked about earlier.

Add all the descriptive attributes you need and relate it to our MoveFact:

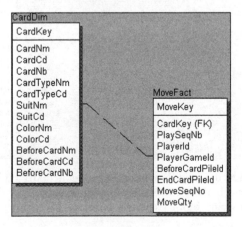

Now do the same thing for the `CardPile`:

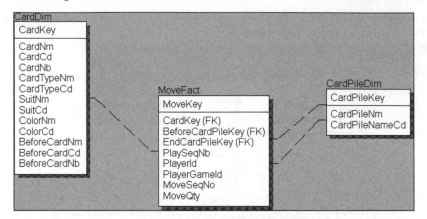

Now look at the `MoveFact` table. `PlayerID` needs to be replaced by relating the `PlayerDim` into the fact table. This is the first time we get to exercise the concept of conforming the dimensions. Doing this means that any analysis based on `Player` will be able to bridge `GameFact` and `MoveFact`.

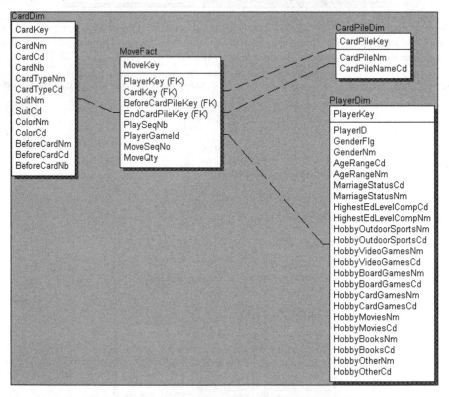

`PlayerGameID` points you to the next dimension. You can actually build a dimension of descriptive information about Games and build a `GameDim`. You would snowflake the relationships that make sense and denormalize the rest. It would build a schema that looks like this:

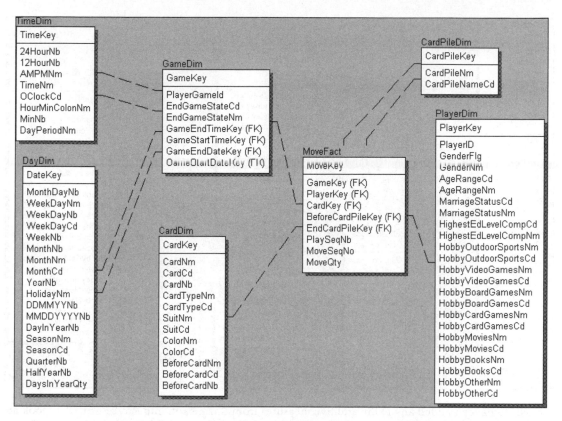

But what if we take the descriptive attributes of Game and locate them in GameMoveFact? This is called putting the facts 'at the wrong granularity'. This can be a very dangerous practice in cases of what look like additive facts. Measures and descriptive facts are 'at the wrong granularity' if they are attributes referring to a different level of detail. When we move data elements that solely describe a Game to a Move, we end up duplicating it as many times as there are Move records for a Game. This deliberate duplication can lead to incorrect reporting.

> **Clients will want to put facts into tables at the wrong granularity. They will want to be able to report on overview or master record values at the same time they are reporting on detail values.**

For example, clients may push to have a measure belonging to an Invoice, the InvoiceTotalAmt, to be put into the InvoiceLineFact. The danger lies in the fact that InvoiceTotalAmt looks like an additive fact, but is replicated numerous times across multiple rows because of the granularity of the fact table. It isn't additive without some added restrictions. Descriptive information like what is in the GameDim however is fairly safe. The Move did happen between the start and end time of the game. The Move was a part of a game that was 'Won' or 'Lost'. You may choose then to design the star schema like this:

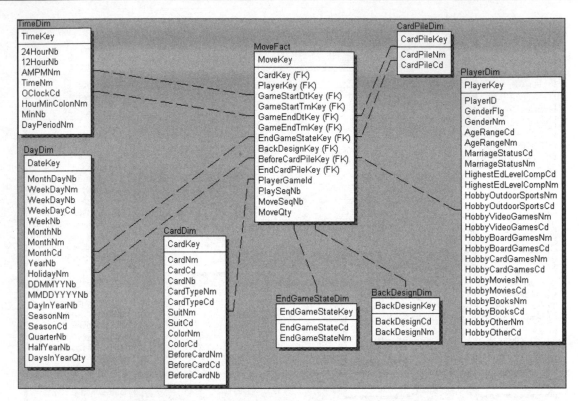

Notice we haven't added any of the additive measures from `GameFact` into `MoveFact`. And look at how many of the dimensions we were able to conform between them. With this many conforming measures we could actually make a good case to the clients that they don't need all the `GameFact` descriptive attributes in the `MoveFact` table. They should be able to select the correct set of `Game` records based on the `Player` records, for instance, and combine `GameFact` and `MoveFact` through the `PlayerDim` table. But we will leave it like this, because this is how the clients want to be able to do their analysis. You should document the fact that several columns in `MoveFact` are at the wrong granularity, however, so they can be removed at a future date if it becomes appropriate.

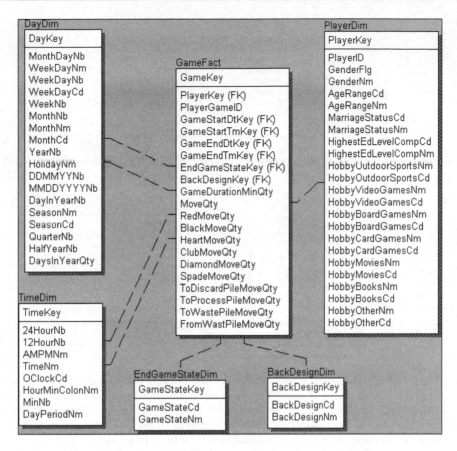

Now there is one more thing we can do to make navigation easier for our clients.

Role Named Dimensions

You will have noticed that we have two dimensions that play multiple roles in the fact table. These can cause havoc in a query tool for the clients. They have trouble remembering which column of the same name, from which table of the same name, is the one they wanted to restrict by. For example, suppose our client wanted to sum the `MoveQty` from `GameFact`, where `GameStartTmKey` was greater than 12:00PM, but the `GameEndTmKey` was less than 1:00PM. If they were using a 'drag and drop' query tool, showing them a picture of the tables, then they can build a query by clicking on `MoveQty`, `GameStartTmKey`, and `GameEndTmKey` from the `GameFact` table. They would then need to go twice to the `TimeDim` to restrict the selection. This gets really confusing and forces a lot of relabel work that you can do upfront for them.

The way to get around this is to build role views, and hide the table from the clients.

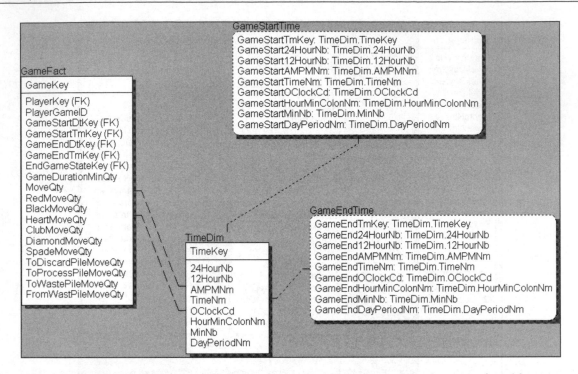

You should name the columns in the role views to match the role named columns in the table, since most of the query tools recognize the similarity and build the join clause for the clients. You need to do this for any dimension that has to fill more than one role. You can see that, along with conforming dimensions, you may want to conform column role names between fact tables to be able to conform the role views as well. Using views for a presentation layer can be very powerful.

Finish Up

And there you have it. As soon as you polish up the entire design with the role playing views, datatype, size, NULL, and all the definitions you have, your second star schema is finished.

Don't forget that these designs need to be reviewed by the team and the clients as well. Polish up all of your deliverables, through the use of color, pictures, and labels, and a little bit of imagination, in order to make it easily comprehensible in the review. Remember to verify both the client needs, and those of the DBA who is physically implementing the dimensional design, once again in the review meeting.

In the grand scheme of things, if this were a data warehouse task you would barely have gotten to first base in the project with this model. This is still a target design to test and improve on. All we have ever been able to do in these exercises is bring you to the point in your analysis where you need to bring in outside help to verify your design. You don't have to be completely finished with the whole model to begin that effort either. You just need to be very comfortable with a section that you can isolate to begin that next phase of validation.

Make sure you keep up with the alterations in definition, documentation, as well as the graphics. You will also need to find ways to communicate those changes to the team.

Summary

Dimensional modeling has just as many special terms as the other modeling techniques we have looked at. Hopefully now you can recognize them in specific instances of design and functionality. The key definitions to remember in this case are:

- ❑ Data mart – a type of data warehouse designed primarily to address a specific function or department's needs

- ❑ Star Schema – design for a data warehouse, comprising a central fact table, linked to a number of dimension tables

- ❑ Fact table – table containing all the required measures of interest

- ❑ Measures – quantities by which attributes are assessed. For example time, data, length, and so on

- ❑ Dimension tables – tables linked to the fact table containing the fact attributes, and appropriate details

- ❑ Granularity – the level of detail held in the fact table. This relates to the hierarchy of information stored (for example in terms of a given time period, store location, sales representative, and so on)

- ❑ Snowflake schemas – variation of the star schema design in which dimension tables are broken down into multiple dimension tables with a hierarchy

We built two separate data marts. Our first data mart (Game) involved the design of a fact table with a bunch of additive measures, while our second example (GameMove) designed a factless fact table with descriptive attributes at the wrong granularity. We looked at the options for designing dimensions, and the power of using conformed dimensions. And we covered Role playing views to help the clients use their query tools. We looked at the different techniques of storing changing values using a change policy.

In the next chapter we will try to retroactively model a system that is already designed and in use.

- Where to Start
- Data Structure Analysis
- Data Analysis
- Front End Analysis
- Historic / Descriptive
- Finishing Touches
- Building a Logical Model
- Finish it Up
- Summary

Reverse Engineering a Data Model

While the majority of this book has focused on designing new systems, from conceptual through logical to physical models, in reality you will often need to document existing database objects and elements. This process is known as reverse engineering, since you are working back from the existing system in order to develop a physical model, which, in turn, can be used to create a logical model. In working backwards you need to compile solid documentation about the data elements, relationships, structure, rules, processes, and quirks of an application. While we can't provide a complete guide to reverse engineering in a single chapter, what we can do is examine various techniques you can use to unearth the data map from an existing database system. In this chapter we'll consider a sample database and work backwards from it to devise both a physical and a logical model. In the course of the example we will:

❑ Look at all the resources available to us – RDBMS library data, database creation script coding, user manuals and training documentation, front-end application screens

❑ See how modeling tools can help you in capturing a physical model of the existing data

❑ See how to develop the same model without using modeling software tools

❑ Work with the physical model to develop a logical one

This kind of 'As-Is' documenting can be used to draw up an inventory of data structures detailing exactly what is in the database. On the other hand it could be trying to get a handle on the actual logical definitions and relationships of the data (from a seriously un-normalized physical design). The physical model you come up with could be used to recreate the data structures in another environment or map data elements for interfacing. It can also be used to compare basic data elements, business rules/relationships, general data types, and definitions in the case of system merges or software replacement.

It's not as easy to come up with a common database, as it was to come up with a common game to analyze. Solitaire is as close to a universal game as I could conceive of, but databases aren't nearly as universally deployed. I have decided to use the Microsoft Access example database Northwind, but I will also throw in some small samples of other types of systems for comparison. I am hoping that most of you have it. It may make the exercise seem tool-specific, but the steps of pulling out the tables, columns, definitions, relationships, and indexes is standard fare no matter what the platform.

Where to Start

Reverse engineering starts by concentrating on building a physical data model. But that is not all you are looking to document. You want to know not only about data objects the system owns, but also what the data elements really are, what other objects it uses, functionality, shortcomings, and problems.

You want to answer questions like 'Where does the data come from?' 'Where does it go?' 'Who uses it and for what?' Plus you want to know not just what data the application was originally designed to hold, but what it has been stretched and forced into managing. You need to concern yourself with what it is today, as well as be able to see a little of where it came from. It's also important to try and get an idea of the applications that use or update this data (and any applications that use those applications) in order to gauge how critical and well-used the database is. How many users would shout if a particular database were switched off?

Most reverse engineering tasks occur in response to a project need. There is a prioritization of necessary information, similar to the analysis we did on the physical-only exercise that will help you decide when to conclude your analysis. You have to document what is there:

❑   Determine the goal of the task. Are you trying to replace, rebuild, restore, or just document the system? Talk to the clients to establish exactly what they want. This will tell you if the product of this task will lead into another one or if it is the goal in itself

❑   Start with the data storage structures – database tables/columns, linked documents and spreadsheet/s, file systems, or any other type of data collection. You need to document the design exactly the way it is currently

❑   Try to find all the unique identifiers – surrogate, natural, concatenated. Plus find any rules that govern their creation, updates, or deletions

❑   Next – try to find relationships between separately stored data sets and between data elements internal to a data set

❑   Profile the data to find definitions. Definitions are an absolute *must* and some of them could be pretty complicated descriptions of 'sometimes it's this and sometimes it's that'

❑   Finally, try to find all the rules of the system incorporated into the screens, back-end code, and reports to find logical data rules that were deployed outside of the data storage structure

Gathering all of this information about an existing system will allow you to provide a model of the physical data structures, and sometimes more importantly, definitions and descriptions of data element management rules in a logical data model.

Resources

The resources you should target in this case are as follows:

- A copy or access to a copy of the system you are reverse engineering is essential. You will need to be able to view everything and exercise the functionality to test your observations. A test copy of some sort that has a good selection of current production data is the best. Working without this handicaps the modeler tremendously.

- Access to RDBMS library or catalog data – This will provide you with information regarding tables, columns, views, triggers, indexes, integrity constraints, relationships, and synonyms (data varies depending on the RDBMS).

- Access to the Code – If you only have a compiled copy of the system, you will find your ability to make quick assessments fairly restricted. You need to look at the code to aid the development of table, column, and relationship definitions (hopefully as notes in the scripts). You should especially look for items such as create scripts DDL (data definition language), procedures and triggers DML (data manipulation language), data access maps (EAI mappings, XML & UML definition files), data move scripts (Load routines, DTS scripts, ETL files), and report code.

- Access to Production Data – You need to know if your assessment of Table/Column name and definition notes is what is really happening in the system. Look for sample data from production databases in order to help determine the nature and diversity of the data contained in the system. You need to gather information about the records and values for the data elements. You have to determine what the population of a data set is. I have reverse engineered hundreds of tables with 0 records. Restrict your efforts to what is being used. You need to look at how many distinct values there are. Is it what you expect? Check on the creativity of the data values. Does it seem that the clients are working around nullability rules or integrity rules by manipulating values?

- Historic / Descriptive – Look for user guides/manuals, Help files, and project notebooks to help you in documenting the local features of the system. Conduct interviews with project team members, and chat informally with programmers or DBAs to aid your research. Attend any training classes pertinent to the job in hand.

You are looking to gather anything that will help you understand, not just the structure of the data, but also how it fits into the ebb and flow of the Enterprise data. You will certainly want to highlight any shortcomings, anomalies, or faults for the team. If you have enough time and resources you should be able to create a credible physical, logical, or even conceptual (if required) data model by working backwards from the original reverse-engineered physical model. You may be able to assist in creating a business process model as well working with what functionality you discover in your analysis.

Data Structure Analysis

The first and probably most important task of a reverse engineering project is to find the data elements, their definitions, and how they are organized. We have a couple of ways of doing this. Automated modeling tools can help you very quickly, using a database connection or by reading the creation scripts. When the modeling tool can't help you, you get to do these tasks manually.

Modeling Tool Support

Many of the modeling software tools available to you, such as Erwin or DataArchitect for example, will connect straight to a database or will read DDL. If you can connect to the database, you can capture almost everything there is to know about it from the structure of the files or RDBMS library/catalog tables on the system.

RDBMS Connection

Almost all RDBMS have a library or catalog where details about the data management/storage/access/manipulation of objects like tables, indexes, views, and procedures is kept. This information is the foundation of your reverse engineering modeling efforts. Bear in mind that building a data model of the current physical structures can only provide a snapshot of the system, since you can bet that very soon some change will have occurred. However, that snapshot can prove useful to you in your reverse engineering work as a starting point for your determination of table and column names and definitions.

As an example, I used Erwin 3.5.2 to take this picture of the `Northwind.mdb` Access file.

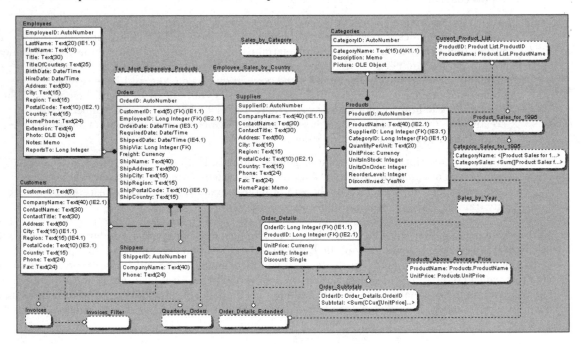

While this model is very useful, there are a number of caveats to be aware of:

❑   The model the software provides is not necessarily in an easily printable format. It took me 15 minutes to rearrange the boxes and lines above to fit the page

❑ There are a number of empty boxes on the model that represent views. The reason why some views have columns and others don't, is that the software can't always make sense of the code within a view. However, it does bring the code into the model for you and creates an empty placeholder

You will get an error report to help you target what the software had a problem with, which will look something like this:

View 'Employee Sales by Country' has been imported as user-defined SQL since
Erwin was not able to parse it.

You can use the software's View Editor to look at the code behind such views. If we take the example of the Order Details Extended view, then the code looks like this:

```
create view "Quarterly Orders" AS
SELECT DISTINCT
    Customers.CustomerID,
    Customers.CompanyName,
    Customers.City,
    Customers.Country
FROM Customers
RIGHT JOIN
Orders ON Customers.CustomerID = Orders.CustomerID
WHERE Orders.OrderDate BETWEEN '19970101' And '19971231'
```

Do stop for a moment to appreciate how rich a stock of information you can capture with such tools. If we remove the views from the model, then we get something that looks like this:

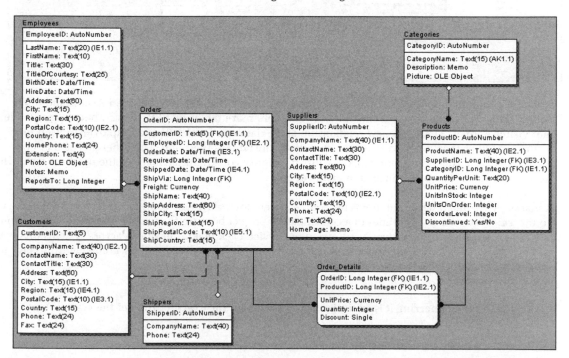

Here we have primary keys, alternate keys, foreign keys, relationships, data types, sizes, and even some definitions (if the database has place for them in the libraries) all captured nearly instantly.

This requires that you have a login to the database you want to take a picture of and SELECT permissions from the DBA.

Let's do this one more time, only this time with Northwind on SQL Server2000.

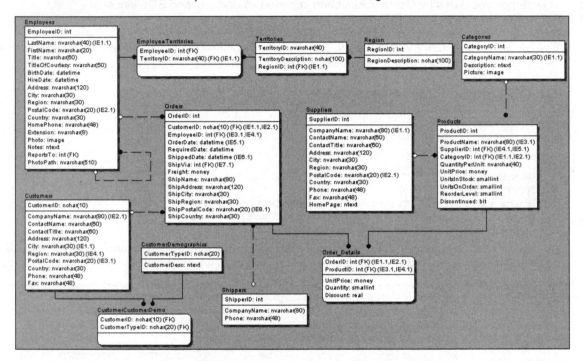

Notice the differences. Obviously the versions of Northwind are different between Access and SQL Server. The data types are different. Not only are there more tables on SQL Server, but also more views (not visible above). There is a new relationship at the database level, relating Employee to itself in a recursion. Other than a new column for PhotoPath, the table is the same. The difference is that now ReportsTo is a role-named foreign key with an integrity constraint managed at the database level. In Access that relationship is managed in the front end.

It matters very much what you use as the source system for your reverse engineering. You may have to do the 'same' system several times in a consolidation project because they aren't really the 'same'. You need to be sensitive to more than just Version or Service Pack level. I have run across systems that were initially the same but over the course of years had been subtly modified in their home environments to support parochial needs.

> **In reverse engineering it is critical that you document the exact location of the system you worked on.**

With a software tool like this you can get very quickly to a complete list of the tables, columns, views, indexes, and integrity constraints that the RDBMS knows about. If your task was to provide a list of database constructs like this, your task (other than some reports) is probably finished. Some reverse engineering jobs are about an hour long resulting in just these lists and a picture.

Unfortunately the RDBMS is in the dark about some things. This may be for any of the following reasons:

❑ The constraints (relationships) weren't built in the database as constraint structures, the front end controls some or all of the integrity, or indeed triggers are used to implement business rules that don't fit easily into the database as constraints. In cases like that, your model will come back without a single relationship line in sight. The definitions don't come back. You have a great list of names but there were no comments put into the catalogs that the software tool can access. This can make some reverse-engineered structures almost useless. The columns aren't named intuitively to help you know what is in them so you still have no idea what or where a data element lives

❑ Data elements are stored in files outside the RDBMS, in either the front end, or sometimes directory structures that can be accessed through other coding techniques

Sometimes you can't use modeling software to help you accomplish even this task. There are various reasons for that:

❑ You can't get the security or communication set up. For instance some software can't use NT authentication and the RDBMS isn't set up for login accounts

❑ The RDBMS isn't on the list of those that your software can connect to

❑ The data structures aren't a RDBMS. Sometimes you are trying to model files like linked Excel, Lotus 123, or Word documents. Other times you will be working with non-relational hierarchical or network type DBMS, which mostly don't convert into relational modeling tools

In cases like that we are stuck with alternative methods, like importing the create scripts or resorting to sketchpad and a pencil.

Data Definition Language Imports

In cases where you simply can't get a sufficient handle on the source to give you an informed snapshot of the database, then you will need to look at the source-code to create a database. Your DBA is generally the best point of contact in finding a code library or providing you with a file that they used to create the tables. This file or files is generally referred to as the DDL (Data Definition Language) of a system, or a **create script**. These files are not always available either. The system may have been created without them, they may have been lost over time, or you may be working with a vendor tool.

> Be careful. Create scripts are not always kept up-to-date with the current objects. There may be a series of 'Alter...' scripts required as a supplement to build current structures.

From this file you have access to all the table names, column names, data types, sizes, precision, and nullability. You may also have access to default values, data object definitions, and comments left behind by those who have maintained the system over the years explaining anomalies, depending upon the age of the create script. In order to be able to import DDL text, your modeling software must be able to read script written for that RDBMS. If that platform isn't supported again, you will have to resort to typing the table descriptions in by hand.

For example, the following code creates two tables named Employees and Orders for an Oracle platform:

```
CREATE TABLE Employees (
    EmployeeID       ROWID NULL,
    LastName         VARCHAR2(20) NOT NULL,
    FirstName        VARCHAR2(10) NOT NULL,
    Title         VARCHAR2(30) NULL,
    TitleOfCourtesy    VARCHAR2(25) NULL,
    BirthDate       DATE NULL,
    HireDate        DATE NULL,
    Address         VARCHAR2(60) NULL,
    City          VARCHAR2(15) NULL,
    Region          VARCHAR2(15) NULL,
    PostalCode        VARCHAR2(10) NULL,
    Country         VARCHAR2(15) NULL,
    HomePhone         VARCHAR2(24) NULL,
    Extension         VARCHAR2(4) NULL,
    Photo         CLOB NULL,
    Notes         LONG VARCHAR NULL,
    ReportsTo        INTEGER NULL);

CREATE UNIQUE INDEX PrimaryKey ON Employees
(    EmployeeID             ASC);
CREATE INDEX LastName ON Employees
(    LastName            ASC);
CREATE INDEX PostalCode ON Employees
(    PostalCode            ASC);
ALTER TABLE Employees
    ADD ( PRIMARY KEY (EmployeeID) ) ;

CREATE TABLE Orders (
    OrderID        ROWID NULL,
    CustomerID        VARCHAR2(5) NULL,
    EmployeeID        INTEGER NULL,
    OrderDate        DATE NULL,
    RequiredDate       DATE NULL,
    ShippedDate        DATE NULL,
    ShipVia        INTEGER NULL,
    Freight        NUMBER DEFAULT 0 NULL,
    ShipName        VARCHAR2(40) NULL,
    ShipAddress        VARCHAR2(60) NULL,
    ShipCity        VARCHAR2(15) NULL,
    ShipRegion        VARCHAR2(15) NULL,
    ShipPostalCode       VARCHAR2(10) NULL,
```

```
       ShipCountry       VARCHAR2(15) NULL);

CREATE UNIQUE INDEX PrimaryKey ON Orders
(    OrderID            ASC);
CREATE INDEX CustomerID ON Orders
(    CustomerID         ASC);
CREATE INDEX EmployeeID ON Orders
(    EmployeeID         ASC);
CREATE INDEX OrderDate ON Orders
(    OrderDate          ASC);
CREATE INDEX ShippedDate ON Orders
(    ShippedDate        ASC);
CREATE INDEX ShipPostalCode ON Orders
(    ShipPostalCode     ASC);
ALTER TABLE Orders
   ADD ( PRIMARY KEY (OrderID) ) ;
ALTER TABLE Orders
   ADD ( FOREIGN KEY (CustomerID)
               REFERENCES Customers ) ;
ALTER TABLE Orders
   ADD ( FOREIGN KEY (EmployeeID)
               REFERENCES Employees ) ;
ALTER TABLE Orders
   ADD ( FOREIGN KEY (ShipVia)
               REFERENCES Shippers ) ;
```

The physical model created by a modeling tool of this DDL looks as follows:

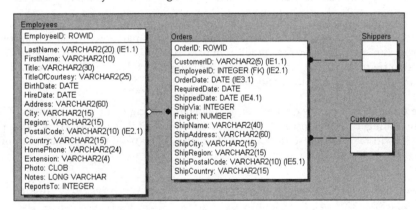

As you can see, we can extract much of the same information we got from the RDBMS Library Catalog. The column names, data types, data size, and nullability come directly from the CREATE TABLE command statement. We can also determine the primary keys of each table by looking at the following lines within the script:

```
CREATE UNIQUE INDEX PrimaryKey ON Employees
(    EmployeeID         ASC);
CREATE UNIQUE INDEX PrimaryKey ON Orders
(    OrderID            ASC);
ALTER TABLE Employees
   ADD ( PRIMARY KEY (EmployeeID) )
ALTER TABLE Orders
   ADD ( PRIMARY KEY (OrderID) ) ;
```

We can determine the foreign key definitions from the following lines:

```
ALTER TABLE Orders
   ADD ( FOREIGN KEY (CustomerID)
               REFERENCES Customers ) ;
ALTER TABLE Orders
   ADD ( FOREIGN KEY (EmployeeID)
               REFERENCES Employees ) ;
ALTER TABLE Orders
   ADD ( FOREIGN KEY (ShipVia)
               REFERENCES Shippers ) ;
```

This explains the empty boxes on our diagram. We have foreign keys that reference the tables Customers, EmployeeID, and ShipVia. However, our create script only creates the Employees and Orders tables, so the software can't determine any structure for the Shippers and Customers tables, and leaves them empty. The DBA can help you determine any synonyms that have been set up in the existing database to reference a table in a different system.

> I should warn you about this. I haven't had much luck getting a clean import from DDL files. Code is often full of so many legal but obscure syntax blocks that the modeling tool is overwhelmed.

Be aware that even scripts auto-generated from sources like Microsoft SQL Server Enterprise Manager seem to build code that is legal in the RDBMS, but not always parsable by modeling software. The resultant errors can give an incorrect model. It may take a bit of trial and error to figure out what changes need to be made in the code to provide a clean import. Review the errors and carefully double-check what results you get with the script itself.

For instance this SQL script was created using the default setting from the **Generate SQL Script** option in Enterprise Manager for Microsoft ® Management Console 1.2, Version 5.0, Service Pack 2. on SQL Server 2000. Erwin 3.5 can't parse the **COLLATE** clause. They need to be removed in order to do an auto-import.

```
if exists (select * from dbo.sysobjects where id = object_id(N'[dbo].[userinfo]')
and OBJECTPROPERTY(id, N'IsUserTable') = 1)
drop table [dbo].[tbcinfo]
GO

CREATE TABLE [dbo].[userinfo] (
   [login_id] [varchar] (255) COLLATE SQL_Latin1_General_CP1_CI_AS NULL ,
   [Name] [varchar] (255) COLLATE SQL_Latin1_General_CP1_CI_AS NULL ,
   [extra] [varchar] (255) COLLATE SQL_Latin1_General_CP1_CI_AS NULL ,
   [location] [varchar] (255) COLLATE SQL_Latin1_General_CP1_CI_AS NULL
) ON [PRIMARY]
GO
```

The exact error is Unable to parse "COLLATE" of line 6. The only thing able to be imported is this:

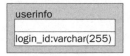

Using an automated tool can be very helpful, but you must be very careful to check the results. The DBAs or programmers who create and manage the DDL may be able to help, by determining what options to use in creating DDL without the bits that cannot be parsed.

Manual Processing

When the software tool can't help, the only alternative is the hard way namely reading and building it yourself. We have a couple of options here. We start with any code that could have been used to create the structures originally. If those don't exist, we move on to reading the structures themselves with whatever is available. You may need to get hold of a designer copy of a software tool to see the back end structures or it may be as simple as opening Excel to see what is there.

Code

In those cases where the RDBMS library/catalog and DDL aren't options for your software, you can at least use the DDL to 'Cut and Paste' the names from the file to prevent typos. Even if you can't write code, you can see that it isn't all that hard to read the create scripts. The name after the word 'Table' is of course its name. The other names are the columns, each with their data type, size, and nullability. Well-developed code, which you'll hope to get you hands on, is nicely organized with a new line for every object and tabs to help the eye see what is going on.

Sometimes you find odd things when you look at code. Note that CategoryID below is NULL allowed from the Access version of Northwind.mdb (this bug is fixed in SQL Server 2000). That is extremely interesting as it is called out later in the script as the unique index. Don't be surprised. Some databases allow one record to have a NULL primary key. Shocked?

As was I when I first found out. When I asked about this 'feature,' I was told that it could be used to process records that are partially completed during data or for some other, currently unknown, process.

```
CREATE TABLE Categories (
    CategoryID              AutoNumber NULL,
    CategoryName            Text(15) NOT NULL,
    Description             Memo NULL,
    Picture             OLE Object NULL
);

COMMENT ON TABLE Categories IS      'Categories of Northwind products.';
COMMENT ON COLUMN Categories.CategoryID IS 'Number automatically assigned to a new
category.';
COMMENT ON COLUMN Categories.CategoryName IS    'Name of food category.';
COMMENT ON COLUMN Categories.Picture IS 'A picture representing the food
category.';
```

```
CREATE UNIQUE INDEX CategoryName ON Categories
(
    CategoryName           ASC
);



ALTER TABLE Categories
    ADD ( PRIMARY KEY (CategoryID) ) ;
```

But there are other types of code that you may have to learn to read. Look at code written for a Network-style database. First, you should know it is pretty challenging reverse engineering databases that aren't relational into a data model. We expect data sets connected by key migration. Many database platforms don't work that way.

Notice that the DDL syntax is different and yet the elements are still there. Instead of 'Table' these are called 'Record'. The data type is in front of the field name (what we are used to calling columns) where the size is behind the field name. A definition note is set immediately after the name (this is probably optional, but very helpful for a modeler trying to reverse engineer this.

Network and Hierarchical systems also don't use primary and foreign key concepts. You won't find those to help you know how the data fits together. The connectivity or relationships are called out in set structures like the one at the very bottom connecting the updte_rec to the bus_date_rec. These are linkages by pointer rather than migrating data values.

There are unique indexes like the cstmr_code in the custmr_rec in the code below:

```
record custmr_rec{
unique key
char  cstmr_code[9];        /* Customer Code */
char  cstmr_name[31];       /* Customer name */
char  cstmr_taxable_ind[2];/* Y=Customer is taxable */
char  cstmr_active[2];      /* N=Inactive */
char  cstmr_reserve_1[4];   /* Reserved for future use */
char  cstmr_reserve_2[4];   /* Reserved for future use */
char  cstmr_reserve_3[8];   /* Reserved for future use */
}

record updte_rec {                 /* Update log record */
long  upd_bdate;            /* Business Date of update */
long  upd_sysdate;          /* Date of update */
long  upd_systime;          /* Time of Update */
long  upd_fld;              /* Field ID of updated field */
char  upd_code[4];    /* Type of update (HIRE, PROM) */
char  upd_userid[9];  /*LoginID of user making change */
long  upd_rec_no;           /* Record number updated */
long  upd_fld_no;           /* Field number updated */
long  upd_old_val;          /* Old value */
```

```
long   upd_new_val;                /* New value */


/* To retrieve records busdate chronogically */
        compound key updbdate_key {
                upd_bdate        ascending;
                upd_sysdate      ascending;
                upd_systime      ascending;
}

compound key updsystime_key {
                upd_sysdate      ascending;
                upd_systime      ascending;
}

set bdate_updte_set{
        order    last;
        owner    bus_date_rec;
        member   updte_rec;
}
```

You have to read this type of code differently, but you can still find the names, sizes, and connections for documentation.

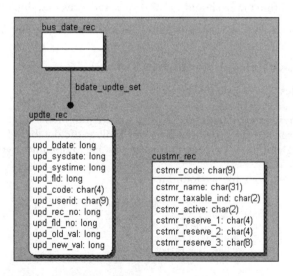

> **A data modeler should learn to read code they work with frequently, even if they don't write it.**

Structures

Then there are the times when you don't even have code to read. You are analyzing data structures that have no concept of create scripts, like simply built structures in a tool like Lotus123 or Excel. In these cases, you are looking for a file type construct with data elements named (hopefully) in labels on top of columns. The further away you get from relational platforms the more difficult it will be for you to reverse engineer a physical data model. The lines start to blur between reverse engineering and just plain business process and data analysis.

Structure Assessment

Many people seem to think that all reverse engineering is about is getting the database structure documented. But without doing some other checking, this first pass could lack quite a bit of knowledge about what is really going on in an application. There are some assessments you can do by just knowing this much:

❏ Do the structures and names suggest a fairly normalized structure or not?

❏ Are there large quantities of columns with obvious repeating groups?

❏ Can you see dependencies internal to the tables (breaking 2nd and 3rd Normal form)?

❏ Does it look like the same data element is in multiple tables?

❏ Do the columns seem to be defined contrary to what you think would be efficient. `Nulls` where you don't think they should exist? Types and sizes that don't make sense?

❏ Can you see business rule problems (based on your understanding from other models) in this structure?

❏ Are there massive quantities of indexes? Or none at all?

❏ Do all the tables have a primary key?

This would be the highest level of analysis. You can't make judgments on the data or how the data is managed. All you can see are the structures that were built at the database level, so you tuck all the physical facts you can glean from the code into what you use to document your models.

Here is just that little category table we found in Access:

```
Categories
CategoryName: Text(15) NOT NULL (AK1.1)
Description: Memo
Picture: OLE Object
```

Look at what we can tell about this table:

Table Name	Categories		
Comment on Table	Categories of Northwind products		
Table Columns	**Comment on column**	**Data Type and Size**	**NULL/NOT NULL**
CategoryID	Number automatically assigned to a new category.	AutoNumber	NULL
CategoryName	Name of food category	Text(15)	NOT NULL
Description		Memo	NULL
Picture	A picture representing the food category	OLE Object	NULL
Primary Key	CategoryID		
Index	CategoryName		

Don't forget the definitions. Just remember they are what the original programmer *thought* was going into those columns. The data stored in these columns may be more complex than the description suggests, since you will need to verify how up-to-date the description actually is. What can we tell by looking at this model of the Northwind.mdb?

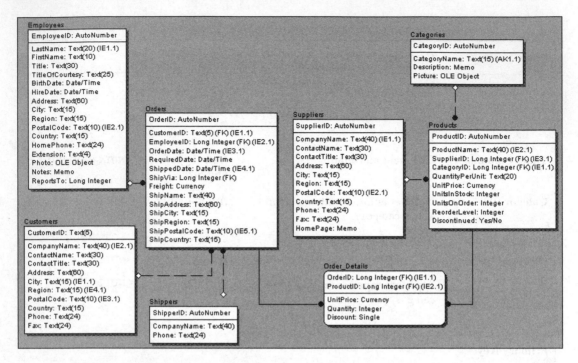

- ❑ Northwind looks fairly normalized

- ❑ There aren't any glaring repeating groups

- ❑ Other than some geographical dependencies in addresses there don't seem to be any glaring Normal form violations

- ❑ Data elements seem to exist only once in the structures, although some of the names wouldn't support that conclusion as there are repeating names like three Region columns. (I am assuming that there simply isn't a modifier in the name to distinguish Employee Address Region from Supplies Region)

- ❑ There seems to be some nullability in the business rules that doesn't make much sense. Products do not seem to require a Supplier nor be in a Category. Orders do not seem to have to have a Customer or Employee overseeing the process

- ❑ There are very few not nulls rules and some null allowed columns are in primary key positions. (Remember this is Access)

- ❑ Indexes seem light to normal

- ❑ All tables do have a primary key

What if it looked like the diagram opposite? Just having a copy of the structure of the tables may not be very useful in determining what the data elements are. I would like to tell you I hardly ever come across tables like the one opposite, but it isn't true. They show up on a pretty regular basis in larger companies with at least 10-15 years of custom development in their environments.

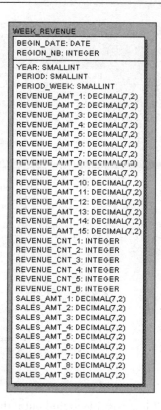

How would you assess this one?

- ❑ Not Normalized

- ❑ Unknown repeating groups – can't tell what the data elements are

- ❑ Looks like a data mart of weekly sales information for each Region in the enterprise, with many measurable facts. This is probably a reporting table. We just don't know what the measures are

- ❑ It looks like an efficient structure – just non-intuitive

- ❑ There is a primary key making a Region Week of sales data unique

But we wouldn't stop there with this structure. There must be more to know than just this. It is quite possible that if you look you will find a view, report, or load routine to help figure out the real data elements in this generalized set of columns. The table was obviously designed to be very flexible. In this case a view holds the key to understanding these data elements.

You need to review the view code if it is possible to find out if there are any restrictions being applied in the WHERE clause that could help you with your definitions. This one is very simple. Everything in the Week_Revenue table is available in the Week_Revenue view.

```
CREATE VIEW WEEK_REVENUE
    BEGIN_DATE,
    REGION_NB,
    YEAR,
    PERIOD,
    PERIOD_WEEK,
    ADJUSTED_SALES,
    SPECIAL_EVENT_SALE,
    MANUAL_PROMOTION,
    PREMIUM_SALES,
    SALES_TAX,
    RETURN_AMT,
    DAMAGE_AMT,
    CREDIT_AMT,
    CANCEL_AMT,
    NET_SALES,
    GROSS_SALES,
    BALANCE_SHEET_AMT,
    VENDOR_DISCOUNT_AMT,
```

```
            PAYROLL_PAYOUT,
            THEFT_AMT,
            TRANSACTION_CNT,
            CREDIT_CNT,
            CANCEL_CNT,
            MASTER_PACK_AMT,
            SINGLE_UNIT_SALES,
            CHARITY_DONATION,
            ASSISTED_SALES,
            INTERNET_SALES,
            CATALOG_SALES)
    AS SELECT
            WEEK_REVENUE.BEGIN_DATE,
            WEEK_REVENUE.REGION_NB,
            WEEK_REVENUE.YEAR,
            WEEK_REVENUE.PERIOD,
            WEEK_REVENUE.PERIOD_WEEK,
            WEEK_REVENUE.REVENUE_AMT_1,
            WEEK_REVENUE.REVENUE_AMT_2,
            WEEK_REVENUE.REVENUE_AMT_3,
            WEEK_REVENUE.REVENUE_AMT_4,
            WEEK_REVENUE.REVENUE_AMT_5,
            WEEK_REVENUE.REVENUE_AMT_6,
            WEEK_REVENUE.REVENUE_AMT_7,
            WEEK_REVENUE.REVENUE_AMT_8,
            WEEK_REVENUE.REVENUE_AMT_9,
            WEEK_REVENUE.REVENUE_AMT_10,
            WEEK_REVENUE.REVENUE_AMT_11,
            WEEK_REVENUE.REVENUE_AMT_12,
            WEEK_REVENUE.REVENUE_AMT_13,
            WEEK_REVENUE.REVENUE_AMT_14,
            WEEK_REVENUE.REVENUE_AMT_15,
            WEEK_REVENUE.REVENUE_CNT_1,
            WEEK_REVENUE.REVENUE_CNT_2,
            WEEK_REVENUE.REVENUE_CNT_3,
            WEEK_REVENUE.SALES_AMT_1,
            WEEK_REVENUE.SALES_AMT_2,
            WEEK_REVENUE.SALES_AMT_3,
            WEEK_REVENUE.SALES_AMT_5,
            WEEK_REVENUE.SALES_AMT_6,
            WEEK_REVENUE.SALES_AMT_7
    FROM WEEK_REVENUE
```

Finding this code would allow you to do a mapping from Table Column to View label. Now, knowing the names of the data elements as they are described in the view, gives you a better chance of gathering a definition for each column in the table.

Column Name	View Label
BEGIN_DATE	BEGIN_DATE
REGION_NB	REGION_NB
YEAR	YEAR
PERIOD	PERIOD
PERIOD_WEEK	PERIOD_WEEK
REVENUE_AMT_1	ADJUSTED_SALES
REVENUE_AMT_2	SPECIAL_EVENT_SALE
REVENUE_AMT_3	MANUAL_PROMOTION
REVENUE_AMT_4	PREMIUM_SALES
REVENUE_AMT_5	SALES_TAX
REVENUE_AMT_6	RETURN_AMT
REVENUE_AMT_7	DAMAGE_AMT
REVENUE_AMT_8	CREDIT_AMT
REVENUE_AMT_9	CANCEL_AMT
REVENUE_AMT_10	NET_SALES
REVENUE_AMT_11	GROSS_SALES
REVENUE_AMT_12	BALANCE_SHEET_AMT
REVENUE_AMT_13	VENDOR_DISCOUNT_AMT
REVENUE_AMT_14	PAYROLL_PAYOUT
REVENUE_AMT_15	THEFT_AMT
REVENUE_CNT_1	TRANSACTION_CNT
REVENUE_CNT_2	CREDIT_CNT
REVENUE_CNT_3	CANCEL_CNT
SALES_AMT_1	MASTER_PACK_AMT
SALES_AMT_2	SINGLE_UNIT_SALES
SALES_AMT_3	CHARITY_DONATION
SALES_AMT_5	ASSISTED_SALES
SALES_AMT_6	INTERNET_SALES
SALES_AMT_7	CATALOG_SALES

Remember that you are just trying to document the system 'As-Is'. Don't try to figure out why the decisions were made to deploy a structure like this, though it may seem like the right thing to do at the time. There may be many good reasons why things were done this way that you are unaware of. It may be part of a security plan, or it could be that this strange structure was required by another part of the system. Document it objectively and with as much detail as you can discover.

Data Analysis

The next step of the process of reverse engineering is to look over or profile the data and verify what we think the definition of the column/table is. Unfortunately Northwind was never a production database, so the data values it contains are polished test system values. In actuality, there are three things that occur to data in Production systems with startling regularity:

❑ The first is that single, simple data columns suddenly become the home of multiple instances of unusual values that they were not originally designed for

❑ A data column is used to store the things it was supposed to, but if some special character is inserted, then it means something else

❑ Conversely the data has dried up and there are no more instances of given data objects in the business. As a result the column 'just doesn't get used anymore'

Common checks are as follows:

SELECT COUNT

How many states in the United States? The number you want here is fifty, unless territories are added. Equally if you only do business in twelve states, the answer should be twelve. If you get 72 there is a problem either with the name/definition of the column or with the quality of the data.

How many months do you expect to find in a 'Year'? 12? I worked with a system that had an 18-month growing year for agriculture. Every other year had 2 Januarys, Februarys through June records. That was a surprise.

SELECT COUNT / GROUP BY

Ratios are also a good indicator. Select the count of the records in the table. Now select the count of specific values in the column. If you have 100 records in the Employee table, and 99 of them have 'N/A' in the LastReviewedByEmpId column you can question if the business rule is really that everyone have a review once a year. Do a group by month for Hire dates. If they all seem to fall in January you can question whether that makes sense. You are searching for things that do not make sense.

SELECT COUNT DISTINCT

How many distinct values for month would you expect to find in a database? If there are more than twelve, or if they are not the twelve you expect because three of them are February misspelled twice and August and November are missing, then you need to find out why; this may be a quality issue, or indeed an unusual data definition.

One of my favorite things to do is find how many ways creative clients have gotten around NOT NULL rules. They put in N/A, Unknown, a series of spaces, and zeros. There are values that you will find in looking at distincts that make you question the definition of the columns.

SELECT MIN

How far back would you expect dates to go in a system? If, for example, you are in a Payroll system and the minimum date in the HireDate field is in the 1500s then there is a problem. Quite likely someone came up with some quirky date to flag employees for some reason. In this case the date I came across was a flag is used to denote the lack of a data value during a data migration effort from years ago. But you need to document it because it is obviously important enterprise data and indeed data of different intelligence than the original intent.

SELECT MAX

How high would you expect a LibraryFineAmt to be? Probably not more than around $100.00 in the worst case. If you find something that far exceeds your reasonability factor you need to find out why. The column could contain dollar values that mean something different to LibraryFineAmt. It may be that the cost of the book is being added for damages. That totally changes the definition of what is populating that column.

What would you think if you selected the Max CreateDate and it was three years ago? You would realize that no one inserts to this data set anymore. It may mean that no one uses it either, but that is a different kind of analysis that requires the DBA to put a trace on query traffic.

SELECT

Sometimes you need to just look at the whole list and see what pops up in front of your eyes. What does it mean when you find people's names in address lines? Usually it is the 'Attention to …' although there are actual George Washington Blvds out there.

What about values that look like `<#name%date&text*number>` in a text field? That means you have probably come across a column that is being used as a junk pile. For some reason, instead of adding new columns, a way was found to cram lots of different data elements into one field. All of those special characters are probably parsed in code to be able to use the separate data elements.

Select columns in one table that you think should make sense together. State and Country. BirthDate and GraduationDate. Look for things like Quebec in India and Graduation dates that are before Birth dates.

Data Assessment

You should be able to take the results of your data profiling and provide some statistics about the quality of the data you found, as well as update the definitions of the tables and columns. You would be able to provide commentary like the following for the small Categories table in Northwind.mdb.

Categories General Assessment – Data quality good – even better than database rules allow				
RowCount Qty 8				
Column Name	**Definition in Code**	**DataType**	**Null?**	**Data Review found**
CategoryID	Number automatically assigned to a new category	AutoNumber	NULL	All rows have a unique number – no nulls
CategoryName	Name of food category	Text(15)	NOT NULL	All names are intrinsically different – no duplication by misspelling
Description		Memo	NULL	All categories have descriptions – no nulls – seem appropriate to the name
Picture	A picture representing the food category	OLE Object	NULL	All categories have Ole objects. I didn't open them to review for appropriateness

Data Rules in Code

Once you have as much as you can glean from looking at the structures and the data you want to go over any other code that may have rules embedded in it.

DML

This is a prime source of business rules. The 'IF ... THEN ... ELSE' structure of procedural code lends itself to easily pick up some of the rules not held in the database structures.

❑ DML – (data manipulation language) Procedures, Triggers (stored procedures that are fired by events in the database such as INSERT or DELETE statements). This code will verify that the data elements behave just the way you thought they did. You may find some denormalization clues in triggers that fire after INSERTs or UPDATEs pointing to extra places the data is stored. This will help you determine what is the base data element, and what is derived.

Look at this interesting macro (script that automates a series of operations that you will perform frequently) that I found in `Northwind.mdb`. If you look at the 'Validate Postal Code' section you can see that there is definitely a series of True/False statements, suggesting a relationship between Country and Zip Code to prevent incorrect values being inserted into the database. You will need to note that in the logical model, since you can't do so in the physical one. Except as notes, there are no physical relationships to support these business rules.

Subroutine Name	Formula	Action	Description
Validate Postal Code	`IsNull ([Country])`	StopMacro	If Country is NULL, postal code can't be validated.
	`[Country] In ("France", "Italy", "Spain") And Len([PostalCode])<>5`	MsgBox	If postal code is not 5 characters, display message...
	...	CancelEvent	...and cancel event.
	...	GoToControl	
	`[Country] In ("Australia","Singapore") And Len([PostalCode])<>4`	MsgBox	If postal code is not 4 characters, display message...
	...	CancelEvent	...and cancel event.
	...	GoToControl	
	`([Country]="Canada") And ([PostalCode] Not Like "[A-Z][0-9][A-Z] [0-9][A-Z][0-9]")`	MsgBox	If postal code not correct for Canada, display message and...
	...	CancelEvent	If postal code not correct for Canada, display message and cancel event
	...	GoToControl	

Reports

You may find that your data elements do some of the strangest things in reports. Look at the expression that inserts data into a block of text on an invoice. It is actually fairly simple to decipher:

```
IIf([Region] Is Null,[ShipCity] & " " & [ShipPostalCode],[ShipCity] & " " &
[ShipRegion] & "  " & [ShipPostalCode])
```

If there is no `Region` find the `ShipCity`, add a space, put in the `ShipPostalCode`; otherwise use `ShipCity`, add a space, put in the `ShipRegion`, add a space, and put in the `ShipPostalCode`.

Look at the sales figure in this report. Do you think the cents were truncated or rounded? You can't tell until you check out the code from the report.

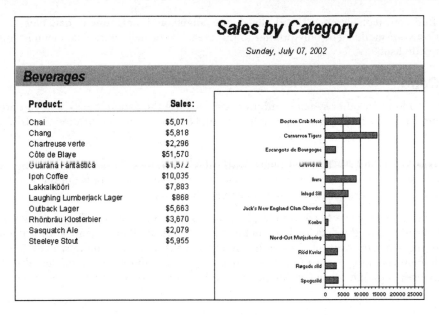

Here is a procedure that creates a Sales by Category screen, and report values that I found in the SQL Server2000 Northwind database. Look at how many functions are being applied to `TotalPurchase`. The answer to our question is rounding among other things. I start to get nervous when I find rounding happening on money. I realize it needs to happen with some strange and bizarre tax and discount rules, but these things make me check data definitions twice to make sure I have noted they are not straight summations. The other thing to notice is that there are many data elements needed to create this value. If it had been in the table structure as a denormalized column in `Order`, we would have needed to note this formula in the definition:

```
CREATE PROCEDURE SalesByCategory
    @CategoryName nvarchar(15), @OrdYear nvarchar(4) = '1998'
AS
IF @OrdYear != '1996' AND @OrdYear != '1997' AND @OrdYear != '1998'
BEGIN
    SELECT @OrdYear = '1998'
END

SELECT ProductName,
    TotalPurchase=ROUND(SUM(CONVERT(decimal(14,2), OD.Quantity *
                        (1-OD.Discount) * OD.UnitPrice)), 0)
FROM [Order Details] OD, Orders O, Products P, Categories C
WHERE OD.OrderID = O.OrderID
    AND OD.ProductID = P.ProductID
    AND P.CategoryID = C.CategoryID
    AND C.CategoryName = @CategoryName
    AND SUBSTRING(CONVERT(nvarchar(22), O.OrderDate, 111), 1, 4) = @OrdYear
GROUP BY ProductName
ORDER BY ProductName

GO
```

You may find your data elements sliced, diced, rearranged, and merged with data elements that don't even exist on your model. The only pointer to the existence of such extra data element ingredients is in the report code itself.

External Code

Don't forget to look for other systems and processes that use the data in the system you are reverse engineering. You may find that even a small, seemingly unimportant application can be a cornerstone of data integration. Keep an eye out for:

❑ Data Access maps – EAI mappings, XML files, UML files. These show how the data has been defined to move to another system. There are more and more tools out there to help connect systems together; take advantage of analysis that is already finished.

❑ Data Move scripts – Load routines, DTS packages, ETL routines. These can also help determine how the data has been defined to move to another system. They are a wonderful source, since they have links to other systems buried in them. You may even find that a data element is coming from a source system that you have thoroughly modeled already. That will give you a definition and all the pedigree information you need.

Front End Analysis

Once you have a foundation of understanding based on the analysis of the back end, you can enhance it by exploring the front end (if one exists) and any products built from the system, like reports, that are available. You want to verify what you learned about the data sets and their relationships to each other. Even simply using the application yourself will help aid your understanding of what the data elements are, and what they are being used for. We are going to verify our assessment of the data elements by mapping a label on a screen, or report to data elements. We'll double-check relationships by looking at the configuration of screens and noting how the data is managed by a system user.

Screen Labels

Screen labels can be very enlightening about the nature of the data element. Sometimes the names and design of the database aren't very helpful in knowing what is really there. Screens labels and report headings are designed to be read and understood by a much larger audience than the tables. As an example, look at this screen from the Access system:

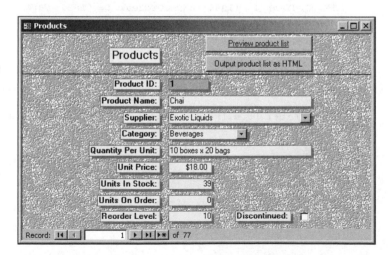

This is a very typical screen in most systems. The screen name is **Products**. You can guess that this maps to the `Products` table. That may not always be true, but it is a good place to start. If there is no Product table, try to match the screen labels to the table most of the product information is in. The data elements map one-for-one and they are even in the same order. The two foreign key IDs are being represented on the screen by the longer names from their parent tables. I italicized the data element for you.

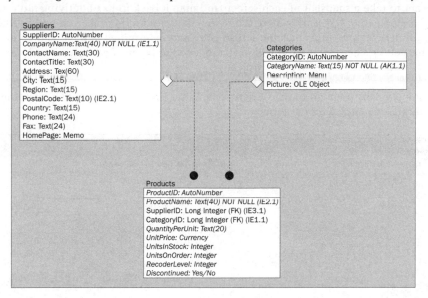

Check off the data elements you have accounted for in some way. This is a good way to double-check the course of your analysis. You could actually create a screen to table map by comparing the data elements to your model. This often gives a more understandable logical name versus the physical name, which might be hard to decipher. Screen to table mappings are handy for documentation assisting maintenance tasks and impact analysis studies. They look like this:

Screen Name	Screen Label	Table Name	Column Name	Type/Size
Products	Product ID	Products	ProductID	Autonumber
Products	Product Name	Products	ProductName	Text(40)
Products	*Supplier*	*Suppliers*	*CompanyName*	*Text(40)*
Products	Category	Category	CategoryName	Text(15)
Products	Quantity per Unit	Products	QuantityPerUnit	Text(20)
Products	Unit Price	Products	UnitPrice	Currency
Products	Units in Stock	Products	UnitsInStock	Integer
Products	Units on Order	Products	UnitsOnOrder	Integer
Products	Reorder Level	Products	ReorderLevel	Integer
Products	Discontinued	Products	Discontinued	Yes/No

This is a very simple mapping, so I will just point out the times when it isn't so intuitive. Notice that `Supplier` comes from `CompanyName` not a `Supplier` name. It can actually be quite a challenge figuring out what fields map to what columns, and even what tables with some database designs. Not all screen mappings are as neat and intuitive as this one, particularly on older mainframe systems.

You may want to take a snapshot of each screen and map it back to its underlying table structure. If you need to dig *really* deep to figure out where the screen data originates from, you will probably need to ask a programmer's help to pull apart the screen code and determine the table and column each field maps to. This can be very tedious and will probably need to be justified for cost and time in the requirements of the reverse engineering project.

Now let's look over the one part of the Orders screen that isn't quite as simple a mapping. Consider the Ship Via check fields circled on the form:

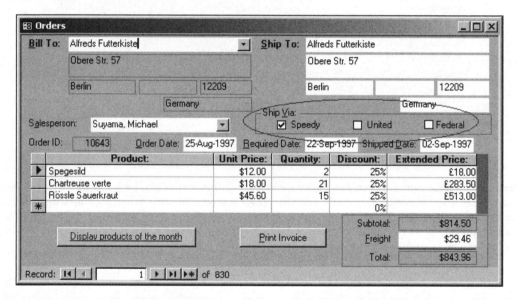

Can you map the Ship Via on the screen to a table? Look at the `Orders` table. Notice that it has a foreign key named `ShippedVia`. We are very fortunate that the constraints for these tables are actually in the database. Quite frequently you will begin your reverse engineering analysis with a pile of disconnected boxes trying to figure out how they fit together.

`ShipperID` changes names as it migrates to `Orders`, and becomes `ShipVia`. It has been role named. But something else happened along the way. Generally data types, sizes, and names are your first clues for foreign keys of relationships. They usually stay the same as they migrate from table to table. The exceptions can be hard to spot. When columns change names, data types, and sizes and they just don't seem to match up, it can make relationships tougher to spot and verify in reverse engineering data modeling. In this case while the data type is still a `Long` integer in reality, it's no longer automatically generated (or noted in the table design) as an AutoNumber in the `Orders` table (as it was in the `Shippers` table) so the data type as well as the column name changes in the two tables.

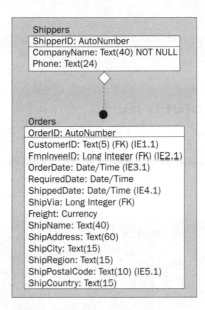

Double-check the values in `Shippers` compared to `Orders`:

		Shipper ID	Company Name	Phone
▶	+	1	Speedy Express	(503) 555-9831
	+	2	United Package	(503) 555-3199
	+	3	Federal Shipping	(503) 555-9931
*		\utoNumber)		

		Order ID	Customer	Employee	Order I	Require	Shippe	Ship Via	Fre
▶	+	10248	Vins et alc	Buchanan	lul-1996	ug-1996	Jul-1996	Federal Shipp	$32
	+	10249	Toms Spez	Suyama,	lul-1996	ug-1996	Jul-1996	Speedy Expre	$11
	+	10250	Hanari Carr	Peacock,	lul-1996	ug-1996	Jul-1996	United Packa	$65
	+	10251	Victuailles	Leverling,	lul-1996	ug-1996	Jul-1996	Speedy Expre	$41
	+	10252	Suprêmes	Peacock,	lul-1996	ug-1996	Jul-1996	United Packa	$51
	+	10253	Hanari Carr	Leverling,	lul-1996	Jul-1996	Jul-1996	United Packa	$58
	+	10254	Chop-suey	Buchanan	lul-1996	ug-1996	Jul-1996	United Packa	$22
	+	10255	Richter Sup	Dodsworth	lul-1996	ug-1996	Jul-1996	Federal Shipp	148
	+	10256	Wellington	Leverling,	lul-1996	ug-1996	Jul-1996	United Packa	$13
	+	10257	HILARIÓN-	Peacock,	lul-1996	ug-1996	Jul-1996	Federal Shipp	$81
	+	10258	Ernst Hand	Davolio, N	lul-1996	ug-1996	Jul-1996	Speedy Expre	140
	+	10259	Centro com	Peacock,	lul-1996	ug-1996	Jul-1996	Federal Shipp	$3
	+	10260	Ottilies Käs	Peacock,	lul-1996	ug-1996	Jul-1996	Speedy Expre	$55
	+	10261	Que Delícia	Peacock,	lul-1996	ug-1996	Jul-1996	United Packa	$3
	+	10262	Rattlesnake	Callahan,	lul-1996	ug-1996	Jul-1996	Federal Shipp	$48

Well, I have to say this is not what I expected to find in the table. Instead of a number in the `ShipVia` column, we see the name of the company. This is because Access 2000 has a list function that translates all foreign keys into user-friendly names derived using the tables they originate from. If we didn't know this, or hadn't double-checked the data type, then we might have thought that the `ShipVia` column contained text rather than a `Long` integer. This illustrates that you shouldn't rest on assumptions when you are doing this kind of analysis. You have to work through all the interesting quirks of every new database platform to find reality.

You will not always find tables for all the data elements on the screens. Data is also stored in small hard coded lists managed by screen objects like 'drop-down' lists. It's important to note these data structures in notes on the model or as part of the definitions since it could be important for the customers of your analysis to know.

Data Relationship Screen Rules

The other thing the front end can help you with is relationships and business rules, especially those that don't show up in back end analysis. Frequently you will find that a simple column in the back is really a fairly complicated structure in the front. Look for labels that look like column or table names, as well as drop-down boxes or checklists, which will give you an idea of the relationship between the various data elements. Take, for example, the Categories screen in Northwind-Access.

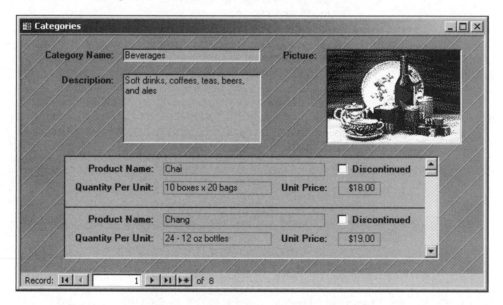

You can easily verify (or derive) the one-to-many relationship of Category to Product based on what you can see here on the screen. There is only one Category name listed at a time on the screen with a scrolling list of Products, so the business rule should be one Category to many Products. You can double-check this by looking again at the Products screen, and verifying that each Product can only be in one Category at a time. Looking back at the table definitions again verifies that this one-to-many relationship looks right.

If the database doesn't have the integrity constraints built, you may have to figure out how the data is actually flowing around. Column names, data types, and sizes are a good first clue. The second is how the screen seems to treat them.

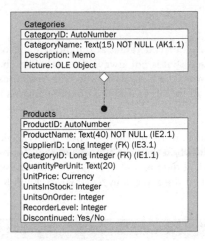

Finding and verifying relationships is another place that you may need to ask for a programmer's support to get to the code that manages the screen.

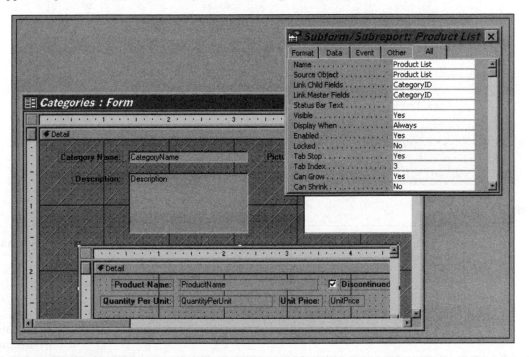

Notice that the designer view of the detail portion of the screen links the child field CategoryID to the master field CategoryID. This proves the foreign key relationship that created the list of Products based on which category is being displayed. The view the user sees was a good hint and this is conclusive evidence.

Derived Values

Northwind does not seem to store derived values at the table level, which makes the task of reverse engineering a lot easier. However, that is not always the case. If such derived values exist in the tables, then you need to go figure out what the formula is, and where the base elements come from that create totals, discounts, averages, and all the other useful math conclusions in databases, and define them for the model.

Those values are especially important to the clients. They rarely look at the tiny bits of detail data needed to create the answers. So when they are concerned that a subtotal has suddenly begun to be sporadically incorrect, the physical data model needs to be able to explain how the subtotal is formed. Here is a nice formula from one of the screens in Northwind. Each formula can also be mapped out for ease of use.

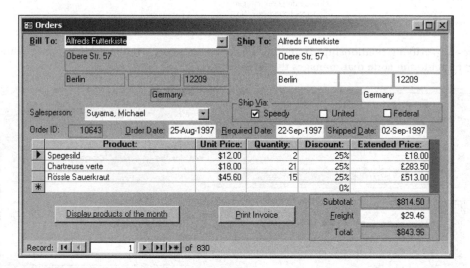

Formula Map

Screen/Report Name	Value Label	Formula	Table Name	Column Name
Orders	Extended Price	CCur([Order Details].[UnitPrice]*[Quantity]*(1-[Discount])/100)*100 AS ExtendedPrice	Order_Details	OrderID ProductID UnitPrice Quantity Discount

In this case, the formula creates the ExtendedPrice value by performing the following calculation:

```
Unit Price*Quantity*PercentageDiscount
```

It then uses the CCur function to convert this value into a currency data type.

Historic / Descriptive

Use whatever existing documentation you can acquire. This can involve some, or all, of the following:

❑ **User Guides/Manuals** – Get a personal copy of anything you can. You will probably be bookmarking, highlighting, and scribbling notes in the margins before you are done. If you can find an old copy that has already been 'enhanced' by a client with their comments, then so much the better. You have access to notes that they felt were important enough to add to the original either challenging a statement or clarifying it further. An even better situation would be to find an older and a newer version of the user guides, since this will give you a clue as to what features have been added to the system over time, and at what point. This will point you in the direction of any properties peculiar to the system

❑ **Help Files** and **Comments in Code** – Look at what the programmers thought was important enough to comment in their code. Consider the following example:

Field Name	Data Type	Description
OrderID	AutoNumber	Unique order number.
CustomerID	Text	Same entry as in Customers table.
EmployeeID	Number	Same entry as in Employees table.
OrderDate	Date/Time	
RequiredDate	Date/Time	
ShippedDate	Date/Time	
ShipVia	Number	Same as Shipper ID in Shippers table.
Freight	Currency	
ShipName	Text	Name of person or company to receive the shipment.
ShipAddress	Text	Street address only -- no post-office box allowed.
ShipCity	Text	
ShipRegion	Text	State or province.
ShipPostalCode	Text	
ShipCountry	Text	

Notice that the `ShipAddress` field isn't suppose to have any Post Office box numbers allowed. I don't know how they plan to prevent it, but it's at least noted here. You should add that to your definitions. Similarly, note that `ShipRegion` is defined in very broad terms as being a State or Province. The original client representative on the development team may help review and critique the Help files. Go through them to get a perspective of how they thought the screens, sections, functionality, and reports were supposed to be like since the actual programmer probably never read the Help text. Compare that description with what else you find

❑ **Project Notebooks** – Any notebooks used by the development team can prove useful. These are generally really hard reading, but sometimes the system you are working with is too old to get anything else helpful. Try to find someone to help you go through it unless you are familiar enough with the system to map the file names to screens or processes. Otherwise you will just get lost

❑ **Training Classes** – Take the time to audit classes on the application or just spend time with the teacher. Get hold of any tutorials and go through them. The more you know about how the data in the system is meant to behave, the easier it will be to notice exceptions to those rules

❑ **Interviews / Informal Conversation** – Find the people who are using the system, and train with them if you can. Listen closely to things that bother them about the system and how they get around it. People have the most ingenious ability to come up with data solutions that don't include approaching IT to make application changes. A typical one would be using multiple-abbreviated terms in text fields to denote attributes not modeled in the data properly, and then doing text searches on these

Find the people who use the data coming out of the system. They will be able to document point by point all the shortcomings of the data itself. They will expound on quality issues of the data.It is very important to document such faults, since they may well cripple future projects.

Find the people who maintain the system, such as the DBA and chief programmer. They will have stories to tell about the system that will probably cause you to wonder how it could have stayed in production so long without being replaced.

Finishing Touches

Make sure that you do all the good things to this kind of model too. Make it easy to read, by adding notes of anything you think is going to be lost from your analysis if you don't write it down.

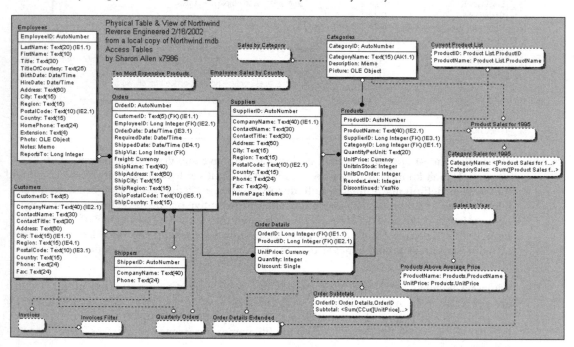

Building a Logical Model

You need to build as complete an understanding as possible of that physical solution before you can try to derive the logical relationships. Deriving a logical model from a physical one is a matter of finding the business rules in the application, whether or not they are in the table design. You must capture what is allowed and not allowed. What sets own the attributes? What identifiers are available whether they are used as keys or not? Can an Employee have multiple titles over time? Can an Order have multiple lines of the same product? Can a Customer be related to other Customers? Do Customers have multiple shipping addresses? The answer to these questions will help to enhance the existing system or compare it to a potential 'off-the-shelf' replacement.

Names

In our Northwind-Access example, we start with the physical model we built from a link to `Northwind.mdb`:

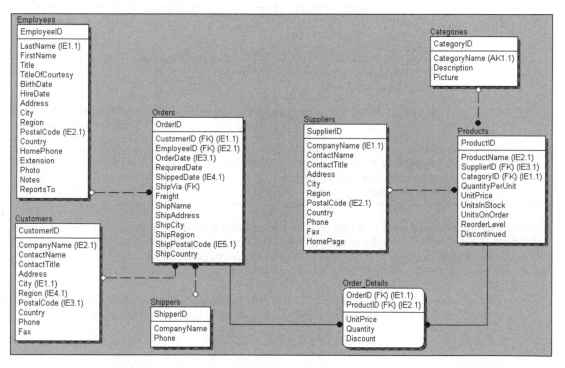

Build a report of the tables and build logical entity names from the physical ones. Entity names are singular and descriptive of the data set. Look over the definitions you found in the RDBMS and start to look for logical data sets. Look for similarities, and use what you learned from the logical modeling chapter. I italicized a few things that should jump right out at you from the very start:

Table Name	Table Comment	Proposed Logical Name	Notes
Categories	*Categories* of Northwind products.	Product Category	Category of Product??
Customers	Customers' *names, addresses, and phone numbers.*	Customer	May be a sub category of Company to include Shipping Companies
Employees	Employees' names, titles, and personal information.	Employee	
Order_Details	Details on products, quantities, and prices for each order in the Orders table.	Order Line	
Orders	Customer name, order date, and freight charge for each order.	Order	
Products	Product names, suppliers, prices, and units in stock.	Product	
Shippers	Shippers' *names and phone numbers.*	Shipping Company	May be a sub category of Company to include Shipping Companies
Suppliers	Suppliers' *names, addresses, phone numbers, and hyperlinks to home pages.*	Supplier	May be a sub category of Company to include Shipping Companies

Customers, Shippers, and Suppliers look like they have quite a bit in common at this point from their definitions. I italicized some of the common elements to point them out. Shared data elements are only a clue, we need to look closer at the primary definitions and the unique identifiers to determine whether these have enough commonality to be grouped into a category.

Next we do the same thing for the columns. We are going to make the names singular, descriptive, and make sure that each one has a class word to help us know the nature of the data element.

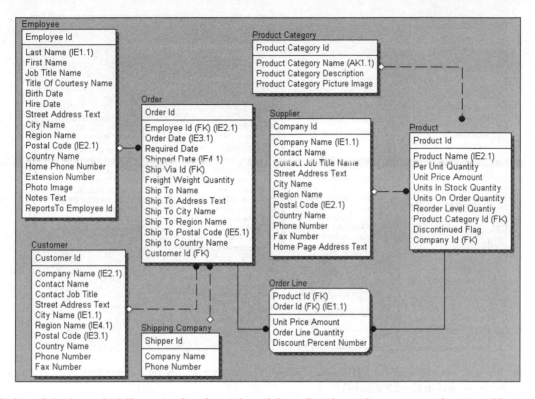

It doesn't look much different to the physical model yet. But this is the important first step. Next we will try to find the natural or candidate keys.

Keys

It becomes very clear from this view that the programmer used surrogate keys, but did not define many alternate (unique) keys. So we may be left doing some actual data validation of guesses about what data elements make a row unique other than the IDs.

> *This model was created using Erwin 3.5.2. The 'IE.1' notes are Inversion entries that denote non-unique indexes in the database. They are not alternate keys. 'AK's are alternate keys in this tool, and are unique indexes.*

See if you can find the natural keys by looking at the data and move one into the PK position. Change the model to match. Surrogate-keys are very rarely modeled logically, so removing them from the model will help you narrow down the data elements.

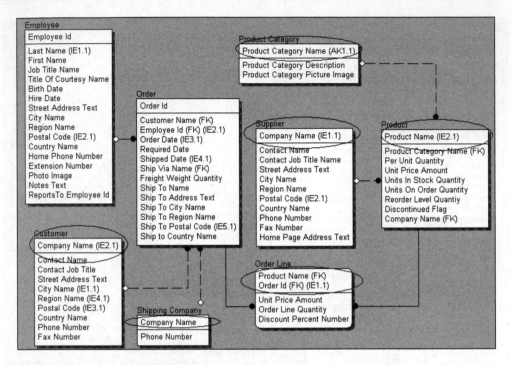

I left the EmployeeID and OrderID as they were. They may actually be the numbers that are used to manage those sets in the Enterprise.

Categories

Now let's look again at the `Supplier`, `Customer`, and `ShippingCompany` tables. We saw from the descriptions of these three tables that the sets had a lot in common, and use exactly the same names for quite a few of the columns. I would say that this is a category structure that the programmer chose to implement with three separate tables, so let's add the category to our logical model:

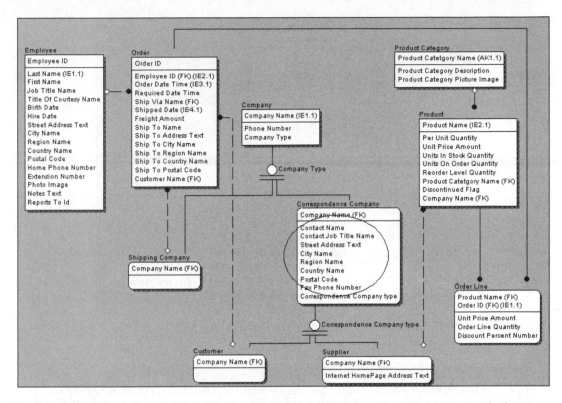

Yes, I could certainly have cheated here a bit and simplified the category. However, the business rules built into the physical design do not allow for Shippers to have the attributes I circled. We needed to make a two-layer category that allowed Company to own Phone as the only completely shared attribute with Shipping Company, Customer, and Supplier. In order to build the second categorization, I created the Correspondence Company super-type entity (it being the set of companies we send mail to) to own all the attributes shared by both Customer and Supplier. It is important, if you are backing into a logical model, that you put in the business rules even if they don't seem to make sense (just be sure to make a note that they don't). That may actually be the point of deriving a logical model off a physical one. This makes it very clear that the application does not treat Shipping Companies the same as other companies.

Below you can see the solution showing how I think the Enterprise probably really works. In reality those attributes dealing with contact and correspondence apply to Shippers also. Someone has to be able to pay them, negotiate fees, and look up lost shipments. But right now, that data must be managed outside of the Northwind.mdb application.

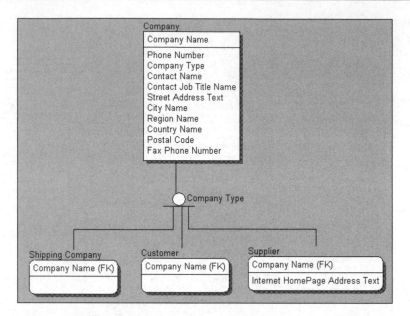

Now let's look at Product Category (`Categories`). With a name like that it should be on the list to review. First look at the actual data.

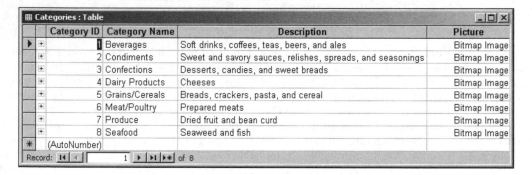

The first thing I notice is that they are very much alike. They have a name to identify them, a description to expand the understanding, and a picture (but that is all). I generally don't show a category structure on a logical model unless the supertype/subtype structure brings value for communication. For instance, some of the subtypes could own different attributes like the temperature needed for refrigeration of cold products, or the shelf-life of perishables. They may also need to be broken out to support detailed business rules like a special relationship for special equipment needs of refrigerated products. We could call this out in a category structure since it does divide Products into groups, but in this case I don't think it is necessary.

You need to make a choice on your logical model. I would tend to say that there is a potential Enterprise need for the categories. Which structure you use would be your choice. This is how it would look if you chose to break it out on your logical model:

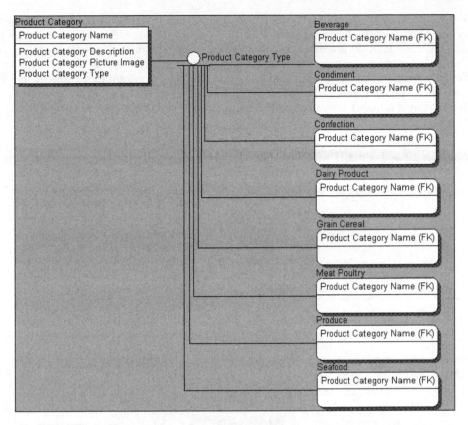

Each of the entities need to be reviewed to check for buried categorization that could be documented. Review Employees and Orders to see if you think they would benefit from a category design.

Other Rules

Look at the last attribute in Employee. Reports To Id certainly implies a recursion to Employee itself. You may want to check the data to verify that the rules are being managed even though we didn't find a constraint at the database level. Add the relationship and make sure you role name the new column.

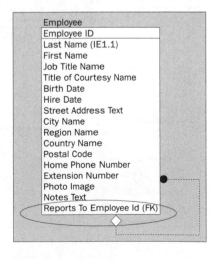

You also want to work through your normalization rules, but only from the perspective of what is really in the system. You have to document the restrictions, not actual data element business rules in the enterprise. This is a logical view of a system with its own business rules. Look for repeating groups, and data value interdependencies between the key and to each other. Remember that we discovered a dependency between Country and Zip Codes in a macro? You may want to dig deeper into how the application maintains that rule and model it out. If there is a quality check in the application somewhere, even if it hasn't been physically implemented as a foreign key to manage the integrity of the rule, then model it in.

	Macro Name	Condition	Action	Comment
				Attached to the BeforeUpdate property of the Suppliers form.
	Validate Postal Cod	IsNull([Country])	StopMacro	If Country is Null, postal code can't be validated.
		[Country] In ("Frar	MsgBox	If postal code is not 5 characters, display message...
		...	CancelEvent	...and cancel event.
		...	GoToControl	
		[Country] In ("Aust	MsgBox	If postal code is not 4 characters, display message...
		...	CancelEvent	...and cancel event.
		...	GoToControl	
		([Country]="Canac	MsgBox	If postal code not correct for Canada, display message and...
		...	CancelEvent	...and cancel event.
		...	GoToControl	

Suppliers : Macro

Physical implementations often pull data sets and rules out of the logical model and manage them in places other than the RDBMS. The rules are managed in front-end code, triggers, and procedures.

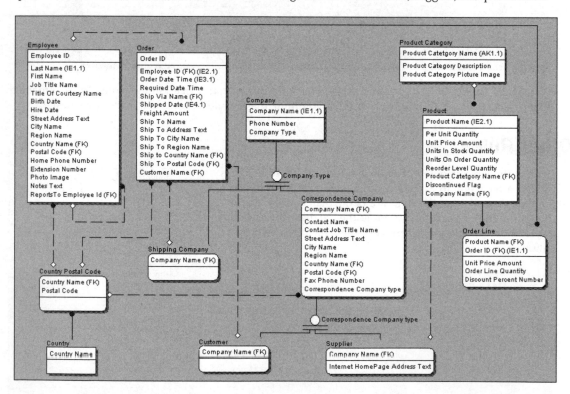

Relationship Names

Finally you will want to add relationship verbs to be able to document business rules. Since this is a reverse engineer model, you will want to interview the clients to make sure you choose appropriate verbs.

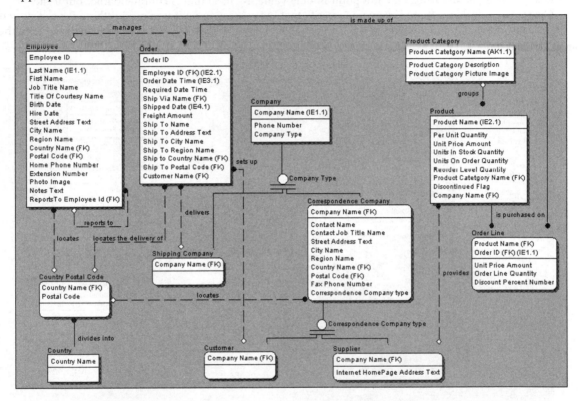

You will want to revisit the cardinality and nullability to verify this is how they were implemented in the system. They may not be the true Enterprise business rules, but we are documenting the 'As-Is'.

Finish It Up

Every step we took along the way adds more value and ability to communicate what a system is and does from the data element perspective. Document every insight for posterity. As always you need to notate the model. Make it clear what this is a model of. Title it. Make sure that any documentation that you derive from it has source notations so that they can be matched like the definitions or mapping documents. Always add dates. In the case of reverse-engineered models, you will want to add the location and name of the database being analyzed.

You should add whatever you need to keep the model a valid reference document. I added some notes to myself in case `Northwind.mdb` comes my way again or continues its lifecycle with some enhancements. The Ship to Recipient is probably a reusable set of 'Ship to' values based on the Customer, not the Order. Country Postal Code can probably be expanded to take on relationships to City and Region. And there is a potential for Order Unit Price Amount to be unable to be verified against Product. This is an assumption on my part. It seems that Unit Price Amount in Product can change. The one in Order Line is a point in time value. By itself that is commendable. But if the Customer complains, there is no way to verify that the correct amount was used if there is no history of the Unit Price Amount changes at the Product level. However that would have to be analyzed with the Business team.

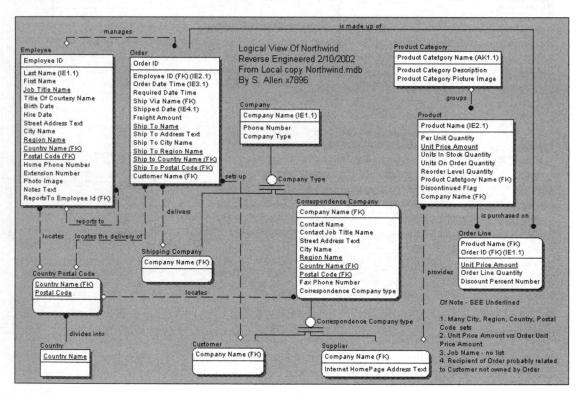

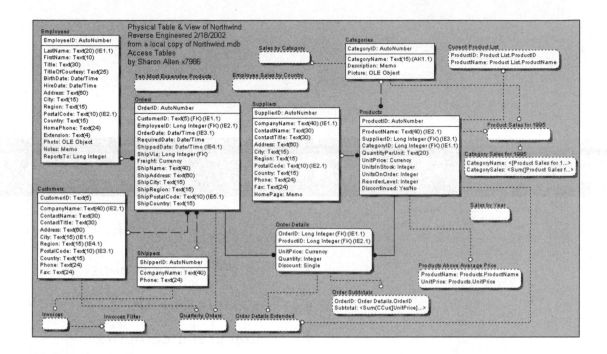

Physical Table & View of Northwind
Reverse Engineered 2/18/2002
from a local copy of Northwind.mdb
Access Tables
by Sharon Allen x7986

Summary

In this chapter we have considered the nature of reverse engineering. It is the process by which we extract information from existing systems in order to work backwards and derive a physical model, and further back to a logical model. The nuances of different database systems and development platforms often makes this process a difficult task. We have seen how modeling tools such as Erwin can help in taking snapshots of existing databases, and producing physical models from which we can begin to verify table and column names. While we can generally discover table and column names through the use of such tools, or by considering database creation scripts, it is the relationships between tables that can prove most difficult to verify. This is where screen analysis, use of documentation, employee know-how, training, and other 'soft' resources can prove invaluable in figuring out exactly how data is being used in the system under scrutiny. Only by learning as much as possible about the use of the application can you determine how the existing data structures are being used, and how this compares with the original design.

Reverse engineering has an important role to play in helping improve the efficiency of enterprise applications (by determining faults in the design), aiding integration of existing systems (by pinpointing table and column definitions and relationships between such tables), and allowing comparisons of existing systems with potential new system solutions.

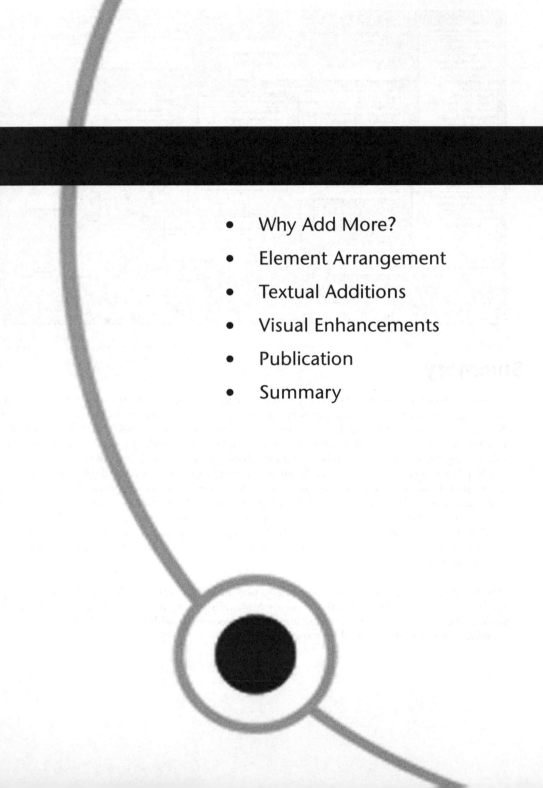

- Why Add More?
- Element Arrangement
- Textual Additions
- Visual Enhancements
- Publication
- Summary

Communication with the Model

This chapter considers various techniques that you can utilize on an optional basis to increase the usability of the data model, and the amount of information you can provide within it. Having been through the process of creating the data model, you want to make it a sought-after deliverable and optimize its abilities to help solve problems. These optional elements allow you to highlight and focus on salient points of interest, or preserve information with the model that tends to become disconnected and lost over time. Not only that but using a detailed publication format can streamline deployment of new data analysis.

In the course of this chapter we'll look at:

❑ **Element Arrangement** – ordering tables/columns or entities/attributes to illustrate rules of precedence that may exist

❑ **Textual Additions** – Use of items such as titles, versioning numbering, and legends to aid swift understanding of the model and what use is being made of it

❑ **Visual Enhancements** – Use of color, images, or font styles to illustrate important information

❑ **Publication Formats** – Producing information on file, for a file library, or over the Web

Why Add More?

Why indeed? You have completed the modeling tasks. All of the entities/tables/views, attributes/columns, relationships/constraints have been polished, detailed, and honed until they meet your quality standard. What more is there to data modeling than that? The answer is that you have a responsibility to the customers of this analysis to make it as simple as possible to comprehend your document, recognize what they are looking for, and make the best use of it.

Data models are syntactically complex documents that amalgamate graphics and text to describe conclusions based on analysis. Modeling uses notations and standards that are known to only a select few in the Enterprise, and yet the model may need to be available to audiences that we are not even aware of. As a result we need to make sure the model can be read without us having to be present acting as the guide.

When we make additions to the model for communication sake we need to stay sensitive to any given requirements, since different Enterprise environments may restrict the use of some of the techniques we are going to cover. Some departments or organizations have requirements for delivered documentation that will tailor for any enhancements. On the other hand if they intend to fax the model to various parties, for example, then we will lose any colorization we might have used in the document. In that case we would need to use some other method of highlighting the pertinent information, such as different font styles. In other cases we may need to stay within strict parameters for text additions, perhaps along the lines of released drawings in manufacturing for instance.

We also have soft requirements that occur during a project. Team building and making yourself, and your models, a welcome addition to the effort may also be an aspect of whether or not you choose to enhance the model. Sometimes what is required is a slightly more personable and light-hearted technique. Other times you will choose an extremely serious approach to emphasize the seriousness of your documentation. Both methods should be conducted with professionalism, and utilized as appropriate for the clients you are working with.

> **Remember that you are developing models for clients, not to suit your own needs.**

Element Arrangement

This is a very basic technique that may make reading your model simpler by implying precedence (rules of existence or order of data creation) from the position of the entities/tables.

Up until now the arrangement of the entities and tables in my examples concentrated more on keeping the box elements (entities, tables, and views) as close to each other with as short a line element (relationships and constraints) as possible while making sure nothing covered anything else. This is a compressed style that keeps the model as small in size as possible. However, let's consider the model that we drew up at the end of Chapter 8:

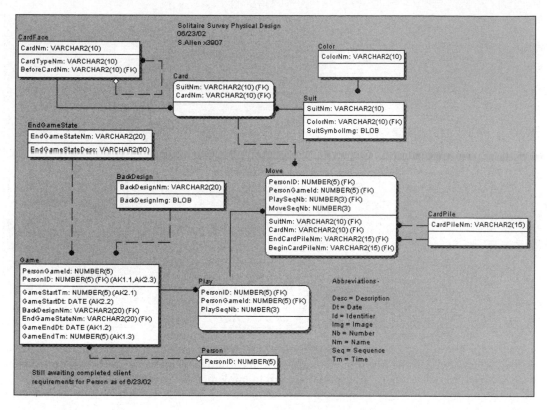

The arrangement of the objects on this model does not make it easy to know what order the tables need to be loaded in. Precedence can be very important to both DBAs and programmers as they implement physical models and develop production-ready applications. Identifying the most important tables, those likely to be accessed most frequently by users, and integrity constraints, helps them to modify the physical design so as to optimize the speed of the application and avoid long (and loud) user complaints when the system goes live.

If we rearrange the model to note precedence we need to move every table that is a parent above its child or children. Look at the next example. You can see that it is now much easier to find the order in which data values must be created to enable support of the integrity constraints. It may also simplify and enhance your ability to 'tell the story' during a model walkthrough, in highlighting the parent tables. You'll also notice the 'independent' ('hard corner') tables, such as `Color` and `Person` in this case, appearing in the top half of the model. These are the simple 'List of Values' tables that are often a useful starting point for the team in their programming tasks.

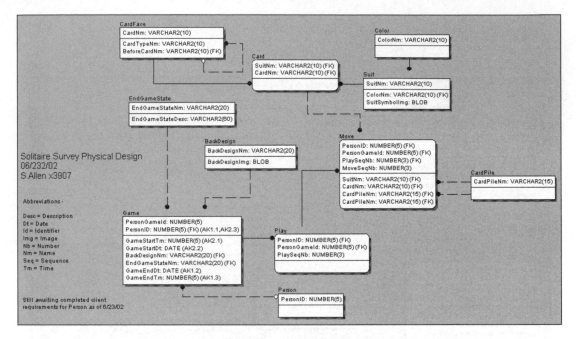

Such element arrangement is often requested for submodels that support the technical team, since as we've outlined, it makes the task of identifying core tables and constraints much easier. This is a very useful and powerful technique, but it becomes hard to implement in very complicated designs.

Textual Additions

What we mean by textual additions in this case is very simple text like headings, notes, and legends that can increase your clients' ability to read and depend on the model you present to them. These extras, when used appropriately and judiciously, help capture knowledge that has a tendency to disappear after a project is completed. This is often information that different members of the project team have in their own heads, but overlook as not being important or useful enough to note down.

Titles and Headings

To illustrate how text can aid understanding of models, let's consider a situation where you are looking through your department's model archive for any work that has been done with Orders in the past. You find a small model named `ShippingOrderTest`. It is a six-table subset of something to do with shipping and orders. Unfortunately there is no way of knowing much of anything else about it. We are left wondering:

❑   Has it been deployed?

❑   Who is responsible for it?

❑   What system is it a part of?

❑   Where are the structures it designed?

❑   When was it last updated?

❑   Is it part of a larger model?

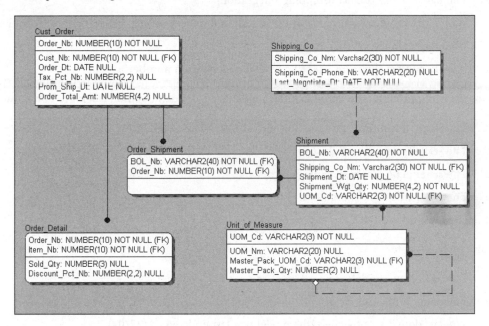

Models are not just stand alone documents. They fit into the processes governing the management of data. You need to add some information to make that link easy to recognize. This is much easier in this case if, instead of the model above, we came across the following:

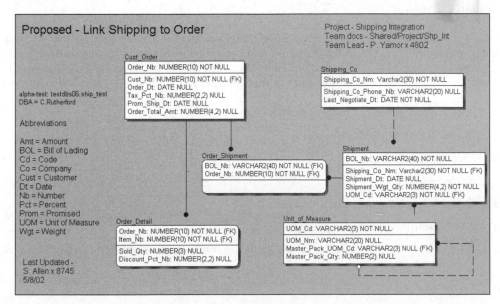

Now you can tell so much more than the first graphic. You know that:

- ❑ This is still a proposed solution (as stated in the model title)
- ❑ The name of the project (Shipping Integration)
- ❑ Where the project documentation is stored (in the `Shared/Project/Shp_Int` folder)
- ❑ Who the team lead is (P.Yamor)
- ❑ How to contact the team lead (the telephone extension number is 4802)

Perhaps more importantly you know that this model has been deployed on a server. You know:

- ❑ The stage of testing at the time this model was created (alpha-test)
- ❑ The server name (`testdbs06`)
- ❑ The schema or database name (`ship_test`)
- ❑ The DBA who is in charge of it (J.Bollinger)
- ❑ How to find the DBA (on extension 4872)

You also have a feel for:

- ❑ The age of the model/project
- ❑ The name of the author or updater (S.Allen)
- ❑ The last date it was touched (the model was last updated 04/27/02)

This second model, with all the extra information added to it, leaves the client with a much higher expectation of the quality of the information being presented, in comparison to the model with all this information omitted.

You may want to come up with a standard set of title elements that are included with every data model for your department. This will add consistency and professionalism to your product. Here is a list of things that I have found to be important to know about any model I pick up. Not all of them are applicable all the time. Again you need to use your judgment to know what is important for your use.

- ❑ Project / Application / Subject Area Name
- ❑ Model or Submodel Name
- ❑ Last worked on Date
- ❑ Name of Modeler
- ❑ Contact details for more information
- ❑ Brief description of model purpose
- ❑ Brief description of method to create model (in other words whether it has been reverse engineered or not)
- ❑ Source of analysis information

This information can be grouped into a block like this:

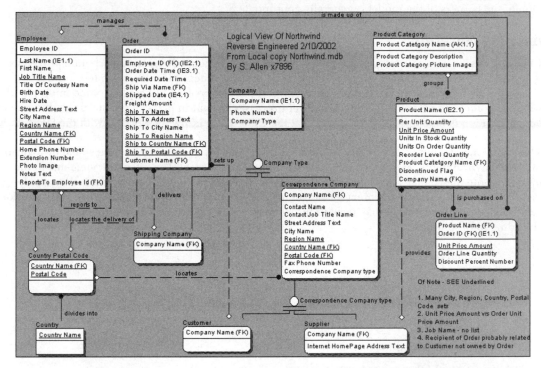

Or you may want to separate and emphasize some parts of the heading with size and font formatting, as in the following example:

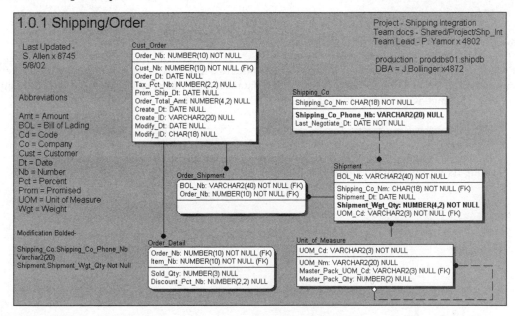

It is a good idea to standardize a location on the model for this information for the sake of consistency. One of the corners of the model is generally appropriate.

Versioning Notation

Change Control, or versioning, of the model can be a very serious, disciplined corporate procedure requiring check out and check in, review boards, and environment (development, test, production) release controls. It may also be a more casual project process created to keep everyone informed of what version of the model is current. Whatever processes are put in place, it is crucial that the project documentation is managed so as to ensure that the entire team is always working with the latest design.

The model may include status notification that it represents levels of analysis (conceptual or logical) or physical environments (Design, Alpha, Beta, or Production release). We often add elements to the model to note the changes in status and use numbering schemes to note new releases. We can also include notes to document the precise changes (or delta) from the previous model. In order to make the version clear to the team, we may need to provide these elements in addition to the normal Title /Heading information:

- ❑ Version Number
- ❑ Brief description of version impact
- ❑ Release-to-environment name
- ❑ Team lead to contact about the release
- ❑ Information for contacting them
- ❑ Location of other supporting documents
- ❑ Release database information
- ❑ DBA in charge of release
- ❑ Information on how to contact them

Let's look at an example of how to notate a data model to support a change to a database with versioned documentation. We'll assume that this is part of a database that was recently released to production, and number it 1.0 since it was the first release.

> **Numbering of releases is a standard that needs to be determined. I have seen standards ranging from X.Y.Z where \<X\> = major release, \<Y\> = enhancement, .\<Z\> = bug fix all the way to simple 1,2,3.**

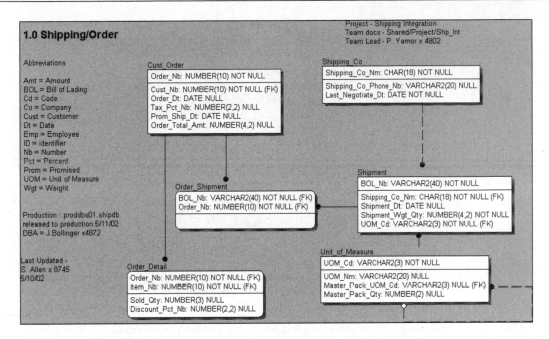

Now that this model has been implemented in a production environment (as noted on the left-hand side of the model) the clients have discovered that this first release had a few shortcomings. While these are small issues, they still need to be cleared up, and the following requests for corrections (we'll term them **Problem Correction** here) have been sent to the team:

- ❏   `Shipment_Wgt_Qty` in Shipment should be NOT NULL.

- ❏   `Shipping_co_Phone_Nb` in `Shipping_Co` should be VARCHAR2(20) (an Oracle variable length character data type)

The clients have also taken this as an opportunity to request new data elements pointing out that this system is already growing and evolving. Their requested changes (we'll term them **Change Request**) are as follows:

- ❏   Add `Taken_By_Emp_ID` to `Cust_Order`

- ❏   Add `Back_Order_Qty` to `Order_Detail`. Populate by checking quantity on hand in inventory at time of order creation.

The modeler may be asked to review any change to the design to find the best solution to data element or rule additions, deletions, and modifications. This provides us with an opportunity to change the model before the database changes. On the other hand, depending on how your organization manages data structure changes, we may be told of the changes after they occur.

In this case you will probably create two submodels so that the Problem Correction and the Change Request can be reviewed and implemented separately from each other. The Problem Correction model will have text to document the modifications that have been carried out in fixing the bugs identified by the client. I sometimes change the font or color of the changed values so that they are easily recognizable to the maintenance team. It may be documented something like this:

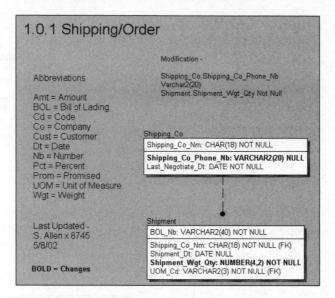

1.0.1 Shipping/Order

Modification -

Abbreviations

Amt = Amount
BOL = Bill of Lading
Cd = Code
Co = Company
Cust = Customer
Dt = Date
Nb = Number
Pct = Percent
Prom = Promised
UOM = Unit of Measure
Wgt = Weight

Shipping_Co.Shipping_Co_Phone_Nb
Varchar2(20)
Shipment.Shipment_Wgt_Qty Not Null

Shipping_Co
Shipping_Co_Nm: CHAR(18) NOT NULL
Shipping_Co_Phone_Nb: VARCHAR2(20) NULL
Last_Negotiate_Dt: DATE NOT NULL

Shipment
BOL_Nb: VARCHAR2(40) NOT NULL
Shipping_Co_Nm: CHAR(18) NOT NULL (FK)
Shipment_Dt: DATE NULL
Shipment_Wgt_Qty: NUMBER(4,2) NOT NULL
UOM_Cd: VARCHAR2(3) NOT NULL (FK)

Last Updated -
S. Allen x 8745
5/8/02

BOLD = Changes

As you can see, in this case I have used bold type to highlight those attributes that have been modified, and added a note at the top of the model to explain what changes have been made.

You will do something a little different with the Change Request. Notice that even this 'simple' enhancement may mean something rather involved. The modeler needed to find the best source for an employee reference. Integration always requires extra sensitivity. You need to be aware of not just the structures, but also the quality of the data, and the processes in place to maintain it. Your database needs may not be easily satisfied by what looks at first glance to be an easy integration solution.

Here is the submodel for the Change Request. Notice the text block outlining the impacts and proposed methods of satisfying the request. You may want to put them here, or you may need a fairly extensive document that explains the proposed techniques for satisfying the request. You may be proposing a solution that will even have a ripple effect into another system.

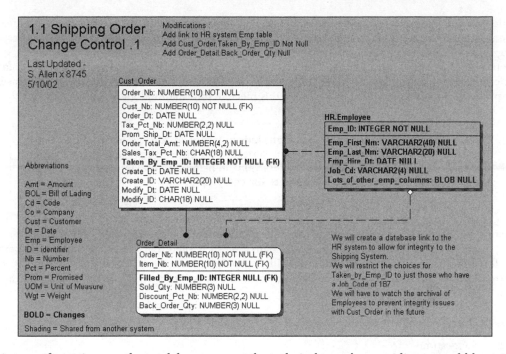

This type of notations on the model can support the technical team by providing a good blueprint of what is about to be impacted. The DBAs and programmers may know of aspects that will cause other issues by being able to see at a glance what is being targeted for change. Reviews like this can prevent one fix causing another problem, like making sure the reports and screens can accommodate the new larger sizes or additional functionality. Changes like this are almost always multi-faceted mini-projects that need analysis and planning of more than simply the database structure to ensure that they don't disrupt, or impede, the success of the project. Your model may need to be matched up with other documents to create a 'Database Change Control Package' detailing all of the implications of the proposed change.

After all the analysis has been done it may be decided to roll several Problem fixes and Change Controls up into one production release. One of the new functions of Erwin 4.0 allows us to consolidate changes up in a single version using a 'merge' function.

Sometimes the data model is not used to update the database, but instead is compared with it, and refreshed accordingly, on a periodic basis. In these situations the data model becomes a snapshot of a moment in time for the database, generally the original creation. The data model may then be notated with the 'Last checked against production' date as a versioning element.

Notes

Notes can be invaluable to those wanting to know more about the model in the future. We can always resynchronize the physical data model with the database in order to determine structure names, or reverse engineer a logical model from a production database. However, what we can't always do is find some of the basics about the model or the project that sponsored it.

While this type of enhancement to the model can clutter the graphic, bear in mind that separate documentation you provide along with the graphic has a tendency to get lost. Again, it is a question of using whatever means you feel comfortable with in order to convey the necessary information effectively. I have taken to adding a 'Text only' page of the model that isn't always printed out for every single meeting or discussion. Do not automatically put a note on the model. Instead, in each case, determine if there is a special need to couple this piece of information tightly with the model.

> **Data model documentation requires high skills in technical editing, in deciding what is important and what is extraneous in the context of the objective. We must justify the inclusion of information on the basis of its value in helping to understand the subject matter. There will never be enough space for everything.**

You can add anything to the model in a note. As we mentioned earlier there is a large amount of information that gets lost to the Enterprise, since it only ever spends time in the minds of the project team, and isn't recorded. I can't tell you how many times I wished that I had the diary of the person who left a model behind for me to maintain. I have contacted a few over the years to try to get information, but in most cases they had already erased that part of the temporary memory in their brain. I have used notes to document:

- Unsolved issues / questions
- Suggestions
- Final choices
- Disclaimers
- Risks
- Warnings
- Policies
- Team communiqués
- Schedule – Milestone Dates, Critical meetings
- Parallel task status
- Particularly complicated Business or Processing rules

Here is an example of a model where some of this type of information is noted:

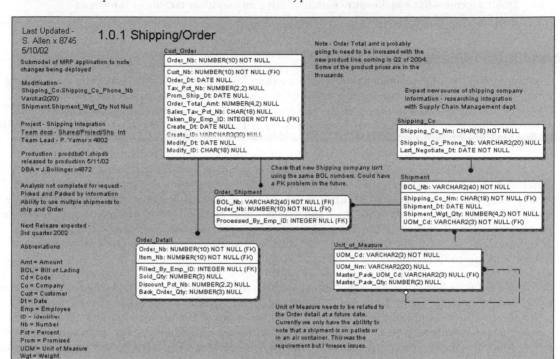

Once again you need to judge your audience before you send out a model that looks like this. It may have too much unnecessary information for them to be able to focus on their task. Some of these comments may not be of interest although they may all be interesting to you. Keep the 'noise' level down by only including what is important to support the task being accomplished with the delivery of a data model.

Legends

Legends are the translation devices in documentation used to explain the meaning of the various model elements we might use, such as:

- ❑ Abbreviations
- ❑ Formatted Text
- ❑ Use of Shading
- ❑ Graphics / Images / Icons

A Legend doesn't have to be a multi-valued list. It can simply be a statement like 'Changes in Red' or 'FKs in italics'. Highlighted features (in any fashion) need to have their meaning documented, otherwise the client will be none the wiser as to what you are trying to convey.

> **Don't assume what you meant to highlight using an emphasis technique is obvious. Build a Legend on the model to document it.**

Abbreviation Legend

You have seen me use this one on many of the examples in this book. It is generally found more often on physical data models since conceptual and logical models try to use the full names whenever possible. But any time you have to abbreviate words you should keep a legend handy. Make sure that this text block can be printed along with the graphic. Having it separately from the model isn't very helpful.

It is also advisable to build a standardized set of abbreviations at least for that model, if not for the Enterprise. Try to keep them intuitive. Some abbreviations or acronyms are so obscure that no one would recognize them without a key. I had to use 'LTLG' and 'GTHG' on one just recently to denote 'Less than lowest level of processing goal' and 'Greater than highest level of processing goal' for targeted percent variance allowances in process grading. If the abbreviations or acronyms I used got lost somehow, then no one will ever figure out (short of reading the code or the definitions) what those letters were meant to convey.

We also need to be careful to watch for abbreviations used for multiple definitions. For example, I have seen 'pt' used to mean 'part', 'participant', 'percentage', and 'partial'. At the other extreme we need to avoid using more than one abbreviation to mean the same thing. For instance 'no', 'nb', and 'nbr' can all be used to mean 'number'. Standardizing can help, but we almost all have legacy issues to contend with, where it is important to stay consistent with what you are working with. Take, for example, this change to an old Shipping department application:

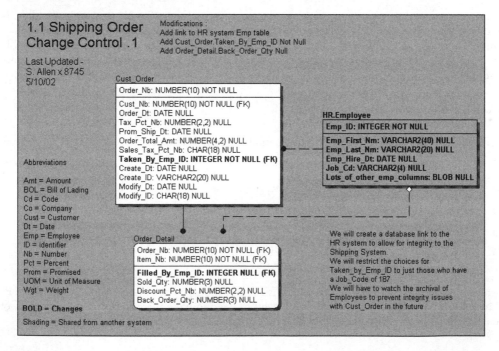

Here is one last word about abbreviating in general. We all like simple things, and short names make coding quicker and easier. However, I find system names tend to be over abbreviated rather than vice versa. Avoid the possibility of confusion in your data element names by using full names wherever possible.

> **Have some sympathy for the future in your naming and documentation of naming conventions. Sponsor and advocate a standard abbreviations list for the department.**

Formatted Text and Shading Legend

It is easy to forget the power that you have available to you in the form of italics, underlining, or bolding to bring an aspect of the model to the forefront. Use of shading on the model is often a powerful way to single out elements for scrutiny. All of these can help in telling people why you want particular elements to be noticed. In this case I often mirror the formatting used on the model in the legend to make it even simpler to understand what I am referring to. For example:

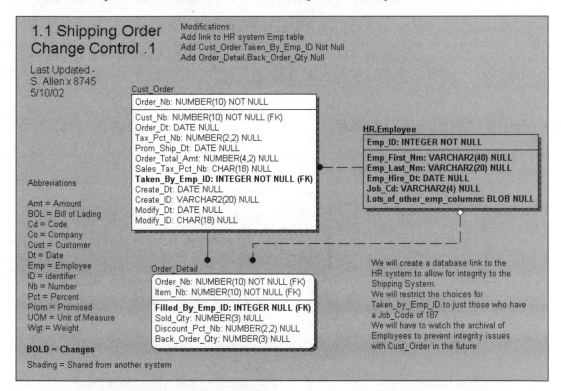

As you can see the legend states, not only what I have highlighted using bold type, but also why I have shaded one of the tables. Documentation is all-important here in enabling effective communication with the person viewing the model.

Visual Enhancements

Models do not have to be simple black and white text maps of table and column names with constraint lines between them. Color, bolding, size, italics, and even strike-through fonts allow us to add dimensions of added value to the model.

> **Use common sense when you choose the way to focus attention. Not everyone has access to color printers and copiers.**

You have seen maps colorized for population, temperature, altitude, AIDS hot spots, and pretty much anything else that has a connection to geography. Data models can be colorized or shaded using the same premise. I wish that I could show you some examples that aren't gray tones, but that is one of the restrictions of publishing. You might consider a colorful presentation version of your work suitable for presentations, with another version gray shaded suitable for normal distribution as photocopies.

One of the really neat functions of computers is that we can colorize or format text. I use color and formats to identify and emphasize attributes and columns that need to be paid attention to. Models get to be so large and complicated that without using some text tricks you waste time finding what you are looking for. Consistency and standardization is a key to making this work. Your modeling tool may be able to help you with this. Visio makes all NOT NULL fields bold for example.

Graphics/Images/Icons

Don't ignore the wealth of small graphics, images, and icons. They can be very helpful in reviewing a design. Remember this little part of our Solitaire modeling project?

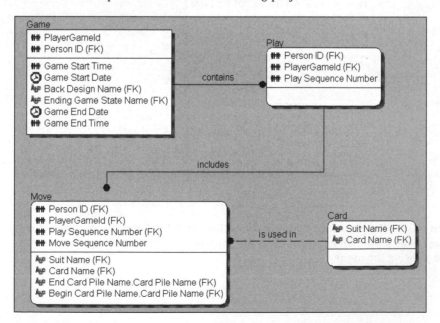

The data domains are noted here with little symbols rather than text. This enables you to review the different data types at a glance, and makes the model more compact than if you display the domains in ordinary text format. The little clock means datetime, ABC is a text field, and the pound sign is a number.

You may be able to increase the provided set of icons by importing ones that are meaningful to your team. You will need to create a legend for these as well to ensure that their meaning is clear to the reader. These tiny pictures may be especially useful to you when you are working at the conceptual and logical levels since they portray concepts very well.

Entity icons are also powerful for use with a reviewing group, in providing a simple definition of the sets you are documenting. This is illustrated in the simple diagram below. You would probably back this model up with additional layering of details allowing everyone to gain understanding of your analysis in an iterative fashion.

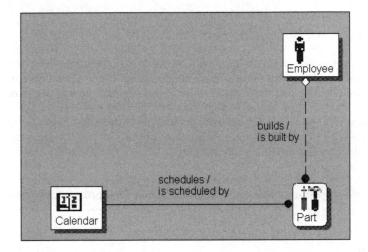

Other Options

We all know that modeling and the management of models is serious work. In this context the next set of enhancements can be seen as gimmicks. They need to be used sparingly to continue to be powerful, in order to avoid the perception that the modeler doesn't take the subject matter seriously.

> **Whatever you choose to use in your presentation should be measured to support context, not hide it, and support your team members, not patronize or antagonize them.**

Highlight a Version

Versioning data models so that people recognize the changes can be tough. They are all the same size. The boxes and lines may be exactly in the same place as the last model you delivered. The differences are so subtle that they are virtually invisible to anyone other than the person who cares very much about that specific change. Generally they are black and white. One doesn't read them like a book. One refers to them when necessary.

I have used many methods of making it easy to recognize a new version of a model. This is especially important during the first weeks after the physical design is completed. You may have changes to the model every two hours, especially if the development team has been divided up to work on different aspects of the project in parallel. Everyone needs to keep up-to-date on the shared objects, and this can prove increasingly difficult if there are numerous model versions piling up in In-Baskets or on desks.

Add something to the model that will make it easy to recognize a change. I have added the following to models with surprising results. The team likes it and they can easily find the latest one on their desks. These enhancements do not replace date and number but these often get to be what the team looks for.

❑ Stickers

❑ Stamps

❑ Vocabulary words

❑ Quotes

❑ Facts – Sports, Weird, Space, and so on.

I just left a meeting today where the developers were referring to the 'Pre-Frog' structure. I thought they were referring to yet another new acronym until they pointed to my latest sticker on their packets of model changes. The ensuing laughter cleared some of the residual tension of the review.

You are going to say that your third grade teacher used to do this stuff. You are right and it worked there too. Be careful not to overdo it, since it can cost your credibility if you pay too much attention to the cute, and too little to getting the job done right.

> **Remember documentation real-estate is prime so don't let informality get out of hand.**

Publication

Publication of models is one of the procedural issues that should be discussed when we have our initial meeting with the client. We generally have several options, but it is up to the modeler to present the model in the format that is acceptable to the client. The pictorial and backup documentation can be presented in the following formats:

❑ Paper – the most widely used form of a data model (big or small)

❑ Electronic files in a shared environment

❑ Database – Model management software

Each situation will generally require some form of security policy regarding access to the models and data management documentation. Clearly models developed using company-sensitive information should only be accessible to those with sufficient authority. However, balancing security with reasonable access is a tough call. The names of the tables and columns in your company can be worth quite a bit to anyone working in serious corporate espionage. On the other hand *ad hoc* query tool support is creating a valid need for our customers to know this information. Like I said, this one is tough.

Model files are usually not accessible without the use of a licensed copy of the software used to generate them so direct access to them is rare. Commonly these files will then be generated in report formats for wider distribution, tailored appropriately for the clients. The graphics may go out as .pdf files, while the reports will be produced in whatever format is standard for your company, such as Word or Excel documents for example.

> **You, and your department, must find a way to establish and maintain a publication policy that provides your documentation consistently and appropriately to your customers.**

Semi and Public Access – The Web

So many of our companies are not housed in the same facilities anymore, and the challenges of supporting a team spread temporally and geographically are huge. We are just now starting to leverage the Web for internal affairs as well as external ones.

Some modeling tools are really getting serious about providing reports in HTML format. For example, Erwin 4.0 has several web-friendly pre-canned reporting options for you. They allow you to extract information from the main file you are working on and link this information to a web page. Since you can provide login controls to such pages, this is a means to distribute selected information to end users. The graphics from your model are stored in a .gif or .pdf format and the model elements are provided in searchable, linked documents. For companies with intranets, and enough technical support for rapid content changes, distributing documentation this way can be ideal. The following screenshot illustrates this facility in the case of a section of our Solitaire model:

FORMATS:	TABULAR	HIERARCHICAL

RTB Table Owner - HTML

Entity

Entity

Name	Definition
Card	One of 52 specific combinations of suit and numbers (or face), usually displayed
Card Pile	A temporary and changeable area used to process a collection of cards, which b
Game	A contest played for sport or amusement according to rules made up of many sr
Person	A potential participant in a study being conducted by the Psychology departme
Play	A Play is completed when the entire set of Available Cards are assessed resultir
Playing Area	The location where a game of Solitaire is being carried out. Example - Home, Wo

Development Access To Files

Some of your customers may actually be partners in adding to, and maintaining, the files. DBAs and data modelers often share the model. The data modeler takes the model to a certain point in the design and then the DBA takes over, generally after the first draft of the physicalization. Programmers may also share physical models, as they work on the code necessary to implement the design, and take advantage of data modeling software such as Visio Professional, Erwin, and DataArchitect, which include functionality for the creation of triggers and procedures attached to the design.

It can get to be quite a challenge with so many people needing to actually update the model. It is fortunate that some software will merge model changes into a single file. Otherwise you need to be very careful not to lose the value you have added to the model through your various enhancements, by overwriting the wrong file.

Archive Access – The Library

Have I convinced you that any company could have hundreds of models? You may have production, test, development, vendor, legacy, enterprise, conceptual, E/R, F/A models of all subjects and supporting all departments. Managing all these models efficiently may well require the creation of a **data model library** (also referred to as a **model repository**).

Creating such a repository could be as simple as collating all the models together on a shared server somewhere. On the other hand, software like Computer Associates ModelMart enables you to store your models in a database, broken down into their own data elements.

You will want to figure out your own naming, indexing, card catalog, and identification system for locating them and knowing what they cover. You may want to create an overview document (index) so that someone could use search criteria to look for a particular model, by department or model type for example.

I have heard some of the vendors at shows also talking about new Enterprise object reuse between models. This is a great boon to our process. We waste way too much time reinventing Address, Employee, Item, and a hundred other entities/tables.

> Modelers, DBAs, Programmers, and Analysts need to be able to reuse model structures the way we reuse code, in other words simply and easily.

Summary

Data models form the foundation documentation for many different types of Enterprise analysis such as database development, reverse engineering, or application integration projects. Such models can be enhanced through judicious use of text, images, color, and formatting in order to help customers focus more easily on important features. This makes impact analysis, data element usage, and changes to the model more immediately obvious, through the various iterations that will inevitably take place. Without a simple means of keeping the whole development team, as well as the clients, aware of the current version of the model, as well as any problems or modifications that are required, confusion will reign.

Models also have to have a reliable publication method tailored to any security and access requirements. This may involve models being published on a company intranet, or the creation of a central model repository. The creation of a repository makes for improved reuse of existing models, and, as a result, a more efficient management of data elements (and their subsequent growth) within a given Enterprise.

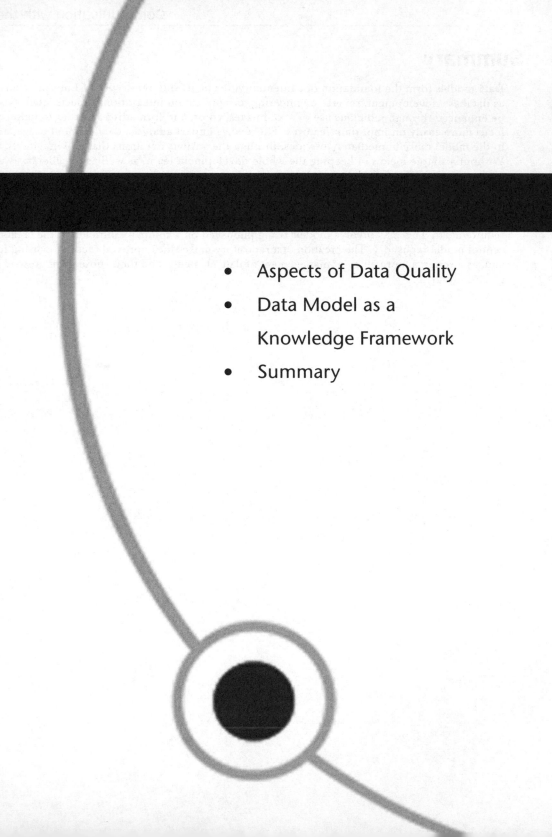

Further Data Analysis

This chapter covers other analysis you may want to do to provide information about aspects of the data that could affect design and security decisions. Often, these aspects of the data elements don't change the logical model but they may need to be thought about when choices are made about denormalization options and physical deployment.

The need of some data to be handled in a special way may cause you to separate it from the table you might otherwise design it to be in. The highly critical need of a data element to be correct at all times, like security privileges and salary levels for example, may cause you to add extra integrity constraints or rethink an integration process. The more you know about the nature of a data element, and its relationship with individuals, the business, and the larger world, the better prepared you are to design a solid, forward-looking, physical design.

There are also some extra types of documentation that use the model as a framework for locating and leveraging other information in the Enterprise. Using the model as a reference point for providing information can help everyone see the data connections in your company.

In this chapter we will cover:

- ❑ Aspects of Data Quality
    - ❑ Fidelity – the integrity, accuracy, and completeness of a data element
    - ❑ Criticality – how correct do the data elements have to be?
    - ❑ Sensitivity and Privacy – moral and legal responsibility to secure data elements
    - ❑ Stewardship – assigned responsibility for data quality
    - ❑ Cross Footing – checking for the same answer using multiple methods
    - ❑ Process Validation – watching how the data is used for appropriateness
    - ❑ Risk and Mitigation – knowing the data problems and lessening their impact
- ❑ The use of data mappings to trace and audit the validity of data elements

Aspects of Data Quality

Gathering facts about the existing and future quality needs of single data elements is often overlooked in our modeling efforts. We data modelers seem to worry more about the size and shape of the containers of the elements than the actual data and yet it is the data itself that tells us the story of rules, relationships, exceptions, and hardships in the processes they support.

Data quality needs a champion in the IT department. The data modeler, by using the normal forms to build a logical and physical model, helps to provide a framework for organization that promotes quality data. But the organization of the data isn't enough. You need to know more about the data than just how to organize it relationally to be able to develop applications that manage high quality data assets. Just because a table design is built to provide a third Normal form schema doesn't mean that the data set itself will actually end up in third Normal form. The people building data have to respond quickly to new data element needs and rapidly changing business rules. They have to solve problems creatively with their applications, and may need to denormalize to do so. However, the more you find out, document, and share with the development team, the better prepared everyone is to build in safe flexibility and safe guards for the Enterprise data.

Don't think that the list of data quality aspects we will cover here is comprehensive. The data world is vast and diverse. Every Enterprise, by their very nature, seems to focus on new data, or different facets of it. It continually fascinates me to see what is important to each new Enterprise I visit. Government vs. private, service vs. manufacturing, entertainment vs. banking military vs. civilian, they all care about different data elements differently. For example, whereas book publishers may guard unreleased book titles jealously, the public library guards the names of people who check out books while happily publishing book titles; both enterprises have different viewpoints as to what is sensitive.

Look over these other aspects of data analysis. They don't exactly fit into a model, other than as notes or additions to your definitions, but they remain extremely important aspects about the data you are modeling.

Fidelity Analysis

Fidelity is a quality of dependableness. How dependent are you on having correct data available at all times? Michael H. Brackett gave a presentation at the Information Quality Conference in 2000 called *A New Perspective for Data Resource Quality*. He said that data fidelity is made up of three parts:

❑ **Integrity** – specifies how the data is maintained after capture

❑ **Accuracy** – specifies how well data stored in the resource represents the real world

❑ **Completeness** – specifies how well the scope of the data resource meets the scope of the business information demand

The data modeler looks to data in existing systems, forms, or reports to find the current state of these aspects. They test data to determine the level of success that can be expected of their design. And finally they need to continually audit new data to check out the levels of fidelity as the Enterprise continues to grow and change.

There are tools out there that can help with some of this type of analysis using automated and systematic examination. Evoke is one of them (www.evokesoft.com). It automates the labor-intensive process of examining the data in the Enterprise systems. The software's data profiling process will highlight any data anomalies and incompatibilities and store them in a repository, ensuring that these issues are dealt with before the data is moved into the target application. So, for example, if you are integrating two systems containing Customer Address information, Evoke will help highlight the fact that 'Street' is used in one system's addresses, while 'St.' is used in the other. You need to be able to recognize that this relates to the same data element. While this is a trivial example, what about if you were documenting colors and needed to know that 'beige', bage', and 'beaje' are all the same? Tools like this can save you time and lower the percentage of error that any manual task adds into a process. Without a tool like Evoke however, you can still comb through a set of data with your own set of checks in a disciplined way. This type of analysis can produce eye-opening statistics that tend to challenge interview answers, written requirements, and even system documentation.

Manual Examination – Profiling

It seems that half my life has been spent in sifting and sorting through piles of data to see what it is really made up of. Profiling is a process of looking for anomalies by going through a set of actual data. It is a good idea to gather this type of data together for the client during the data analysis stage. You may be looking at old reports or spreadsheets that are the tools being used in the business process now. Even the clients may not always be aware of how the end users (data input operators, transaction-level operators) use the systems. It may be that the end users have worked out a quick, cheap, viable solution to an issue in an inflexible application tool. However, you could certainly label this as a problematic solution because they did it without considering any data requirements past their immediate needs. Now the Enterprise has data element fidelity problem/s that could easily ripple to other places.

To get a profile of the data, you should try and determine the following details regarding the columns of a table:

- ❏ Minimum value
- ❏ Maximum value
- ❏ Number of instances of NULL, 0, N/A, <spaces> (NOT NULL columns can be tricked)
- ❏ Number of unique values
- ❏ verify that similar values really are the same
- ❏ Number of each unique value in the table
- ❏ Random sampling

Don't forget to count the total number of records in the table too, in order to provide a statistics set for each column that looks something like this:

Table Name	Employee	
Column Name	Hire_Date	
Column specification	DATE, NOT NULL allowed	
Row Count	1500	
Expected Range	03/17/1998 (company established) – current day	
Check	Value	Quantity
MIN	09/09/1099	276
MAX	01/01/3999	36
COUNT – null, 0, N/A, \<spaces\>		0
COUNT unique		216
SELECT unique	09/09/1099 03/17/1998 03/18/1998 . . . \<there would be 216 distinct dates here – I'm not showing them for brevity\>	216
SELECT COUNT unique hire_date GROUP BY	216 – 09/09/1099 15 – 03/17/1998 1 - -03/18/1998 and so on. 43 – 01/01/3999 \<there would be 216 distinct dates here – I'm not showing them for brevity\>	216

What does this tell us? It tells us that even a NOT NULL with data type DATE can be manipulated to hold values that mean something other than what your data definition would suggest. In this case we have discovered two nonsensical employment dates (09/09/1099 and 01/01/3999) being used as flags for something unrelated to the definition of a Hire_Date. For example, you may find out that all Employee records where the Hire_Date = 09/09/1099 were loaded from a previous system where the data was missing. The date was chosen to be absurd on purpose, and became an identification of records that have a problem. The code removes these records from certain reports using this absurd date for identification. This is probably not a customer-driven data quality issue, but rather an IT decision during a data migration effort. However, don't be surprised if there's no one left amongst the clients who remembers why this weird date was used in the first place. You may well have to make your own decision as to what to do with the data, but at least you've spotted the problem now, and so minimized the impact on the rest of the data.

You may find that the other absurd date, 01/01/3999, is being used for records of contractors. The system forces the clients to put in a date, though the contractors haven't been hired. Why are the contractors in the Employee table you might ask? Perhaps HR discovered that the Employee table has been integrated into several systems (such as e-mail). So without an Employee record an e-mail account couldn't be set up. They found a quick workaround by inserting this nonsensical date to bypass the data rules built into the tables. You have to give them credit for innovation.

These answers are not uncommon or ridiculous. They happen every day to every data element in your models. The only way you can find out what is really happening is by checking yourself. In this case the Enterprise concept of Work Force grew and nobody questioned if the systems that were in use could handle the new definitions and business rules. The original analysis may have been complete and accurate at the time, but almost nothing (including data rules) remains stable forever.

In this example the client faced database rules requiring that the workforce for the Enterprise fit into the concept of Employee. It had been complicated by different departmental rules that depended on everyone in the intricate web of communication having a record in the Employee table. That forced contractors and temporary help into the Employee table just so they could get an e-mail account. Forcing those records into that system then caused the Hire_Date to become something it wasn't originally intended to be, namely a flag of employment status.

Data profiling can help you identify the reality of:

- Natural Keys – true uniqueness (don't be fooled by ID numbers that were not backed up with stored procedures to avoid duplicates occurring)
- Data types – true set of values
- Nullability – true rules of required or not (watch for values like spaces, N/A, and absurdities)
- Embedded multi-values – data in columns delineated with commas or special characters
- Definitions – the data set doesn't match the column name or definition

Criticality Analysis

Criticality has to do with the importance of that piece of data being right. It may be that your middle initial isn't very important to the company but your social security number is critical. Critical data often has extra checks and audits to try to prevent data corruption. The checks could be in the front end (within the user interface screens) or back end (within the database itself). Those decisions will be made by the development team. What is important is that extra checks be considered.

While some organizations have status, risk, and criticality catalogs, there doesn't seem to be one industry standard that I can pass on to you. Instead, what I'll give you here is a personal method I developed to help identify the criticality of data. It uses a simple one to four scale, with one being the most critical. Tagging your data elements this way allows us to focus on 'Mission Critical' data elements.

Remember that what is important to one company will be unimportant to another. You need to find out what is critical to your customers and respond accordingly. It always seems to me that if the data was worth collecting, someone is depending on it being right. However, it's a reality that not every data element is maintained with the same levels of quality. This type of analysis provides the understanding of what the impact will be to the Enterprise and customer if it's wrong.

> **Criticality classification is not an excuse to allow bad data. It simply allows you to focus extra care on those data elements which will have a severe impact on the system if they aren't stored appropriately.**

Sometimes the real trick here is not in classifying data elements but identifying effective and appropriate methodologies of maintaining compliance by preventing data in the first level from falling below the fidelity level required. In fact you can use some of the statistics you generate from your fidelity analysis to test whether a data element classified as highly critical is over 95% (or whatever is determined to be appropriate) accurate. If you can create a fidelity test that provides you with the ability to monitor your first-level data you can at least highlight the need for procedural changes to help keep the data at the best fidelity possible. In this way the data modeler can participate in helping identify potential problems.

Here is a suggestion for levels of criticality. You may need to tailor a set to work for you in your enterprise.

Level One – Absolutely Necessary

The data *must* be correct. It is process stopping since you can't complete a legal or vital function if this data element is incorrect. This data is probably never NULL allowed. It should have some type of list of values, format mask, or ability to check against alternative sources. Data values that fall in this category are fixed when there is an identified problem, even if it entails extensive manual intervention. These data elements can't be wrong, and it's often catastrophic if they are.

Examples of this include:

- ❑ The Ground Positioning System longitude and latitude plus the altitude reading of a plane in flight for the Air Traffic Control systems

- ❑ The drug name, dosage, and patient ID of a prescription in a Pharmacy

- ❑ The traffic light controls that prevent both directions being Green at the same time

Level Two – Important

This data is expected to be correct. It will cause issues if it's needed and found to be wrong. The difference between this and level one is that level one data is mandatory for processing that constantly happens, while level two data is used for processes occurring less frequently. Not having it correct is a risk. Data values that fall in this category will be fixed when there is an identified problem, but generally not as an emergency like level one. Since they aren't so critical, there is usually time to clean these up when they are discovered.

These are generally data values that have some repercussions if they are wrong. It *will* cause an anomaly to summation reporting, cause special handling, create annoying duplication of effort, or leave a final process unable to complete due to the inaccuracy. Usually this type of data finds its way to a 'Clean Up' process after the fact.

Examples include:

- ❑ Sales Total on an Invoice for a Retail firm

- ❑ Address on a delivery for a Freight company

- ❑ Beneficiary information for processing death benefits in a Company

Level Three – Good To Have

This data should be correct. If this data element is wrong the error may cause some statistical issues but won't create anything other than some reporting anomalies. It will only be fixed if there is minimal effort needed. These are data values that are informational only as a rule, and generally have few repercussions if they are wrong. They *may* cause an anomaly to summation reporting, require special handling, create annoying duplication of effort, or leave a final process unable to complete due to the inaccuracy. But generally these things are just ignored and explained as + or – accuracy percentages. This type of data is seldom 'cleaned up' and causes the data warehouse team headaches later on.

Examples include:

- ❑ Zip Code for addresses used in bulk mailings for an Advertising firm.
- ❑ Reprint date for books in a Library
- ❑ Car Color for Rental firms

Level Four – Nice To Have

This data may be correct but if it isn't there it has probably no impact. There is very little worry over whether this data is accurate or not. It is usually NULL allowed and is often a text block for some kind of note. However, this data can't ever be used to trace or substantiate any conclusion, as it has no controls. This will probably never be fixed.

Examples include:

- ❑ Age of pet on application for a Dog or Cat License
- ❑ Visiting from Location gathered in the Guest book at an Antique Store
- ❑ Color of Hair for the Department of Motor Vehicles

Sensitivity and Privacy Analysis

We are becoming more and more aware of the need to protect the privacy of people's data. Companies can now be sued for privacy breaches if someone has their identity stolen and it can be proved to be due in part to negligence on their behalf. This is not just an issue of security. It is an issue of awareness. We legitimately give people security privileges to data that they do not seem to recognize as sensitive. They behave as though their privileges extend to creating and publishing data that should have been noted as being 'For your eyes only'. The theft of information is often not a breakdown of security but a breakdown of awareness of responsibility.

> **Data is an asset, a resource just like inventory, money, and energy. We have to protect the assets of our Enterprise.**

Publication or access to some data elements has to be restricted. Noting them as requiring special handling is another aspect of data analysis. You can apply pretty much the same levels to sensitivity and privacy that we did to criticality. Again this is a suggestion of a way to categorizing the sensitivity of your data elements. You need to make these aspects of the data elements available to your development team so they can address the extra security needs.

First Degree – Legally Protected Private

This data *must* be protected. This data could be damaging to the livelihood, security, or reputation of the company or individual if it were stolen or published. These are things that have legal ramifications if they get out. They may be encoded inside the database itself, or indeed stored separately from the rest of the data in a secure area, such as a server in a walk-in safe for example. Access to this data may need to be justified through a manager.

This data may involve financials, personal information (pay rate, reviews, complaints), R&D concepts (Research and Development), political contributions, negotiations, staffing level scenarios, medical issues, or security monitoring. Examples include:

- ❏ Tax identification numbers
- ❏ Personal financial information
- ❏ Medical test results

Second Degree – Enterprise-Defined Private

This data is *expected* to be protected. You can probably base this level of privacy on what you expect to be able to keep from your co-workers. Item names for sold product is public but the names of what is in Research and Development should be restricted until R&D and Marketing allow the information out. This is pretty much the same data as the previous one, but it has less potential for legal damage, although serious damage to the Enterprise can still be done if this information becomes widely distributed. Examples include:

- ❏ The next season Marketing plans
- ❏ Test results for research before publication
- ❏ Product formula and processes

Third Degree – Morally-Defined Private

This data should be private. Day and month may be OK but let's keep year of birth slightly private. Some people get unhappy when everyone knows how old they are. While the name of the city you live in may help promote the car-pooling program, we need to keep street and address number quiet so no one gets an unexpected visit from a co-worker. Examples include:

- ❏ Age of Children living at home – actually any information about children not volunteered
- ❏ Names of people who checked out a book at a library
- ❏ Family connections to famous / infamous people – unless volunteered (political, criminal, celebrity)

Fourth Degree–Public

This data is public. We fully expect everyone to know our product line and hours of business. In fact if it isn't public we have other problems. Similarly, if the dates and times that a consultant is available to meet clients isn't made public, then arranging appointments with them will be problematic. By this level of the game you may also have legal requirements to make certain information public. These may be data elements that need to be in the company prospectus. Depriving access to some data can be as detrimental to the Enterprise legally as not protecting data that should be protected.

Stewardship

Another aspect of data analysis is determining who has responsibility for the validity of a bit of data. For example, we assume that HR is ultimately responsible for the Employee list therefore they must have tools to be able to audit the list, or be involved in any decisions about intended use of the list. We don't know that about all the data in our systems. For many years we divided stewardship up by application boundaries. If your department owned an application it owned the quality of the data elements. Unfortunately that doesn't work in a world full of integrated data.

> **Stewardship should at least be available at the entity or table level (sometimes it will be more specific like the credit level of a vendor). Or it may even be a partition within the data set itself (like region or pay level).**

One of the things we seem to have lost over time is the sense of responsibility for the validity of data. Trying to establish ownership, or at least stewardship, of data elements at least tries to address that loss. You may want to build a 'proposed ownership of data' list for your tables that looks something like this:

Table	Table Definition	Owner – Department or specific	Access available to
Color	Stores the list of valid values for color type. Example 'Black & White', 'Colorized', 'Color'.	Manufacturing	DBA
Contract Text	Stores reusable Riders, Clauses, Footnotes, and Terms & Conditions.	Legal	Application Owner
Geo	Stores the valid list of Geographic areas or Territories. Examples: 'Western Europe', 'France', 'Lyon'.	Shipping	Application Owner
Grade	Stores the valid list of Grades used to qualify a product. Examples 'A++', 'B'.	M. Martin	End Client
Language	Stores the valid list of Languages. Example 'German', 'Spanish'.	Legal	Application Owner

Alternatively you may want to create typed lists within tables, as in the following example where all the status lists were implemented in one table called Status, using a type code to differentiate them.

Status Lists	Status Definition	Current Known Values	Owner
Activity Status	The status of an Activity Remark as it is routed for review.	Open, Resolved	Unknown
Company Status	The status of a company record.	Active, Inactive	Finance
Geo Status	The status of a geographic area record.	Active, Inactive	Shipping

Table continued on following page

Status Lists	Status Definition	Current Known Values	Owner
Product Status	The status of an existing product.	Active, Inactive	Marketing
Proposal Sales Order Status	The status of a Proposal Sales Order through its lifecycle.	Pending, Signed, Unsigned, Clean, Unclean	Sales

Stewardship should not be confused with security privileges. Having sufficient privileges to change data values is very different from whether you have responsibility for ensuring that they are right. The security privilege to add parts to the Part table may be owned by someone different to the person assigned stewardship of the accuracy of that Part table, although they may be closely coupled.

Cross-Footing

Cross footing has to do with double-checking using a different method to get to supposedly the same answer. It is a truth test for data. The more ways we have of verifying the quality of the sets in our systems, then the more power and value the data assets can wield.

Derivations

We have many data elements that are created over and over again in different systems, especially when integration is playing a role in the Enterprise, without the checks and balances that need to keep everything in sync. There are, for example, derived values in our reports. Sometimes we even store them in tables, especially data warehouse tables. One way to mitigate the risk of keeping derived values is to provide cross-footing validation from other sources. You may want to create a cross-footing analysis like this:

Data value	Formula	Cross-Foot Formula
Monthly Gross Sales Amount	Sum(Daily Gross Sales Amount) for all sales falling within one calendar month as defined in the *Daily Sales Summary* procedure.	Sum(Transaction level: Sale Amount + Tax Amount – Discount Amount) for all sales falling within one calendar month for all departments

Look at the formula and cross foot formula above. You may find out that the validation consistently has a larger number than the formula currently being used. When you dig it out you find that the Daily Sales Summary procedure doesn't remove transactions typed 'Returns' from the summation, or that it never added in the Parts department sales to Rework.

> **You can prevent serious audit problems by doing a double-check using different sources of what should be the same data. Your team will have to determine what the correct frequency of this would be, whether for every transaction, daily, weekly, or monthly for example.**

Reasonability Checks

You may be able to set up 'reasonability' checks. These checks enable us to avoid gross errors in data by setting maximum and minimum limits on the data. Such checks may be that the weight of a patient is always between 1 and 1000 kilos, or that the equivalent weight in pounds will always be a larger number than in kilos, for example. All of this can be managed in domains added to the database creation coding, though it may be that triggers will be needed in some cases to check for validity.

Table	Column	Reasonability Rules
Employee	Hire Date	Never earlier than company origin date Never later than today
Item	Master Pack Quantity	Never equal to or less than 1
Shipment	Bill of Lading Total Weight	Never greater than equipment weight rating

Process Validation

Process validation deals with the fact that you as the modeler probably know the business rules in the model better than anyone. You can test for them by exercising the front-end screens, reports, and querying the tables to watch for appropriate data behavior. You may want to take the business activity descriptions (sometimes called **use cases**) and follow a record through from creation to deletion to verify it is being handled as intended. Sometimes there is a slip-up in the deployment of the plan. Catching it before it goes to production can save enormous analysis later.

Make a checklist of your relationship / cardinality statements. Open the application tool and test it out by exercising the functionality that has been provided. Look over the screens and reports and check for the ability to create and report multi-valued relationships even when normally there is only one (like E-mail Address below). You may even need to try the screens and then dive into analysis in the database tables to verify that what you think should be happening is indeed the case.

Every Employee may be contacted at Zero, One, or Many E-mail Addresses?
Every Item must have One or More Item Versions?
Every Organization must be staffed with One or More Employees?
Every Department may be located in Zero, One, or Many Staffed Sites?
Every Site may be the location of Zero, One, or Many Staffed Sites?

You analyzed the processes that helped build the tools. Sometimes that makes you a valuable resource to the test teams who verify that the requirements of your design make it to the implementation.

Risk and Mitigation Analysis

There is also the need to document anything that you find that makes you nervous about a proposed data management technique. Most risks fall into a potential breakage of one of the data quality checks above. You see a potential for data issues dealing with current or future:

❑ Table / Columns not being used as designed

❑ Data not being recognized as being 'Mission-Critical'

❑ Data not being recognized as being 'Enterprise-Sensitive'

❑ No one being responsible for data quality

❑ No checking data values for reasonability

❑ No double-checking calculated values

❑ No ongoing verification of growing Enterprise data concepts being handled correctly

❑ Data being collected without any understood business need or projected future use (the 'let's record everything' syndrome)

Risk and mitigation analysis combines what you found in the previous analysis and:

❑ Prioritizes the issue into High, Medium, or Low risk

❑ Justifies the prioritization with a potential impact statement

❑ Documents the actual solution to remove the risk

❑ Suggests methods of mitigating or reducing the risk by means other than the present solution

Mitigation has to do with making something less severe. It doesn't fix the problem; it just makes the results hurt less. You may want to encourage a 'Suggestion Box' type of form or add an 'On-Line problem reporting' application to the corporate tool set to gather intelligence from around the company about data shortcomings due to inadequate functionality, rule shortcomings, or changed business processes. Gathering and reviewing the options can help IT manage responses by providing possible solutions and mitigation plans.

You may want to provide something like these examples. This type of analysis can help build strong communication ties between the business clients and the data management team. The brainstorming that has to occur between the groups to solve the issues is an opportunity to stay in touch with the evolution of the data elements, both in terms of definition and usage.

Potential Data Management Issue/Risk #1	
Description	Customers with 'Unsatisfactory' credit rating still available in the pull down list on the Order screen. New Orders are allowed to be created for them
Potential Impact	High

Potential Data Management Issue/Risk #1	
Impact Analysis	There could be an increase in severely Past Due billing and / or eventual bad debt that the company will need to absorb by ($ to be determined)
Solution	Remove Customer name from the list on the pull-down list until credit rating on or above 'Satisfactory'
Mitigation Options	❑ Allow ($ to be determined) worth of orders while still in 'Unsatisfactory' credit rating. Will need to check rating and billing amount and status of 'Open' orders ❑ Allow manager overrides to system rules ❑ Allow Accounts Receivable to suspend and reinstate Customer order privileges

Potential Data Management Issue/Risk #2	
Description	Region Managers have only one contact phone, e-mail in the system
Potential Impact	Medium
Impact Analysis	There is often an urgent requirement to communicate with the Region managers. One phone and one e-mail are not enough ways to contact them
Solution	Add a 'Many' table for both Phone and E-mail for Employees
Mitigation Options	❑ Manage extra contact information data to be managed outside the current system to be secured and accessed by rules within the Operations department ❑ Expand the current field lengths and change the definition of the fields to mean Phone Contact Information and E-mail Contact Information. This will allow the clients to add however many they want. ❑ Get all the Region Managers 24/7 pagers and use the pager number in the phone field

Potential Data Management Issue/Risk # 3	
Description	Order system is susceptible to being 'offline' on weekends and evenings. IT doesn't provide 24/7 help support.
Potential Impact	Medium

Table continued on following page

Potential Data Management Issue/Risk # 3	
Impact Analysis	The Order department has to revert to a manual system when this happens and then input the orders later. There is always a potential for 'Lost' orders and bad data written on the forms without the access to the data integrity of the system.
Solution	Add a 24/7 Help desk to the IT charter.
	Fix whatever it is that is impacting the Order system.
Mitigation Options	❑ Have a floating 'Primary' support assignment for the IT department. Person on 'Primary' to carry a pager for the duration of the assignment.
	❑ Develop a 'Roll-over' application support that allows the clients to use a 'Back-up' system to be merged back invisibly when the system problem has been diagnosed and returned to 'On Line' status

Data Model As a Knowledge Framework

I realize that I am biased about the potential importance of a high quality data model to an enterprise. At the onset of developing a data model, I can almost envision the potential connections that can grow from each of those high-level entities. Each conceptual entity can become the basis for many logical entities. The logical entities can be combined into either single or multiple physical tables. The tables can be deployed in multiple locations and installations. They can be the foundation for many applications, code blocks, screens, reports, and web sites. Each of the concepts, entities, and tables has an owner and a steward. Highly skilled technicians maintain them. Business processes would grind to a halt without them.

Maintaining the connectivity between elements, as well as the ability to trace and audit them, makes one corner of our chaotic world of information systems into a quiet and respected library where anyone can research a question and have faith that the answer is correct. **Mapping** is a manual method of trying to provide some indexing and tracking, and we will look at it briefly here.

Data Maps

Way back at the beginning of this book we found out that data elements come in several varieties, namely conceptual, logical, and physical. You saw how those could be followed through a maturing process from concepts to actual columns in tables. It is easy to conceive of those levels of maturing being tied to each other in **mappings**. What may not be quite so obvious is their relationship to other concepts and other logical or physical elements.

You can map to:

❑ Machines (Development, Test, Production, Backup, individual desktop PCs, routers, printers)

❑ Code (screens, reports, procedures)

❑ Documents (project, standards, change control)

❑ Locations (geographic, virtual)

- ❑ Models (sources of shadow entities/tables, versions, submodels)
- ❑ Organizations (sponsor, interested party, security)
- ❑ Pathways (network, DTS, load/sync routines)
- ❑ People (authorship, stewardship, support)
- ❑ Processes (feeding, originating, referencing, supporting)

Mappings note relationships from one thing to another. The discussion here highlights how the data models can be used as a starting place to make such connections and maybe inspire you to develop some of your own. Building and maintaining this type of documentation can save a serious amount of time at the beginning of a project by being able to research known business processes, data element definitions, and data relationship rules. We can also save time doing impact analysis by being able to trace a change through all of the hardware, software, networks, code, screens, and clients that utilize them. We may be able to justify budget or staff by being able to provide an overview of the complexity of the data management environment. We can assist in smooth data loading in the event of upgrades, new applications, or company merges.

> **Mappings are indexes to data in terms of structures, definitions, owners, concepts, hardware, applications, and so on. We do them to help us get the job done faster.**

When you accumulate your mappings into some type of repository you will be able to come up with a 'Where Used' report something like this:

Data table. Data element: EMPLOYEE.EMPLOYEE ID		
Definition: The non-significant, system-generated, surrogate key that uniquely identifies an Employee.		
General purpose of element in Main Computing System	**General Hardware Use Description**	**Hardware Name**
Original Creation on	Production box	STDHP001
3 year Backup on	Backup box	STDHP006
Final Archive	To disk	Off site disk storage location 2
Release test area	QA – Beta Test box	STDHP003
Development test area	Integration – Alpha Test box	STDHP010
Development area	Programmer development box	STDHP015
Development area	Programmer development box	SQLSERV008
Development area	Programmer development box	SQLSERV010

Table continued on following page

Data table. Data element: EMPLOYEE.EMPLOYEE ID		
Definition: The non-significant, system-generated, surrogate key that uniquely identifies an Employee.		
General purpose of element in Programming Code	**Code Type**	**Code Name**
Production Creation	Screen	`EmpStartInput`
Production Query	Screen	`EmpFind`
Production Report Restriction	Screen	`EmpHistoryReportParam`
Employee History Identification	Report	`EmpHistoryRpt`
Payroll Check Identification	Report	`SalaryCheckCreationRep`
Security Privilege allocation	Procedure	`AssignPriv.sql`
General purpose of element in Document	**Document Type**	**Document Name**
HR application description	Training Manual	People Manager 2.5 Training Guide
Integration review for merging international and domestic applications	Project Proposal	Human Resource Consolidation in 2009
Company Standards	Data Format Standard	IT Data Element Development Standard 1.9
Change to format from Number to Text to allow for more characters in company acquisition – legacy data	Change Control	CC 2345345.5
General purpose of Model	**Model Type**	**Model Name**
In work Human Resource consolidation analysis	Conceptual	HRConsolidation Preview
Reverse Engineer of People Manager 2.5	Physical	PeopleManager25
As-Is and To-Be analysis for change control CC 2345345.5	Physical	CC2345345AsIsToBe

This is of course a very restricted and simplified example. Employee ID is the type of data element that would have pages upon pages of mappings. Mappings of this type would not have to be driven from the data element, since they are flexible enough to support going from any of the elements noted above and pulling the detailed connections into an index that allows an overview of that subject.

I always remember the panic we faced around the Y2K crisis and think of the time savings we could have gained by having dependable documentation of this type.

Mappings To the Conceptual Model

You will recall that conceptual models have a tendency to be rather high level. That being the case they map mostly to high-level visions in the enterprise. You can do mappings at different levels even within the model. Are you mapping the entities or the model itself? Are you mapping to a version (point in time) or a virtual (up to date) concept that was documented in the model? You have many choices because the conceptual model contains many information facets itself, any of which can be used as one end of a mapping:

❑ Itself – scope, purpose, sponsor, date, time

❑ Entities – concepts, definitions

❑ Relationships – business rules

❑ Notes – interesting issues

Your conceptual model can map to:

❑ New company initiatives like a data warehouse project, or CRM (Customer Relationship Management) system. It could document the expected data foundation (scope) that the project would cover.

❑ Subject area models that add a certain level of detail to the highest conceptual thoughts. Subject areas often overlap each other so you may need to note more than one.

❑ Documentation in the form of projects that were spawned from it, vendor information (if that area of data is being managed by a purchased software package), or even white papers and analysis documents organized in an effort to rethink the way we currently do things.

A mapping can be set up to note that the entire scope of a department's responsibility (or charter) lies in this portion of the conceptual model. You can start at these upper levels and then drive the mapping into higher and higher resolution (lower and lower detail).

> **The hardest thing about this type of documentation is knowing when to begin, when to stop, and how to keep it accurate.**

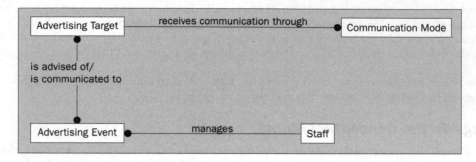

Remember this conceptual model from earlier in the book? Let's see what we could map parts of it to.

Model Name	Enterprise Intitiative	Status	Reason
MarketingConceptual	CRM	In review	Possible enhancement to the marketing application giving more visibility to the planned and actual advertising targets by event

Or we could take it to a more detailed level:

Model Name	Entity Name	Entity Definition	Logical Entity
Marketing Conceptual	Advertising Event	An Advertising Event is a communication activity sponsored by an Enterprise, carried out by an Enterprise, that announces opportunities to an Advertising Target through one or more communication modes.	CommunciationsLogical – Communique AdvertisingLogical – Advertising Message
Marketing Conceptual	Advertising Target	An Advertising Target may be a Person, Family, or an Audience. Each target receives communications about Advertised Events through an Advertising Model	MarketingLogical – Client AdvertisingLogical – Household CommunicationsLogical – erson CommunicationsLogical – company CommunicationsLogical – Contact

Model Name	Entity Name	Entity Definition	Logical Entity
Marketing Conceptual	Communication Mode	A Communication Mode is a method of deploying and disseminating information either with a specific receiver (such as Mail and Phone Call) or to an intended audience as in Bill Board, Radio, or Television.	AdvertisingLogical – Address AdvertisingLogical – E-mail AdvertisingLogical – Phone
Marketing Conceptual	Staff	A Staff member is an Employee or Contractor who is working with the Enterprise to plan, deploy, manage, and review Advertising Events.	HRLogical – Employee EnterpriseLogical – Work Force

It's easy to talk about mapping but another thing to do one. It is exacting, tedious, and brilliant when you just want to figure out something like what we are thinking about when we use the concept 'Communication Mode'. Sometimes it is hard to justify until you have a need to know something like this *fast*. Y2K would not have been such a worry if we had just known how big the problem was going to be. Without documentation somewhere along these lines everything is an unknown factor and requires research. We should be able to refer to documentation like this and at least get a feel for the answer to a question, even if it isn't the whole answer.

Mappings To the Logical Model

The logical model is getting a little closer to data elements that we recognize in the physical world. Here you can see the logical model at the hub of a bunch of other logical, conceptual, and physical models. It is also the beginning of mappings to real-world connections, especially people, processes, departments, budgets, justifications, and schedules.

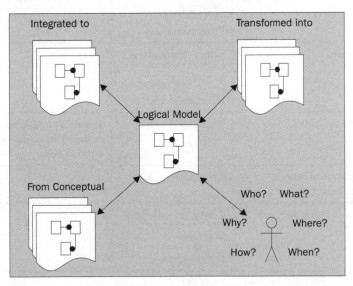

Here again you have to choose what you are mapping to in the model. Is it the model itself, the entities, attributes, relationships? An example of what a logical mapping may look like is as follows:

```
Address
Communication Address ID (FK)
Building Number
Room Type Name
Room Number
Street Name
City Name
State Name
Country Name
Postal Code
```

For this entity you may want to map what the expected data source will be. Entities without data sources are difficult to deploy in an application. How can we maintain quality data if no one wants to load or maintain a data set, but simply wants to use it?

Entity Name	Attribute Name	Data Source	Note
Address	City Name	Phone Solicitation Web Site Purchased List	
Address	Street Name	Phone Solicitation Web Site Purchased List	
Address	State Name	Phone Solicitation Web Site Purchased List	
Address	Country Name	Phone Solicitation Web Site Purchased List	
Address	Postal Code	Purchased List	We don't use manually collected zip codes. We always use the latest vendor file
Address	Communication Address ID	System	
Address	Room Number	Phone Solicitation Web Site Purchased List	

Entity Name	Attribute Name	Data Source	Note
Address	Building Number	Phone Solicitation Web Site Purchased List	
Address	Room Type Name	Phone Solicitation Web Site	

Mappings To the Physical Model

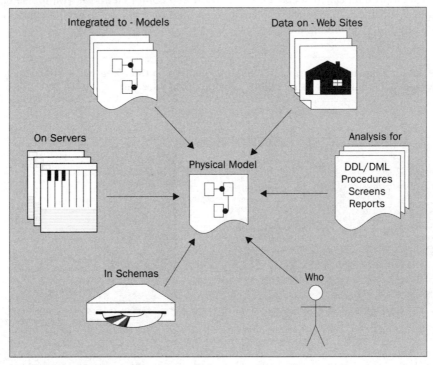

Mappings for the physical elements are the most common in use in Enterprises today. They are found in many IT groups. DBAs have mappings of applications to servers and servers to boxes. Programmers have mappings of code blocks to database names and databases to test and production boxes they have been loaded on. The infrastructure team has mappings of virtual addresses to the various computing locations throughout the enterprise.

Unfortunately we don't always share the mappings and find that efforts are duplicated between groups. The DBAs want to know what data elements are on what server. The programmers want to know what data elements are in what code. The network team wants to know what data elements are moving across the T1 lines from the web. Everyone has a little different need, but they all basically want to know where data elements are now, where they are going to be in the future, and the means by which they move between the client and the servers.

Using the model as a starting place for all mappings creates a central starting point. It also makes it absolutely necessary to keep the model valid at all times with the environments. The modeling software Erwin (and a few of the others as well) offers a great function called 'Compare' that will auto-synchronize all the elements in a model with what it finds in the database library tables. This will actually synchronize in both directions, either making the model like the database, or the database like the model.

Admittedly, it is those very database library tables that are used more frequently than the models as the source data for physical mappings. However, sometimes access to those tables is restricted. The model is usually public access and the team that manages them is usually not locked in code rooms behind cipher locks like DBAs. The challenge here is how to bring all this mapping information into a repository that provides flexible reporting and the correct security all at the same time. I have recently been looking at a product called MetaCenter (www.dataag.com) that allows you to use named Erwin objects (entities, attributes, and so on) and set up mappings to database objects, documents, in fact pretty much anything you would like.

> **New data management software is constantly coming on line. You will want to keep up with new tools that might be available to help you do your job.**

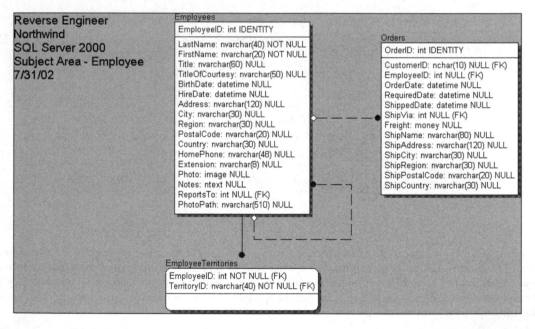

Here is a small subject area model of the Employees table reverse engineered from the SQL Server 2000 version of Northwind (that we looked at in Chapter 11 *Reverse Engineering*). A physical mapping of the table/column to the logical attribute and stored procedure name could look something like this:

Table Name	Column Name	Data Type	Attribute Name	Stored Procedure Name
Employees	EmployeeID	int	Employee Id	EmployeeIns.sql EmployeeUpd.sql EmployeeDel.sql JobChangeUpd.sql BadgeUpd.sql
Employees	LastName	nvarchar(40)	Employee Last Name	EmployeeIns.sql EmployeeUpd.sql
Employees	FirstName	nvarchar(20)	Employee First Name	EmployeeIns.sql EmployeeUpd.sql
Employees	Title	nvarchar(60)	Employee Job Title Name	EmployeeIns.sql EmployeeUpd.sql JobChangeUpd.sql
Employees	TitleOfCourtesy	nvarchar(50)	Employee Title of Courtesy Name	EmployeeIns.sql EmployeeUpd.sql
Employees	BirthDate	datetime	Employee Birth Date	EmployeeIns.sql EmployeeUpd.sql
Employees	HireDate	datetime	Employee Hire Date	EmployeeIns.sql EmployeeUpd.sql
Employees	Extension	nvarchar(8)	Employee Phone Number Phone Type = Company	EmployeeIns.sql EmployeeUpd.sql
Employees	Photo	image	Employee Photo Image	EmployeeIns.sql EmployeeUpd.sql BadgeUpd.sql
Employees	Notes	ntext	Employee Note Text	EmployeeIns.sql EmployeeUpd.sql
Employees	ReportsTo	int	Manager Employee Id	EmployeeIns.sql EmployeeUpd.sql JobChangeUpd.sql
Employees	PhotoPath	nvarchar(510)	Employee Photo Access Path Text	EmployeeIns.sql EmployeeUpd.sql BadgeUpd.sql

Remember that you would expect many more values in the stored procedure column in a real-world application.

All of the columns are part of the INSERT and UPDATE procedure but only the EmployeeID is needed in the DELETE procedure. There is a process to update the EmployeeID badge image into Northwind that uses EmployeeID, Photo, and PhotoPath. And finally there is a procedure to change job classification that also uses EmployeeID, Title, and ReportsTo.

This type of mapping allows you to see potential impact on code if the table structure changes. You can see at a glance that EmployeeID changing could potentially cause the most impact whereas Notes would impact less.

Pedigree Mappings

Ever wonder where a bit of data you find on a report came from? There is a story about a CFO who asked four different Vice Presidents separately the same question. 'What was the Gross sales from the Western Region last quarter?' Does it surprise anyone that he got four answers? No, probably not. What is astonishing, however, is that each of them brought him an *IT- produced report*!

You will find yourself in requirements meetings where everyone spends hours trying to nail down *which* Net Sales figure to use from a choice of many different reports. I don't mind that there is a need to build three different summations of Sales totals. But it does bother my orderly soul that we would publish them all with the same labels creating an opportunity for bright analysts to compare the numbers and decide that IT can't add. A simple label change would correct all that, or a note in the footer of the pedigree of the value.

How important is it to know just what is in a derived value after all? Ask the data warehouse team. They deal with all those disparate Gross and Net Sales figures from different systems. The only way to deal with them is to trace the pedigree of the data back to its source and determine why they are different. Part of my career was spent with a highly successful data warehousing team. However, our managers spent a good deal of their time proving the figures in the reports we were providing were correct especially for the first few months after going live. All of our customers had legacy reports with summations, averages, and totals that disagreed with the ones we were providing. We knew where ours came from; the challenge was to figure out where theirs came from and then explain the differences in formula, source, or timing.

Until I became a data modeler, I never realized that data spent so much time wandering in and out of systems. Data management of a data element may seem to be simple but chances are it is not. We often overlook what data goes on to become, and that is: information. Information of course is central to management controlling an organization, so a data modeler has a very important role to play. Data tends to begin life simply, generally in a nice mainframe style OLTP system, and is then summed, truncated, rolled up or down, averaged, factored, apportioned, parsed, and basically chewed up and pressed into a mold by the time it hits reports viewed by upper management. Data moves from mainframe, to client server, to desktop, through Excel, back to mainframe, and finally out through a printer.

Pedigree mappings look something like this:

Pedigree for Total Quarter Manufacturing Hours on the Finance Budget Quarter Report		
System	**Process Step**	**Note**
Payroll database and Manufacturing database	Add together the worked hours for each shift in the work month	
Payroll database and Manufacturing database	Calculate the overtime hours and multiply by 1.5	Finance wants to see hours in terms of pay rate
	Add in the inflated overtime hour quantity	
Rework database	Minus hours used for 'Setup', 'Maintenance', 'Rework'	
MRP database	Add 20% management hours	For overhead adjustment

I'm sure you will have much more interesting examples of your own. I just want to give you a sample of what a pedigree would look like. You might even want to document the procedure or report code block that eventually places it on the report.

Role Name Mappings

This is one of the most useful (after pedigree) mappings that you can spend time and energy doing. Everyone wants to be able to follow database relationships. They want to know how many places the most common keys are migrating to. But sometimes they are not easily recognizable because many of them will change their name to a role name once they get there.

This type of mapping follows the path of a key through its travels. It may migrate to the same table, as in the Supervisor of an Employee being an Employee also. It may migrate to another table as an 'Inspected by' for the Item table. It may even migrate to another system or application through integration. Then you can really lose sight of it.

> **Keep track of where data elements are migrating to and what they are called once they get there. It will save you hours when you need to do an impact analysis for changes to that column.**

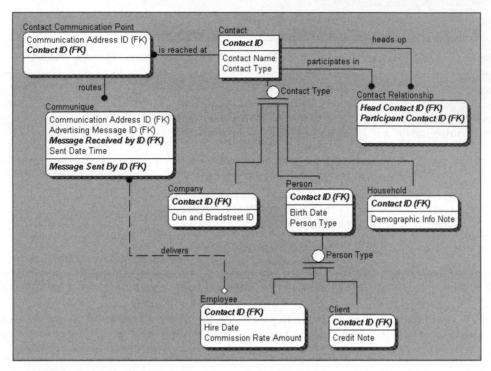

Look at this portion of the Marketing logical model. See the attributes that have been italicized? Those are all `Contact ID`, even the ones that don't look like it anymore. A map of it looks like this:

Migration and Role name Map		
Source Entity = Contact		
Primary Key = Contact ID		
Entity Name	**Attribute Base Name**	**Role Name**
Person	Contact ID	Contact ID
Client	Contact ID	Contact ID
Company	Contact ID	Contact ID
Contact Communication Point	Contact ID	Contact ID
Household	Contact ID	Contact ID
Employee	Contact ID	Contact ID
Contact Relationship	Contact ID	Head Contact ID
Communiqué	Contact ID	Message Received by ID
Communiqué	Contact ID	Message Sent By ID
Contact Relationship	Contact ID	Participant Contact ID

Look at how easy it is now to recognize all the Contact IDs in this system. Sometimes role naming is a very valid part of designing. Sometimes however, the name just seems to change without much thought. At least with this type of map you can see all the places the data element has migrated to and what it is called once it gets there. This is just the logical model. You can do the same thing with the physical design, and have another useful product.

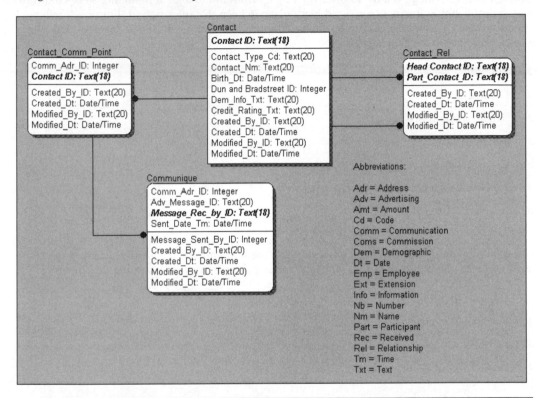

Constraint and Role Name Map		
Base Table = Contact		
Primary Key = Contact_ID		
Table Name	**Column Base Name**	**Foreign Key Column Name**
Contact_Comm_Point	Contact_ID	Contact_ID
Communique	Contact_ID	Message_Rec_By_Id
Contact_Rel	Contact_ID	Head_Contact_ID
Contact_Rel	Contact_ID	Part_Contact_ID

Summary

We looked at some other aspects of data that are useful to know about. These are all the data quality issues that we often leave till last in our analysis. These are suggestions of extra data understanding that you add to the list of things you try to discover way up front in the logical modeling step. Unfortunately none of the modeling software I have used has a place to keep this information. I'm sure it will be included someday. Each entity and table, each attribute and column will have a place to note what you have discovered about its:

- ❏ Fidelity
- ❏ Criticality
- ❏ Sensitivity and Privacy
- ❏ Stewardship
- ❏ Cross-Footing
- ❏ Process Validation
- ❏ Risk and Mitigation

We also looked at how many things are related to the information stored in data models. Keeping the information in mapping documentation is a stop-gap method until we have really inserted meta data management into our Enterprises. We looked at many different facets of mapping that include:

- ❏ Logical Mappings
- ❏ Physical Mappings
- ❏ Pedigree Traces
- ❏ Data Element Roles

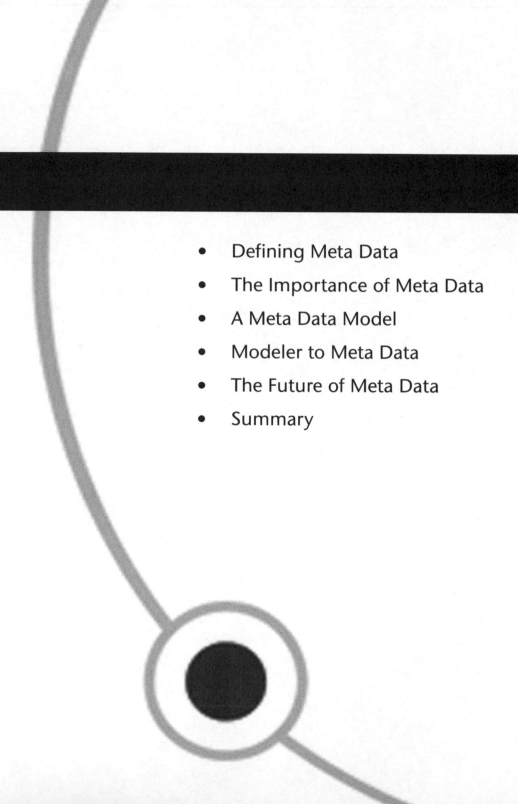

Meta Data Modeling

In this chapter we're going to look at meta data, a topic that has grown over the past few years and gained an independent body of knowledge of its own in Data Management. It is the information that gives us an overview *about* software/business process solutions rather than the data values organized *in* such solutions. Gathering it together into a repository is often instrumental in our ability to manage the full scope of tasks, goals, and strategies taking place in data management teams.

In this chapter we will focus on meta data and how, from a data modeler's perspective, this is just another project, another set of clients, and another set of data. But this time we are part of the client group, contributing our own requirements and business processes to the project.

In particular we will look at:

❑   Definitions of meta data

❑   Uses of meta data

❑   Data models of meta data

❑   Meta data research

Defining Meta Data

Most often you will hear the definition of meta data as 'Data about Data', but it could just as easily be 'Knowledge about Knowledge', or maybe 'Information about Information'.

These definitions have a certain appeal in their simplicity. Think of all the resources in the public library, which exist only to help you find the places that have the answers to questions. Those tools are the starting place for most research. You use the *'Guide to Periodicals'* to find articles about subjects or by authors. You use encyclopedias and bibliographies, the card catalog and computer search tools, dictionaries and anthologies. These are tools that contain collections of pre-built sets of 'Knowledge about Knowledge' organized in a way that helps reduce your time to find an answer.

Meta data exists at many levels in the library. Individual books have indexes and tables of contents that help you find what you are looking for at a more detailed level than the card catalog. Even chapters inside the books often have a bulleted summary of the contents of just that one chapter. These are all meta data elements. They are not always aggregated into a single place like a repository but they all serve the same function, namely to provide pointers to locations of more information, or to sum up an aggregation of some aspect of the details in the form of statistics. You will actually hear people refer to Meta Meta Data data, in other words, information regarding information about data.

> **A Meta Data Repository is the Enterprise Data Card Catalog.**

In David Marco's *'Building and Managing the Meta Data Repository – A Full Lifecycle'*, (ISBN 0-471-35523-2), he gives us a fuller, more comprehensive definition of meta data:

Meta data is all physical data (contained in software and other media) and knowledge (contained in employees and various media) from inside and outside an organization, including information about the physical data, technical and business processes, rules and constraints of the data, and structures of the data used by a corporation.

From this definition you can see that everything we have been talking about analyzing, developing, or modeling in this book is part of the body of meta data for the Enterprise. If you can't research your Enterprise's physical data, business processes, rules and constraints about the data, and organization of data structures, then we are doomed to have to waste time rediscovering and rebuilding things that were known once but are lost.

> **Reinventing anything that exists wastes time, money, and resources. Duplication is sometimes needed for performance, but it needs to be *managed*, not accidental.**

You could look at meta data as by-product information from everything we do. There is information to be gleaned from our plans, designs, actual implementations, and how things behave after we set them in place. But we have such a disparate set of media and environments to gather data from. We have everything from Mainframe use statistics to video traffic citation data stored as:

❑ Desktop Data
❑ Paper data
❑ Visual, Aural, and Animated data
❑ Mainframe data
❑ Server data
❑ Models, mappings, and definitions
❑ Web site data
❑ People and memory

Meta data Management is the means by which we fit this 'data puzzle' together. While we'll always have a need for different solutions to different problems, utilizing the diversity and uniqueness of each data platform and tool, we need to maintain virtual connections to all the Enterprise data sources so that the puzzle stays valid and up-to-date:

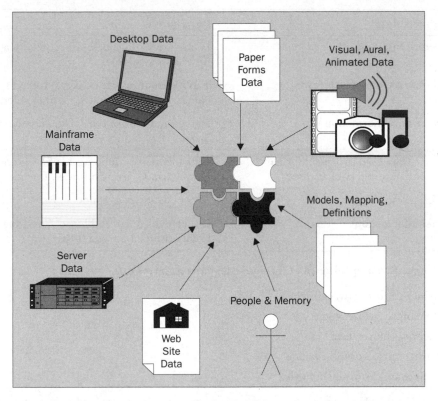

Development of such an **Enterprise Meta Data Repository**, such as the card catalog in the public library, can allow this to happen. If you start every project with a trip to the repository you may find that, other than some integration and possible alterations to existing structures, a great deal of what you have been tasked to provide already exists.

Meta data can be gathered about every process and procedure, and involves more than just facts about tables and columns. It can be information from lessons learned, gained from experiences and trial projects, and is generally divided into two major groupings, technical and business.

Technical Meta Data

Technical meta data refers to information about applications, tools, and systems supporting the Enterprise data management solutions. It includes, for example, information about database structures, front-end objects, networks, hardware, software, and the relationships between them.

This information supports designers, developers, and administrators during development, maintenance, and management of the information technology environment. Meta data documents the connections of tools, applications, and systems that combine to provide answers to information needs.

Here is a list of examples of technical meta data:

Technical meta data	Description
Infra-structure Information	Hardware, Software, Connectivity, Capacity (used and available)
Deployed data storage structures	Table /Column names, Keys, Indexes, Domain values, Archiving strategy, Purge rules
Programs / Code information	Names and descriptions, Dependencies, Schedules
Integration – Data load process information of internal and external data sources	Data elements, Mapping source to target, Frequency, Conversion rules, Encoding rules
Report and query	Access patterns, Frequency, Execution time
Data model information	Conceptual, Logical, Physical, and the Relationships between them

Technical meta data also relate all of the above together in terms of:

- ❑ Relationships between them
- ❑ Versioning information
- ❑ Security information
- ❑ Audit controls and balancing
- ❑ Project and team relationships

You can see that this data encompasses machines, networks, and managing business data. We use this information to be able to generate our own statistics, trends, and overviews of the workings of the IT world. We also use it as a resource to streamline the processing of data requests by being able to easily locate and target solution requirements.

Business Meta Data

Business meta data focuses on making technical meta data understandable and usable by the business community. It provides explanations, mappings, road maps, and translations of the technical solutions and the business needs. This type of meta data is built with the help of the business community. This helps them know how to tap into the rich data resources available to them. These would include:

Business Meta Data	Description
Dictionary of Names, term translations, and definitions	Physical structure to Business terms, Technical terminology, Business terminology
Subject areas information	Definitions, Content, Location
Data Quality information	Rules and statistics, pedigree mappings in terms of relative values of particular data sets, data restriction/domain rules

Business Meta Data	Description
Rules for pre-processed data elements	Description of exact rules for summations, derivations, and formulations. Justification of what data sets are included in aggregations, and those that are excluded
Data element business parameters	Stewardship assignments, criticality assessment, sensitivity assessment
General data processing information	Refresh dates, error handling, archive strategy, purge rules

You are right of course if you sense a bit of overlap. Business meta data generally supports clients who need to understand the business implications of data rather than the details of collecting and storing it. These are often data miners doing *ad hoc* querying from the decision support structures, or they may be power users who need to identify and locate the correct sources to use to answer their questions.

Live Meta Data

There are other things referred to as meta data that are not created just as reference collections of facts about data. These meta data values serve as critical variables inside actual code and tools.

One of the challenges of any meta data repository is dealing with the fact that once the data values are collected they are disconnected from the processes they describe. There is a danger that they fall out of step with reality. It takes serious discipline to maintain meta data outside of actual processes like the meta data found in .NET, XML, ETL (Extraction, Transformation, and Loading) tools, and operating software catalogs. Some meta data repository applications try to solve these issues by maintaining connectivity to, or simply providing visibility of, these sources rather than build a separate collection of meta data information.

We have document management tools that maintain lists and hierarchies of their contents. There is even data model management software like Computer Associate's ModelMart that keeps the models and their contents in a database.

> **Gathering and reporting meta data from live sources guarantees a certain level of validity with reality, whereas keeping separate lists of meta data can get out of sync.**

.NET & XML

In .NET and XML meta data is defined as self-describing data, which is built so that we don't need a guide to go find out what it is about. In other words meta data tells us what it is about. The most common examples of meta data in current vogue are XML code files and .NET assemblies. For example, a .NET assembly contains its own meta data and can provide information about itself to an operating system, so that the Windows operating system no longer has to look up in the Windows Registry (or catalog) to find out about the assembly. This is not the case with COM objects, which have no meta data, and so are not self-describing. Their description is held or registered separately in the Windows Registry: HKEY_LOCAL_MACHINE.

445

These structures are often used in EDI (Electronic Data Interchange) tasks where the source and target need cooperative data standardization for two parties to be able to interact with each other. The definition or understanding of what the data elements *represent* (the meta data) is as important as the values themselves.

ETL & EAI Tool Catalogs

ETL software creates maps and processes that move data from source/s to target/s. Each mapping includes any rules for error handling and conversion that is needed to move and consolidate records. These tools are frequently used to supply ODS (Operational Data Stores), DSS (Decision Support Systems), and DW (Data Warehouses) with their data. They are being coupled with EAI (Enterprise Application Interchange).

These files, or **mappings** as they are called, are considered meta data sources and are often tapped into directly to provide business views of data pedigrees and technical views of integration structures.

DBMS Library Catalog Tables

I am referring here to database management systems in the most generic sense. Any type of data storage system, such as Relational, Hierarchical, and Network, that includes its own content management capability. Most of us are very familiar with gathering information about tables and columns from these structures. Depending on the catalogs other information may also be available. Some carry statistics of use, definitions of the tables and columns, create information, or even meta data about itself referring to version, build, and license date information.

The Importance of Meta Data

Why do we have indexes, bibliographies, outlines, tables of contents, and concordances? We have them because it is too difficult to *remember* all the things we might ever want to know about a subject. In fact it is impossible to tell what subjects are going to be the *most* important ones to even narrow down the scope of the information. We have the challenge of determining the scope of what meta data elements we are going to manage for use by a wide customer base, because different things are important to different customers.

Here are some of the focuses we use to determine what to gather, organize, and provide for the Enterprise:

Data use Customers (Data Miners, Decision Support Analysts, Ad Hoc report writers) see importance in:	Meta Data may provide:
Empowerment to help themselves as much as possible	An Enterprise card catalog for researching
Targeted, quality information	Location of targeted data elements
	Definitions of subtle differences if the same data element occurs multiple times
	Who to go to if the data values don't seem to be what the customer expects

Data use Customers (Data Miners, Decision Support Analysts, Ad Hoc report writers) see importance in:	Meta Data may provide:
Speed –To their goal faster	Complete location information
	Who to go to for access support
Backup details – Explanation of what was used to create the data that their decisions are based	Descriptions of pedigree, stewards, and processes creating data
	Detail descriptions of formula
	Schedule information of when data was created

Data creation Customers (Input Operators, Application Administrators) see importance in:	Meta Data may provide:
Inventory of data elements they are responsible for	A list of data elements stewardship assignments to be reviewed periodically for accuracy
Domain descriptions and business rules regarding their processes.	Visibility to definitions
	Visibility to constraints
	Visibility of data element to data element business rules
Archive schedules	Schedule information and who to see if retrieval is necessary
Knowing interface/integration details to help troubleshoot data values	Description of ETL, EAI, data movement processes and who manages them
	Mapping of source and targets

Data Environment management (DBAs, Programmers, Data Modeler) Customers see importance in:	Meta Data may provide:
Research into addition / modification / deletion of structures	Visibility to missing, duplicated, or unnecessary data elements both by name and definition
Analysis documentation providing design specifications	The conceptual, logical, and physical model element mappings
Inventory of data objects/elements in systems, applications, etc. that they support	A list of tables, procedures, and so on, mapped to applications and environments

447

Data Environment management (DBAs, Programmers, Data Modeler) Customers see importance in:	Meta Data may provide:
Domain descriptions and business rules regarding their processes.	Visibility to definitions
	Visibility to constraints
	Visibility of data element to data element business rules
Archive schedules	Schedule information and who to see if retrieval is necessary
Knowing interface/integration details to help troubleshoot process problems	Description of ETL, EAI, data movement processes and who manages them
	Mapping of source and targets
	Schedule of interfaces and the error handling
Upcoming changes	Visibility to both 'As-Is' and 'To-Be'

Enterprise Organization (Senior management) sees importance in:	Meta Data may provide:
Corporate knowledge	Better knowledge survival in the event of loss, relocation, or promotion of staff
Empowerment to help themselves as much as possible	An Enterprise card catalog for researching especially things like location of reports
Profitability	Visibility to missing, duplicated, or unnecessary data elements both by name and definition

We have a vast amount of information at our fingertips. We need to figure out how to organize it and use it to our advantage to save time, resources, and money.

A Meta Data Model

So considering the scope and charter of meta data, how do you get your arms around it? It obviously isn't new. As corporate organizers, researchers, and managers of data we in the information technology field have worked hard to build and keep list after list in documents, charts, spreadsheets, and databases to help us get our jobs done. Even I keep a huge spreadsheet of every table, column, size, definition, and location that I have worked with. It gives me a starting point for familiar structures, a beginning place to look for integration points, and a sanity check for standard names and sizes.

However, these types of documents haven't been very user-friendly to our business customers who want to know some of the same things. They want more *ad hoc* access to their data, and now have more user-friendly data access/manipulation tools that use simple point, drag, and click functionality (like Brio and MicroStrategy for example). They made the data, they want to use it, and they have come to believe that just querying it won't hurt anything (not true but it's hard sometimes to explain to them).

This is where the Meta Data Repository comes into play, as a comprehensive Enterprise library of what we know about our data environments. Building such a repository is similar to building any other business process. You start with a clear understanding of what you want to accomplish, how you will know if you were successful at it, and where you intend to draw the boundaries. You document the processes, analyze the needs, and provide solutions. From that you build the scope and requirements for your Meta Data Repository. With these the data modeler can begin to document the data elements and business rules between them. Like I said in the introductory paragraphs, to the modeler this is just another subject area needing to be analyzed.

Conceptual Meta Data Model

We have talked about how the conceptual model can be a tool to help the wonderful problem-solving, brain-storming, creative-questioning activity that happens at the onset of any project. A Meta Data Repository project should start this way also. The absolute first question that needs to be answered is who will use the Repository? Every department or team mentioned needs to have a representative on the project from that moment on.

The biggest problem with modeling meta data is that the business process of gathering and storing meta data is fairly complicated. It is a mix of locking into sophisticated stores of meta data (like the catalog in SQL Server or tables managing Informatica scripts), finding and referencing manual data stores (like spreadsheets, files, and documents), and gathering currently non-existing data elements and relationships.

The who, when, why, and wherefore of gathering and managing meta data are still nebulous. What it means to your organization should be discussed and agreed upon. However, some of the areas you might want to look at are the things we talked about in the *'Data Maps'* section of the last chapter.

- ❏ Machines (Development, Test, Production, Backup)
- ❏ Code (screens, reports, procedures)
- ❏ Documents (project, standards, change control)
- ❏ Small Machines (individual desktop PCs, routers, printers)
- ❏ Locations (geographic, virtual)
- ❏ Models (sources of shadow entities/tables, versions, submodels)
- ❏ Organizations (sponsor, interested party, security)
- ❏ Pathways (network, DTS, load/sync routines)
- ❏ People (authorship, stewardship, support)
- ❏ Processes (feeding, originating, referencing, supporting)

Starting at that high level helps everyone define the direction, so what you are attempting to accomplish is important to determine up front. Begin meta data conceptual modeling with questions like:

- ❏   What data is involved?
- ❏   What will some of the reports be?

Is the goal to:

- ❏   Follow the development cycle of data for the Enterprise
- ❏   Find Integration opportunities
- ❏   Lift the Data Quality in existing systems
- ❏   Manage redundancy
- ❏   Catalog the Systems, Applications, Tables, Columns, Triggers, Procedures, Indexes, and so on
- ❏   Create feedback to the data sources to be acted on
- ❏   Provide an entry point for non-IT clients to find data support objects – reports, data elements, formulas?

You might start with a conceptual model that looks something like this:

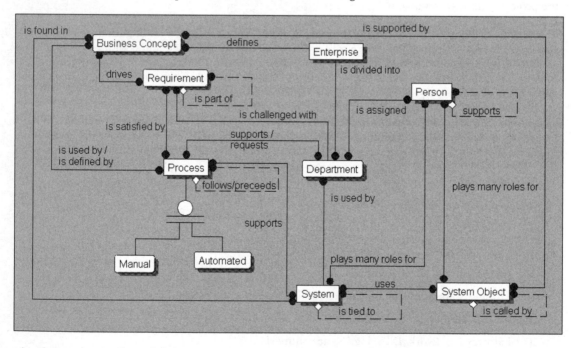

As always you need good definitions to make head or tail of a conceptual model. Here are the definitions of the entities in the conceptual model:

Entity Name	Definition
Business Concept	A thought, idea, or definition used by our Enterprise. This may be our definition of Gross, Net, Profitability, or Security for example.
Department	A business unit that is a permanent or temporary grouping of people in the Enterprise. Generally requires a budgeting aspect.
Enterprise	The aggregation of business units required in order to satisfy our customers. This may include vendors linked to us by process as in our Supply Chain Management star vendors, for example.
Hardware	A piece of machinery used to support Enterprise data management.
Location	The address, geographic or virtual, where something can be found.
Person	An individual connected in some way to our Enterprise. These may be employees, contacts, contractors, temporary help, and customers.
Process	An act or series of acts proceeding from one to the next accomplishing a goal. These are either Manual or Automated.
Requirement	A goal, or necessary action to accomplish a goal.
System	An orderly, interconnected, complex arrangement of parts, principles, and procedures. A system may be as simple as the filing cabinets in our legal department, or as complex as the new MRP bar code task management system.
System Object	An element used by a system. These are filing cabinets, cash registers, procedures, tables, databases, routers, networks, and so on.

If this seems terribly high-level, remember the conceptual model is just a starting place. The more we work with the definitions, the better detail we end up with. Remember also that this model is not a generic one, simply one that I have drawn up here based on the mapping concepts that I have found to be important to data modelers over time. You would need to go through the process with your team and listen to their needs, in order to build your own model.

Even if your team stops here with the modeling effort, you will have a great deal more information to work with when comparing various vendor meta data tool packages, such as Computer Associates PLATINUM Repository, IBM Information Catalog, and Cognos Informatica MX2.

Logical Meta Data Model

We can use our conceptual model from the previous section to work towards a logical model, in the same way in which we converted our Solitaire conceptual model into a logical one. We begin to drive the meta data repository requirements towards a greater level of detail. The team will carve out a piece of the conceptual model and call it the scope of a meta data project. We go through all the steps to create a logical model based on all the requirements and data integrity rules that can be determined from the customers.

From the modeler's perspective this is just another analysis of data sets important to the enterprise. It will probably be run like any other project. I am going to warn you also that this model can get to be huge; several hundred entities if you take it all the way to the logical-fully attributed level of analysis. Your logical model can stop at Enterprise analysis detail, with some attribute definition, if you are working with a vendor's product, but will have to be more detailed if you are developing an entirely custom-built solution.

One of the complaints that I hear about relational modeling, is how complicated it can get to be. Remember the logical model is just organizing the sets of data. It doesn't mean that we are planning to physically store them that way. The only data element model that I have found you can really verify with customers is the logical-fully attributed one. I know that it can get to be really busy and complex, but that is why you never really use the big one for anything other than wallpaper in your office. Model deliverables need to be scoped to include only what is necessary for the person or task at hand.

As an example of a logical meta data model, consider the following model that I drew up for some DBAs. It only covers one tiny corner of meta data, in this case information regarding the places, operating systems, and upgrade installations for a set of SQL Server instances on a number of different Servers.

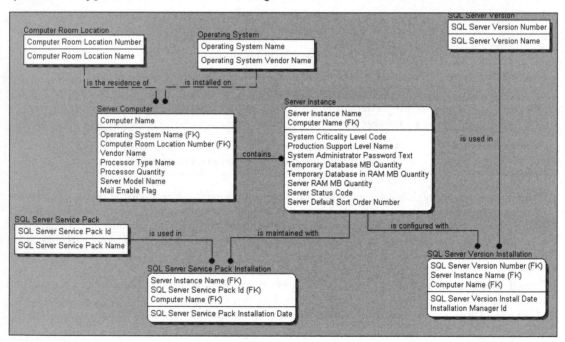

One of the other areas where meta data models prove useful is in developing, and maintaining, Decision Support Services (DSS). In David Marco's book that we mentioned earlier, he states that people frequently need meta data sources in these cases for:

❑ Query access patterns, frequency, and execution time

❑ Report names and definitions

❑ Audit controls and balancing information

❑ The system of record feeding the DSS (interfaces)

- ❑ Mappings, transformations, encoding or conversions to the DSS
- ❑ Data Model information – logical and physical
- ❑ Database information – tables, columns, keys, indexes
- ❑ Relationships of the Data Model to the implemented system
- ❑ Extract criteria and history
- ❑ Archive criteria and history
- ❑ Job dependencies
- ❑ Program code names and descriptions
- ❑ Version history
- ❑ Security needs, grants, and roles
- ❑ Subject area contents
- ❑ Business names and definitions
- ❑ Rules for Drill-Up, Drill-Down, and Drill-Across

Many of these concepts deal with the heavily pre-aggregated data in data warehouse and decision support systems (DSS). This is generally the world of dimensional models. Drill-Down is the act of exposing progressively more detail by making selections of items in a report or query. In other words taking a Quarterly report, for instance, and uncovering all the Period details that went into making up those numbers. Drill-Up is exactly the opposite. It is the act of combining by time or location or some other aggregation dimension. Drill-Across is the act of combining different subject area data by using a conforming dimension. For example, taking Sales data by day and adding Receipt data by day to be able to report on storage volume flows as merchandise moves in and out of a store.

But meta data can be about any business process in the enterprise. DSS is only one of them. The actual requirements of your enterprise would need to be explored and subjected to the rigor of a project team.

Physical Meta Data Model

What happens if your project team decides that they need to build an Enterprise Meta Data Repository rather than buy one? You will need every scrap of your determination, creativity, perseverance, and sense of humor to design a physical model that will not only satisfy the need for data integrity but will address issues of usability, complexity, expandability, and maintainability. Having said that, the process steps that you need to take here are the same as those that we looked at in taking our logical model and turning it into a physical model in Chapter 8. It is important to also bear in mind that the world of meta data is a large area, and there is a lot of work going on out there that you may be able to tie into.

Modeler To Meta Data

Up until this chapter on meta data, we have been talking about data modeling in terms of supporting business client needs. Once we move into the subject of 'data about data' we discover that we are our own best clients. This is data about what the modeler does, and we are both the steward and the customer of these data elements.

Data Modeler – Contributor to Meta Data

We have talked in general about software that can assist in your modeling efforts throughout this book, such as Computer Associates Erwin 3.5.2, which I've used to generate all the model graphics. You can create electronic documentation that behaves as mini-databases of information elements related together to make a comprehensive story. The elements either own information, or share information, through relationships. Entities relate to attributes in a one-to-many relationship. Data types relate to columns in a one-to-many relationship. Attributes own their definition. Models own their notes. All that information is meta data. Some modeling tools work with model management applications that are databases unto themselves and store meta data about models (like Computer Associated ModelMart).

A good portion then of your analysis and design products contributes to Enterprise meta data. What would a conceptual model of our meta data look like? Maybe something like this? I wanted to bring out the names of things we have been talking about all along, so I broke out Data Model Elements into a level where you can recognize their names. This (plus a whole lot of other things) is the meta data we contribute to the Enterprise:

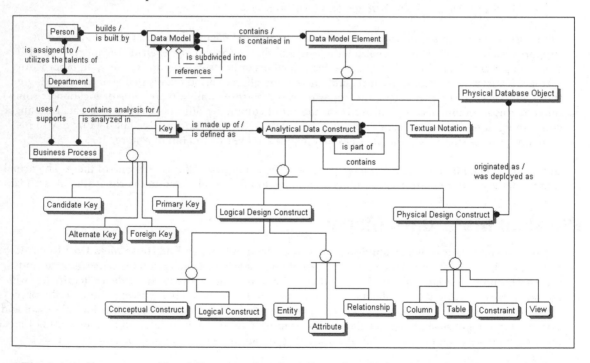

This is just the conceptual level. Imagine what the fully analyzed logical model would look like if it were fully attributed!

Data Modeler – Customer of Meta Data

We could take the model above and use it to help build a Data Model Meta Data Repository. Once it was built, the data modelers would become one of its best customers. A new step in the interviewing and analysis during the modeling activity would become researching through what already exists.

You could use any information relating to the business processes that you are trying to support. Past project documentation would be available, searchable, and gain new importance as a bank of knowledge. We don't want to loop back to old solutions that didn't work, and equally, we need to get a feel for the strengths and weaknesses of a process during our present analysis. We can reuse portions of other models to drive Enterprise standard structures and definitions. Reuse of those structures reduces the time to market for any project, even if they are only used as a beginning place to be verified and/or modified as the need arises, based on custom requirements. We could even load models from people we have networked with, or the 'Common' structures templates that can be purchased. We can look at table designs to help steer our own by looking at both the similar and the unique to inspire new solutions.

This data collection could become an oracle of information about the state of the data foundation of the enterprise. It can provide the ability to just see what is and has happened, not at the data value level but at the data management level.

The Future of Meta Data

The future of meta data management is firmly tied to the future of data management in general. Here it is 2002 and what do we see from our IT viewpoint? We still have disconnected islands of data, separated by storage type, application boundaries, data style, and disjointed data management vision.

Our tools need to find a way to communicate with a central repository. There are organizations that are striving to bring some commonality and standards to our chaos. The recently merged Meta Data Coalition (MDC) and the Object Management Group (OMG) are attempting to define an industry-standard version of the meta models. OMG is a vendor independent consortium who has made it their goal to try to build the finished puzzle in the middle and to lend a hand in standardizing new custom development. Anyone more interested in common meta data models will find a growing set of open information models, now referred to as Model-Driven Architecture and the Common Warehouse Meta model. These are platform-independent models that are trying to document the commonality of data elements and give us standard names to work with between industries and teams. This should serve to help us leverage work already accomplished and make us more productive. More information on this subject can be found on the web at www.corba.org.

Summary

In this chapter we have considered the nature of meta data, the 'knowledge about knowledge', or 'data about data', which is becoming ever more crucial in Enterprises. If we take the example of an order entry system, we have seen that meta data is not the orders in the order entry system, but rather information regarding:

- ❑ statistics about the orders
- ❑ information regarding their make-up
- ❑ how they are organized and stored
- ❑ who can access them
- ❑ to do what
- ❑ where does the data flow to
- ❑ how does it get there
- ❑ what were the origins of the structure of an order
- ❑ who created it
- ❑ for what project
- ❑ to solve what problem
- ❑ and on and on ...

The importance of meta data lies in our challenges today with staff, clients, and resources. We need to be striving to serve everyone better and in a more cost-efficient way. We need to provide higher quality tools, faster and more acceptable to the customers. To do that we need to be able to refresh our memories with the successes, failures, existing solutions, and abandoned efforts so as to be able to make intelligent decisions about data management choices. We need to recognize the ability to manage the shared environment of our data as being important to the enterprise.

- Worst Practices
- Team Blocking Tactics
- Stalling a Schedule
- Model Mismanagement
- Best Practices
- Keeping to Schedule
- Understanding Data and Design
- Project Lessons
- Summary

Data Modeling Working Practices

In this last chapter, I am going to share some of the lessons I have learned from my twelve years of data modeling. In that time I have mainly been a relational database modeler, and had the opportunity to work as employee and consultant, government and industry, entertainment and trucking, international and domestic, and for large and small companies. That gives me at least a potpourri of experiences in data modeling challenges. I will break the chapter into two parts:

- ❏ The first half will consider the nature of a data modeler's work practices, both in terms of good and bad habits. While it isn't possible to give you an absolute formula for success, what I can do is highlight a best practices checklist to adhere to in your modeling work. Equally, the list of bad practices should act as a warning signal should you find some of them familiar during the course of your work.

- ❏ In the second half of the chapter, I will share some of my thoughts regarding the planning and development of your own modeling projects, in terms of the lessons that I have learned over the years. We will consider:
    - ❏ Custom Solutions
    - ❏ Purchased Solutions
    - ❏ Legacy and Forensic work

We'll begin by considering worst practices, and move on to look at best practices.

Worst Practices

I came across this information from a quick survey of several teams. Managers, project leads, and programmers shared with me their observations of things that a data modeler can do to become a handicap rather than an asset. Some have caused so many negative results, that having any modeler assigned to a project becomes an unwelcome addition. The following practices will result in poor team cooperation, broken schedules, and model mismanagement.

Team Blocking Tactics

A data modeler always works with other people; it's one role that can't work completely independently. The clients, development and maintenance programmers, database administrators, managers, and data management staff are all vital relationships that a modeler needs to cultivate.

Maybe I am wrong, but my experience is that data modeling is more dependent upon the person modeling than some other skills. If a programmer can't deliver a good program, they are replaced with someone who can. If a modeler can't deliver good analysis and design, then the modeling step is removed along with the modeler. All of these ways of behaving will ultimately silence the voices around you. Keep these techniques up for a while and no one will ever visit your office or invite you to participate in a project again.

Arrogance

I would say that the number one thing a team member can do to break up a partnership is just plain not listen or respect anyone. Arrogance in this case leads to the assumption that you don't need to:

- hear the needs of a client because you modeled something like it before
- listen to the project manager because you have been on a development project before
- spend time with the DBA because you have designed for this platform before
- work with the programmers because you don't care how they implement anyway
- go to conferences, read articles, or network because you know it all
- learn anything new because the old way works just fine

Uncompromising

Another thing that can cause teamwork problems is by being *uncompromising*. An individual who won't back down, even in the face of legitimate needs by the team, will protect the design at all costs. Their general stance is one of:

- My way or the highway
- I'm the data modeler and always know best
- There is only one right answer, namely mine
- Normal forms must be protected at all costs
- Standards are the law
- All-or-nothing implementations
- All short-cuts are bad

Such a stance can involve being a perfectionist when delivery is the crucial deliverable, objectionable in blocking every suggestion or compromise, and generally be inflexible and rigid in your approach. It can also mean knowing that there is a problem but ignoring the expected outcome.

Obstructive

I heard over and over from people that the modeler didn't want to let anyone see their formative work, like a touchy portrait artist. They are *obstructive* with the analysis and leave the team in the dark until they are ready to publish a completed work. An obstructive modeler hides the model because it:

❑ Isn't fully detailed

❑ Doesn't have all the definitions

❑ Hasn't been reviewed

❑ Doesn't contain all the subject areas

❑ Has crossing relationship lines

❑ Isn't pretty yet

❑ They are unresponsive to questions regarding the model, and avoid confronting any difficult issues they may have uncovered in their analysis. They might even wait until the last minute to provide the answer which you have known about for weeks.

There are a lot of reasons for not sharing. Lack of trust is the most common. If you don't trust your team then how are they going to trust you?

Defensive

This has to be one of the hardest to avoid. We wouldn't commit a solution to paper if we didn't think it was a good one. The pride of ownership gets in our way of being a team player. It can be extremely difficult not to take suggestions and responses about our analysis as criticism. Don't get *defensive*. It isn't personal; it's business. However, we can naturally:

❑ Be hostile about non-modelers' observations

❑ Interpret all suggestions as criticism

❑ Protect the design because it is yours

❑ Treat all suggestions as a threat to the design

❑ Make the team uncomfortable questioning your design

❑ This can lead us to push everyone around with threats and dire predictions, subtly take out other options by making jokes of them, or be condescending and patronizing

Avoidance

Modelers are usually part of the 'core' team of projects but they don't always make 'just being there' a priority. Delaying scheduling, being perpetually late to and early from, or a classic 'no-show' after agreeing to come to meetings are *avoidance* techniques. This can stall the analysis for so long that you may even force a reduction in scope. In doing so you'll say things like:

- ❑ Mañana – Tomorrow
- ❑ … I promise
- ❑ I'm getting to it as fast as I can
- ❑ Just as soon as 'X' does 'Y'
- ❑ I'm still thinking about it
- ❑ You got it! (aloud) Not in your lifetime, buddy! (in your head)

Being slow, or over-committing yourself so that you can't find any time to satisfy anyone, will both impact on the project schedule and the team. Equally, you can slow progress by refusing to meet until the model is 'just right', avoiding asking for help until it is too late, taking more pride in nursing an issue than in fixing it, or the requirements are done, the review has happened, it is signed, and so on.

Bluff To Your Team

You know bluffing has its place in Poker, but it's a form of *deceit* since it means you are not telling the whole truth. It's a little like paying on credit; you get the cash now but you had better make good on it really soon or the penalties could be more than you want to pay.

Bluffing about the completeness of your tasks or your ability to meet deadlines can make the schedule look better (for a little while), and involves communicating to your team with:

- ❑ Little white lies
- ❑ Half the story
- ❑ Impractical recommendations
- ❑ Techno-babble jargon
- ❑ Silence when you should speak up
- ❑ Irrational suggestions when you should be quiet

This leaves you being perceived as a hypocrite (due to misrepresentation of facts), two-faced (in sending ambiguous messages on purpose) or a troublemaker (by causing trouble when your real opinions are acted on by outside forces). It's possible you'll be perceived as all of these.

Thoughtless

This is a matter of *disrespect.* You can show your disrespect by:

- ❑ Interrupting constantly
- ❑ Being patronizing
- ❑ Making assumptions
- ❑ Making personal comments
- ❑ Generalizing with 'always', 'never', 'all', 'none' statements
- ❑ Being unwilling to share in the 'grunt' work

Criticize

You are in a unique position of being pretty much in contact with every group, skill, position, and client involved with the team. This means that you have the power to *criticize* everyone if you wish.

This is a great technique to use if you need to shift the spotlight off you to someone else's issues. This involves constant:

- ❑ Blaming instead of solving
- ❑ Keeping score like it was a contest
- ❑ Sarcasm at every opportunity
- ❑ Being overly sensitive and using it as an excuse to launch an attack

Incomprehensible

This one came up a lot in my survey. Unfortunately for us we have a pretty large body of 'reserved' words. Some of them sound so familiar to people that they get confused when we seem to be using them to mean something completely different in conversation. Others are as alien as a whole different language. This technique renders the model and the analysis *incomprehensible* whether you mean to or not. What use is it then? It fails at its most basic need.

Talking fast and using data modeling terms without explaining them can reduce any audience to complete silence. Spraying words such as entity, attribute, relationship, primary key, category, and foreign key without regard for your audience will leave everyone nonplussed and frustrated.

Passivity

Refusing to take the initiative and portraying an attitude of *passivity* can be intentional in a 'Passive Aggressive' rebellion, or it can just be a lack of drive or confidence in what to do next. You can frustrate everyone around you if you have to have clear directions for everything that you do. In this respect you can:

- ❑ Follow the project plan like stereo instructions
- ❑ Speak only when spoken to
- ❑ Never offer to help, to learn, to participate
- ❑ Never introduce new concepts, clients, techniques
- ❑ Never follow your nose

Stalling a Schedule

Having a team member who contributes to stalling the schedule is one of the worst nightmares for a project manager. The data model has exactly the same function on a project as the foundation of a building. *Everything* is based on the rules, names, and definitions captured in the model.

DBAs can't decide on a platform, estimate size, or brainstorm support until at least the logical model is done. Programmers can draft up screens but need the physical design completed before they can do much in the way of data manipulation. Even the Network team need to know the size, shape, and frequency of the data movements in order to know if they have enough bandwidth. This places the data modeler right in the critical path for a project. Ignoring that for very long can have devastating results.

Fall into Analysis Paralysis

Ever try to paint a sunrise? It changes so quickly that it is almost impossible to paint. You can capture it with a camera but we don't have Enterprise data cameras yet. So you are left with returning each morning at dark and attempting to catch a little more day by day.

You are thinking that Enterprise processes are more long-lived than sunrises and should be easier. I used to think so too, but I have seen process changes increase in frequency so much that almost every new project is hard pressed to deliver anything before it becomes partially obsolete. We try to build in expandability but even that is based on our impressions about future needs. We also succumb to delivering 'throw-away' applications, reports, and data collections in order to keep up with the flood of needs around us.

So the impression that our customers have of us is that we get stuck analyzing. From their perspective, we get 80% complete, realize that we missed something, go back and analyze it, find out that it impacts what we thought we had captured, alter it, and start all over again. They get the most frustrated when it's the logical modeling. I can't tell you how many times I have heard the question 'When can we start coding?' But if you don't know yet how the data fits together logically, you are really guessing what the best design is for the physical tables.

Endless Analysis

Endless analysis will leave your team stuck in the mud going nowhere. It can be a result of scope creep, an over-abundance of options, or an uncompromising viewpoint that the team has to provide an 'all or nothing' solution.

Don't Communicate

One thing about data models is that they look great on paper. There is no way from glancing at them to know how good they are. Your team takes for granted that you have it right just because they have a wonderful graphic in their hand. They make assumptions about what they need to do from conversations with clients, so if you don't take them back to the actual data elements and relationships from time to time, they may be misleading themselves as to the complexity coming.

A great way to blow a schedule is by not communicating constantly with the people who need to know. You need to revisit not only the clients who gave you the data rules but also the programmers as their code matures. All of a sudden someone is going to realize they didn't make room for something, didn't realize that an option had to be multiple (rather than single), didn't modularize their tasks enough to prevent a huge ripple from occurring when a change needs to be made.

One Task At a Time

This may be pretty simple, but I have known people who just can't multi-task. Unfortunately the tasks in modeling are pretty parallel by nature. But there are ways to take shortcuts in the event of a schedule issue. It is easy to slow up a project simply by forcing clients to tell you one more time what an address, e-mail, or name looks like, rather than using your own experience to develop the names yourself. It is true that clients have to be stewards of the data elements they ask us to provide storage and manipulation tools for. They need to take responsibility for the definition, size, and rules surrounding their data elements. However, they are busy generally doing their 'real' jobs and have trouble fitting tasks like creating definitions for 300 data elements into their schedules. You can easily stall a team because you can't quite get the clients to commit to something, and aren't willing to make some best guesses for them.

Never Admit You Are Wrong

We all get things wrong from time to time. The absolute worst thing for a schedule is having someone know something is wrong and being afraid to admit it. Generally the farther you get then the worst it is going to be to correct. Models are not good places to leave an error. Someone will trip over it eventually. Refusing to ask for help will inevitably lead to problems in the long run. What, for example, will happen if you assume that modeling for a financial application can't be any different to a manufacturing application, despite the fact that you've never modeled one before?

Equally, you won't be truly effective in your workplace if you never consider the possibility of using new tools, or going on training classes. Not spending any time with the clients, DBA, and/or developer(s) means that you won't grasp the finer details of the system you are trying to model.

Model Mismanagement

What else impacts a project? 80% of our models are simply used to document and communicate information about Enterprise data. They are information repositories and storyboards living in our department, but published to a group of customers who count on them. These are the things that my survey tells me are the most annoying to our customers (in no particular order):

- ❑ **Reorganize** – it can be very disorienting to our customers if we move their boxes with every model revision. You would think we do it on purpose so that they can't find anything. Inconsistent placement of entities or tables on your diagrams, in combination with poor documentation of these data elements, will lead to client confusion and frustration

- ❑ **Make it Legible** – shrinking models down drastically in order to fit them on a page, using tiny font sizes, will make the model illegible to the client

- ❑ **Information Provision** – if the model, which is complicated already, is too filled with extras, the customer may be frustrated trying to read it. W.T.M.I. (way too much information) can make the model into busy wallpaper

    If too much information is bad then so is too little. I have changed jobs enough to know how frustrating it is to come into a department and not be able to discover anything about a model I found. Model customers have this problem too, mostly with versions of the same model. It can be incredibly frustrating to have six versions of the model in your In-Basket and not be able to tell which one is the current release

- ❏ **Data Element Library** – providing a collection of information about any aspect of the models, applications, or data elements for the client is a good ideas. However, it will quickly become a useless resource if it isn't kept up-to-date

- ❏ **Denormalization For the Sake of It** – denormalization without appropriate thought to the rules of normalization will lead to data integrity problems. Working with the attitude of 'never denormalize' or 'always denormalize' will lead to problems

- ❏ **Be Inflexible** – this is a suggestion that the letter of the law is not always the best choice. A company standard just means that it is normal, and has been agreed upon by some group of people. So use standards under normal circumstances. You will always trip over unusual circumstances where you'll need to be flexible with these standards in order to provide a tailor-made solution. Sticking rigidly to your tried and trusted procedures will result in a poor model. However, bear in mind that you will also damage the model if you don't apply any naming standards whatsoever. Five different tables containing the quantity 'Product' will lead to data integrity problems sooner or later

- ❏ **Don't Back Up Your Work** – this is something that nobody forgets to do, right? Well, let's just say that it's something that is easy to forget. Your client isn't going to be very happy if you turn up for a review meeting without a model to present, because there was a power cut and you lost all your work

Best Practices

Having considered the worst practices that you can bring to the modeling world, here is a list of the best practices. They directly parallel the list of worst practices, guiding you as to how to avoid the pitfalls we have already outlined.

Listen To Colleagues

Listen everywhere; in the lunchroom, over walls, in one-on-ones, in chartering sessions, in brainstorming sessions, on the internet, in articles, on bulletin boards. Keep finding ways to tailor your skills to meet the changing data world around you, since you never know where a good idea is going to come from, so keep your ears open.

Compromise

Obviously there are some issues that it is difficult to compromise on. Security, quality, integrity, project critical objectives, and even standards are tough to make flexible if there are opposing sides. As an example, you may well have been given a list of users and the permissions they have in accessing the data. However, the DBA may have reasons as to why such a security 'policy' will be unworkable. You need to talk over the problem and find a solution. Sometimes you are right to dig your heels in, but sometimes you have to be a little flexible. Find a way forward. That doesn't mean you have to give up on what is important to your department or you personally, but there are almost always ways to make both sides happy.

Accessible

Note your reservations, difficulties, and stages of development on the model. Create a disclaimer, status the stages of evolution, and then publish them. Even formative models are the property of the team. Letting the team see the model helps everyone get a feel for how big, complicated, and far along the model is. It also allows everyone to see how the model has evolved, and what decisions have been made along the way. This can reduce tension and provide a visual status of the analysis.

Receptive

Let go of ownership. You may have done the analysis but it is always an Enterprise-owned solution. Make sure someone in the Enterprise was brought along the way to support the design afterwards. Sometimes you have to take a step back to let go. I find that providing more than one solution upfront helps reduce the 'my model' emotions.

Punctual

Modelers should probably be optional invitees to almost every meeting in a development project. They should find a way to attend at least 75% of them. The small unnoticed comments, frowns, politics, and hesitations are critical indicators of the completeness of the analysis and the soundness of the model. Make it a point to hang out with the team as much as possible. Even being able to document areas or aspects where you can tell there is a problem, can be very valuable when making a decision later on.

Transparent

Be upfront and as truthful to your team as possible. There are times when you need to choose the correct moment to break bad news. But keeping everyone updated on how things are going is the best way to prevent nasty surprises. The earlier the team knows about potential stumbling blocks and pitfalls, the more time they have to find a practical solution to overcome them.

Respectful

A great team-mate is blind to everything other than the talent of the person next to them. We need to simply respect everyone on the team for lending us their unique perspective and talents. We need to help create a comfortable and safe environment for everyone. Utilize all the talent available to the team; if a colleague can perform a task faster and more efficiently than you then let them do it.

Reserve judgment and do your research before you criticize any team members. Always offer a compromise, alternative, or suggestion to fix what you think is a problem. Blaming individuals won't fix whatever problem you perceive there to be.

Communicate Effectively

You have to be able to communicate with your team or they will eventually assume that they can't tune into your frequency and back off. Clients are worse. They will dread having to talk to you at all and avoid you at all costs if you aren't able to connect with them, even at the cost of a less successful project. Put together a five minute 'What I mean when I say ...' presentation and begin your model sessions with it. Even those who heard it before will probably appreciate the refresher.

467

Self-motivated

You need to be self-managed in many ways. No one, not even I, can tell you what directions to work first. The thing I like best about modeling is that each analysis is an adventure. Imagine what the early explorers would have done if they had to wait until someone told them what to do next. You need to be willing to act like a sponge, soaking up ideas and thoughts from within the organization, or department, that you are working in. Be dynamic and get out front. Hang out with the clients and allow your curiosity to help you absorb information to aid you in your modeling.

Keeping To Schedule

Analysis paralysis is something to avoid whenever possible. Having said that there are times when you have to accept that your schedule will be delayed. Most of my modeling career has been spent helping data customers tell me requirements. The frustrating thing is that they want to concentrate on their suggested solutions instead. We have to gently turn them around again and again to focus on the problem at hand, cataloging and documenting them to the fullest and then look at ways to fix them.

Change requests, application suggestions, and purchase proposals are almost always solutions. They are usually what goes through review committees and gets approved before the technical team is ever approached. Then the team is obliged to try to work with that solution.

Most necessary temporary paralysis happens when you figure out that you have been given a solution, rather than requirements, and the solution isn't going to work for any number of reasons. You have to circle back and find out what the solution is trying to solve. Then you have to take those obstacles one by one to the clients and find a solution that will work.

Other delays happen when you find that the requirement to upgrade, change, modify, integrate, or enhance existing systems has a huge impact on satellite systems. Take, for example, a company that is going international, but still wants to use the existing HR system. The requirement is to change the Social Security Number to be NULL-allowed, which means that not all employees will have them now. The project team gets started, only to find that Social Security Numbers are integrated with the Payroll system, Quality Control for inspectors, Security for ID numbers, and the Internet team for primary key of accounts. Each of the new discoveries expands the analysis to unexpected realms. This type of temporary paralysis is important. The team could have gone forward with the solution to make Social Security Number NULL-allowed and caused impacts on other systems.

> **You can't be so focused on the scope that you refuse to notice or point out that you are sawing off the limb you are sitting on.**

Pareto's Rule

Pareto's rule states that a small number of causes are responsible for a large percentage of the effect, in a ratio of about 20:80. So 80% of the benefit will come from 20% of the effort. Modelers cannot generally act independently in applying this principle, but in helping the team to keep on schedule someone needs to draw a line in the sand and call the analysis complete.

The best thing to do is to find the appropriate 20% (according to Pareto) and call it a day. The biggest trick is finding the right 20% to concentrate on. A 'Where Used' analysis finding every screen, procedure, table, report, and code block where a data element is used, or a 'Criticality' matrix that focuses on the necessity of having a data element 'correct' at all times sometimes helps. You can consider the rule in terms of:

- ❑ 20% of requirements generate 80% of the functionality

- ❑ 20% of one's functionality will absorb 80% of the resources

Or you can say that:

- ❑ 80% of the requirements will be satisfied with 20% of the model

- ❑ the remaining 80% of the model will only support 20% of the requirements

> **Avoid getting stuck on some small return issue that will impact the schedule. Isolate it and phase it in if you can.**

The Law of Diminishing Returns

This is the other thing that is good to keep in mind. It is also called the law of decreasing returns and the law of variable proportions. It says that 'if one factor of production is increased while the others remain constant, the overall returns will relatively decrease after a certain point'. This is mathematically represented in a sort of 'lazy S' showing that you have to exert more and more effort to achieve incrementally less and less. In fact, after a certain point you can work as hard as you want and basically get nowhere, while in the initial stages a small amount of effort results in a disproportionate amount of benefit.

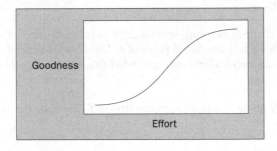

When the modeler finds the logical modeling running to hundreds of entities, it's time to consider phasing in an approach to avoid getting trapped in this type of 'less for more' scenario. You can break your modeling effort up into subject areas (banking vs. sales) or functionality (Assigning a Cashier to a Register vs. Creating a Deposit). Only you will know that the working model is getting too big to handle, or how to partition it so you can focus better.

Manage Expectations

You have to help everyone know where you think things might change, might need extra security, or might be wrong. They can work around those areas until you have a better feel for them. It's your product, and you need to take responsibility as if you are solving problems of your own making, whilst keeping everyone informed as to where you are. Share as much as you can, not only about the model, but your gut feelings about the analysis as well to help keep people out of minefields as long as possible.

Use Your Initiative

Draw up what you know in your models, since it makes the process go faster. People are quicker to tell you something is wrong than tell you what looks right. Remember that waiting around for clients to give you name formats or table abbreviations will impede the pace of the project.

There are other applications where you work, so look up how their `Address_tb` is designed. Even if you think it is not the best design, it will have the advantage of being totally integratable in the future. Check out the bought package data structures, and look at what the particular SAP, PeopleSoft, or Oracle Apps solution for data design is.

What about previous models and how you solved the security requirements there? Was it similar? Can you steal not only the structures, but the documentation as well?

Do you ever make friends with other modelers? Network them and see if they have a fast solution to your needs. None of us knows everything, and it can be a pretty lonely place out there sometimes. I have worked in companies where I was the only one on staff who knew what relational theory was.

Try to find a way to piece patchwork structures together to help shorten the creation cycle. Build a 'Best of ...' solutions for your Enterprise and use it. Use the dictionary to give 'Best guess' definitions. Don't force the clients to tell you what a City name is. Again give them a target that they can shoot at. Do some of the work for them and put notes in the model if you have to, explaining that this is still waiting for agreement with the clients.

Start a collection of data dictionaries from every source you can think of. Pull definitions from every model you can lay your hands on and build yourself a 'Meta Definitions' document. Use it whenever you can to help build a common understanding of what those data elements are to the Enterprise.

> Add a task to every project to build common lists of definitions for you and the team to use in the future.

Ask for Assistance

Asking for help or explaining a difficulty is not necessarily a sign of weakness. It takes some strength to admit to needing training, extra time, or a helper. The funny thing is that you would probably never let a co-worker drown in tasks if you knew they were struggling. So let someone help you out once in a while. We spend our lives trying to make tools that will help other people get their jobs done faster. Why don't we ask once in a while for it ourselves? Even the DBAs and programmers are good at this. We could really gain some time in simple, and sometimes even cheap, ways if we could just work up the courage to ask.

> **What saves time generally saves money. You can model on paper but you can increase your productivity enormously with a modeling tool to help.**

A few days learning how the client does their job can be invaluable. Finding out the methods a DBA has to performance-tune one of the platforms can help you understand what they are facing in the physical design world. Even taking a basic class in one of the programming languages will help you know when to push back when a programmer says something cannot be done. Even knowing the wonders of UML, Object-Oriented design, and Data warehousing techniques makes you a much more valuable asset to your Enterprise.

> **Knowledge about nearly anything is power in modeling.**

Try to get a book budget for one or two books a year, and build a department library, picking up modeling texts, software books, and specialist dictionaries. That way you have a good chance of building your definitions with due regard for specific 'Industry Standards'.

Keep project documentation in soft as well as hard copy, especially if there are hand-written notes. You would be surprised how often an application needs to be altered and no one knows anything about who/what/where/when/ or why it was created in the first place.

Model Management

Here is a list of best practices, directly related to the bulleted list of model mismanagement we provided earlier:

- ❑ **Consistency in models** – from our perspective position means nothing. Having an entity in the top left, center, or right bottom has no meaning. However, to avoid confusing the customer, be as consistent as possible in the position of entities on your diagrams, and document any changes so that they are clear to the client. If you use submodels for most of your publication, you may be able to keep most things in their usual place. On the big model you may need to use color or text formatting to help people see where the box went. Finally you can add a note to provide directions to the new location if need be. You might even want to create a placement standard in your department

- ❑ **Readable Models** – we all struggle with models that are too big for the paper size we have to put them on. But in your quest to fit everything on the page, take pity on everyone and keep the font size of your model easily readable. If you are shrinking to fit a paper size, never go lower than 70%. Anything less than that leads to the customer thinking that you are unaware, or uncaring, of their inability to use your document

- ❑ **Appropriate Information** – I provided you with all kinds of suggestions for things you might want to put on a model. Now I am going to retreat backwards a bit. Some of the modeling software will actually allow you to create a reusable library of notes so you can create and store all those things, but manage what shows up on one print of the model. Add the extras judiciously. Have an eye to visual presentation since you don't want people to get tense just by looking at your model

At the other end of the scale, don't omit important levels of detail. No matter how much of a draft you think the model is, at least add the following information before you publish it anywhere:

- ❑ The name of the project / application
- ❑ What it is a model of – Enterprise Logical or Production Physical or Test Data Mart
- ❑ Your name and extension
- ❑ The date the model was last updated (not printed)
- ❑ And find a way to version it so that someone could find the right one out of the six at a glance

❑ **Data Element Library** – one of the most powerful tools you can provide your department with and perhaps others customers is a data element library. If you decide to provide a collection of information about any aspect of the models, applications, or data elements, you need some way of keeping them accurate. You may need to audit them from time to time, wipe out and refresh the information, or simply add methods for the library customers to check for themselves. You should never publish this type of information and allow it to get stale. I know that can be very difficult. It is better sometimes to force a request for this type of data if you are not confident in its upkeep. Creating a tool and not maintaining it can be as dangerous as giving your teenager a car and not providing either training or maintenance of the brakes. You never know when someone is going to make an Enterprise-critical decision based on your library

❑ **Judicious Denormalization** – just because we can denormalize, doesn't mean that it's always the answer. Every time it seems important to break one of the rules of normalization, especially one of the first three, you should question whether there is another way to approach the problem. What risks are involved in denormalizing, and what benefits will we gain? This is where discussions with the DBA and developers will help in determining what is best for the system you are currently working with. Denormalization should be a last resort to a relational modeler, except in the case of dimensional modeling. Try to use common sense to make the decisions and have a good reason for doing so

❑ **Be Flexible** – when unusual circumstances crop up, create a standard 'Bypass the Standard' technique. You don't want to lose total control, you just need to bend it a little. You may even have written the standard in the first place. Make it a living process also, subject to evolution as the need arises. And realize that some of your standards are more open to flexibility than others. The Laws of Normalization aren't very flexible in creating a logical design; but the options available for performance tuning that requires some amount of denormalization are pretty boundless

---

> **Be prepared to have to bend your own rules.**

At the opposite extreme, ensure that you never deliver your products without any naming standard whatsoever. I have certainly had to work with physical names that made me wonder if someone came up with them by using Scrabble letters. Even the most common of abbreviations were used multiple ways to mean the same thing, or they used the same abbreviation to mean multiple things. Not every Enterprise has a 'Common Abbreviations' list. Not all the abbreviations in it may suit your needs. Try at least to be consistent within the confines of a project

❑ **Back up your work** – do what you recommend to everyone else and protect your most valuable assets in at least two ways. Probably one off your system in a department-shared environment and the other in a disaster recovery mode, hopefully offsite.

Having considered an overview of what constitutes best working practices for a data modeler, let's look in more detail at some factors that will help you plan and develop your own modeling projects.

Understanding Data and Design

I have tried through this book to help you become aware that the task of analyzing and designing repositories for data is not just a plugable formula process. The data itself, what is captured in spreadsheets, forms, and documents are *only* the physical manifestations of what we are trying to manage. If you are modeling a distribution warehouse and have never seen one, stop what you arc doing and check out the reality, go kick a few tires, and then start modeling. Once an expert reviews a model then a fudge or bluff has no hiding place. As modelers we need to have 'vision', in being able to understand the detail, the exceptions and the mechanism by which a domain functions. By understanding data problems, we can find beautiful and simple ways to solve them.

Logical To Physical Transformations

One of the greatest mysteries in my professional career is the relationship (or sometimes lack thereof) of the logical to the physical model. I find myself baffled by what is implemented in comparison to what I thought I documented in the logical model. The departure of one from the other is sometimes astonishing. My advice to you is to stay in touch as much as you can. Do your best to determine what is actually happening with the data, rather than what the team or clients either *perceive*, or think *ought*, to be happening. Don't make assumptions about your designs being used the way you planned them to be used. People often use tools to fix problems creatively. Toasters make great paperweights, while buckets make good stools. If someone can force data into a field, they might do it regardless of the intent of the field.

Keep the model updated, create and maintain risk-assessment documentation, and try to maintain the mapping of logical to physical along with a list of design decisions. And make sure you stay in touch with not only the design team, but the clients as well. The key is to minimize the opportunity for a data element to be used in a way that is not part of the game plan. Point out that a new data element may need to be created rather than use the old one. They may both describe facts that aren't in sync with each other.

The physical model can take on a life far beyond your ability to manage. It depends very much on the organization, custom development processes, qualifications for a successful project, and the Enterprise disbursement of data architecture authority. If 'On Time' and 'On Budget' are the highest criteria for success, then the database design may be more subject to changes to support fast, cheap solutions than if 'Customer Satisfaction', 'Enterprise Architecture Standard', or 'Sustainable Data Quality' are the criteria. However the mark of a good data modeler is being able to spot false economy, and pointing out and convincing decision makers that a short-term saving could result in a long term cost. I admit that I end up breaking more of my data standards to support fast and cheap solutions than I do to support real performance gains.

Fallacies About Physical Data

It took me years of working in IT to make these discoveries. Maybe I am just not that bright, but these shook the very foundations of my world when I figured them out. I thought these rules were understood to be set in stone. I didn't realize what they implied:

❑ **Application owners own their data** – I hear members of the computer services group constantly say that they take care of the machines and software, but that the users own the data. They wash their hands of all bad data events the way that auto manufacturers and the highway builders often try to lay 100% of the blame for accidents on the drivers. Data is an Enterprise asset owned by the entire company, not just one portion of it. If something is occurring systematically at the data creation stage then the whole company suffers in the long run. We are all in this together. If 'bad' data happens it should be up to IT to help try to find out the cause and fix it if it is in their power, or bring the problem to someone else's attention if it isn't

❑ **Application owners control all their data** – there are just too many data values that act as logic points in applications for the application owners to be able to claim that they control all of the data. If the value for affirmative changes from 'Y' for yes to 'J' for ja many applications lose their ability to process 'IF ... THEN ... ELSE' statements that depend on finding a 'Y'. Lots of code depends on finding certain values. Most of these types of data values lie in the 'Lists of Values' type of data, although even procedures that are counting on finding dates can give incorrect results when faced with text or numbers. The application owners have to follow certain laws in their own tool or it will cease to function correctly. That means they don't control all of the data

❑ **Designs can be flexible** – designs can be flexible to a point. You can make the list of 'Type' codes flexible enough to include new ones, or create client-controlled lists so that Vehicle_Type can grow to anything the client wants to add. There are two problems that I have run across:

  ❑ There is generally a great deal of logic surrounding the values of these types of lists. Even innocuous things like lists of Countries, Colors, or Departments can cause breakage. You have to verify that there is *no* logic based on the values of these data entities for them to be truly flexible. It can't matter whether a Product is 'Red', 'Green', or 'White', unless you can capture the rule for Color logic, and describe it as a relationship on the model. Otherwise a programming change has to happen for a new Color 'Silver' to be treated the same as 'White'

  ❑ You have to choose a design sometime, and all designs have some restrictions associated with them. Some have less than others, but I have never run into a completely 'Flexible' design

Approach the concept of flexibility as shades of gray. Look over your choices and decide what can't be done if you design it that way. I often add a note to the models of each of the Physical designs to point out implied restrictions using that structure. Being as normalized as possible, or using OODB object-oriented database design helps, but nothing is truly flexible other than Jello. This simply illustrates that data modeling provides a snapshot of ever-changing business requirements

❑ **Primary keys never change** – I started data modeling living under the incorrect assumption that primary keys cannot be updated. They *can* be in most if not all RDBMSs. Not only that, but some designers expect to be able to. Countries, rock bands, web sites change their names (which I always thought of as their natural key). An acre of land once identified by a lot number is divided up into development lots. Also Known As (AKA) and Previously Known As (PKA) abound in the real world. The thing, person, or event is still what it was when it started, but now it has a new natural primary key. This is one of the best arguments for surrogate keys. Coding gets tricky when the programmers have to deal with the change of a migrating key. They have to change all foreign keys to match, or you lose the links during the update. Some tools provide a CASCADE UPDATE function, or they have to write triggers and stored procedures to fire automatically to take care of this event. Again you have to watch for logic points. If reports have been programmed to look for 'USSR', but our business now needs to look for 'Russia' there will be problems when the update happens.

I have been left wondering if there is a real *natural* key in the world that is not subject to change

❑ **Primary keys are never NULL** – I don't think they are logically, but some RDBMS (mostly older versions) allow a single NULL to exist in the primary key. Primary key has been implemented to simply mean unique. A single instance of NULL is unique. I have also come across interesting uses of non-significant identification in what I thought was supposed to be a natural primary key. Creative clients uses words like 'N/A-1, N/A-2, …' to make up uniqueness when you meant them to put in a Contract_Number. This probably means that there isn't enough validation in the design, but it can be hard to prevent creative people from doing creative things

Project Lessons

I have probably been involved in a hundred projects over the course of 12 years. Some ran as long as two years, while others were as short as a week. I am going to write down some of my best guesses about the average length of time that the various stages of projects take. These are only guides to give you an idea of what sort of ballpark you are playing in; it isn't possible for me to give you absolute numbers, and you shouldn't take them as such. I will break the thoughts up into Custom development, Purchased solutions, and Forensic work.

Custom Solution Projects

In these kinds of projects, you get to start from scratch and find a solution. You draw from everything you know, everything you learn, and everything you want to be, in order to come up with a series of products that help the project team build an application. You will be asked to provide an estimate of duration for most project plans. Here is what I think after many years of working with teams, based on the workings of a modeler with some experience.

Remember that the modeler should stay with the project from start to finish. This means being present when the initial project chartering session takes place, and attending the post-deployment assessment and evaluation meeting, as well as all the work in between. Ongoing and sustaining effort isn't easy to estimate, but as a rough rule of thumb my formula is:

❑ Eight hours per programmer per week prior to test build

❑ Four hours per programmer per week for the duration of the project

475

So if the Project plan calls for 20 weeks of Planning and Developing and another ten for Testing and Implementation using four programmers, the modeler could estimate:

```
(8 hours x20 weeks x4 programmers)
+
(4 hours x10 weeks x 4 programmers)
or 640 + 160 = 800 hours
```

or 20 weeks full time for a 30 week project.

My simplest estimation is that the data modeler is on a custom development project from start to finish for 75% of the time, although they will move to full time during some phases and into half time in others. A small project such as a web page development will only need half a day a week. Some of that will just be meeting to touch base; some will be to respond to action items. Sustaining support requires you to stay in touch:

❑   Update the model as necessary

❑   Maintain the documentation appropriately

❑   Publish and deliver new documentation

❑   Stay abreast of new discovery in development and testing

Here is a table summarizing what I consider to be reasonable definitions of small, medium, and large-scale projects. The durations given are in terms of achieving a first reviewable draft. Remember that all models are iterative, so I have included the time spent updating them, to a final version in the ongoing time.

Quantity	Small	Medium	Large
Duration	Anything less than three months	More than three months but less than six months	More than six months
Number of Entities	Less than 20 entities	More than 20-50 entities	More than 50 entities
Size of Team	Any size team less than five	A team of between five and seven	A team of more than seven
Conceptual Modeling time	10 hours per business process	20 hours per business process	40 hours per business process
Logical Modeling time	10 hours per subject area	20 hours per subject area	40 hours per subject area
Physical Modeling time	One hour per non-operational attribute	One hour per non-operational attribute	One hour per non-operational attribute

Phrases To Watch Out For

These are the warning signs in a custom development project. It means that you need to heighten your sensitivity to the team and the customers. You may need to manage expectations, speed up your response, spend some time explaining what you are doing, or dig your heels in a bit to prevent your work from being pushed aside.

When Can We Have the Database Design?

This will generally come from the programmers on the team chomping at the bit. Don't feel that you have to have the whole design done in order to give them some of the design. Programmers want to get started and need to be supported. What you should be very leery of is letting them start coding without the team approving the part of the physical design they would like to start with.

Once programmers start using names and structures, it is very difficult to change their code. You have to use some level of reasonability about the maturity of the design and manage expectations that some things will be likely to change all the way until you get out of Test.

Why Do We Need To Do a Logical Design?

The answer to this question is three-fold:

- ❏ So that the data elements can be stored in the most appropriate structures
- ❏ So that the enterprise has a view of what data elements are in this project
- ❏ So that we can identify the correct source of all the data elements

The problem has always been that logical modeling takes time. If these things are not important to the person asking the question, or they feel they already know the answers to these concerns, you will not be able to defend it. A logical model isn't universally regarded as a 'Value Added' process.

What Is So important About Third Normal Form?

Be careful with this one. This is usually questioning data modeling in general, rather than whether third normal is the appropriate level of modeling. In fact nine times out of ten they don't know what third normal form is. Try to find out their level of understanding before you answer. Never go on the defensive. Question back to find out what they really want to know or what their opinion is. People only believe something is true if they find out for themselves. You can give them information but they have to make up their own mind.

What Development Needs?

During the course of a project, I have heard clients state:

- ❏ We'll never need to share this data with anyone
- ❏ We'll never need to store that much data
- ❏ We'll never have that many users
- ❏ We'll never have to support international access
- ❏ We'll never have to provide 24/7 support
- ❏ We'll never need to modify that

❑   We'll never need to report that way

❑   We'll never need to capture data to that level

And they are almost always short-sighted about their needs (sorry about that guys!)

Try to provide structures that your feelings tell you will support additional needs in the future. If you are overruled on something you feel passionate about, then make sure that your alternative design stays with the program documentation somehow along with a risk assessment. That way a future team will have a head start. On many occasions when clients utter these sentences the very opposite is true!

We Always ...

In a similar vein, I have heard clients state that:

❑   We always have that information when we create this record

❑   We always report that way

❑   We always take the weekend off

❑   We always need to have a person on call

❑   We always provide this information on this report

❑   We always send this data to that department

❑   We always ship US domestically

❑   We always have only one phone number

❑   We always buy in US dollars

❑   We always have a manager for a department

Always and never are to be suspect at all times. You are allowed to not believe them, and provide extra functionality in the form of many products per order vs. one, space for international addresses (even if they don't think they will ever use it), etc. Your goal as a modeler is often to turn these always and never statements into "Until we had this new application, we always USED to ...". Help them to recognize that they used to do it that way because they had to. You are helping them design a brave new world of data rule possibilities.

Purchased Solution Projects

Logical and physical data models for bought applications are interesting concepts. The vendor generally tells you that they don't exist, often for proprietary reasons. If I thought they really don't exist, I would be questioning the database design from the very onset.

Sometimes a data modeler will be asked to support a team deploying a purchased application such as Oracle Financials, Lawsen, SAP, PeopleSoft, or the smaller packages. Sometimes they would like you to look at the structures with an eye to helping with the first data load or custom report building, or indeed in data conversion issues. While it can sometimes be hard to work with such bought packages, since you may not be able to readily access the definitions of the tables and columns that the enterprise data resides in, you can bring all your 'reverse engineering' skills into play. Granted, some systems are so complicated that you would be foolish to manipulate data using anything other than the means provided by the software tools. However, that doesn't mean that we can't work to integrate purchased solutions with existing systems, or develop the means for users to develop their own *ad hoc* queries of a data warehouse, for example.

Estimating Support

Find out what the team wants. Sometimes it is just a simple reverse engineer of the tables, to aid reporting on the database objects. You have to manage expectations of what a model will be able to do for them. I have worked with vendor packages that have no constraints created at the database level. That means the model is just a collection of boxes. Sometimes the naming convention is totally alien to what they are used to; SAP for example has abbreviated German. A data model like this provides very little to the general meta data of the company. It is difficult (at least for me) to offer a model without definitions, relationships, and a key to naming conventions but we do try to help where we can.

No Model Available

Always ask the vendor for a model. Even if the physical design is proprietary, then the logical design shouldn't be. The business rules of what they are providing is in the logical model. I fully admit to being almost constantly turned down by vendors. But if enough of us ask, maybe some day it will be provided without us having to nag for it.

Logical

The only way to build a logical model (which documents the data elements, definitions, and business rules without any physical denormalization to cloud the fundamentals) from most vendor packages is from the front end. You have no access to the code and the database design isn't usually much help due to proprietary issues. This is reverse engineering analysis with a lot of shortcomings. My estimate is something like:

- ❑ Two hours per setup screen (application configurables)
- ❑ Four hours per List of Values screen
- ❑ Eight hours per Transaction screen

So if the Application has two screens to set up security and application management configurables, with nine different lists to be set up, and 20 transaction screens, the modeler could estimate:

```
(2hours x 2 set up screens)
+
(4 x 9 LOVs)
+
(8 X 20 OLTP screens)
or 4 + 36 + 160  = 200 hours
```

or five weeks full-time for the vendor app.

Physical

Building a physical data model is a pretty straightforward task, unless you are being asked to document constraints that are being managed in the front end, or through stored procedures. A physical model generation can be achieved quickly, based on your software tool's ability to connect to the RDBMS the application is installed on, whether it is designed to read from that platform, and what is actually available for it to read in the RDBMS catalogs. Here are my suggestions for getting just a physical model out.

- ❑ Hand type – One hour per table
- ❑ Automatic Reverse Engineer – Four hours to clean up the graphic
- ❑ With relationships that aren't in the DBMS – two hours per table

So if the Application has 20 tables and your software can access it, it would be about four hours to get out a picture. If you are typing it out (assuming tables of an average of 15 columns) it would take about a week (40 hours).

Definitions

Definitions (comments) may or may not be provided at the database level. If they are, then your software will bring them in from the dictionary tables of the RDBMS. Or you may be able to find them in a DDL file as comments. If not, then 1/2 hour per column is a good benchmark, with a caveat that you will probably not be able to provide all of them (some will be a mystery forever). If this application had 20 tables averaging 15 columns each, you might need about four weeks to get all the definitions together based on data profiling, and testing your ideas by exercising the screens and reports to verify your analysis.

Non-Normalized Designs

Don't expect to understand the physical design of a bought application. I have been overwhelmed by what is provided as the table designs of really respected software companies. Some of them are aggregations of older, previously independent applications, possibly modified from previous Hierarchical or Network designs, patched together with a new front end for backward compatibility. My other thought is that the database is deliberately designed to be a total mystery as part of the security measures of the vendor.

So unlike other types of data element analysis, don't expect to come out of a vendor product analysis understanding the underlying structure of the data.

No Naming Legend

Generally vendor structures don't come with a list of abbreviations or terms used in the data structures. This means that the only way to create a data dictionary or set of table/column definitions will be a full database data profiling. The tables and columns will not necessarily be named to help you search for something. I find columns named NAME or DATE without any clue as to which name or date. But by far the worst recognition has to do with abbreviations and surrogate keys. Without constraints at the database level, non-significant numbers representing foreign keys to somewhere are useless. And without some naming standard to work with, figuring out abbreviations is nothing more than an educated guess.

Questions To Ask

Sometimes the DBA or Data modeler is invited to preview vendor software before the decision is made to buy it. If you are asked to review it, then try to bring up these issues before the purchase has been committed to.

❏ **Can we integrate**? You need to know if there will be enough understanding of the data structures to allow other enterprise system integration. If this is a new HR system, then can you use the employee data for other systems directly, or do you need to build an intermediary system that is basically duplicated data just to be able to access and use it correctly? Depending on the criticality of the Enterprise data to be managed in a vendor application, I would give very low marks to an application that can't be integrated into the Enterprise data concepts.

❏ **Can we bulk load**? Most vendors provide some start-off functionality that assists in launching a newly deployed system. Ask if you can do it more than once without bothering the existing data. Will it check for duplicates of the members of the set, rather than surrogate key uniqueness (this is pretty rare)? You generally feel pretty comfortable bulk loading custom-designed systems (even if you have to truncate and reload part of the system more than once) because you understand all of the nuances of the data design. This isn't usually the case in Vendor designs. At least make people aware that after the initial load, there is a potential that even large quantities of data will need to be hand-keyed in order to use the data integrity checks that are only at the screen level.

❏ **Can we write our own reports**? This is generally a crucial question for me. Don't let the vendor say 'Yes if you use our report writer'. Many provided report writers are slimmed down for client usage and cannot support more complicated queries, formatting, security, merging of other system data, or logic tree analysis that many companies require. You want to know if you can write reports, query the data, basically access the data through a programmatic method by using the tools currently standard in IT. This means you can capitalize the reporting tricks already in use in the database without having to translate them all into another tool.

Legacy and Forensic Analysis

Sometimes this type of analysis reminds me of those deep-sea submarine exploration shows. You are totally in the dark and funny looking objects keep swimming into your meager spotlight. The time it takes to unearth and document a legacy system is very dependent on how long it has been used and modified, how integrated to the enterprise it is, and how large is it.

This is an extremely general estimate (just to give you a starting place) for most analyses. My size definitions for a large, medium, and small legacy system are as follows:

Quantity	Small	Medium	Large
Number of Tables	Less than 20 tables	20 – 50 tables	More than 50 tables
Number of integration sources/target	0 – 1 live integration source/targets	More than 2 live integration source/targets	More than 5 live integration source/targets
Number of database code objects	Less than 10 database code objects – triggers, procedures, etc.	More than 10 database code objects – triggers, procedures, etc.	More than 20 database code objects – triggers, procedures, etc.
Conceptual Modeling time	4 hours	4 hours per 10 tables	8 hours per 10 tables
Logical Modeling time	1 hour per non-operational attribute	1 hour per non-operational attribute	may be impossible – 2 hours per non-operational attribute
Physical Modeling time	1 hour per non-operational column	1 hour per non-operational column	1 hour per non-operational column

You may totally disagree with all of my estimate factors, but I always feel it is easier to take someone else's estimate and say that it is wrong, than to invent one in the first place. So leverage these thoughts to come up with your own formulas.

Questions To Ask

I believe that all knowledge is valuable to the Enterprise. Some of it is just more valuable than others. Take the task of documenting a legacy system for instance. You need to ask some questions:

❑ **Is it worth analyzing**? Why this system? Why not another one? Is it due to be replaced? Are you trying to find the data scope? What is the desired knowledge goal in dissecting this application or suite of applications? Just how complicated would this analysis be? What is the cost benefit from knowing this information?

❑ **When was it last used**? Some applications die natural deaths. The last customer gets transferred or the business process changes. Monitor the activity of the database, and see whether it is being used by a significant number of users, or whether you are actually wasting time reviewing a data desert. How important is this system to the Enterprise? Who can you talk to who was employed here when the system was first deployed?

❑ **Is there any documentation**? Search code libraries. Ask for training documentation, programmers manuals, even the code itself may have notes in it. Try to find the original project documentation. Sometimes (although not often) you will find an original data model physical design that you only need to create delta documentation from. Do be careful though, since any documentation you find will need to be validated before you can rely on it to make any decisions

Expectation from Data Profiling

The best way to get definitions for a legacy system is simply to match table/column name assumptions with the data actually in the column. Then you can say with certainty that although the column says `Employee_First_Name` you don't think that Mr., Mrs., Dr. are really first names. Most legacy systems have been performing their jobs for a long time and having odd data values (like titles in the first name column) doesn't always cause serious problems. Many data anomalies have been accepted by the Enterprise because nothing stopped on account of it.

Chasing IDs

Surrogate keys have been around for a long time. They are almost the rule rather than the exception. Unfortunately for a data modeler trying to trace data, they add a level of complexity to your task. You either need a skilled programmer at your elbow for a while, or you need to learn how to query that RDBMS. I have had very helpful DBAs port the data and data structures into a neutral environment (such as Access) where I can work without screwing up the live data, only to find that I still can't figure out what is going on.

Human Intervention

Have you ever looked at a report out of an application and been confused because the things being reported don't seem to exist in the system you are analyzing? I have. I have had to take the reports apart to figure out that there has been some translation or aggregation code added to change values into what the customer wanted to report, rather than change the original data values at source.

You may find instances where the data values in the legacy system never seem to be reported, caught, fixed, or cause problems. There is some human intervention going on that causes dissimilar values to be grouped, dramatic changes from one value to another, and even masking and filtering that seems to change critical enterprise totals.

If you are doing a legacy analysis you need to be aware that the whole data story does not lie in the database design. Suggest that someone needs to pull apart the reports, screens, and interfaces as well to get a whole picture. I have tried to follow data values as they move through the Enterprise. They are created in one system, transferred to another, and report out to a desktop. On the desktop they are sifted, sorted, rounded, truncated, mutated, and modified. From there they are moved into an aggregated view in Focus, Lotus 1-2-3, or Excel. Then they are loaded back into other systems, which move them again. Finally they end up in the data warehouse or ODS with no history of how they came to be.

Legacy systems have been around long enough to become an intrinsic part of what can be termed the 'great data dance'. You will need to pay special attention to the interfaces that take place, when, using what logic, from what source, and to what target. Without that view of the lifecycle of the data elements, you have an incomplete picture of the data structure.

Model Reviews

Model reviews are critical. This is where you get buy-in, validation, and approval of your discoveries. Bad models can be fixed in a moment, but poor model reviews will take a toll on your credibility that may take years to repair. Good model reviews can open doors, build strong relationships, and help your career goals. Take them seriously. Realize that model reviews have goals and objectives as much as the models themselves do. Focus on what you want to accomplish. Then do everything you can to help make it a success. Make sure that everyone with an interest in the project is invited, and that they all receive whatever documentation you need them to read prior to the meeting. This is your time to explain what you have discovered. You need to present with confidence, and at a technical level appropriate for your audience. Don't bore the project manager with table definitions, or the DBA with definitions of entities and attributes. Remember to ensure that notes are taken of the meeting, paying particular attention to any issues, points of contention, or action items that arise. Writing them down will convince the audience that these are important enough to spend more time on than you have in the model review. It also allows you to follow up any points raised following the meeting.

Experience Counts

Data modeling, project management, programming, and database administration are all skills that mature over time. They are not simple classroom knowledge skill sets. They benefit from time in real problem-solving situations. I don't expect this book to do anything more than provide a framework for someone who wants to build, read, or review a data model. You have to have done it a few times to get comfortable with the language.

Don't get frustrated if it doesn't seem to be easy. It isn't always easy. But it is simple. Remember learning soccer? The rules are simple enough. The ball movement is simple enough. Winning a game is not necessarily easy, but it *is* based on simplicity. The more you play then the more comfortable you are with the challenges, and the more confident you are about your choices.

> Be passionate about gaining experience, model everything you can lay your hands on, review what you did with the programmers, DBAs, clients, project managers, and soak up everything they tell you. But keep returning to the concepts of normalization to check the results.

Responsibility vs. Authority

Unfortunately we are frequently asked to be responsible for things that we have no authority to control. Data modelers are generally given the responsibility to analyze, document, and provide documentation about the Enterprise data. They are generally relied on to provide a beginning database design. However, they are rarely given authority to enforce that any of their designs, suggestions, or analysis conclusions are acted on. Therefore they are not independently authorized to build an integrated, safe, secure, well-managed data environment. Instead, data modelers are simply part of the chain of authority; the DBAs may have the authority to approve or disapprove a database design, while the programmers may have the authority to change the design in order to meet schedule or budget.

I have seen authority for the database designs lay in many places, and I have also seen no authority framework provided at all, in a sort of data management free-for-all. Perhaps worst of all has been the times I have witnessed a data management group given authority for the data structures of the company that have created a bottleneck, brick wall, legalistic, ivory tower department that is avoided at all costs. I have watched departments literally buy their own servers to avoid having to deal with data management authority. How sad. Instead of bring about a better data world they have created a world which includes data sharing resistance, revolution, and civil war.

You need to find out what your authority is, what the authority of the team members you work with is, and how to provide the best product you can within that framework. Talk with your manager about it. Draft out a process model of how data analysis fits into the processes of data management in your world. You may even find ways to improve what is currently happening to the betterment of everyone's common data.

Summary

Team building, maintenance, and support are crucial to the success of any project. We have seen in the first half of this chapter how bringing attributes such as arrogance, defensiveness, obstruction, and an inability to compromise to the team will impair its ability to function efficiently. We should instead aim to be open minded, willing to listen to other inputs, and exacting in our production of definitions and concepts, in order to draw up the highest quality data models.

Don't negatively impact the schedule if you can help it. Recognize and deal with 'analysis paralysis' by knowing if you have hit something that really needs extra time or if you are just stuck. Try to find the right mix of perfectionism, communication levels, educated guessing, requesting assistance, tools, training, and research material to get the job done.

And finally treat your models as the best product in your line. Deliver it with quality and aplomb. Make sure the customers are comfortable with the:

- ❏   Placement of the objects
- ❏   Readability of the text
- ❏   Amount of information available
- ❏   Quality of information
- ❏   Denormalization choices
- ❏   Standards
- ❏   Security measures for protecting the model

In the second half of the chapter I have attempted to provide a distilled version of some of my experience with data and design. I told you about the surprises I have had about data, especially in my expectations of how it behaves. We looked at some 'best guess' formulas for determining how long projects involving custom design, or modeling our purchased systems might take you. Of course I can't add in anything that is unique to your world, so you may want to take my number and double it! We finished off by looking at some of the 'softer' issues around your modeling work, including model reviews and authority for data management.

Data modeling is something that will provide you with constant challenges and opportunities to learn. It's a great job, and is a position full of opportunities to explore new business processes, try out new technical tools, and potentially make a lasting difference in managing data assets. It is a job that not enough people take seriously, resulting in badly designed, inefficient databases, full of data anomalies, costing companies time, money, credibility, and losses of opportunity in a fast-moving world. As a data modeler, it's your mission to eradicate these brakes on useful data, and lead your colleagues to a world where well-behaved, predictable, and usable data becomes the norm.

With a grasp of basic relational theory, and practice in drawing up definitions for entities, attributes, tables, columns, and relationships, you, as a data modeler, can become a powerful and valuable asset in helping deliver well-designed, robust, and high-performing applications within any organization.

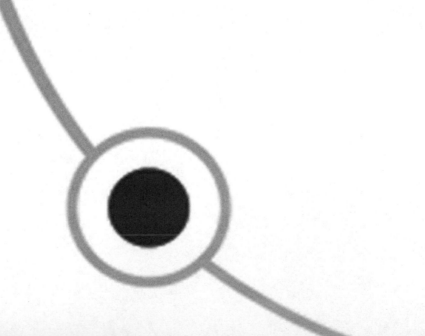

Index

A Guide to the Index

The index is arranged hierarchically, in alphabetical order, with symbols preceding the letter A. Most second-level entries and many third-level entries also occur as first-level entries. This is to ensure that users will find the information they require however they choose to search for it.

Notes

Notes

Notes

Notes

Notes

Curlingstone Publishing writes books for you.
Any suggestions, or ideas about how you want
information given in your ideal book will be studied by our team.
Your comments are always valued at Curlingstone Publishing.

Free phone in USA 800-873 9769
Fax (312) 893 8001

UK Tel.: (0141) 341 3340   Fax: (0141) 341 3400

Registration Code: | 70026MF744M63Z01 |

Data Modelling for Everyone – Registration Card

Name _____

Address _____

_____

_____

City _____ State/Region _____

Country _____ Postcode/Zip _____

E-Mail _____

Occupation _____

How did you hear about this book?

❑ Book review (name) _____

❑ Advertisement (name) _____

❑ Recommendation _____

❑ Catalog _____

❑ Other _____

Where did you buy this book?

❑ Bookstore (name) _____ City _____

❑ Computer store (name) _____

❑ Mail order _____

❑ Other _____

What influenced you in the purchase of this book?

❑ Cover Design ❑ Contents ❑ Other (please specify):

_____

How did you rate the overall content of this book?

❑ Excellent ❑ Good ❑ Average ❑ Poor

What did you find most useful about this book? _____

_____

What did you find least useful about this book? _____

_____

Please add any additional comments. _____

_____

What other subjects will you buy a computer book on soon?

_____

What is the best computer book you have used this year?

_____

Note: This information will only be used to keep you updated about new Curlingstone titles and will not be used for any other purpose or passed to any other third party.

Check here if you DO NOT want to receive support for this book ■

Note: If you post the bounce back card below in the UK, please send it to:

Curlingstone Publishing Ltd
116 West Regent Street
Glasgow G2 2QD. UK

Database Book Publishers